cook simply
everything

Step-by-step techniques & recipes
for success every time from the world's top chefs

EDITOR-IN-CHIEF
JILL NORMAN

**LONDON • NEW YORK • MELBOURNE
MUNICH • DELHI**

Senior Project Editors
Annelise Evans, Michael Fullalove, Pippa Rubinstein

Consulting Editor
Norma MacMillan

Senior Art Editors
Susan Downing, with Alison Donovan

Editors
Lucy Heaver, Caroline Reed, Frank Ritter

Designer
Alison Shackleton

Art Director
Carole Ash

Publishing Director
Mary-Clare Jerram

Publishing Manager
Gillian Roberts

DTP Designer
Sonia Charbonnier

Production Controller
Joanna Bull

Photographers
Steve Baxter, Martin Brigdale, Francesco Guillamet, Jeff Kauck,
David Munns, William Reavell

First published as *The Cook's Book* in Great Britain in 2005
by Dorling Kindersley Limited, 80 Strand, London WC2R 0RL
Penguin Group (UK)

Cook Simply Everything first published in 2007
Project Manager and Editor Claire Tennant-Scull **Project Designer** Elaine Hewson

Copyright © 2005, 2007 Dorling Kindersley Limited
Text copyright © 2005, 2007 Dorling Kindersley Limited except:

Text copyright © 2005 Introduction: Jill Norman; Flavourings: Peter Gordon; Stocks
& Soups/Poultry & Game Birds/Fruit & Nuts: Shaun Hill; Chinese Cooking: Ken Hom;
Breads & Batters: Dan Lepard; Eggs & Dairy Produce/Pasta & Dumplings:
Michael Romano; Fish & Shellfish/Vegetables: Charlie Trotter.
The moral rights of these authors have been asserted.

2 4 6 8 10 9 7 5 3 1

A CIP catalogue record for this book is available
from The British Library

ISBN 978 1 4053 2030 6

Colour reproduction by GRB, Italy
Printed and bound by Star Standard, Singapore
Discover more at
www.dk.com

CONTENTS

FOREWORD

EVERY COOK COLLECTS RECIPES THAT PARTICULARLY APPEAL TO THEIR PERSONAL PALATE, AND IT IS THESE RECIPES THAT THEY PARTICULARLY LIKE TO SHARE WITH OTHERS. IN THIS BOOK, 13 TALENTED CHEFS FROM VARIOUS COUNTRIES IN EUROPE, NORTH AMERICA, ASIA, AND AUSTRALIA HAVE EXPRESSED THEIR TASTES AND DISCOVERIES THROUGH THE TECHNIQUES THEY HAVE USED AND THE SIGNATURE DISHES THEY HAVE CREATED, MANY OF THOSE IN THEIR OWN RESTAURANTS. WHILE SOME RECIPES MAY TOUCH ON CLASSICAL GREATS, EACH IS ENHANCED BY A MODERN TWIST. THE RESULT IS A RELIABLE REFERENCE BOOK THAT IS EQUALLY AT HOME ON THE SHELF OF ANY CHEF DE CUISINE AND IN THE KITCHEN OF ANY WOMAN OR MAN WHO APPRECIATES THE ARTS OF COOKING, WANTS TO KNOW MORE, AND IS KEEN TO DEVELOP COOKING SKILLS.

COOK SIMPLY EVERYTHING BEGINS WITH THE BUILDING BLOCKS OF ALL CUISINE, THE SIMPLE AND CLASSICAL STOCKS, AND PROGRESSES THROUGH THE WHOLE SPECTRUM OF COOKERY, FROM SAUCES, MEATS, AND VEGETABLES TO BAKING AND DESSERTS. ALONG THE WAY IT VISITS TECHNIQUES BOTH MODERN AND TRADITIONAL AS WELL AS SAMPLING DISHES DRAWN FROM THE GREAT CUISINES OF THE WORLD, FROM EUROPE TO INDIA, THAILAND, CHINA, AND THE AMERICAS.

I RARELY NEED TO FOLLOW RECIPES NOW, EXCEPT WHEN MAKING PASTRIES AND OTHER FOODS THAT REQUIRE STRICT MEASUREMENTS. BUT WHEN I DO USE A RECIPE BOOK, I LIKE THE AUTHOR TO COME TO THE POINT AND MAKE IT CLEAR WHERE THE RECIPE IS HEADING, WITHOUT ENDLESS AMOUNTS OF CHAT. *COOK SIMPLY EVERYTHING* CERTAINLY MEETS THAT REQUIREMENT. THE TECHNIQUES ARE WRITTEN CLEARLY AND MANY HAVE STEP-BY-STEP PHOTOGRAPHS THAT GIVE AN EXCELLENT PICTURE OF HOW TO COMPLETE EACH STAGE – IT IS SO MUCH EASIER TO COMPARE YOUR PROGRESS AND TECHNIQUE TO PHOTOGRAPHS THAN TO WORDS ALONE. THIS BOOK HAS BEEN CONCEIVED AND WRITTEN AS A DETAILED REFERENCE TOOL, SO THE COOK CAN RETURN TO IT TIME AND TIME AGAIN FOR TECHNICAL CLARIFICATION OR SIMPLY INSPIRATIONAL DISHES FROM AROUND THE WORLD.

SO MANY PEOPLE HAVE TOLD ME THAT THEY CANNOT COOK, DO NOT HAVE THE TIME TO COOK, OR SIMPLY DO NOT LIKE TO COOK. *COOK SIMPLY EVERYTHING* CHANGES ALL THAT BY MAKING IT SIMPLE FOR EVERYONE. AS YOU ARE GUIDED THROUGH THE COOKING PROCESSES STEP BY STEP, YOU BECOME MORE CONFIDENT, YOUR SKILLS IMPROVE, AND YOU ARE ABLE TO COMPLETE THE DISHES SMOOTHLY AND WITHOUT A HITCH. *COOK SIMPLY EVERYTHING* REALLY CAN GUARANTEE SUCCESS EVERY TIME.

MARCUS WAREING

INTRODUCING THE CHEFS

WHEN THE IDEA FOR THIS BOOK WAS FIRST PUT FORWARD IT SEEMED OBVIOUS THAT CHEFS FROM DIFFERENT PARTS OF THE WORLD SHOULD BE INVITED TO PARTICIPATE. THE GLOBAL KITCHEN IS INCREASINGLY A REALITY. CHEFS TRAVEL FROM ONE CONTINENT TO ANOTHER TO TALK AND WORK TOGETHER, TO DEMONSTRATE THEIR SKILLS, TO DEVELOP THEIR EXPERTISE, AND TO CREATE NEW IDEAS.

THE FIRST PERSON I APPROACHED WAS THE INFLUENTIAL CHARLIE TROTTER IN CHICAGO; HIS IMMEDIATE ENTHUSIASM MADE THE PROJECT SEEM POSSIBLE, RATHER THAN ABSURDLY AMBITIOUS. HIS ENCOURAGEMENT AND SUGGESTIONS ABOUT OTHER CHEFS HAVE BEEN INVALUABLE. THROUGH CHARLIE I MET TOP PARISIAN PÂTISSIER PIERRE HERMÉ, WHOSE CREATIONS SPARKLE LIKE JEWELS IN THE WINDOWS OF HIS BOUTIQUES. IN PARIS, I ALSO TRACKED DOWN AN OLD FRIEND, KEN HOM, WHO AGREED TO WRITE THE CHINESE CHAPTER. THE ITALIAN ROOTS AND MODERN AMERICAN APPROACH OF NEW YORK CHEF MICHAEL ROMANO MADE HIM THE NATURAL CHOICE TO WRITE ON PASTA.

IN THE UK, SHAUN HILL, PAUL GAYLER, AND MARCUS WAREING BROUGHT THEIR MANY TALENTS TO THE BOOK, FOLLOWED BY SKILLED BAKER DAN LEPARD AND INVENTIVE YOUNG INDIAN CHEF, ATUL KOCHHAR. NEW ZEALANDER, PETER GORDON, LONG A RESTAURATEUR IN LONDON, DREW ON HIS ECLECTIC FUSION FOOD TO ILLUSTRATE THE TECHNIQUES OF FLAVOURING. HAMBURG PÂTISSIER, STEPHAN FRANZ'S KNOWLEDGE OF DIFFERENT TRADITIONS ENABLED HIM TO WRITE ON GERMAN, FRENCH, AND AMERICAN CAKE MAKING. SOME OF THE MOST INTERESTING FOOD TODAY IS AUSTRALIAN AND I WAS DELIGHTED WHEN TWO AUSTRALIAN CHEFS AGREED TO JOIN US: CHRISTINE MANFIELD, WHO HAS AN INSTINCTIVE FEELING FOR WORKING WITH ASIAN INGREDIENTS; AND DAVID THOMPSON, MASTER OF CLASSIC THAI COOKING, WHO TEACHES EVEN THE THAIS. THE CHEFS HAVE COLLABORATED, EXCHANGED IDEAS, AND ALWAYS BEEN MUTUALLY SUPPORTIVE. WORKING WITH SUCH TALENTED AND CREATIVE PEOPLE HAS BEEN VERY REWARDING. I AM VERY GRATEFUL TO THEM ALL FOR THEIR UNSTINTING COMMITMENT TO MAKING *COOK SIMPLY EVERYTHING* A REALITY.

Jill Norman

JILL NORMAN

STEPHAN FRANZ

I AM FASCINATED BY HOW THE ORIGINS AND TRADITIONS OF SWEET CAKES AND PASTRIES ARE STILL REFLECTED IN BAKING TODAY.

A Berliner, Stephan Franz discovered a love of pâtisserie during his apprenticeship at that city's Hotel Intercontinental. He took courses in pâtisserie and then gained further experience working as a practical trainee in the Hotel Negresco in Nice, France. Eventually he undertook specialist training in the Konditorei-Café Widmann, Germany's finest cake shop.

Stephan worked under Hans Haas, the two-star Michelin chef at Tantris in Munich, then in the Aubergine restaurant in Munich with three-star Michelin chef Eckhart Witzigmann. He and Witzigmann collaborate on various book and television assignments.

In 1997, as head pastry chef of the newly rebuilt Hotel Adlon in Berlin, Stephan Franz was able to develop fully his creativity and special talent. He also wrote the recipes for the dessert section of *Cooking Art of the Adlon*, the hotel's new cookery book.

In 1999 he was chosen as best pâtissier by the Association of Master Chefs in Berlin. He was lauded in 2003 by the *Gault Millau* food guide, which informed its readers that "the greatest pastry chef in Germany sparkles and enchants with his light, inspirational, and imaginative desserts". In 2005 another food and travel guide, *Aral Schlemmer Atlas*, acknowledged his work with the accolade of "outstanding pâtissier of the year".

PAUL GAYLER

HOW CAN ANY COOK BE TIED DOWN TO ONE SPECIFIC CUISINE WITH ALL THE WONDERFUL WORLDWIDE PRODUCE AT OUR DISPOSAL?

Paul Gayler began his cooking career at the tender age of 12 while assisting his mother with their family-run outside catering business. At the age of 16 he attended a local catering school where he passed with the highest achievable honours. He later honed his career by working in some of the finest hotels and restaurants in the UK and Paris.

Paul then took up the position of chef at Inigo Jones, one of London's finest and most exclusive restaurants, where he gained an enviable reputation for his high-quality food. He also introduced a gourmet vegetarian menu, the first of its kind in the UK.

In 1991 Paul was invited to head the team of the newly opened Lanesborough Hotel, overlooking Hyde Park in the heart of London. In a short space of time the Lanesborough, a member of the St Regis Group, has become one of the most exclusive hotels in the world.

Paul oversees all food preparation within the hotel, supervising a strong kitchen brigade of 40 chefs. He describes his style as "global contemporary", a careful blending of flavours while maintaining classical French disciplines.

Paul has received numerous awards and is in constant demand to appear on television and radio shows. His first cookery book was published in 1995 and he has since written some 12 books on various cookery subjects.

PETER GORDON

MY PHILOSOPHY IS BASED PURELY ON FLAVOURS FROM AROUND THE GLOBE, IGNORING POLITICAL BOUNDARIES.

Peter Gordon was born in Wanganui, New Zealand. At 18 years he moved to Melbourne, Australia, where he apprenticed himself for four years as a chef during the exciting days at the birth of modern Australian cuisine.

After travelling through Asia and Europe for a year during 1985–86, Peter headed back to New Zealand to set up the Sugar Club kitchen in Wellington. He had realized that a wealth of ingredients had become available and was waiting to be played with. Peter was in turn led in the direction of creating what he can only describe as fusion cuisine.

Peter sees the world as full of flavours and textures, each a delicious treat that should be made the most of. He believes that he should not be limited in the kitchen by regional cuisines that have no relevance to his own personal life – his Maori and Scottish ancestors, an Antipodean childhood, and a year of Asian culinary experimentation – and which are based on political boundaries drawn by people long deceased.

It is the challenge of what to do with a new ingredient that excites Peter, rather than the fine tuning of a recipe created by someone else many years ago. These days, Peter is based at The Providores restaurant in London, with consultancies in New York, Istanbul, and Auckland, New Zealand.

PIERRE HERMÉ

I IMAGINE PASTRIES THAT I WOULD LOVE TO EAT MYSELF. FOR ME, THE MOST IMPORTANT THING IS TO PLEASE THE PALATE.

Descended from four generations of baker-pâtissiers, Pierre Hermé began his career at the age of 14 as apprentice to Gaston Lenôtre, becoming head pâtissier at the age of 20. At the end of 1996 he left Fauchon to set up Pierre Hermé Paris with his associate Charles Znaty. Their first shop opened in Tokyo in 1998 and was followed by a tea room in July 2000.

Opened in 2002, Pierre Hermé's pâtisserie at 72 rue Bonaparte in Saint-Germain-des-Prés was an instant success. At the end of 2004 he opened a second shop, with highly innovative décor, at 185 rue de Vaugirard, as well as launching a training workshop in partnership with the prestigious Ferrandi school. In early 2005 he opened a new Pierre Hermé Paris pâtisserie in the Omotesando district of Tokyo, where the shops of international fashion brands that have a presence in Japan are clustered.

Celebrated in France, Japan, and the US, the man whom *Vogue* has dubbed "the Picasso of pastry" has brought taste and modernity to pâtisserie. With Pierre Hermé, decoration is simpler and techniques have been re-thought. Conceived as sweet indulgences for adults, Pierre Hermé's pâtisserie has shed old references to childhood and has entered the world of gastronomy.

SHAUN HILL

COOKING IS ALWAYS PERSONAL, WITH THE HOPE THAT MY VIEW OF WHAT MAKES A GOOD DISH WILL COINCIDE WITH YOURS.

London Irish by birth and an inhabitant of the English countryside by choice, Shaun Hill is married to Anja, a Finn, and has a son, two daughters, and five grandchildren. His early cooking experiences were in the restaurants that thrived in London in the late 1960s: Robert Carrier's eponymous, ground-breaking restaurant in Islington, the Gay Hussar in Soho, and the Capital Hotel in Knightsbridge. More recently, Shaun worked for nine years at Gidleigh Park on Dartmoor, and then 10 years cooking unassisted at the stoves of the Merchant House in Ludlow, Shropshire.

Shaun was made Egon Ronay Chef of the Year, and received the Catey Chef Award (awarded by the restaurant trade), and the *AA Restaurant Guide*'s Chef Award, all in 1993. The latter is decided by a poll of the 1000 chefs who gain an entry for their restaurant in the guide. The Merchant House, which closed its doors in February 2005, held a Michelin star throughout its 10 years and was voted 14th Best Restaurant in the World in a 2003 poll of international food writers and chefs.

Shaun Hill was awarded an honorary fellowship at the Classics department of Exeter University, where he has co-written translations and commentaries on the foods of antiquity. He also works as menu consultant to British Airways.

KEN HOM

TRANSFORMING RAW INGREDIENTS INTO A DELICIOUS, MOUTHWATERING DISH IS SO SENSUOUS AND REWARDING.

Ken Hom is the author of a number of award-winning cookery books that, published in 12 languages, have sold over two million copies worldwide. He has been described by Craig Claiborne of *The New York Times* as "one of the world's greatest authorities on Chinese cooking". His numerous celebrated television series have been shown throughout the world. He is a household name in over 59 countries and is best-known for his popularizing of the use of the Chinese wok.

Born in the US, Ken speaks several languages, has studied medieval art history and film, and was formerly a professional photographer and freelance television producer. Several years ago, he revamped all the menus for Cathay Pacific Airways. In 1990, he was inducted in the prestigious *Who's Who of Food and Beverage in America* as recognition of significant and lasting achievement in the culinary industry.

Today Ken is a sought-after food and restaurant consultant with clients throughout the world, most recently the Oriental Restaurant Group. He travels the world, conducting cooking demonstrations and appearing on radio and television shows. He also contributes frequently to many publications throughout the world, including *The Financial Times*.

ATUL KOCHHAR

WHEN I DECIDED TO BECOME A CHEF, MY FATHER TOLD ME, "WHATEVER YOU DO, IT SHOULD BE NO LESS THAN PERFECTION."

Atul Kochhar was born in Jamshedpur, northern India, where his father ran a catering business. He trained at Oberoi School of Hotel Management in Delhi, then worked as sous chef at the Oberoi Hotel in New Delhi. In 1994 he travelled to London, to open his restaurant, Tamarind. The restaurant immediately won the Best Newcomer Award of the Curry Club of Great Britain™ and many other awards, culminating in Atul becoming the first Indian chef ever to be awarded a Michelin star, in 2001.

In 2003 Atul left Tamarind to pursue his most ambitious venture to date, becoming chef-patron of Benares restaurant, in Mayfair. He has been instrumental in changing the perception of Indian cuisine in the UK.

Atul's recipes have appeared widely in magazines and newspapers, and he demonstrates regularly on food shows in the UK and internationally. He also works as guest lecturer for various prestigious culinary schools across the globe. In 1999, Atul helped Thames Valley University open the Asian Academy of Culinary Arts, in Ealing.

In 2004 Atul wrote *Indian Essence*, a collection of original recipes from across India. His food is a reflection of India today – vibrant and colourful – and he frequently returns to India to research further his country's cuisine.

DAN LEPARD

I STILL SMILE WHEN A LOAF COMES OUT OF THE OVEN LOOKING GREAT. THAT SWEET BUZZ THAT YOU FEEL DOESN'T GO AWAY.

Dan Lepard was born in Melbourne, Australia. Abandoning a political studies degree at Monash University, he moved to London and worked as an actor and photographer. He then donned an apron and started work in the kitchens of Alastair Little.

Still not sure whether baking was for him, Dan left for the US and worked for a year as personal chef to the artist David Hockney, and a further year as a grill chef in New York. While there he realized that top-quality bread is an essential part of the perfect meal.

Returning to London, Dan worked as head pastry chef and started the bakery at St John Bar and Restaurant in October 1994. He left there to work for Giorgio Locatelli on the opening of Zafferano, and that position began a relationship that defined his baking.

After a spell in other bakeries and kitchens, he started work for Phillipe Dadé and Gail Stephens at Baker & Spice in London. He opened the bakery at Locanda Locatelli, and worked with Jim Webb on the bread for Ottolenghi in Islington, London.

Dan is co-author of *Baking with Passion* with Richard Whittington, which won the Guild of Food Writers Book of the Year 2000 and was short-listed for the André Simon Award 1999. *The Handmade Loaf*, published in 2004, was his first solo book.

CHRISTINE MANFIELD

CONSIDER CAREFULLY EVERY MORSEL YOU PREPARE AND EAT. YOUR DESIRE FOR FABULOUS TASTES WILL BE REWARDED.

Christine Manfield is one of Australia's most celebrated chefs, a perfectionist inspired by complex flavours and a writer whose books, *Paramount Cooking*, *Christine Manfield Desserts*, *Spice*, and *Stir*, have coloured the lives of cooks from Melbourne to Manchester and Manhattan. She is currently writing her fifth book, due to be published in 2007.

After working with some of Australia's best restaurateurs, Christine opened Paramount Restaurant in Sydney with partner Margie Harris in 1993. The restaurant established her international reputation, being regarded as one of Australia's finest by critics and the dining public alike. Since its closure at the end of 2000, she has broadened her global food interests, working alongside respected chefs around the world and hosting gastronomic tours to destinations such as Morocco, India, Spain, and Southeast Asia.

In 2003 Christine opened East @ West, a new restaurant in the heart of London, serving a unique kaleidoscope of Asian tastes and textures. The restaurant closed in early 2005, but not before receiving several awards, including *Tatler*'s Best New Restaurant, Best UK Menu at the Catey's Awards, three rosettes at the AA Restaurant Awards, and runner-up for the Best Vegetarian Menu at the *Time Out* Restaurant Awards.

MICHAEL ROMANO

OF ALL THE ARTS THAT BRING PLEASURE TO PEOPLE, COOKING IS THE MOST INTIMATE: THAT'S WHY I LOVE TO COOK.

Michael Romano's career began in 1971 at Serendipity restaurant. While there he was introduced to the renowned James Beard, who advised him on his culinary career. Jobs at the Hotel Bristol in Paris and Hotel Pierre in New York were followed by a spell under the tutelage of Michel Guérard at his three-star restaurant in Eugenie-les-Bains. After holding several other prestigious positions, Michael became chef de cuisine at the venerable La Caravelle in New York, then in its 25th year.

New York's Union Square Cafe (USC) became Michael's home in 1988, and six months later *The New York Times* elevated it to three stars. He became a partner in USC with Danny Meyer in 1993, and from a 21st ranking in the *New York City Zagat Survey* the restaurant achieved No.1 Most Popular Restaurant in 1997–2002 – a record. In 2003 USC's sister restaurant, Gramercy Tavern, made No.1, to be toppled by USC in 2004.

To share with others their passion for gastronomic pleasures, Danny and Michael collaborated in writing two cookbooks, *The Union Square Cafe Cookbook* and *Second Helpings*. Among many nominations and awards, Michael won the James Beard Foundation's Best Chef in New York City in 2001. Other restaurants he has opened include Tabla (1998) and Blue Smoke (2002).

DAVID THOMPSON

THE BALANCE OF FLAVOURS IN THAI CUISINE IS UNIQUE. TO ME, OTHER CUISINES SEEM ORDINARY BY COMPARISON.

In the late 1980s, David Thompson travelled to Thailand and became enamoured of the country, its people, and their culture. During his stay he met an elderly woman, Khun Sombat Janphetchara, whose mother was attached to one of the palaces of Bangkok and was thus heir to a tradition of great culinary refinement. It was from her that David learned the fundamentals of Thai cuisine.

In 1993 David and his partner, Peter Bowyer, opened Darley Street Thai in Sydney, Australia, followed in 1995 by Sailors Thai, also in Sydney. David was made *The Sydney Morning Herald* Professional of the Year in 1999. In 2000, he was approached to start a restaurant in London – Nahm, which opened at the Halkin Hotel in 2001 and was awarded a Michelin star in 2002.

Also in 2002 David published *Thai Food*, which won The Guild of Food Writers Award, the André Simon Award, the Glennfiddich Food Book of the Year, and the James Beard Award. At the Tio Pepe ITV Awards, David was made London Chef of the Year.

David returns to Thailand regularly to continue his researches. In that country, memorial or funerary books, "ngan seu ngaan sop", record the interests of the departed, and in these he has found long-forgotten recipes that he is able to draw on in his restaurants.

CHARLIE TROTTER

I COOK AS MILES DAVIS PLAYED HIS JAZZ. IT'S ALL ABOUT CREATING SOMETHING IN THE MOMENT THAT IS UNIQUELY MINE.

Charlie Trotter started cooking professionally in 1982 after graduating with a degree in political science from the University of Wisconsin, USA. At that time, he embarked on an intense four-year period of work, study, and travel, including stints with Norman Van Aken, Bradley Ogden, and Gordon Sinclair. He lived in Chicago, San Francisco, Florida, and Europe "reading every cookbook I could get my hands on and eating out incessantly".

In 1987 Charlie opened Charlie Trotter's in Chicago. Now recognized as one of the finest restaurants in the world, it has received five stars from the *Mobil Travel Guide*, five diamonds from AAA, and seven James Beard Foundation awards. *Wine Spectator* named it Best Restaurant in the World for Wine & Food (1998) and America's Best Restaurant (2000).

Charlie is author of 14 cookery books and the subject of two management books. He also hosts the TV series *The Kitchen Sessions with Charlie Trotter*. He produces a line of gourmet products under the Charlie Trotter brand name. In 1999 he founded the Charlie Trotter Culinary Education Foundation, which awards funds to individuals seeking careers in the culinary arts. Charlie was recognized at the White House for this work and was named as one of only five "heroes" to be honoured by Colin Powell's charity, America's Promise.

MARCUS WAREING

INSPIRATION FOR A DISH CAN COME FROM CONVERSATION, A BOOK, A FLAVOUR – ANY OF THESE CAN PLANT A SEED.

Marcus Wareing's culinary training began at Southport College, Merseyside. At the age of 18 he moved to the Savoy Hotel in London, and then worked at the Michelin three-star restaurant Le Gavroche under Albert Roux and Michel Roux Jnr. Marcus next worked at the Point, a luxury resort in upstate New York; at the Grand Hotel in Amsterdam; and at Gravetye Manor, East Sussex. On his return to London, Marcus was part of the starting brigade at Aubergine, working beside Gordon Ramsay from 1993 to 1995. He was proud to be named Young Chef of the Year by the Restaurant Association in 1995.

After working under Daniel Boulud in New York and Guy Savoy in Paris, Marcus became head chef at L'Oranger in London, gaining his first Michelin star at the age of 25. In 1999 he opened Pétrus with Gordon Ramsay in St James's, London, regaining his Michelin star, and in 2007, Pétrus gained a second. Pétrus relocated to the Berkeley Hotel in 2003 and Marcus returned to the starting point of his career with the relaunch of the Savoy Grill and Banquette at the Savoy Hotel. In 2003 the Savoy Grill also earned a Michelin star.

In 2006 Marcus cooked for the Queen as part of the Great British Menu television series. His first book *How to Cook the Perfect...* is published by Dorling Kindersley.

USEFUL INFORMATION

The following reminders will help you to make the most of this unique guide to cooking, drawn from some of the top restaurant kitchens of the world. Specific terms, unfamiliar techniques, and less-common ingredients are explained in the glossary on p482.

USING THE RECIPES

Recipe introductions provide background on the dish, its origins, preparation, and serving suggestions. Read through the recipe to ensure you have all the necessary ingredients and equipment.

- Each recipe serves four unless an alternative number is given.
- Measurements are given in both metric and imperial. Use either in any one recipe, as they may not always be exact conversions.
- Spoons refer to measuring spoons (not table cutlery) and these should be level unless otherwise stated.
- Ovens should be preheated to the temperature specified at the appropriate point during preparation of the recipe.
- Cooking times are a guide. They can vary according to the ingredients (for example ripeness or tenderness), or the individual oven or equipment, such as type of pan. Check cooking progress at the first suggested time, or at intervals during cooking.
- When a recipe can be partly or fully prepared in advance, instructions are included at the appropriate stage. Follow the instructions for chilling, storing, and finishing as appropriate.
- Check your freezer before preparing recipes that have to be frozen. On an ice cream machine turn on the appropriate setting in advance, following the manufacturer's instructions.

Accurate measuring

- Balance scales are fine for measuring larger quantities, but electronic scales are more accurate, particularly for measuring small quantities or delicate mixtures.
- Use a clear measuring jug for liquids and stand it on a level surface, then check the quantity at eye level.
- Do not pour liquids into a measuring spoon over the food you are preparing in case excess overflows into the mixture.

Ingredients

The quality of the ingredients is always reflected in the finished dish, and therefore all foods should be in prime condition. Fresh produce, fish, meat, and poultry should be just that – fresh. Frozen ingredients should be of good quality and adequately packed as a safeguard against deterioration during storage (by freezer burn, which dries out the surface of food). The foods you use should not be out of date. Dried or store-cupboard ingredients, such as flour, grains, nuts or seeds, should be in good condition: discard items that are stale or beyond their use-by date. Oils and vinegars deteriorate in flavour when stored in very warm or light conditions and when they are well beyond their use-by date. Similarly, herbs, spices, and other seasonings should be stored in cool, dark conditions and used comparatively quickly.

Follow recipe instructions and tips on choice of ingredients, for example on the size and ripeness of fruit. Essential preparation or cutting instructions are given in the ingredients list. When preparation is included before the ingredient, this should be completed before measuring the quantity. For example, chopped herbs are often measured after preparation.

- Unless otherwise stated all vegetables and fruit are assumed to be medium in size. They should be washed, scrubbed, or peeled as usual unless alternative instructions are given.
- Ingredients that discolour or deteriorate once prepared should be cut at the appropriate stage in the recipe.
- Use the type of flour suggested, either strong, plain, or self-raising, as they are not interchangeable.
- Use the type of sugar specified.
- Herbs are fresh unless dried herbs are specified by the recipe.
- Use the type of oil suggested in the recipe.
- Vinegars have markedly different flavours and preservation qualities, so cook with the type listed – avoid substitutions.
- Use type of milk specified, for example full-fat milk.
- Use large eggs, unless otherwise stated. Eggs vary, so in some recipes weights are also given for greater accuracy and success.

Note It is recommended that young children, or the vulnerable should avoid recipes made with raw or undercooked eggs.

EQUIPMENT

A well-equipped kitchen should have at least a small selection of good-quality basic equipment that is maintained in good working order. As a general rule, the simpler the tool and the more frequently it is used, the better quality it should be. Knives, pots, pans, and chopping boards are used the most frequently but, with care, high-quality items will give good service for many years. Mixing bowls, whisks, spatulas, spoons, and similar items are less expensive and there is less need for them to last a long time.

Personal choice is important so that you have implements that are comfortable and practical for your requirements, skills, everyday quantities, and style. Equipment should work well together; pots, pans, and ovenware should complement the cooker in type, size, and shape. Check manufacturer's guidelines when planning your selection of cooker, pots, and pans – some materials do not work on certain types of hob. Select one or two small electrical appliances for a range of tasks rather than having several items that double up for the same jobs. The best advice for equipping a kitchen from scratch is to start with a few essential, high-quality items and build on these as your cooking repertoire develops.

Note Some types of cling film or sealable plastic bags are unsuitable for use with heat. Check manufacturers' details before use in any recipe that calls for these items in cookery.

Pots and pans

Aluminium This conducts heat well, so it heats up quickly. It is a reactive material and, in modern cookware, is used in combination with another material, typically stainless steel or enamel. Old-fashioned uncoated aluminium pans should be replaced.

Cast iron This also conducts heat well and heats up quickly. It is heavy and retains heat well, which can be an advantage for long, slow cooking. Uncoated cast iron, for example used for griddles, rusts if not oiled or "seasoned" after washing.

Copper Another good conductor, this reactive metal is usually lined with tin, when it is referred to as tinned. Copper and aluminium are a traditional combination. As with aluminium, traditional uncoated copper pans are not recommended.

Stainless steel This is often used with a layer – or sandwich – of aluminium or copper in the base. Aluminium or copper conduct heat well while stainless steel does not react with food, making it suitable for cooking all types of ingredients. High-quality, sandwich-base stainless steel pans are responsive to heat, non-reactive, durable and, with care, they have a long life.

Vitreous enamel This is a coating applied to metals. Lightweight, painted enamelware is not durable and it tends to chip easily. Vitramel™ is the trademark for good-quality enamel cookware, including baking pans and roasting tins.

Earthenware and ceramics These do not conduct heat well and are usually reserved for oven use. However, a heat diffuser mat is sometimes used with certain types of fireproof glazed earthenware.

Fireproof and ovenproof glass Used mainly in the oven, for which glass is practical, durable, versatile, inexpensive, and available in many styles. Fireproof glass casseroles are not suitable for all hobs.

Non-stick cookware There is a wide choice of varying quality. As a general rule, non-stick coatings do not withstand high heat well. Most manufacturers recommend that non-stick coated pans are used over medium temperatures and not high heat.

Knives

From the vast choice available, select a small number of knives according to quality and material. The safest knife is a sharp knife; a blunt one is far more dangerous. The best knives are made from one piece of metal that can be seen to go right through the length of the handle. A large cook's knife at least 20cm (8in) long; a short cook's knife; a small to medium serrated knife (good for tomatoes and thin-skinned fruit); and a serrated bread knife make a good basic kit. A sharpening steel or stone is essential.

Storing knives A block or rack will prevent the knives from rubbing together and damaging each other.

Carbon steel Rarely used alone in modern knives, this sharpens well and is durable, but being a reactive metal it discolours fruit and vegetables, and can taint their flavour. It also rusts.

Stainless steel This is non-reactive but it does not sharpen well.

High-carbon stainless steel This combines the qualities of carbon and stainless steel – it can be sharpened, is durable, and does not rust. High-quality knives are expensive but they will last for years.

Specialist utensils

Select specialist utensils according to the use you intend to give them. A food thermometer is useful for checking cooking fat and syrups. Zesters and graters for preparing citrus fruit are also invaluable, and a siphon is essential for making foams.

Food processor A food processor will chop, purée, blend, knead, and crumble or combine foods but does not whisk or cream well. Discs for slicing, shredding, grating, and cutting julienne are optional, along with a wide variety of attachments for many purposes, including juicing. Among the many features a pulse setting is useful.

Food mixer A hand-held mixer will whisk air into ingredients, cream fats, and beat mixtures. This complements a food processor. A heavy mixer, with a stand, can be used for large cakes and whisking large quantities of egg whites. They have a range of attachments for carrying out many of the techniques a processor will fulfil but these are not as easy to use or wash.

Blender A blender produces smoother puréed liquids than a food processor. Blenders may be in the form of a goblet or hand-held. The latter is useful for puréeing ingredients in a pan or container.

Ice-cream machine A machine that churns and freezes mixtures to make ice cream is not essential, but if you like to make ice cream or sorbet often it would be a good investment.

HYGIENE

Any chopping boards, knives, or utensils used in the preparation of raw poultry, meat, or fish must be cleaned thoroughly with hot soapy water before being used again. Many professional kitchens colour code their boards to avoid the risk of cross-contamination.

SAUCES & DRESSINGS

PAUL GAYLER

Most home cooks appear to regard sauce making as some secret or mystical exercise, exclusively reserved for temperamental chefs in posh restaurants. During my many years in top kitchens I have often been asked, "How do you know what goes with what?" and "How do you make sauces?" Admittedly, at first sight the sauce-making aspect of cooking is enough to send any cook into despair; the repertoire of classic sauces alone is so vast that a mere listing of their names can baffle a beginner. However, sauce making is not rocket science, and learning a few of the basic sauces (called mother sauces) will give you the ability, freedom, and confidence to produce many more. For any cook, sauce making can become one of the most rewarding branches of cookery.

What is a sauce? A sauce is best described as a flavourful liquid, made from a variety of bases that have been lightly thickened. Stocks of all flavours should be made with the utmost care and attention, as they ultimately form the base flavour, quality, and success of your sauce. Ideally, I suggest making your own stocks, whether meat, fish, or vegetable. Although a little time-consuming, they are well worth the effort. If your time is limited, use a dehydrated bouillon or consommé. Instructions for making stocks are in the chapter Stocks & Soups, p54.

Sauces can be thickened by a simple reduction (rapidly boiling to evaporate excess liquid) or by the addition of a little starch. The majority of the classic sauces are made with one form of starch or another, but sauces are also thickened by other means. Hollandaise or mayonnaise sauces are emulsified with eggs; butter sauces with butter; cream sauces are finished with cream; and vegetable sauces are thickened with puréed vegetables. There are even some sauces thickened with animal blood, although these are somewhat rare nowadays. Complex sauces are the basis of great French cuisine and the glory of any dinner party or special occasion. They may be time-consuming, but in terms of flavour they really pay dividends in the finished dish.

The variety of sauces The term sauce covers a very wide range of accompaniments. There are the many classic French sauces, such as white béchamel, blond velouté, brown veal and chicken jus sauces, warm white butter sauces (beurre blanc and beurre fondu), and cold savoury butter sauces. There are the salsas of Mexico and Spain and the hot and spicy sauces of the Far East. Also included are light vinaigrettes (French dressings) for salads or fish dishes and the relishes and chutneys synonymous with old England.

Over the last decade or so our eating patterns have changed dramatically. Our knowledge of world cuisines has increased, with many of us travelling and eating out more often than ever before. Today's chefs are responding to demands for lighter sauces that are simpler, less rich, and more easily prepared than those of the past, whether they are for everyday use or for special occasions.

Marrying sauces with foods Whatever sauce you choose to make, it is extremely important that it complements, highlights, and enhances the flavour of the dish it accompanies, whether it be eggs, fish, vegetables, meat, poultry or game, salad, or a dessert. The sauce should never overpower the food or be overpowered by it. Generally, a sauce must have a clear flavour, good texture, and a glossy appearance. In this chapter you will find the basics of good sauce cookery, suggestions for sauce variations, and some sauces in new styles for your enjoyment.

Today, supermarkets offer an increasing range of ready-prepared sauces, but nothing can compare to the flavours of fresh sauces made in your own kitchen. One last thought: I always teach my cooks that the refinement of flavour of any sauce, or dish for that matter, depends on the seasoning, which in turn depends entirely on the taste buds of the cook. A good sauce always can be achieved if it is frequently and appreciatively tasted during its making. I wish you "Bon appetit!" as you go forward and improve your knowledge and appreciation of great sauces.

BASIC SAUCE-MAKING TECHNIQUES

Successful sauce-making relies on one or more of the following professional techniques, according to the type of sauce you want to prepare. The techniques are not difficult and they will ensure that you achieve superb results. Equipment such as whisks, spatulas, skimmers, and fine sieves will prove invaluable to the process. I have found it vitally important to use the right piece and size of equipment for the job or task in hand – it certainly makes cooking, and in particular sauce-making, much easier.

Whisking

Rapid whisking will emulsify and blend ingredients, aerate and add lightness to sauces containing egg yolks or cream, and make white sauces smooth and glossy. You can either use a supple, slim balloon whisk or a flat coil whisk.

To incorporate the maximum air, whisk from the bottom of the bowl or pan up, working round the sides and across the middle.

Cooked sauces that contain egg yolks are usually whisked in a bowl set over a pan of simmering water to prevent them from curdling.

Skimming

One of the most important and often overlooked steps in sauce-making, skimming removes fat, foam, and other impurities, which would otherwise spoil the flavour and appearance of a sauce.

Skim regularly during the cooking process, using a shallow perforated skimmer to remove any foam or other impurities from the surface of the sauce.

Brown sauces made in advance can be chilled and any excess fat that solidifies on the surface can be skimmed off with a spoon.

Straining & sieving

Straining removes solid ingredients and sieving helps emulsify liquids to make elegantly smooth sauces.

To sieve, hold a fine sieve over a pan or bowl and pour in the sauce. Using the back of a ladle, press the sauce through the sieve. Discard solids remaining in the sieve.

Reducing

Reducing a sauce will decrease its volume through evaporation and thus intensify its flavour. To reduce, cook in an uncovered pan over a high heat, stirring occasionally.

Deglazing

Pan sauces and gravies are made from the deglazed caramelized juices released from roasted or fried meat, poultry, and vegetables.

To make a pan sauce, remove the food from the pan and spoon off excess fat, then deglaze the caramelized juices by adding stock, water, or wine and stirring to loosen the particles and incorporate them into the liquid. Reduce and finish as required. Making a sauce like this gives a richness and depth of flavour that cannot be achieved just by simmering ingredients.

Clarifying butter

When butter is heated gently, the milk solids will separate from the butterfat and the clear liquid fat – clarified butter – can be poured off. Unsalted butter is better for clarifying than salted butter.

Clarified butter can be heated to higher temperatures than ordinary butter, so is often used for sautéing. I also like to use clarified butter for hollandaise and béarnaise sauces.

1 Cut butter into cubes, put into a pan, and heat gently just until the milk solids have separated from the fat (left). Do not let the butter get too dark or its fresh taste will be destroyed. Skim off any froth.

2 Carefully pour the clear liquid butter into a bowl (right). Discard the milk solids in the pan. Skim off any impurities on the surface of the clarified butter.

WAYS TO THICKEN A SAUCE

Most sauces are given body and consistency by combining a flavoursome liquid with one or more thickening agents. Some are added at the beginning of the sauce-making process, while others are added at the last minute. In addition to the thickeners below, sauces can also be thickened with blood (for poultry and game dishes) and colourful fruit and vegetable purées.

Blending

Many sauces can be quickly made in a blender. Hollandaise and pesto are examples. Blenders – goblet or hand-held – are also great for blending purées and liquids together for light, last-minute sauces.

Seasoning

Salt and pepper are necessary to enhance the flavours in a sauce, but they should be used in moderation. Before serving, taste the sauce and adjust the seasoning, if necessary. White pepper is preferable to black in pale sauces.

FLAVOURINGS

■ Always use fresh herbs in sauces. Soft herbs, such as chives, tarragon, and basil, should be chopped and stirred in at the last moment. Hardy herbs, such as rosemary and thyme, can be cooked in the sauce.
■ Freshly crush or grind spices and add sparingly at the start of cooking. Taste and add more later, as needed.

Roux

This cooked mixture of butter and flour is used to thicken white sauces such as béchamel. Melt butter in a pan until foaming, stir in an equal weight of flour, and cook, stirring, for about 40 seconds. Stir in milk and simmer until thickened.

Butter

Chilled butter whisked into a hot sauce gives body and shine. Be sure the butter does not get too hot or it will separate.

Take the finished sauce off the heat and gradually whisk in small cubes of well-chilled unsalted butter.

Bread

Bread is sometimes used to thicken sauces – bread sauce is a familiar example. Around the Mediterranean, bread is widely used with nuts in sauces such as Turkish tarator, Italian salsa di noci, and Spanish romesco (p44).

Beurre manié

Beurre manié (or kneaded butter) is a paste of butter and flour added at the end of cooking. To make it, use a fork to mix soft butter with plain flour in a ratio of two to one. Gradually whisk small pieces into the hot sauce until it thickens.

Arrowroot, potato starch & cornflour

These forms of starch are first "slaked" – mixed with a little cold liquid – before being added to a sauce at the end of cooking. They will thicken it immediately. Arrowroot and potato starch (fécule) are used in brown sauces and to thicken rich, reduced broths, while cornflour is the normal thickener in Chinese dishes and sweet sauces.

As a general guide, 1tsp starch will thicken 200ml (7fl oz) of sauce. Slake the starch, then whisk into the sauce and simmer gently for 2 minutes to thicken. Do not cook longer or the sauce will tend to become thin again. Finish the sauce as required and serve.

Eggs & cream

Eggs, particularly the yolks, are the thickening base of many emulsion sauces. Hot emulsified sauces such as hollandaise are cooked in a bowl over a pan of simmering water to prevent the yolks from overheating. Egg yolks mixed with cream (to make what is called a liaison) are sometimes used to enrich and thicken classic velouté sauces. A liaison is added at the end of cooking.

To thicken with a liaison, put the egg yolks and cream in a bowl and whisk in a spoonful of the hot sauce. Add this mixture to the rest of the sauce in the pan, off the heat. Return to a very low heat and cook, stirring constantly, until the sauce coats the back of the spoon. Do not allow the sauce to boil or it will curdle. Serve immediately.

EMULSIFIED SAUCES

Chief among emulsified sauces are mayonnaise, hollandaise, and beurre blanc. They are made by forming an emulsion of droplets of fat such as oil or melted butter in a liquid such as water, vinegar, or lemon juice. Egg yolk is often present to hold the emulsion stable.

Emulsified sauces have a certain notoriety for separating and curdling. The key is to create – and maintain – the emulsion correctly: the speed at which the fat is added and sustaining the right temperature throughout the process are important.

MAYONNAISE

A smooth and delicious sauce made from egg yolks, oil, vinegar, and mustard, mayonnaise is perhaps the most popular of all cold sauces and forms the basis of numerous variations. It is especially good with poached and deep-fried fish, cold fish and shellfish, and cold meats.

Olive oil can be rather overpowering in mayonnaise, so I recommend the use of an unflavoured oil such as sunflower or canola.

Being a bit of a traditionalist, I prefer to make mayonnaise using a whisk and bowl but, for those keen on saving labour, I have also included a method using a blender or food processor.

Before you start, make sure all ingredients, especially eggs and oil, are at room temperature. They are difficult to emulsify when cold. To establish the emulsion right from the beginning, add the oil literally drop by drop to start with.

Makes 300ml (10fl oz)
2 egg yolks
1tsp Dijon mustard
1tsp white wine vinegar
250ml (8½fl oz) sunflower or canola oil
2tsp lemon juice

BLENDER MAYONNAISE

Mayonnaise can be made successfully in a blender or a food processor, but always make at least 300ml (10fl oz). I have learnt from experience that a small amount does not blend properly.

Place the egg yolks, mustard, vinegar, and a pinch of salt in a blender or food processor. With the machine switched to the lowest speed, blend these ingredients together. With the machine still running, trickle in the oil in a steady, slow stream through the hole in the lid until the mayonnaise is thick and emulsified. Add the lemon juice and blend briefly, then adjust the seasoning to taste.

1 Place the egg yolks, mustard, and vinegar in a mixing bowl. Add a pinch each of salt and pepper (for preference, white pepper).

2 Steady the bowl on a dampened tea towel and pour in the oil – drop by drop to begin with, then a drizzle – whisking all the time.

3 Add the oil in a steady stream as the sauce begins to thicken, whisking continuously to keep the emulsion stable.

4 When all the oil has been incorporated and the mayonnaise is thick, stir in the lemon juice and adjust the seasoning to taste.

Classic mayonnaise-based sauces

Aïoli (garlic mayonnaise)

Add 4 crushed garlic cloves to the egg yolks, then continue as for the master recipe. Perfect with hot or cold fish and as a dip for vegetables.

Rouille (chili mayonnaise)

Add a pinch of saffron and ¼ tsp cayenne pepper to aïoli (above). Traditionally served with the Mediterranean fish soup bouillabaisse.

Tartare sauce

Add 25g (scant 1oz) finely chopped gherkins, 25g (scant 1oz) rinsed and chopped capers, 2tbsp chopped parsley, 2tbsp chopped chervil, and 2 chopped shallots to the finished mayonnaise. Good with deep-fried and pan-fried fish.

Rémoulade

Add 1 finely chopped anchovy fillet and 2tbsp chopped tarragon to tartare sauce (left). Serve with cold meats, cold fish, and fried fish.

Truffle mayonnaise

Replace 1tbsp of the sunflower or canola oil with truffle oil, then add a little finely shaved truffle to the finished mayonnaise. Great with fish, vegetables, and cold meats.

Thick, glossy, and unctuous – perfect mayonnaise

Rescuing curdled mayonnaise

When mayonnaise separates into coagulated flecks of egg and oil, it has curdled. (In the trade this is also known as splitting.) Curdling can happen for several reasons. Here are the most likely causes of curdling:

- The egg yolks or oil were too cold.
- The oil was added too rapidly to begin with.
- Too much oil was added.

Happily, curdled mayonnaise is easy to rescue.

1 Place 1 egg yolk or 1tsp Dijon mustard (this will affect the flavour slightly) in a bowl, then trickle in the curdled mayonnaise, whisking.

2 Continue whisking in the curdled mixture until it is all incorporated and smooth.

HOLLANDAISE SAUCE

For me, hollandaise is the best of all sauces – wonderfully smooth, light, and delicate. A good, well-made hollandaise has a rich yellow colour, a slightly tart flavour, and a fluffy texture – somewhat like a warm mayonnaise in consistency. It is the perfect match for poached fish or vegetables, and egg dishes. Hollandaise is sometimes made using simple melted butter, but I find that clarified butter gives a richer, smoother flavour.

A curdled hollandaise can be returned to respectability by placing a fresh egg yolk in a clean bowl and whisking in the curdled sauce a little at a time.

Makes 600ml (1 pint)

2tbsp white wine vinegar
2tbsp water
1tsp lightly crushed white peppercorns
4 egg yolks
250g (8½oz) unsalted butter, clarified (p26)
juice of ½ lemon
pinch of cayenne pepper

1 Place the vinegar, water, and peppercorns in a small heavy-based pan and bring to the boil. Lower the heat and simmer for 1 minute, or until reduced by one-third (to about 2½tbsp).

2 Remove from the heat and leave until cold, then strain the liquid into a heatproof bowl. Add the egg yolks to the liquid and whisk together.

3 Set the bowl over a pan of simmering water: the base should be just above the water. Whisk the mixture for 5–6 minutes, or until it thickens and is ribbon-like, creamy, and smooth in texture.

IN A BLENDER

If you are short on time, you can make hollandaise in a blender.

Follow step 1, then leave the vinegar reduction until cold. Strain the mixture and add a pinch each of salt and pepper. Place with the egg yolks in a blender and blend for a few seconds. Heat the clarified butter. With the machine switched to its highest setting, trickle in the hot butter and blend until thick and fluffy. Add the lemon juice and adjust the seasoning.

Hollandaise sauce – a warm emulsion of butter and egg yolks

4 Place the bowl on a dampened tea towel. Slowly add the clarified butter, pouring it into the mixture in a thin stream and whisking until the sauce is thick and glossy.

5 Add the lemon juice, then season with salt, white pepper, and cayenne pepper. Serve at once. If you need to keep the hollandaise warm, use a bain-marie (p33) or transfer it to a thermos flask.

BÉARNAISE SAUCE

Made in exactly the same way as hollandaise, béarnaise sauce has the addition of tarragon and shallots infused in the vinegar. It is one of France's best-loved sauces, enduring the test of time, even in these days of modern sauces. It is usually served in its simplest form, as an accompaniment to grilled steaks and fish.

To make béarnaise sauce, at step 1 of the basic hollandaise recipe, add 2tbsp roughly chopped tarragon and 2 chopped shallots to the vinegar reduction. Then stir 1tbsp chopped tarragon and 1tbsp chopped chervil into the finished sauce before serving.

Hollandaise-based sauces

A hollandaise can be flavoured with a variety of ingredients.

Foyot sauce
Boil 150ml (5fl oz) dry sherry to reduce by half. Cool, then add to the finished sauce. Serve this with grilled meats, fish, and vegetables.

Maltaise sauce
When blood oranges are in season, there is no better sauce than Maltaise to accompany vegetables, particularly asparagus. Simply add the grated zest and strained juice of 2 small blood oranges to the finished sauce instead of the lemon juice.

Mousseline sauce
Fold in 75ml (2½fl oz) semi-whipped cream just before serving. It is good with steamed asparagus or poached fish. Try adding 1tbsp chopped herbs too, such as tarragon, chives, or chervil.

Mustard sauce
Stir 1tbsp Dijon mustard into the finished sauce. Serve with grilled fish or chicken.

Noisette sauce
Add 50g (1¾oz) beurre noisette (p31) to the finished sauce. The nutty flavour of noisette sauce goes well with fish.

Olive sauce
Add 1 heaped tbsp chopped good-quality black olives to the finished sauce. This is great with asparagus and egg dishes.

Saffron sauce
Add ½tsp saffron threads to the vinegared water when starting to make the hollandaise.

Watercress sauce
Add 100g (3½oz) chopped watercress leaves to the finished sauce and stir to mix.

Béarnaise-based sauces

Like hollandaise, béarnaise sauce has many variations. The following are some of my favourites.

Balsamic sauce
Replace half the white wine vinegar with balsamic vinegar, then add 1tsp balsamic vinegar to the finished sauce in place of the lemon juice. This sauce is ideal with grilled or roast meats or fish.

Choron sauce
Add 2tbsp well-reduced tomato sauce to the basic recipe. The tomato sauce (p40) must be well reduced and thick, otherwise it will thin the basic béarnaise too much. A well-reduced passata could also be used. Choron is good with grilled steaks, lamb, chicken, or fish.

Horseradish sauce
For the classic accompaniment to roast rib of beef, stir 1tbsp horseradish cream into the basic sauce. This is also good with grilled steaks or grilled fish, especially salmon.

Paloise sauce
Replace the chopped tarragon with chopped mint. Paloise goes very well with lamb.

BEURRE BLANC

Beurre blanc – also known as white butter sauce – was one of the first sauces I made when I became a professional cook many years ago and it still stands the test of time. It is another classic emulsified butter sauce, rich in flavour and simple to prepare. It is great with poached and grilled fish. Lightly salted butter makes a slightly thicker sauce than unsalted butter. It is a matter of taste.

Makes 300ml (10fl oz)

2 shallots, finely chopped
3tbsp white wine vinegar
4tbsp dry white wine
2tbsp cold water
200g (7oz) unsalted or slightly salted butter, chilled and diced
squeeze of lemon juice

1 Place the shallots, vinegar, and wine in a small pan and bring to the boil.

2 Lower the heat and reduce the contents for about 2 minutes until only 1tbsp liquid remains. It should have a light syrupy consistency.

3 Over a gentle heat, add the water, then whisk in the butter a little at a time until completely emulsified. Season with salt, white pepper, and lemon juice.

Variations

The flavour of beurre blanc can be varied by changing the vinegar or wine and by including other ingredients.

Beurre rouge

For a red butter sauce, replace the white wine with 6tbsp good-quality red wine and the white wine vinegar with 1tbsp red wine vinegar.

Herb beurre blanc

Add 1tbsp finely chopped fresh basil, tarragon, or rosemary with the shallots.

Saffron beurre blanc

Add a pinch of saffron threads to the vinegar and wine reduction, then proceed as for the basic recipe.

Usually served unstrained, beurre blanc can be strained for a smoother sauce

OTHER BUTTER SAUCES

Composed butters – also known as hard-butter sauces – are simple to prepare and work well with various flavourings. After blending in the flavourings, roll the butter in greaseproof paper into a cylindrical shape and chill in the refrigerator or freezer until ready to serve. Enjoy composed butters with grilled meats, poultry, and fish. Simple sauces like beurre noisette or beurre noir for fish or vegetables are made by heating butter on its own or, in the case of beurre fondu, by adding a little water and lemon juice.

CAFÉ DE PARIS BUTTER

This composed butter is particularly good with grilled steak and fish.

Makes 300g (10½floz)

2tbsp tomato ketchup
1tsp Dijon mustard
½tsp chopped capers
1 shallot, finely chopped
1tsp chopped fresh chives
1tsp chopped fresh tarragon
2 anchovy fillets, rinsed and chopped
1tsp Cognac
1tsp Madeira
1tsp Worcestershire sauce
pinch of paprika
150g (5½oz) unsalted butter, softened

1 Place all the ingredients except the paprika and butter in a bowl and mix together well. Season with salt, pepper, and the paprika. Leave to stand for 24 hours in a warm place to allow the flavours to infuse.

2 Using a wooden spoon, beat the infused mixture into the softened butter. Roll the butter in greaseproof paper into a sausage shape, secure the ends, and chill until required.

3 To serve, place a slice of the butter on the meat or fish. The butter will slowly melt over the food and add a wonderful flavour.

BEURRE NOISETTE

For beurre noisette (brown butter sauce), heat 50–75g (1¾–2½oz) salted butter in a pan over medium-high heat for 2 minutes until it foams and turns nutty brown. Add a squeeze of lemon juice. Serve with vegetables or pan-fried fish.

BEURRE NOIR

Beurre noir (black butter sauce) is cooked in the same way as a beurre noisette, but for 20–30 seconds longer. Traditional with pan-fried skate.

BEURRE FONDU

Bring 4tbsp water to the boil in a small pan. Off the heat, whisk in 150g (5½oz) cubed, lightly salted butter until emulsified. Add a squeeze of lemon juice. Serve with asparagus or other vegetables, alongside or instead of hollandaise.

WHITE SAUCES

Easy to prepare and endlessly adaptable, white sauces have been the base of classic European cooking for many years. Béchamel and velouté – the two basic white sauces – are made by combining flour and melted butter to make a roux, then adding differing quantities and combinations of milk, cream, and stock. There are countless variations of these basic sauces, as well as modern adaptations and quicker versions for time-pressed cooks. Here I give the recipe for a classic béchamel sauce, followed by a modern version of velouté sauce, which is made without a roux. The white sauce in its many guises is here to stay.

BÉCHAMEL SAUCE

Béchamel is the king of white sauces and the one from which many others derive. Contrary to general opinion, it is better to add the milk all at once, rather than little by little, to avoid a lumpy sauce. This recipe gives a medium béchamel, which can be enriched with cream before serving.

Makes 600ml (1 pint)

1 small onion, halved
4 whole cloves
600ml (1 pint) full-fat milk
1 small bay leaf
45g (1½oz) unsalted butter
45g (1½oz) plain flour
freshly grated nutmeg
100ml (3½fl oz) double cream (optional)

ALL-IN-ONE

For a quicker version of béchamel, use this all-in-one method, which omits infusing the milk and making a roux. The result is still good, although less refined.

Melt 45g (1½oz) unsalted butter in a pan. Mix together in a jug 600ml (1 pint) full-fat milk and 45g (1½oz) plain flour. Add to the melted butter, whisking until the sauce thickens. Bring to the boil, then reduce the heat and simmer for 5–6 minutes. Season with salt, pepper, and nutmeg. Strain before use. Makes 600ml (1 pint).

1 Stud the onion with the cloves. Place in a saucepan with the milk and bay leaf. Bring almost to the boil and simmer gently for 4–5 minutes. Allow to cool and infuse.

2 In another pan, melt the butter over a low heat. Add the flour and cook gently for 30–40 seconds, stirring frequently with a wooden spoon, until the roux is pale yellow.

3 Remove the pan from the heat. Strain the cooled milk into the roux and whisk vigorously to mix in smoothly.

4 Return the pan to a medium heat and continue whisking for 4–5 minutes until the sauce thickens and comes to the boil. Reduce the heat and simmer gently for 20–25 minutes. When the sauce is smooth and glossy, season with salt, white pepper, and nutmeg.

The ideal coating consistency for a béchamel sauce. Enrich with the cream before serving, if liked

The right consistency

The correct consistency for a béchamel sauce – whether thin, medium, or thick – depends on how you intend to use it.

■ A thin béchamel is ideal for lightly coating vegetables, fish, and meat and for adding body to soups.

■ A medium béchamel is also used for coating vegetables, particularly in a Mornay sauce for cauliflower cheese. And it is the one for gratins and pasta dishes like lasagne.

■ Thicker béchamel sauces are used to bind ingredients for fillings and stuffings and for soufflé bases.

The quantities of flour and butter you use to make the sauce largely determine its consistency, although a béchamel that is too thick can ultimately be thinned with a little more milk and a sauce that is too thin can be thickened by whisking in beurre manié (p25). No matter what consistency of béchamel you are aiming for, if it goes lumpy, whisk vigorously or transfer the mixture to a blender and blitz until smooth.

Thin béchamel

For a thin béchamel, reduce the quantity of butter and flour in the master recipe to 15g (½oz) each. The sauce should have the consistency of pourable single cream and only just coat the back of a spoon. If the finished sauce is too thin, whisk in a little beurre manié to thicken it.

Medium béchamel

The sauce produced by using the 45g (1½oz) each of butter and flour specified in the master recipe has a consistency that coats the back of a spoon well but still flows easily. Adjust as necessary with a little beurre manié, to thicken, or more milk, to thin.

Thick béchamel

By increasing the amount of butter and flour to 60g (2¼oz) each, the sauce becomes thick enough to bind a mixture but still flow when a spoonful is knocked against the side of the pan. Thin down a sauce that is too thick by stirring in a little extra milk.

Variations

Medium béchamel is the basis of three classic sauces.

Mornay sauce

Add 75g (2½oz) grated Cheddar or Gruyère cheese and 1tsp Dijon mustard to the sauce off the heat. Stir in 2 egg yolks mixed with 4tbsp double cream. Good with cauliflower.

Parsley sauce

Add 3tbsp chopped fresh parsley and a squeeze of lemon juice to the sauce.

Soubise sauce

Blanch 2 large chopped onions and sauté in 50g (1¾oz) butter. Add the béchamel, seasoning, and a pinch of sugar. Cook for 15–20 minutes, then blend. Stir in 2tbsp double cream. Serve with lamb or pork.

KEEPING SAUCES WARM IN A BAIN-MARIE

To keep sauces warm until ready to use, a bain-marie (water bath) is ideal, especially for warm emulsified sauces such as hollandaise and beurre blanc, which are less stable than white and brown sauces.

Place the pan or bowl of sauce in a saucepan or roasting tin of barely simmering water (the bain-marie). The temperature of the sauce must remain below boiling point. A double boiler (right) serves the same purpose.

To prevent a skin from forming on the surface of the sauce while it is being kept warm, cover with a piece of lightly buttered greaseproof paper before placing it in the bain-marie.

VELOUTÉ SAUCE: a modern interpretation

The classic velouté sauce is based on a roux, like a béchamel. However, chefs nowadays prefer a richer, creamier sauce, made without a roux and derived simply from natural flavour reductions.

The liquid required for a velouté is fish, chicken, or veal stock (as appropriate) plus wine and cream. When I'm making a velouté with chicken stock, I like to add a little delicacy to the sauce by sweating some thyme with the shallots.

Makes 500ml (17fl oz)

4 shallots, finely chopped
sprig of thyme (for chicken velouté only)
15g (½oz) unsalted butter
300ml (10fl oz) dry white wine
75ml (2½fl oz) vermouth
375ml (13fl oz) well-flavoured chicken, fish, or veal stock
375ml (13fl oz) double cream

1 In a covered saucepan, sweat the shallots and thyme, if using, in the butter over a low heat until softened. Add the wine and vermouth. Increase the heat and bring to the boil, stirring.

2 Reduce the heat and simmer, uncovered, for about 25 minutes, or until the liquid has reduced by two-thirds and is syrupy in consistency. Stir occasionally during simmering.

INCREASING THE FLAVOUR

■ For a sauce lacking in flavour, add a splash of wine or champagne to a velouté made with fish stock, or port or Madeira to a velouté made with chicken stock.

■ If the sauce lacks piquancy, whisk in a squeeze of lemon juice at the end.

5 After reduction, the sauce should be thick enough to coat the back of a spoon. If it is too runny, reduce for a further 5 minutes.

6 Before serving, strain the sauce through a fine sieve. If the sauce is not to be used immediately, keep it warm in a bain-marie or double boiler (p33).

3 Add the stock, stir to combine, and return to the boil. Cook, uncovered, over a high heat for 20 minutes, or until reduced by half.

4 Add the cream and stir to combine. Bring back to the boil, then reduce the heat and cook, uncovered, until the sauce has reduced by over half and thickened.

The rich creaminess of velouté sauce

Velouté-based sauces

Here are some of my favourite variations on velouté sauce. Use chicken, fish, or veal stock for the basic velouté, according to the dish with which you are serving the sauce.

Aurore sauce
Add 100ml (3½fl oz) fresh tomato sauce (p40) or passata to the finished velouté. Serve with poached chicken or veal.

Caper velouté
Make the basic velouté with the stock used for poaching gammon or lamb. Stir in 2tbsp rinsed, drained capers and 4tbsp double cream and simmer gently for 5 minutes. Serve with the gammon or lamb.

Champagne velouté
Add 60ml (2fl oz) champagne with the wine and vermouth. Serve with turbot and sole.

Curry velouté
Five minutes before completion, stir ½tbsp curry paste into the velouté. The curry flavour should be mild and delicate.

Mushroom velouté
Add 100g (3½oz) sliced button mushrooms to the cream and simmer for 5–6 minutes before adding to the reduced stock. Serve with chicken, pork, veal, eggs, or pasta.

Mustard velouté
Add 2tsp Dijon mustard to the sauce at step 5. Do not re-boil, as this can make the sauce slightly buttery. For extra flavour and colour, stir 1tsp chopped herbs such as parsley or tarragon into the finished sauce. Serve with salmon, mackerel, and herring.

Saffron & tomato velouté
Add a good pinch of saffron strands to the stock and simmer to infuse, then make the velouté as normal. Add 2 peeled, seeded, and chopped tomatoes plus, if liked, 1tbsp chopped basil, to the finished sauce. This goes wonderfully with white fish and shellfish.

Tarragon velouté
Stir 1tbsp finely chopped tarragon into the finished sauce. This is especially good with grilled fish or white meat dishes.

BROWN SAUCES

The original brown sauce – the espagnole – was the fundamental sauce in French haute cuisine. Made from rich brown stock thickened with a brown roux, it took two to three days to make and was the base for countless other classic sauces – chasseur and bordelaise among them.

Today, most cooks and many professional kitchens consider the espagnole too time-consuming and uneconomical to prepare. They prefer in its place a simple jus lié (usually shortened to jus), such as light veal jus or chicken jus. The product of a slow reduction of a well-flavoured stock enlivened with meat trimmings, a jus is thickened with a starch such as arrowroot, potato starch, or cornflour towards the end of cooking. Although lighter than the classic espagnole, the modern-day jus is developed into brown sauces in exactly the same way – by the addition of flavourings, such as mushrooms, mustard, shallots, or Madeira, and by mounting them with butter.

As a general rule, light veal jus is best suited to meat-based dishes and chicken jus to poultry and fish-based dishes. When a jus for lamb or duck is required, replace the base stock accordingly. A vegetarian jus uses vegetable stock.

LIGHT VEAL JUS

The jus most favoured by professional cooks – rich, refined, and glossy, it forms the base of many excellent brown sauces for meat.

Makes 600ml (1 pint)

3tbsp vegetable oil
340g (12oz) veal trimmings, cut into small pieces
150g (5½oz) chicken wings or carcasses, chopped into small pieces
2 shallots or 1 onion, chopped
100g (3½oz) mushrooms or mushroom trimmings, chopped
1 medium carrot, chopped
1 garlic clove, chopped
½tbsp tomato purée
sprig of thyme
1 bay leaf
300ml (10fl oz) dry white wine
600ml (1 pint) water
1.5 litres (2¾ pints) veal or dark chicken stock
1tbsp arrowroot, mixed with a little water

BROWNING BONES

When browning the meat bones and trimmings, it is important that they are cooked until deep golden brown. This, together with the caramelizing of the vegetables, will achieve the correct colour for the finished jus. Insufficient browning gives a pale jus.

1 Heat the oil in a large pan. When smoking, add the veal and chicken and fry over high heat for about 20 minutes, moving the pieces around until they are golden brown all over.

2 Add the vegetables and garlic and fry for 10 minutes, or until they are golden and caramelized. Add the tomato purée, thyme, and bay leaf and cook for a further 2–3 minutes.

3 Pour in the wine and water and bring to the boil, scraping the sediment from the bottom of the pan with a wooden spoon to release the caramelized juices.

4 Boil, uncovered, for about 25 minutes, or until the liquid is reduced by two-thirds.

5 Add the stock. Bring back to the boil, then boil, uncovered, for about 20 minutes to reduce again by half, regularly skimming off any impurities. When reduced by half, stir in the arrowroot mixture to thicken the liquid.

6 Cook for 2 minutes, then strain through a fine sieve. The resulting jus should be thick enough to lightly coat the back of a spoon.

Light veal jus –
the professionals'
basic brown sauce

LIGHT CHICKEN JUS

The delicate flavour of this jus makes it ideal for chicken or pan-roasted fish or for braising vegetables like celery and Jerusalem artichokes.

Makes 600ml (1 pint)

3tbsp vegetable oil

1kg (2¼lb) chicken wings or carcasses, chopped into small pieces

2 shallots, chopped

100g (3½oz) mushrooms or mushroom trimmings, chopped

1 garlic clove, chopped

3 tomatoes, quartered

1tsp tomato purée

sprig of thyme

1 bay leaf

300ml (10fl oz) dry white wine

600ml (1 pint) water

1.5 litres (2¾ pints) dark chicken stock

1tbsp arrowroot, mixed with a little water

1 Heat the oil in a large pan. When smoking, add the chicken and fry over high heat for about 20 minutes, or until golden brown all over.

2 Add the shallots, mushrooms, and garlic and fry until golden and caramelized. Add the tomatoes, tomato purée, thyme, and bay leaf and cook for a further 6–8 minutes.

3 Pour the wine and water into the pan and bring to the boil, scraping the sediment from the bottom of the pan with a wooden spoon to release the caramelized juices. Boil, uncovered, for about 25 minutes, or until the liquid is reduced by two-thirds.

4 Add the stock. Bring back to the boil, then boil, uncovered, for about 20 minutes to reduce again by half, regularly skimming off any impurities that rise to the surface.

5 Stir in the arrowroot mixture to thicken the jus and cook for 2 minutes, then strain through a fine sieve. The resulting jus should be thick enough to lightly coat the back of a spoon.

Mounting with butter

In professional kitchens, brown sauces are always finished with a knob of butter, just before serving. This important technique is called monter au beurre (mounting with butter). The butter acts as an emulsifier and serves to make the sauce richer and smoother, as well as adding sheen. It can also be used to correct a sauce that is too sharp in flavour.

To mount with butter, add small pieces of chilled, unsalted butter to the finished sauce and whisk them in. Once the butter has been added, the sauce should never be re-boiled as this will cause the butter to separate and float to the surface, thus making the sauce greasy. To correct a sauce if this does happen, remove the surface layer of fat with a small ladle.

1 Cut a chilled knob of butter into cubes. Take the pan of sauce off the heat and whisk in each cube of butter before adding the next.

2 When all the butter has been whisked in, the sauce will be glossy and smooth.

PAN SAUCES

Pan sauces are generally made at the last moment while the meat is resting. Once the meat or poultry has been roasted or pan-fried, it is removed and any excess fat in the pan is skimmed off. Liquid, such as a simple stock, jus, or wine, is then added to the hot pan and stirred into the caramelized juices. This is known as deglazing.

These juices are then reduced and wine, cream, or butter is stirred in to finish the sauce. Shown below are the steps in making a pan sauce after roasting a chicken.

Gravies made from simple roasts are also prepared in this way and may be thickened with flour or another form of starch or by reduction of the pan liquid.

1 Remove the chicken from the pan and skim off most of the fat. Put the pan on the hob over medium heat and add 200ml (7fl oz) white wine. Scrape up the juices and boil until syrupy.

2 Add 200ml (7fl oz) chicken or vegetable stock and boil until syrupy. Add about 1tsp beurre manié (p25) and stir until the mixture thickens, then cook for 1–2 minutes.

3 Stir in 1tsp Dijon mustard and 2tbsp single cream. The sauce can be strained at this point, if preferred. Season to taste and add chopped soft herbs, such as tarragon, if desired.

Venison with cherries, cinnamon, and walnuts

Ever since I discovered dried cherries I have been experimenting with them in different dishes. They are great with poultry and game, as here in one of my favourite recipes, which I love to serve during the short game season.

Scrape up the caramelized juices to deglaze the pan

2tbsp vegetable oil

4 medallions of venison loin, about 175g (6oz) each, seasoned

3tbsp sherry vinegar

4tbsp cherry brandy

120ml (4fl oz) full-bodied red wine

1cm (½in) cinnamon stick

150ml (5fl oz) game or veal jus

50g (1¾oz) dried cherries

1tbsp redcurrant jelly

4tbsp port

2tbsp broken walnut pieces

10g (¼oz) unsalted butter, chilled and cut into small pieces

Heat the oil in a large pan. Add the medallions and sauté for 3–5 minutes, or until golden all over. Remove from the pan and keep warm.

Drain excess oil from the pan. Add the sherry vinegar and deglaze the pan. Bring to the boil and cook until the vinegar has boiled off.

Add the cherry brandy, red wine, and cinnamon stick and cook for 3–4 minutes, or until the wine has reduced by half.

Pour in the jus and add the dried cherries, then simmer for 5 minutes.

Remove the cinnamon stick and add the redcurrant jelly, port, and walnuts. Whisk in the butter, piece by piece, then season to taste. Pour the hot sauce over the venison to serve.

VEGETABLE & HERB SAUCES

With just a few simple processes, you can create colourful, fresh-tasting sauces based on vegetable and herb purées. Vegetables can be cooked or used raw and you can purée in a blender or food mill, press through a sieve, or pound with a mortar and pestle. The addition of a little cream and/or butter will smooth the texture and add richness. Sauces like this are superb served with anything from pasta and fish to meat and poultry dishes. Here are a few of my favourite vegetable and herb sauces.

TOMATO SAUCE

This simple yet versatile sauce is perfect with fish, meat, poultry, and vegetables. Rather than puréeing the sauce in a blender, I sieve it. This keeps the rich colour and removes the tomato skins. If the sauce is a little bitter, add more sugar.

Makes 600ml (1 pint)

25g (scant 1oz) unsalted butter
1tbsp olive oil
2 shallots, chopped
sprig of thyme
1 small bay leaf
3 garlic cloves, crushed
1kg (2¼lb) fresh, over-ripe plum tomatoes, seeded and chopped
2tbsp tomato purée
1tbsp caster sugar
250ml (8½fl oz) water
100ml (3½fl oz) tomato juice (optional)

1 Place the butter, oil, shallots, thyme, bay leaf, and garlic in a saucepan. Cover and sweat over a low heat for 5–6 minutes, or until the shallots are soft but not browned.

2 Stir in the tomatoes, purée, and sugar. Cook over a low heat, uncovered, for 5 minutes. Add the water and tomato juice, if using, raise the heat and bring to the boil.

3 Reduce the heat and simmer, uncovered, for 30 minutes. Season, then use a ladle to press the sauce through a sieve. Return to the pan and reheat before serving.

VARIATIONS

Rustic style
For a more robust tomato sauce, do not sieve it and remove the bay leaf and thyme just before serving.

Italian style
To produce a simple Italian-style sauce, add 1tbsp chopped basil or oregano just before serving.

Spicy
For a fiery kick, chop a hot chili and add with the tomatoes.

Slow-simmered tomato sauce, smooth and rich

WATERCRESS SAUCE

Here's a good example of a sauce created simply by mixing cream and butter with a vegetable purée. Variations are limitless – instead of blanched watercress, try 450g (1lb) asparagus, broccoli, Jerusalem artichokes, or leeks, chopped into 2.5cm (1in) pieces. The watercress sauce is superb with poached salmon or turbot.

Makes 450ml (15fl oz)

450g (1lb) watercress, stalks removed
200ml (7fl oz) vegetable or light chicken stock
200ml (7fl oz) double cream
25g (scant 1oz) unsalted butter

1 Plunge the watercress into a pan of boiling water to blanch for 30 seconds. Drain in a colander, then refresh in a bowl of iced water. Squeeze the watercress in a piece of muslin or a tea towel to remove all excess water.

2 Put the watercress in a medium-sized saucepan with the stock and cream. Bring to the boil, then reduce the heat and simmer for 10 minutes, stirring occasionally. Transfer to a blender and process to a smooth purée.

RED PEPPER SAUCE

This sauce is great with fish, vegetables, and pasta.

Makes 450ml (15fl oz)

2 red peppers, seeded and chopped
40g (1½oz) unsalted butter
200ml (7fl oz) water or vegetable stock
sprig of thyme
100ml (3½fl oz) double cream

1 Put the peppers in a saucepan with one-third of the butter. Cover and sweat over a low heat until the peppers are slightly softened. Add the water or stock and thyme. Bring to the boil. Reduce the heat and simmer gently, uncovered, for 15–20 minutes. Discard the thyme.

2 Transfer the mixture to a blender and process to a purée. Press through a sieve back into the pan. Reheat, then whisk in the cream, remaining butter, and seasoning to taste.

MOREL SAUCE

The perfect choice with steaks and veal chops.

Makes 300ml (10fl oz)

10g (¼oz) dried morels
300ml (10fl oz) hot chicken stock
2 shallots, chopped
25g (scant 1oz) unsalted butter
splash of Cognac
100ml (3½fl oz) dry white wine
60ml (2fl oz) double cream
90ml (3fl oz) Madeira

1 Soak the morels in the stock for 30 minutes. Remove them. Strain and reserve the liquid.

2 Put the shallots in a saucepan with one-third of the butter. Cover and sweat over a low heat until soft. Add the morels and sweat for 2 minutes, then add the Cognac, wine, and liquid from the morels. Simmer, uncovered, for 15 minutes, or until reduced by half.

3 Transfer to a blender and process to a purée. Return to the pan. Reheat, then add the cream, Madeira, remaining butter, and seasoning.

3 Press the purée through a fine sieve back into the pan. Bring to the boil, stirring, then remove from the heat and whisk in the butter and seasoning to taste. Serve hot.

PESTO ALLA GENOVESE

In addition to pasta dishes, pesto sauce is good with fish, meat, and vegetables. The version here is quick, but if you prefer you can make it more traditionally using a mortar and pestle.

Makes 150ml (5fl oz)

75g (2½oz) basil leaves
2 garlic cloves, crushed
1tbsp roughly chopped pine nuts
2tbsp freshly grated Parmesan
100ml (3½fl oz) extra virgin olive oil

1 Place the basil, garlic, pine nuts, and cheese in a blender. With the motor running, pour in the oil in a slow stream through the feed tube.

2 Process until a smooth sauce is formed, then season with salt and pepper. Alternatively, pound the basil, garlic, pine nuts, and cheese in a

mortar with a pestle, then slowly work in the oil. Pesto can be kept in the refrigerator for up to 1 week, although it will lose flavour and colour.

CHIMICHURRI

One of my favourite steak sauces, chimichurri from Argentina is made in the same way as pesto. Blend together 75g (2½oz) flat-leaf parsley leaves, 2 crushed garlic cloves, 2 small, seeded and finely chopped red chilies, 2tbsp wine vinegar, 1tsp chopped oregano, and 100ml (3½floz) olive oil.

HORSERADISH SAUCE

This piquant sauce is the classic accompaniment for hot or cold roast beef, steak, and smoked fish.

Makes 450ml (15fl oz)

150g (5½oz) fresh white breadcrumbs
120ml (4fl oz) milk
5cm (2in) piece of fresh horseradish root
2tbsp white wine vinegar
½tsp made English mustard
100ml (3½fl oz) double cream

1 Place the breadcrumbs in a bowl, pour in the milk, and leave to soak for 20 minutes.

2 Scrub and peel the horseradish. Finely grate it into a bowl. Add the vinegar and mustard.

3 Squeeze excess milk from the breadcrumbs, then add them to the horseradish mixture.

4 Whip the cream until slightly peaked and fold into the horseradish mixture. Season to taste with salt and pepper.

MINT SAUCE

The traditional partner for roast or grilled lamb, mint sauce is incomparable when freshly made from mint leaves just picked from the summer garden. This is one of the few recipes where the pungency of malt vinegar is called for. The amount of vinegar you add will depend on the consistency preferred for the final sauce. Mint sauce will keep, chilled, for several days.

Makes 150ml (5fl oz)

100g (3½oz) mint

1tbsp caster sugar

2tbsp malt vinegar, or to taste

1 Remove the leaves from the mint stalks. Place in a mortar with the sugar and crush to a pulp with the pestle.

2 Leave for 30 minutes, by which time the sugar will have extracted the juice from the mint. Give the sauce a final pounding, then add malt vinegar to taste and stir to combine.

RAW TOMATO SAUCE

Light, fresh, and slightly tangy, this uncooked tomato sauce is the essence of summer. Do not be tempted to boil the sauce and serve it hot – raw tomato sauce is completely different in make-up from the cooked version. It is good with grilled fish and marinated vegetables.

Instead of using a food mill, you can purée the sauce in a blender and then press the purée through a sieve to remove skin and seeds.

Makes 450ml (15fl oz)

450g (1lb) very ripe, soft tomatoes, chopped

1tbsp tomato purée

10 basil leaves

1tbsp caster sugar

2tbsp sherry or raspberry vinegar

100ml (3½fl oz) olive oil

1 Combine the tomatoes, tomato purée, basil, sugar, and vinegar in a bowl. Cover and leave for 2 hours at room temperature. Purée the mixture by working it through a food mill.

2 Slowly add the oil to the tomato mixture, whisking constantly. Season to taste with salt and pepper. Serve at room temperature. The sauce can be kept in the refrigerator for up to 3 days.

Raw tomato sauce –
the fresh taste of summer

NUT SAUCES

Sauces based on nuts can be found all over the world, with each region having its own favourites – peanut sauces in Southeast Asia, for example, almond sauces in regions of India, walnut sauces in the Middle East, and coconut sauces in the Caribbean.

In Europe, all kinds of nuts are used, often blended or pounded with bread and garlic to make wonderful smooth sauces that are served with pasta, fish, and simple grilled dishes. Three of the most popular and simply made nut sauces are described here.

SALSA DI NOCI

In Liguria, a region of northwest Italy, this sauce of pounded walnuts is traditionally served with pansotti, a pasta stuffed with local wild herbs, but it goes well with other types of pasta too.

Makes 300ml (10fl oz)

2 garlic cloves, crushed

125g (4½oz) walnut halves, blanched and skinned

3tbsp fresh white breadcrumbs

4tbsp olive oil

25g (scant 1oz) Parmesan, freshly grated

4tbsp soured cream or plain yogurt

milk to thin, if needed

1 Place the garlic, walnuts, and breadcrumbs in a mortar. Add the oil and, using the pestle, pound to a rough purée.

2 Mix in the Parmesan, soured cream or yogurt, and seasoning to taste. If the sauce is too thick, thin it by stirring in a little milk.

ALMOND TARATOR

This Turkish sauce is great with grilled and deep-fried foods.

Makes 300ml (10fl oz)

3 slices white bread, crusts removed

4tbsp milk

175g (6oz) whole blanched almonds

3 garlic cloves, crushed

120ml (4fl oz) olive oil

juice of 1 lemon

Sprinkle the bread with the milk and leave for 30 minutes. Purée with the almonds, garlic, oil, and lemon juice in a blender. Season.

ROMESCO SAUCE

This spicy red sauce from Catalonia is wonderful with grilled shellfish, oily fish, and meats. If you prefer a milder sauce, remove the chili seeds.

Makes 300ml (10fl oz)

2 small dried red chilies

150ml (5fl oz) olive oil

3 garlic cloves, crushed

25g (scant 1oz) whole blanched almonds, roughly chopped

20g (¾oz) blanched and skinned hazelnuts, roughly chopped

2 slices white bread, crusts removed and cubed

100ml (3½fl oz) tomato juice or passata

2tbsp white wine vinegar

pinch of smoked paprika

1 Soak the chilies in boiling water for 10–15 minutes. Drain and chop, removing the seeds, if you like. Heat 3tbsp of the oil in a frying pan, add the garlic and all the nuts, and fry until golden. Remove with a slotted spoon to drain.

2 Add another 3tbsp oil to the pan. When hot, add the bread cubes and fry until golden. Remove with a slotted spoon and drain on kitchen paper. Pour the tomato juice or passata and the remaining oil into the pan to warm through.

3 Put the fried garlic, nuts, and bread cubes in a blender. Add the white wine vinegar, warmed tomato juice and oil, and chopped chilies and blend to a purée. Season with the smoked paprika and salt to taste.

Char-grilled mackerel with orange romesco

Mackerel is one of the unsung heroes of our seas. It has never really been renowned as a delicacy, which I feel is a great pity and far less than it deserves because it is cheap and nutritious and has a wonderful flavour. Mackerel is best grilled and in this recipe the spiciness of romesco sauce beautifully cuts the richness of the fish.

1 bulb of fennel, trimmed and cut into 8 slices or wedges

4tbsp extra virgin olive oil plus extra for brushing

4 mackerel fillets, about 175g (6oz) each

juice of 1 orange

grated zest of ½ orange

150ml (5fl oz) romesco sauce (see opposite)

12 red cherry tomatoes, halved

12 black olives, pitted and quartered

Blanch the fennel in boiling, salted water for 2–3 minutes, then remove with a slotted spoon to drain.

Heat 2tbsp olive oil in a large, ridged cast-iron grill pan over medium heat. Season the fennel slices and place on one side of the pan. Cook, turning regularly, until tender and golden.

At the same time, season the mackerel and brush all over with oil. Place in the pan alongside the fennel and cook for 3–4 minutes on each side, or until cooked and lightly charred all over.

Meanwhile, combine the orange juice, zest, and romesco sauce in a bowl.

Heat the remaining 2tbsp oil in a small pan and gently warm the cherry tomatoes and olives for 1 minute. Season to taste.

To serve, arrange the fennel, olives, and tomatoes on 4 warmed serving plates, top with the char-grilled mackerel, and spoon over the orange romesco sauce.

SAVOURY FRUIT SAUCES

For centuries, the British have served savoury fruit-based sauces with their food to add a contrast in flavour and texture. Traditional partners for simply roasted joints of meat and poultry, served hot or cold, include apple sauce with pork or duck and Cumberland sauce with goose or ham. Many of these savoury fruit sauces are simply made by simmering fruit with flavourings and sugar and are eaten straightaway. Chutneys and relishes, though, are usually left to mature for a month or more, which improves their flavour.

AUTUMN FRUIT CHUTNEY

For the best flavour, leave in a cool, dark, dry place for 1–2 months before serving.

Makes 2kg (4½lb)

900g (2lb) cooking apples, peeled, cored, and chopped

450g (1lb) pears, peeled, cored, and chopped

400g (14oz) onions, chopped

1 garlic clove, crushed

250g (8½oz) raisins

1 litre (1¾ pints) cider vinegar or white wine vinegar

1tbsp ground ginger

1tbsp ground cinnamon

2tsp ground turmeric

25g (scant 1oz) salt

450g (1lb) dark brown sugar

1 Place the apples, pears, onions, garlic, raisins, and vinegar in a preserving pan. Bring to the boil. Simmer for 20 minutes, or until the apples and pears are soft but still keeping their shape.

2 Add the spices, salt, and sugar and stir until the sugar has dissolved. Reduce the heat and simmer for 45–60 minutes, or until most of the liquid has evaporated and the chutney is thick.

3 Ladle the chutney into sterilized preserving jars and seal well. Label and date the jars.

OLD-FASHIONED APPLE SAUCE

One must never contemplate eating roast pork without apple sauce. Here is a favourite recipe of mine, dating back to the early 18th century.

Makes 300ml (10fl oz)

450g (1lb) cooking apples, peeled, cored, and thickly sliced

strip of lemon peel

75ml (2½fl oz) cold water

25g (scant 1oz) caster sugar

15g (½oz) unsalted butter, chilled and diced

1 Place the apples in a medium-sized saucepan with the lemon peel and water. Cover and simmer gently for 10–12 minutes, or until the apples have softened. Stir in the sugar, then remove from the heat and leave to cool.

2 Remove the lemon peel. Press the apples through a sieve or purée them in a blender. Return to the pan and reheat gently, then stir in the butter. Serve the sauce warm.

GOOSEBERRY & MINT SAUCE

This tart sauce is wonderful with roast pork and goose. I also like to serve it with oily fish.

Makes 450ml (15fl oz)

400g (14oz) under-ripe or frozen thawed gooseberries, topped and tailed

4tbsp cold water

90g (3¼oz) caster sugar, or to taste

100ml (3½fl oz) sweet muscat wine

small bunch of mint, chopped

1 Put the gooseberries in a heavy-based saucepan with the water, half the sugar, and the wine. Bring to the boil, then reduce the heat and simmer, uncovered, for 10 minutes, or until the fruit has softened.

2 Transfer to a blender and process to a purée. Add the remaining sugar, or more to taste. Allow to cool. Before serving, stir the mint into the sauce and season to taste.

CUMBERLAND SAUCE

The most refined of all savoury fruit sauces, Cumberland is a particular favourite at Christmas time, served with cold meats such as ham, duck, or goose. The sauce can be kept in the refrigerator for 2–3 days. When in season, use a blood orange for even richer colour.

Makes 300ml (10fl oz)	250g (8½oz) redcurrant jelly
1 small orange	1tsp Dijon mustard
1 lemon	75ml (2½fl oz) port
1 shallot, finely chopped	½tsp ground ginger

1 Using a zester or vegetable peeler, take the zest off the orange and lemon. Cut the zest into julienne strips. Put the strips and shallot in a small saucepan of boiling water and blanch for 2 minutes, then drain in a sieve and set aside.

2 Combine the redcurrant jelly, mustard, port, and ginger in the saucepan and stir over low heat until the jelly melts. Do not boil. Add the juices of the orange and lemon, the zest, and shallot. Season. Serve at room temperature.

HOT & SPICY SAUCES

These kinds of sauces will delight the adventurous, heat-seeking cook because they add zip and intensity to the culinary repertoire. In the realm of hot ingredients, it is undoubtedly the chili that wears the crown, but other interesting hot flavourings, such as mustard seeds, horseradish root, and fresh ginger, also have an important part to play in spicing up sauces.

SPICY TOMATO & HORSERADISH KETCHUP

Make this ketchup during the summer when ripe, juicy tomatoes are at their peak. Unlike other ketchups, it can be used immediately. Stored in a cool, dry place, it will keep for up to 6 months. Once opened, refrigerate it.

Makes 700ml (1 pint 3½fl oz)

2kg (4½lb) ripe plum tomatoes, cut into large pieces

1tbsp tomato purée

200g (7oz) onions, finely chopped

250g (8½oz) cooking apples, peeled, cored, and chopped

6 whole cloves

1tsp mustard seeds

1 cinnamon stick, broken into pieces

½tsp celery seeds

250ml (8½fl oz) distilled white vinegar

25g (scant 1oz) sea salt

250g (8½oz) light brown sugar

7.5cm (3in) piece of fresh horseradish root, peeled and grated

Spicy tomato & horseradish ketchup is superb with fried fish, grilled steaks, and hamburgers

1 Put the tomatoes, tomato purée, onion, and apples in a preserving pan with the cloves, mustard seeds, cinnamon stick, celery seeds, half of the vinegar, and the salt. Slowly bring to the boil, then reduce the heat to a simmer.

2 Cook for 1–1½ hours, stirring occasionally, until the tomatoes are soft and pulpy and the mixture has reduced by one-third. Using the back of a ladle, press the mixture through a fine sieve into a clean pan.

3 Add the remaining vinegar, the sugar, and horseradish. Cook over a low heat until the sugar dissolves, then simmer for 30–40 minutes, or until the ketchup is thick. Pour into sterilized jars and seal. Cool before using.

BERBERE

Add a spoonful of this fiery-hot sauce from Ethiopia to beef stews and lentil dishes. Berbere will keep for 3 months in the refrigerator.

Makes 300ml (10fl oz)

6 dried ancho chilies

3tbsp groundnut oil plus extra for brushing

2tsp cumin seeds

1tsp black peppercorns

2tbsp smoked paprika

1tsp ground cardamom

½tsp ground allspice

½tsp ground cinnamon

½tsp ground coriander

½tsp ground ginger

1 onion, grated

2 garlic cloves, crushed

1 Preheat the oven to 230°C (450°F, gas 8). Place the chilies on a baking tray, brush with oil, and roast for 6–8 minutes, or until charred all over. Peel the chilies while warm, then place in a bowl and cover with boiling water. Leave to soak for 30 minutes.

2 Dry-roast the cumin seeds and peppercorns in a frying pan.

3 Drain the chilies, reserving the soaking liquid, and put them in a blender with the whole and ground spices, the onion, and garlic. Add 5tbsp soaking liquid and the oil and process to a smooth sauce.

4 Transfer the sauce to a small pan and cook over a low heat for 10 minutes, or until thick. Cool before serving.

SMOKY YELLOW PEPPER SALSA

Scotch bonnet chilies are extremely hot. If you prefer a milder salsa, use a Dutch variety of chili instead.

Makes 300ml (10fl oz)

3tbsp olive oil

2 yellow peppers, seeded and quartered

½ Scotch bonnet chili, seeded and chopped

3tbsp chopped coriander

2tbsp lemon juice

½ small onion, finely chopped

1tbsp maple syrup

1 Heat 1tbsp oil in a ridged cast-iron grill pan. Add the peppers and cook for 5–6 minutes, or until tender and slightly charred. Cool.

2 Coarsely chop the peppers. Put in a bowl with the remaining ingredients, mix, and season.

DIPPING SAUCES

Middle Eastern hummus, Indian raita, Mexican guacamole, and Mediterranean tapenade are just a few examples of sauces designed to be dipped into using bread, crisp breadsticks, or pieces of raw vegetables and fruit. Dipping sauces can also be spooned onto canapé toasts to eat with drinks before a meal or served as side dishes with grilled meats and fish and with curries. They are great for picnics too. To allow the flavours to develop, make dipping sauces in advance and keep them in the refrigerator.

RAITA

A cooling, yogurt-based dipping sauce, this is traditionally served with most Indian meals.

Makes 300ml (10fl oz)

1 cucumber, peeled
½tsp salt
½tsp cumin seeds, dry-roasted
120ml (4fl oz) plain full-fat yogurt
½tsp caster sugar
1 garlic clove, crushed
1tbsp chopped mint
1tbsp chopped coriander

1 Finely grate the cucumber. Toss with salt and leave for 1 hour.

2 Squeeze out as much liquid from the cucumber as you can.

3 Crush the cumin seeds to a fine powder in a mortar with a pestle. Add to the cucumber with the remaining ingredients, mix, and chill.

TOMATO TAPENADE

This vegetarian-friendly, flavour-packed dipping sauce, served with a basket of warm breads, has been on my menu at The Lanesborough for over 5 years. It is also excellent with grilled fish and lamb.

Makes 250ml (8½fl oz)

100g (3½oz) oil-packed sun-dried tomatoes, drained and roughly chopped
1tsp Dijon mustard
25g (scant 1oz) capers, rinsed and drained
25g (scant 1oz) pitted green olives
2 garlic cloves, crushed
1tsp chopped rosemary
1tsp lemon juice
90ml (3fl oz) extra virgin olive oil

1 Put all the ingredients in a food processor. Using the on-off pulse button, process to a coarse purée, but not until smooth.

2 Season the tapenade with salt and pepper to taste. Serve at room temperature.

VINAIGRETTES

In broad terms, a dressing is a sauce for salad and much of the success of a salad lies in the harmony and balance of its dressing, which should flavour and complement, never dominate. The most common salad dressing is vinaigrette, or French dressing, which at its simplest is a blend of good-quality vinegar and a non-scented oil. Over the past decade, chefs have begun using all manner of vinaigrettes, both to dress exciting salads and as an alternative to the heavier sauces of classic French cuisine.

CLASSIC VINAIGRETTE

Vinegars can vary in acidity, but I find a ratio of three or four parts oil to one part vinegar will produce a pleasing dressing, suitable for most uses. If it is to be served over fish or meat and vegetables, six parts oil to one part vinegar is better. Be sure to have all ingredients at room temperature. Larger quantities of vinaigrette can be made in advance and stored in a sealed jar at room temperature. Shake well before use.

Makes 150ml (5fl oz)

2tsp Dijon mustard
2tbsp good-quality vinegar (champagne or white wine)
65ml (2¼fl oz) vegetable oil
65ml (2¼fl oz) olive oil

1 Combine the mustard, vinegar, and a little salt and pepper in a bowl.

2 Gradually add the oils in a thin stream, whisking constantly. Check the seasoning.

CRUSHED TOMATO VINAIGRETTE

This tasty dressing is a perfect partner for grilled fish or vegetable salads.

Makes 150ml (5fl oz)

1 quantity classic vinaigrette (left)
115g (4oz) ripe cherry tomatoes
pinch of caster sugar
1 garlic clove, crushed

Place all the ingredients in a blender and process to a smooth purée. Thin slightly with a little warm water, if necessary.

Vinaigrette variations

Classic vinaigrette can be transformed into a host of other dressings by adding a few simple flavourings. Here are three.

Orange & rosemary

Add the grated zest and juice of 1 orange and 1tsp chopped rosemary to classic vinaigrette. Leave to infuse overnight before using.

Honey & ginger

Add 1tbsp clear honey and 1tsp grated fresh ginger to classic vinaigrette. Leave to infuse overnight before using.

Truffle & Madeira

Place 100ml (3½fl oz) Madeira and 1 chopped shallot in a small pan and boil to reduce until thick and syrupy. Allow to cool, then add to classic vinaigrette with 1tsp truffle oil. Leave to infuse for 1 hour, then strain. For a real treat, add ½tsp chopped fresh truffles to the dressing just before serving.

WARM & CREAMY DRESSINGS

During the colder months, it makes a change to prepare a salad with a warm dressing or to use a warm dressing to sauce fish, shellfish, or meat. Warm dressings can be made in advance or at the last minute with the pan juices from cooking fish or meat.

Creamy-textured dressings, made with single, double, or soured cream or mayonnaise and cheeses of all kinds, are quick and simple to prepare. They are ideal for dressing crisp salad leaves or as a sauce for cold shellfish and poached fish.

SAUCE VIERGE

Toss this version of vinaigrette with warm vegetables or serve it with grilled fish or shellfish.

Makes 300ml (10floz)

1 garlic clove, crushed
1 shallot, finely chopped

100ml (3½fl oz) olive oil
100g (3½oz) tomatoes, skinned, seeded, and finely diced
juice of ½ lemon or 1tbsp balsamic vinegar
pinch of caster sugar
2tbsp chopped basil leaves

1 Put the garlic and shallot in a small pan with the oil. Warm gently until soft, but do not fry.

2 Add the tomatoes and cook on a low heat for 4–5 minutes. Add the lemon juice or vinegar.

3 Add the sugar and the chopped basil to the sauce and stir to mix. Season to taste with salt and pepper. Keep the sauce warm until ready to use.

 A PAN DRESSING

Remove sautéed fish or meat from the pan and keep warm. Heat 1tbsp olive oil in the pan. Add 75g (2½oz) fresh wild mushrooms and sauté until golden. Add 1 crushed garlic clove and 2 finely chopped shallots and cook for 1 minute. Pour in 4tsp champagne vinegar and 2tsp balsamic vinegar and cook for 1 minute. Remove from the heat. Swirl in 2tbsp chopped flat-leaf parsley, 3tbsp olive oil, 2tbsp walnut oil, and seasoning to taste. Pour over the fish or meat or use to dress salad leaves to serve alongside.

ROQUEFORT DRESSING

Use this to dress salad leaves with crispy bacon crumbled over.

Makes 300ml (10floz)

75g (2½oz) Roquefort cheese
90ml (3fl oz) double cream
2tbsp sherry vinegar
4tbsp olive oil
1tbsp warm water

Purée the cheese in a blender. Add the cream, vinegar, oil, and water and process again briefly to mix. Season to taste and serve.

Bresaola with soft goat's cheese dressing

We have long enjoyed creamy dressings based on blue cheeses, but other cheeses are now being widely used. My creamy goat's cheese dressing is a good example, here served with the Italian cured beef, bresaola.

100g (3½oz) soft goat's cheese, crumbled

1tbsp sherry vinegar

4tbsp single cream

75ml (2½fl oz) olive oil

1tsp Dijon mustard

350g (12½oz) bresaola

75g (2½oz) rocket leaves

2 bunches of watercress

2tbsp white truffle oil

Put 75g (2½oz) of the goat's cheese in a blender. Add the vinegar, cream, olive oil, and mustard and process until smooth and creamy. Season with salt and pepper.

Arrange the bresaola on 4 serving plates. Place a small bouquet of rocket and watercress in the centre of each plate and drizzle over the creamy dressing.

Sprinkle the remaining goat's cheese on top. Drizzle with the truffle oil and serve immediately.

STOCKS & SOUPS

SHAUN HILL

A well-made stock is the basis of a good sauce or soup – without it, most lack power or finesse. Depending on the type of sauce or soup being made, the cook may need good butter, cream, olive oil, and vinegar, but in most cases the heart of a good sauce or soup is a clear stock that sings out the taste of its principle ingredient, as well as those of the other ingredients with which it was made. Stocks have an indispensable role, especially in the restaurant kitchen. Restaurants tend to use prime cuts of meat and fish – such as fillets and chops, Dover sole and sea bass – that are cooked only briefly. Anything only just cooked or, in the case of red meat, undercooked, preserves its tenderness and fine texture. The element lacking in this luxurious, last-minute cuisine is any intensity or depth of flavour from the meat or fish being used. Strong flavours come only from prolonged and thorough cooking. In cooking, the considerations of texture and flavour must always be balanced. A lightly boiled carrot retains its crunchy texture but lacks flavour when compared to one that has been cooked to a mush but strongly tastes of itself. The trick is to aim for the best of both worlds.

Depth and intensity of flavour In the classic French kitchen, compensation for the shortfall in depth of flavour in briefly cooked prime cuts, such as a grilled chicken breast or turbot fillet, is provided in the form of the gravy or sauce that partners it. All the bones and scraps are used to make good, strongly flavoured basic stocks for this purpose, as well as to give a layer of complexity to soups that may otherwise be made largely from starch and vegetables.

The humble ingredients that go into the stockpot belie its vital importance in cooking. The cook should resist any tendency to use it as a swill bin for whatever needs tidying away. Meat bones need to be roasted carefully to prevent blackened tips from imparting bitterness to the stock; fish bones should be gently sweated in oil or butter so that some deepening of colour can take place. This sweating process, technically known as the Maillard reaction, alters the surface proteins, caramelizing them for a more pronounced and significantly altered flavour. It accounts for the difference, say, between a boiled chicken and a roast one, or a poached sole and a grilled one. Some characteristics are true of all stocks, irrespective of their main ingredient. They should be clear and relatively fat-free, because fat boiling in a stock will emulsify, creating a cloudy texture and a muddy taste. However, meat and fish stocks should become gelatinous enough to set when cooled, so that the sauces and soups made with them have a more substantial and sticky feel in the mouth. No salt should be added at any stage – stocks are building blocks rather than finished dishes. Stocks are usually reduced at some stage, concentrating any saltiness they may have, and they may be added to ingredients with their own salty properties, such as cheese.

Soup making While sauce making, with veal stock as its cornerstone, is viewed as the apex of cooking expertise, soup making is often seen as basic, as though its preparation represents a lesser skill. Perhaps people have become too accustomed to the bland offerings of commercial soup companies. Soup also has an image as a vehicle for recycling leftovers, being at best a rustic rather than a refined starter. This poor reputation is entirely undeserved, for the craftsmanship needed to make a superb soup is exactly the same as that needed to create a subtle sauce. The cook has to draw on both skill and personal taste to decide on balance, seasoning, texture, and even the optimum cooking temperature as the flavours are blended into a liquid.

As this chapter will illustrate, there are four main styles of soup: those in which the ingredients are turned into purée; those in which meat or vegetables are suspended in broth; those thickened by egg yolks and cream; and finally consommé, which is the celebration of the stock as the star of the show. For many of these soups chicken stock is the main player, and a clear and well-made stock is a great start in making a classic, well-flavoured, mouth-satisfying soup.

CHICKEN, VEAL & FISH STOCKS

Chicken stock is easily achievable for the home cook. There are two styles, and the initial choice is whether to make a dark stock, which I simply call chicken stock, or a lighter version, which I call white stock. They are ready in hours (rather than the days needed for veal stock). They do not, however, keep well so must be made when needed. Otherwise, once cooled they have to be frozen or regularly reboiled. Either type, or veal stock, serves as the base for a fine soup. Use fish or chicken stock for fish soup.

CHICKEN STOCK

Roasting the bones gives dark chicken stock an intense flavour. It is particularly good for gravy and for consommé. The stock is clear and concentrated as most of the chicken fat is rendered away during roasting.

There is a school of thought that likes the vegetables as well as the bones to be roasted until light brown, but I have found this unnecessary. How much the bones are darkened has an impact on the finished stock in much the same way as the degree to which coffee beans are roasted affects the beverage produced. Darker means stronger but perhaps slightly bitter, too.

The ratio of bones to water in the recipe is a guideline and the general rule is the more bones the better, especially if you want a powerful stock. Prolonged cooking will produce little improvement in the depth or concentration of the stock. If you want to strengthen it, either use more bones or strain the finished stock into a clean pot, skim away as much fat as possible, then simmer until the liquid has reduced by whatever margin you feel appropriate.

There is little strength or flavour in a stock made with skin and backbones. Whole carcasses, raw or cooked and cut up, or winglets are best.

Raw carcasses are generally supplied free of charge by butchers who sell chicken separately as breast fillets and legs. You can buy boiling fowl very cheaply if no bones are available. Such fowl are generally older birds. The meat is not much good, but use it and cook the carcasses to the point of disintegration for the extra body and flavour they give to stock.

Makes about 1.5 litres (2¾ pints) stock

1kg (2¼lb) raw or cooked chicken bones
3 litres (5¼ pints) water
1 onion, quartered
1 leek, coarsely chopped
1 carrot, coarsely chopped

1 Preheat the oven to 200°C (400°F, gas 6). Place the bones in a roasting pan and roast for 20 minutes. Transfer to a large pot or pan.

2 Pour any fat from the pan, then add 500ml (17fl oz) of the measured water. Bring to the boil, scraping up any burnt-on residues.

3 Pour this deglazing liquid over the roasted bones in the pot or pan. Pour on the remaining measured water and bring to the boil.

4 Skim off any foam, then add the vegetables. Simmer, uncovered, for 3 hours, or until the bones begin to disintegrate. If the water level drops below the ingredients, top it up.

5 Strain the stock into a jug or bowl, then leave the pot and contents for a minute or so. Any stock held in the bones will drop to the base, leaving another ladleful of liquor.

COOLING STOCK FAST

Let stock cool naturally before refrigerating or freezing it. If you have made it on a summer's afternoon or evening, you may need to cool it more quickly so that it can be refrigerated before bedtime. Use the sink as a makeshift ice bucket. Half-fill it with cold water and some ice cubes, then place the bowl or jug of stock in this to cool. Any remaining fat will rise to the surface and set into a soft white slush, which is easy to remove with a large metal spoon. Underneath should be chicken stock, now jellied.

6 Leave the stock to cool – covered with a tea towel, if necessary. When it reaches room temperature, skim off any remaining fat with a large spoon, and then refrigerate. Once chilled, the stock should jelly: the more leg bones used, the more gelatinous it will be.

WHITE STOCK

White stock is made from unroasted bones and is good for pale, velouté-like sauces to partner poached chicken. It has a more subdued flavour than chicken stock and tends to be greasier and cloudier because no fat is rendered away by roasting. As with any stock, do not add any salt or strong spices.

Makes about 1.5 litres (2¾ pints) stock

1kg (2¼lb) raw chicken bones, about 4 carcasses
3 litres (5¼ pints) water
1 onion, coarsely chopped
1 leek, coarsely chopped
1 carrot, coarsely chopped
few parsley stalks

1 Place the bones in a stockpot or large saucepan and pour over the water. Bring to the boil.

2 Skim away any foam that rises to the top, then add the vegetables and parsley stalks. Simmer, uncovered, for 2 hours.

3 Strain the resulting liquor into a bowl or jug and allow to cool. When the stock is cool, refrigerate overnight. In the morning most of the fat will have solidified at the top of the container. Spoon this away and then reboil the stock to clear any remaining foam. If refrigerated again for later use, the stock will jelly when chilled.

VEAL STOCK

This is the king of stock. It is the most expensive to make, the most time consuming, and easily the most important item in a good restaurant's cold room. It can be made at home, but is only worth the effort if made in quantity. It keeps well and freezes without any loss of quality.

Veal bones are available from the butcher. Bones from adult animals are not as gelatinous as those from calves, and the stock from them is rather strong, usable only with beef dishes. Veal stock, on the other hand, can be made into jus (p36), which is the base sauce for confections that do not always involve either veal or beef.

Makes about 3 litres (5¼ pints) stock

3kg (6½lb) raw veal bones
6 litres (10½ pints) water
500g (1lb 2oz) onions, coarsely chopped
300g (10½oz) celery sticks, coarsely chopped
300g (10½oz) carrots, coarsely chopped

1 Place the bones on a roasting pan and roast in an oven preheated to 200°C (400°F, gas 6) for 30 minutes. Pour off the fat, then transfer the bones to a large stockpot or saucepan. Add 500ml (17fl oz) water to the pan and bring to the boil on the stovetop, scraping up any residues. Pour over the bones. Add the remaining water.

2 Bring to the boil. Skim off any foam, then add the vegetables. Simmer, uncovered, for 8 hours, topping up the water level and skimming as needed. As stockpots are large, the pan may not be directly centred on the heat. The fat will accumulate at the coolest edge of the pot's surface, making it easy to remove.

3 Strain the stock into a jug or bowl and allow to cool. Once refrigerated, it will jelly.

VEGETABLE STOCK

There are no vegetables that give stock the slightly thickened, gelatinous quality imparted by meat or fish bones. The best that can be hoped for is a well-flavoured if watery liquor. This is the only case where judicious use of commercial stock cubes may be superior to anything you produce yourself.

■ My advice is to buy a top-quality product and make it up in exactly the proportions indicated. Bring the stock to the boil along with chopped aromatic vegetables, such as onion, celery, carrot, and leek, to avoid any commercial or artificial aftertaste.

■ Never crumble stock cubes directly into a soup or risotto – the taste will be harsh.

■ Often, water is fine for diluting vegetable dishes that need liquid. While it adds nothing to the overall taste, it will not detract from the main flavours either.

FISH STOCK

Fish stock is the swiftest to make – an hour at most is all that's needed. Fish bones are available from a fishmonger, but not all make good stock. Those from white fish are best, so sole, turbot, hake, and whiting are the first choice. Second best are from fish that are only a little oily, such as salmon or bass. Bones from oily fish, such as herring or mackerel, are of little use.

The fish bones need gentle sweating in butter to heighten and bring out their flavour before any water is poured over. They are prone to catch and burn so take care to stir the pan base constantly during this part of the process.

Fish stock is the least versatile, good with fish but not with anything else, whereas chicken stock works just as well in a fish dish as in a chicken or vegetable one.

Makes about 2 litres (3½ pints) stock

2kg (4½lb) raw fish bones (see above)
25g (1oz) butter
250ml (8½fl oz) white wine
1 leek, chopped
1 onion, chopped
1tbsp black peppercorns, crushed
few parsley stalks
3 litres (5¼ pints) water

1 Wash the bones in plenty of cold water. Discard any bloody bits near the heads. Gently warm the butter in a stockpot or large saucepan. Add the bones and stir until you can smell cooked rather than raw fish. The bones should not brown.

2 Add all the remaining ingredients and bring to the boil. Skim away any white foam. Simmer gently, uncovered, for 40 minutes then strain into a jug or bowl. There will be little or no fat to skim off, but discard any impurities that drop to the bottom as the stock cools.

The texture of fish stock is thin, the flavour restrained

JAPANESE FISH STOCK

Dashi is a tuna and seaweed-based fish stock used for Japanese soups. It is generally sold dried. Like any commercial stock mixture, it needs to be reconstituted in the exact proportions advised on the packet, or it will be too salty. If you want a milder flavour, add chicken or fish stock to the dashi. If you have access to dried bonito tuna flakes and kombu seaweed you could make your own dashi. Do not boil the dashi for long periods, as evaporation concentrates the stock and it loses its delicacy.

CLEAR SOUPS

If you have made a particularly good stock, a clear soup is the finest and most sophisticated way to show it off. Consommé is the last word in clear soup. Careful manipulation of the stock's temperature during cooking and thorough straining through muslin afterwards are essential to achieve a crystal-clear result. The stock must heat gently and only just come to the boil. If it reaches a rolling boil, the delicate framework of the clarification mixture will break up into the stock rather than clarify it.

CHICKEN CONSOMMÉ

Consommé regularly has some garnish or herb to lend interest, but it is the quality and clarity of the soup itself that is at its heart.

The reduction of the stock as it clarifies means you must begin with about a third more liquid than you expect to end up with. Choose a pot that is deep and narrow. The crust formed by the clarification ingredients has to cover the whole surface, so a narrow pan makes things easier.

To garnish the soup, a few strands of pasta or some chopped or whole chervil is ideal. The formal end of the classical kitchen repertoire adds more exotic items, such as poached quail's eggs or chopped truffle, and I used to slip slices of raw white scallop meat into hot consommé to make a stylish first course for grand meals.

2 large egg whites
1tbsp passata or 1tsp tomato purée
1 chicken leg, boned and either minced or finely chopped
1 onion, chopped
1 carrot, chopped
1 leek, chopped
1 garlic clove, chopped
1tbsp chopped parsley
2 litres (3½ pints) cold chicken stock
chervil, to garnish

1 To make the clarification mixture, whisk the egg whites just enough to loosen them and form a few bubbles. Add the passata or tomato purée and mix thoroughly with the egg whites.

2 Place the chicken, vegetables, garlic, and parsley in a bowl, add the egg white mixture and mix thoroughly – use an electric mixer with paddle attachment if need be. Refrigerate until well chilled.

3 Combine the stock with the clarification mixture in a large saucepan. Heat slowly, uncovered, until the stock comes to the boil. Gently stir to stop the egg sticking.

5 When the consommé is clear and the clarification ingredients cooked, widen the gap and strain the soup through a muslin-lined sieve into a clean container. Season the consommé, garnish with chervil, and serve.

SOUPS WITH SOLID INGREDIENTS

Soups with solid ingredients suspended in a stock base may be a meal in themselves rather than a prelude. Minestrone is a hearty Italian classic and Scotland's Cock a leekie, a chicken broth spiked with prunes and leeks, is in the same chunky style. Oriental soups tend to be delicate and quick to prepare and cook. Fish soups may be close to a stew or more like consommé with a substantial garnish.

PRAWN & SEA BASS SOUP

This clear seafood soup uses dashi (p61) as its base. It is flavoured with soy sauce, which should be the genuine Japanese article, brewed and then aged. Many firms make cheaper products in Singapore for the foreign market. Tamari may be substituted for those avoiding gluten in their diet.

100g (3½oz) spinach, blanched (p482)

1 litre (1¾ pints) dashi

100g (3½oz) sea bass fillet, cut into 4 cubes

4 large raw prawns, peeled and deveined

1tsp soy sauce

½ small red chili

1 spring onion, chopped

1tbsp arrowroot

few drops of lemon juice

1 Squeeze out as much water as possible from the blanched spinach then cut into strips.

2 Bring the dashi to the boil in a saucepan and add the fish and prawns. Cook for a few moments, then add the soy sauce, chili, and spring onion.

3 Whisk the arrowroot with 1tbsp cold water in a bowl. Stir into the soup, bring to the boil, then remove the chili. Add the lemon juice and spinach and serve.

THICKER SOUP

Adding arrowroot, cornflour, rice flour, or the Japanese thickening agent kuzu, gives a soup body. Arrowroot is not an authentic oriental ingredient like kuzu but is easier to find. It acts rather like a hot liquid counterpart of gelatin, giving body to a clear stock. Cornflour or kuzu is used in much the same way as arrowroot, diluted in a little cold water then whisked into the hot soup.

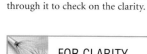

4 Once the stock reaches boiling point, turn the heat right down and leave to simmer gently for at least an hour, or until a white crust forms. When it is hard, poke a gap through it to check on the clarity.

FOR CLARITY

■ Chill the clarification mixture so that the cold egg whites shrink on to the other ingredients and help bind them. Some chefs add ice cubes to the mix to chill it effectively.

■ Before it boils, gently stir the stock while heating it so that the ingredients stay evenly distributed and the egg white does not burn on the base of the pot or saucepan. But once boiling, do not stir it or the consommé will be cloudy. Leave it at a bare simmer.

■ Muslin is very fine. Carefully straining the consommé through a sieve lined with muslin ensures a totally clear result.

THAI CHICKEN SOUP

Thai and Vietnamese ingredients are so widespread that even my rural greengrocer stocks galangal and lemon-grass. This recipe uses coconut milk as its base and key Thai flavourings but makes no pretence at authenticity. Bruise the herbs with the flat side of a heavy knife to help release their juices. They have fibrous textures but wonderful flavour and I strain them out before serving. Nam pla, a sauce made from fermented fish, is salty so needs no extra salt.

4 stalks of lemon-grass, cut into 1cm (½in) lengths

200g (7oz) galangal, peeled and diced

5 lime leaves, washed

1 chicken leg

500ml (17fl oz) water

2 small chilies

1 litre (1¾ pints) coconut milk

1tbsp nam pla

juice of 3 limes

3 spring onions, finely chopped

2tbsp chopped coriander leaves

COCONUT MILK

■ It is best to use the dried or block form, which is always unsweetened. The packet will advise dilution according to whether thin or thick coconut milk is needed. It is the thin version that's needed here, but make allowance for any reduction of water when cooking the main ingredients.

■ Coconut milk separates if heated too much or too long and will rise to the top of the soup if cooled. If this happens, pour it into a blender with some of the chicken and mix it back to a more homogeneous state.

1 Place the herbs, chicken, and water in a saucepan and bring to the boil. Simmer, uncovered, for 30 minutes until the chicken is cooked. Remove it, dice flesh, and reserve. Add the chilies to the pan.

2 Bring the soup back to the boil. Pour in the coconut milk and heat slowly. You need the soup to become hot enough for the flavours to infuse the coconut milk, but do not let it boil.

3 Strain the soup into a clean pan or tureen, then add the nam pla, lime juice, spring onions, coriander, and chicken. Taste in case any seasoning is needed. Cut the strained chili into slivers and use as a garnish, if wished.

MINESTRONE

One of the world's great soups – there are many versions, most of which are probably authentic to some region of Italy. The consensus is that the soup should be thick with ingredients, an almost solid mass rather than garnish swimming in clear broth. It should have pasta, cabbage, and tomato in there somewhere and lots more vegetables besides. Use whatever is in season and keep to the spirit of the recipe rather than the precise list here. Asparagus or courgettes make fine additions in spring or summer as do basil leaves instead of parsley. This recipe calls for bacon – combined with green cabbage it lends a satisfying background to the other ingredients. Vegetarians can keep the dish meatless by omitting the bacon and substituting water or vegetable stock for the chicken stock.

2tbsp olive oil

1 small onion, finely chopped

1 leek, finely chopped

1 celery stick, finely chopped

1 carrot, finely chopped

2 smoked streaky bacon rashers, cut into 2cm (¾in) strips

¼ Savoy cabbage, coarsely chopped

1 small potato, peeled and coarsely chopped

20g (¾oz) dried haricot beans, soaked overnight in cold water then boiled for 1 hour, or until tender

3tbsp tomato passata

1.5 litres (2¾ pints) chicken stock

25g (1oz) dried pasta, short or stubby shapes, otherwise broken into small lengths

1tbsp coarsely chopped flat-leaf parsley

To serve

freshly grated Parmesan

1 Heat the oil in a large saucepan and gently fry the vegetables (except for the cabbage and potato) and the bacon. When the vegetables start to soften, stir in the cabbage, potato, beans, and passata.

2 Season with salt and pepper, then continue cooking on a low heat for 10 minutes, stirring from time to time. Add the stock and bring to the boil.

3 Add the pasta and bring back to the boil. Simmer, uncovered, for 7–8 minutes, or until the pasta is just cooked. Add the parsley and check the seasoning. Serve with Parmesan on the side.

COCK A LEEKIE

This is a substantial soup: enough for a full lunch. It's Scottish in origin, and its essence, in contrast to anywhere else's chicken soup, lies in the use of prunes to flavour the broth – not such a bizarre idea when you think of the successful pairing of rabbit or pork with prunes. Its other singular aspect is the inclusion of beef or beef stock. The soup may be likened to pot au feu with the meat – here beef and chicken – either eaten along with the broth or as a separate course after it.

This recipe feeds six or eight people and it is hardly worth making the soup for fewer. If you do not have a pan large enough to hold the whole chicken and beef as they cook, dismantle the chicken into legs and breasts. Add them 15 minutes later because they will cook more quickly.

Remember that the cooking liquor is to be drunk so don't be tempted to oversalt. Add whatever extra may be needed at the end of cooking.

500g (1lb 2oz) piece of beef brisket

1.5 litres (2¾ pints) chicken stock or water

1 small chicken, about 1.25kg (2¾lb)

1kg (2 1/4lb) leeks, cut into 3cm (1¼in) lengths

250g (8½oz) pitted and ready-to-eat prunes

1 Place the beef and stock or water in a large saucepan. Bring to the boil and simmer, uncovered, for 30 minutes. Add the chicken and simmer for another 30 minutes. Use a large spoon to skim off any froth that rises to the surface. Top up the liquid level with water, if necessary.

2 Add the leeks and prunes then simmer for a further 10 minutes. Check for seasoning.

3 Lift out the meat and cut into small pieces. Place these in deep bowls and then ladle on the broth and other ingredients.

THICKENED SOUPS

Success in soups thickened by a liaison of whole eggs or egg yolk and cream lies in restraint, especially with the cream. Use no more than an equal volume of egg to cream and add a little at a time to the hot broth. Do it away from direct heat in case the egg cooks into omelette-like threads before you have a chance to incorporate it. The objective is to make a slightly thicker, smoother soup. Once this is achieved, more cream and egg will only make the soup too rich to be consumed by the bowlful. Avoid prolonged reheating after adding the liaison. The silky texture isn't stable enough to withstand boiling – this is a last-minute technique before serving.

AVGOLEMONE (BEID BI LAMOUN)

This lemon, chicken, and rice soup is claimed by countries across the eastern Mediterranean but is most famous as a Greek dish. It is thickened with eggs and lemon juice and makes a refreshing, sharp, and tangy summer soup. The soup sounds deceptively simple but two major aspects need particular care. The stock must be well flavoured, made with plenty of chicken, or it will not withstand the lemon juice. And the broth must not boil once the eggs and lemon are added. They must be gently and briefly cooked at a temperature safely below boiling point.

50g (1¾oz) long-grain rice
1.2 litres (2 pints) well-flavoured chicken stock
3 eggs
juice of 1 large lemon

1 Bring the rice and stock to the boil in a saucepan. Simmer, uncovered, for 15 minutes, or until the rice is completely cooked.

2 Whisk the eggs and lemon juice in a bowl until the mixture becomes frothy. Add a ladleful of hot stock and continue to whisk.

3 Remove the soup from direct heat. Whisk the egg, lemon, and stock mixture into it. Continue to whisk until the texture is velvety. Season and serve with lemon wedges.

NORTH SEA FISH SOUP

The fragile nature of the finished soup comes from the egg and cream liaison and is part of its appeal. The freshness and texture of the seafood are central, so it must all be just cooked and no more. Not all fish cook at the same speed: cut denser-fleshed species into smaller pieces or add them earlier.

The choice of fish is a guideline. Buy what is best on the day. Three different fish and one shellfish make an interesting soup. Use only fillets of fish and remove pin bones – the line of little bones head to tail along the centre of some fish.

500g (1lb 2oz) fish fillets and shellfish, – such as red mullet or bass, haddock or cod, salmon or turbot, peeled, raw shrimps or shelled scallops

1tbsp lemon juice

600ml (1 pint) fish or chicken stock

60ml (2fl oz) white wine

2 shallots, chopped

1 egg yolk

1tbsp double cream

1 tomato, skinned, seeded, and chopped

1tbsp chopped parsley

croûtons, to garnish

1 Skin the fish, if necessary, and cut into 2.5cm (1in) pieces. Season and add lemon juice. Bring the stock, white wine, and shallots to the boil in a large saucepan.

2 Add the fish in the order it takes to cook – red mullet or bass first, 2 minutes later the turbot, if using, followed by the haddock, cod, or salmon, and finally the shrimps or scallops.

3 Simmer the soup uncovered for up to 10 minutes. Cooking times may vary slightly. As soon as the fish is cooked, the soup is ready to be finished and served.

4 Stir the egg yolk and cream together in a bowl. Take the soup from direct heat, stir the mixture in, then add the tomato and parsley. Serve with croûtons.

MAKING CROÛTONS

Small dice of white, crustless bread are fried until crisp. Fry in whatever is appropriate to the soup: here, a little sunflower oil and butter is best. Otherwise use clarified butter. It does not burn as quickly as whole butter and makes the finest croûtons. Heat the oil or butter in a small frying pan and add 2 slices or 50g (1¾oz) diced bread. Shake the pan so the croûtons colour and cook evenly, then spoon them out onto kitchen paper and pat dry.

PURÉED SOUPS

Soups that are blended to a thick, smooth purée are the easiest to make. Most use pulses or another carbohydrate to give body, taste, and texture. Any soup that is thickened with potato is best if blended as soon as the potato is done and before it becomes overcooked and glutinous. So the size of the potato pieces and the timing of their addition to the stock are important.

SAFFRON SOUP

This soup is an advance on leek and potato soup and was a regular item at Robert Carrier's London restaurant where I worked in the 1970s. It has not dated and can be jazzed up with lobster or shrimps or served with sippets (see below).

1 tbsp olive oil

1 large onion, sliced

200g (7oz) leeks, cut into 3cm (1¼in) lengths

150g (5½oz) potatoes, peeled and diced

1 tsp saffron threads

1 tsp ground cumin

1 litre (1¾ pints) chicken stock

2 tbsp white wine

2 tbsp double cream

1 tbsp lemon juice

snipped chives to garnish

SIPPETS

Use the thin French stick known as a ficelle (string) rather than a baguette for sippets. Preheat the oven to 180°C (350°F, gas 4). Cut the bread into thin slices and spread on a baking sheet. Place on the lower shelf of the oven for 20 minutes, turning them over once the upper sides have dried. When you turn them, you can rub the upper sides with raw, peeled garlic, pounded anchovies, or a herb paste. Pound any mixture of thyme, chives, parsley, basil, and tarragon with olive oil and a little salt. At the end of cooking, sippets should be dry, not soggy.

1 Heat the oil in a heavy-based pan and gently fry the onion until soft. Add the leek, potato, saffron, cumin, and stock. Season with a little salt and pepper, then cover so that the soup cooks without too much reduction.

2 When the potato is soft the soup is ready – check after about 10 minutes. How long it takes to cook varies according to the type of potato and the size of the dice. Do not let the potato disintegrate into the soup.

3 Blend the soup with the white wine. Add the cream and lemon juice and check for seasoning. If the soup is too thick, dilute it with more stock or water. If it is too thin, add more olive oil. Garnish with snipped chives.

Chickpea & langoustine soup

I first came across this soup in Tuscany years ago, and it has appeared regularly on my menu ever since. The earthiness of the background chickpea blend is a good foil for the sweetness and extravagance of the shellfish. Dried chickpeas need a lot of soaking. If preferred, use canned chickpeas. Replace the water with stock; just bring the chickpeas to the boil and blend with the onion and garlic mixture.

200g (7oz) dried chickpeas

1 litre (1¾ pints) water

1 onion, chopped

2 garlic cloves, chopped

4tbsp olive oil

1tsp coriander seeds, crushed

4 raw langoustines, crayfish tails, or large whole prawns

200ml (7fl oz) white wine

1tbsp lemon juice

1tbsp snipped chives

Soak the chickpeas overnight in plenty of cold water. Drain and rinse, then add to a saucepan with the litre of water and bring to the boil. Do not add salt. Skim away any foam that rises to the surface as the water comes to the boil. Turn the heat down to low, cover, and simmer for 30–40 minutes, or until the chickpeas are tender.

Fry the onion and garlic in half the oil in a frying pan until soft but not brown. Add the coriander seeds and langoustines. Cook gently for a further 3–4 minutes, then add the white wine. Remove the langoustines, crayfish, or prawns and shell them.

Add the cooked onion and garlic mixture to the chickpeas and their cooking liquor and blend, in batches if necessary. If the soup is too thick, add more water or stock. Season with salt, pepper, and the lemon juice.

Serve the soup in warmed bowls with a langoustine, a scattering of snipped chives, and a drizzle of olive oil on top.

FLAVOURINGS

PETER GORDON

What is flavour? Is it a physical or an intellectual thing? Is it defined by region, or purely by individual taste? How do we learn to like a flavour, and can we learn to dislike a flavour? At what point in a child's life does the taste of Gorgonzola cheese become more appealing than that of apple purée? Flavour is generally defined as the sensation experienced when food comes into contact with the taste buds on the tongue. Four basic tastes – sweet, salty, sour, and bitter – are detected and identified by groups of specialized taste buds located on different parts of the tongue. Another sensation, called unami, has arisen from Japanese cuisine, a flavour coming from naturally occurring monosodium glutamate in some mushrooms, seaweeds, and other foods.

In my opinion, flavour is the combination of physical and cerebral sensations derived from anything we put in our mouths. A chunk of mango gives a slightly differing flavour to a purée of the same mango, which I put down to the textures and sensations the fruit in these two forms gives to the tongue. While the flavour of mango can be recreated in a laboratory from chemicals called ketones, nothing but a real mango can give the sensation of a mango in the mouth.

Regional preferences I am intrigued as to why people living in certain areas have a liking for one type of flavour over another. Why, for example, are lime juice and tamarind used so often in the salads, soups, and curries throughout Southeast Asia? Why is it that Thai people enjoy sour flavours usually tempered by sugar or sweet ingredients, while followers of French haute cuisine choose delicate buttery sauces? Spices have been travelling into Europe for many centuries yet few European cuisines utilize these in anything other than baked products. In India and the Middle East, cinnamon and cloves are as at home in a savoury stew as they are in a dessert. Is it simply that ingredients producing these flavours are available regionally, or are there genetic or practical reasons for such preferences? I cannot provide a definitive explanation, but I have observed over many years of cooking in restaurants that flavours can strongly evoke early episodes in people's lives.

Many customers have brought elderly parents to the restaurants where I have been cooking, to give them the opportunity to sample different kinds of foods. In the past I expected such clients to offer some resistance to my culinary ideas, but that has not proved to be the case. Instead, I have shaken the hands of many appreciative men and women who were transported back to their youth, serving in foreign offices in Asia or the Middle East. One dish of braised pork cheeks with star anise and black cardamon had a gentleman reminiscing about his time in Burma. He had never eaten pork cheeks during his time there, but the flavours reminded him strongly of living in the country. Even more than visual reminders, flavour seems to have the ability to recall a bygone time. Somehow the brain keeps a record of a flavour locked away, and a mouthful of a sauce with tamarind and chili can bring back all the memories associated with tasting the flavour in the distant past.

Flavours for the occasion Visiting a new, unfamiliar environment can have a powerful influence on our appreciation of flavour. When I set off on my Asian travels in 1985, I was no great fan of the chili or the raw banana. But after two weeks in Bali I would often have a couple of bananas for breakfast, and at intervals during my morning letter writing I would dip a chili into a bowl of sugar and munch it, washing it down with my kopi Bali. Arriving back in the UK a year later, I lost my appetite for raw bananas (I still love them cooked into a cake or fritter) but retained a love of chili. I can only put down these changes to eating "the right food in the right place". Take away the palm trees, the heat, and the sense of being on holiday, and you can also diminish the pleasure of the flavour. Likewise, a bratwurst and sauerkraut in a bun might seem the best thing ever in a snowy Berlin winter, but try eating it on a sunny beach in New Zealand and the flavours could not seem more wrong.

HERBS

Herbs are the leaves and stalks of edible aromatic plants; essential oils in these leaves and stalks give each herb its distinctive flavour.

I divide herbs into two groups – hard and soft. Hard herbs can withstand cooking for reasonable periods without losing impact. In fact, some benefit from cooking to mellow their flavour. In this group I include rosemary, sage, thyme (once the stalks are woody),

bay leaves, kaffir lime leaves, curry leaves, pandan leaves, lemongrass, and the larger leaves from older oregano.

Soft herbs are best used raw in a dish or added in the last few minutes, or seconds, of cooking. They include chives, the basil and mint families, chervil, parsley, coriander, tarragon, and young thyme, marjoram, and oregano.

Chopping herbs

When herbs are chopped they release their flavour more readily than if they are used whole. For some herbs, the leaves are stripped (see right), while for others – such as chervil, basil, and dill, which have tender and flavoursome stalks – the whole herb is chopped. If chopping whole herbs, gather up the sprigs into a bunch, then chop with a rocking motion, rotating the knife and pushing the herbs back into a pile. For herbs such as chives, rather than chopping just snip them with scissors.

Once chopped, herbs deteriorate quickly, so try to chop them at the last minute, or keep in a covered jar in the refrigerator until needed.

1 To chop herb leaves (a mixture or a single variety, such as the basil leaves shown in the photographs), gather them together and then roll them up tightly.

2 With 1 hand, hold the rolled herb leaves on a board. Using a large knife, slice across the roll to cut the herbs into shreds (this is called a chiffonade). Gather into a pile.

3 Using either the knife or a mezzaluna, chop the herbs using a rocking motion, turning the pile 90° halfway through, until you have the size you want.

Stripping leaves

Stripping is a quick way to remove herb leaves from the stalks. It is particularly suited to herbs with woody stalks, such as rosemary (shown here). Hold the stalk 5cm (2in) from the end and run thumb and forefinger of your other hand along the stalk to rip off the leaves. Then pick the leaves from the softer stalk at the tip.

Pounding herbs

Herbs are often pounded in a mortar and pestle when making marinades, pestos, and some sauces. The pounding action forces the flavour of the herbs into the other ingredients. Good examples of pounded mixtures are pesto sauce (with basil) and Thai-inspired marinades (lemon-grass and chilies).

Drying herbs

Some herbs dry better than others, retaining their taste and scent. For hard herbs, rinse and pat dry, then gather and tie the stalks together with string. Hang up in a cool to warm (not hot) room with plenty of air-flow. Once dry, leave in bundles or strip off the leaves.

For softer herbs, lay them on kitchen paper on trays. Leave in a cool to warm room (if hot or humid, the herbs might go mouldy).

Store in airtight containers and use within 4 months of drying, or while they still smell fragrant. Dried herbs are more concentrated than fresh, so use sparingly. A good rule of thumb is that for every 1tsp fresh herbs you can substitute – where appropriate – ½tsp dried.

Freezing herbs

Frozen herbs can be preferable to dried herbs, depending on what you're planning to do with them. For example, if I didn't have fresh basil I'd rather use frozen basil in my tomato linguine than dried.

You can either buy frozen herbs (keep an eye on expiry dates) or freeze them yourself. Wash the herbs and spread on kitchen paper to dry, then place on a tray lined with cling film. Freeze, uncovered, for about 3 hours. Once frozen, strip the leaves from the stalks. They'll keep for up to 6 months.

MEASURING HERBS IN CUPS

When adding large quantities of herbs to a recipe, I like to measure by volume rather than by weight, using a 250ml (8½fl oz) measuring cup. Lightly pack herbs in the cup, filling it full (1 cup), half full (½ cup), or whatever is required. A little more or less herbs won't dramatically affect the result.

HERB MIXTURES

Herbs are an intrinsic part of any cuisine. They can add a freshness, cleansing quality, or a deep earthy flavour to many different meals. Herbs are also often used together to create a rounded flavour and complexity. They are great team players that are well worth experimenting with.

BOUQUET GARNI

A bouquet garni is a bundle of herbs used to flavour "wet" dishes, such as soups and stews, where you want to remove the herbs after the dish has finished cooking. The classic combination of herbs is bay leaf, thyme, and parsley, although bouquet garnis can also contain sage, rosemary, and occasionally spices, such as cloves or allspice.

To make a bouquet garni you can either tie the herbs together with string, using bay leaves as the outer wrapper, or tie everything up in a small muslin bag.

GREMOLATA

This Italian salsa is traditionally sprinkled over cooked dishes such as osso bucco as they are served. I also like it on scrambled eggs and salmon at a weekend brunch, and with poached chicken and veal.

1 tightly packed cup flat-leaf parsley leaves

1 garlic clove, crushed

finely grated zest of 1 large lemon

Finely chop the parsley, then add the garlic and chop together. Mix in the lemon zest. Store, covered, in the refrigerator for no more than a few hours before using.

SALSA VERDE

This sauce is traditionally served with poached or grilled meats and fish. You can either make it by hand, chopping with a knife, or use a small food processor, blitzing the herb leaves with the oil first. Substitute other soft herbs in place of any of those suggested, if you prefer.

½ cup flat-leaf parsley leaves	1tbsp small capers, rinsed
½ cup basil leaves	¼ cup snipped chives
½ cup mint leaves	1 spring onion, finely sliced
¼ cup chervil leaves	125ml (4fl oz) extra virgin olive oil
⅛ cup tarragon leaves	1tsp whole grain mustard
3 cornichons, rinsed	grated zest and juice of ½ lemon

WASHING HERBS

Herbs bought from a supermarket will already be washed, but bunches from the local farmers' market will probably contain the odd twig, leaf, or insect. Fill a deep bowl with cool water and plunge in the herbs, holding by the stalks. Shake around a bit, then drain in a colander or give them a few good swings outdoors. Gently pat them dry in a tea towel before chopping.

1 Chop the parsley, basil, mint, chervil, and tarragon. Roughly chop the cornichons and capers or, if the capers are very small, leave them whole. Put in a bowl with the chives, spring onion, oil, mustard, and lemon zest, and mix together. Finally, stir in the lemon juice and season to taste.

2 Leave the salsa to sit for at least 30 minutes at room temperature so that the flavours can develop. Stir before serving.

THAI BASIL & CORIANDER MARINATED SQUID

This starter is quick to make on 2 counts: the marinade is assembled in seconds, and the squid needs only brief marinating and cooking. White pepper is used for its distinctive flavour, so don't replace it with black. You can also use the marinade on sliced chicken or turkey breast or fish fillets.

1½ heaped tsp white peppercorns
½tsp salt
1 garlic clove
handful of Thai basil
handful of coriander, including roots, stalks, and leaves
400g (14oz) squid, cleaned and body finely sliced into rings and tentacles separated
2tbsp groundnut oil
1tsp nam pla (fish sauce)
2tsp finely chopped or grated pale palm sugar

1 Lightly pound the peppercorns, salt, and garlic in a mortar with a pestle until combined. Add the basil and coriander and work into a chunky paste. Put the squid into a bowl and coat with the paste. Leave at room temperature for 15 minutes.

2 Heat a wok until smoking. Add half the oil and swirl it around. Add half the squid and cook over high heat for 30 seconds, tossing it a little. Tip the squid into a bowl. Wipe the wok clean, then cook the remaining squid in the same way.

3 Return the first batch of squid to the wok and add the fish sauce and palm sugar. Toss together and cook for a further 20 seconds.

Serve the squid immediately, with chunks of peeled cucumber and lime wedges.

GREEN HERB OIL

This vibrant green oil, fragrant with herbs, is great to drizzle over grilled swordfish, goat's cheese salad, or poached chicken breast. My favourite herbs to use are oregano, basil, mint, and tarragon, but a combination of several can be inspiring. Store the oil in the refrigerator or a cool, dark place – it stays fragrant for a week.

You can use the sediment to brush on grilled fish when almost cooked, or mix it into mashed potatoes for colour and a subtle flavour.

Makes 250ml (8½fl oz) oil

| 1½ cups tightly packed herbs of your choice |
| 150ml (5fl oz) light-tasting oil (grapeseed, sunflower, or light olive oil) |
| 100ml (3½fl oz) extra virgin olive oil |

1 Bring a large pan of water to the boil. Plunge the herbs into the boiling water and stir gently, then leave for 5 seconds.

2 Drain the herbs in a sieve, then tip them into a bowl of iced water. Leave to cool for 20 seconds, stirring gently once.

3 Remove the herbs from the iced water and drain well in the sieve, then pat dry with a tea towel or kitchen paper.

4 Place the herbs in a blender and add the light-tasting oil. Blend for 20 seconds, then set aside for 10 minutes.

5 Strain the oil through a fine sieve and funnel into a clean bottle or jar. If you like, reserve the sediment for later use (see above).

6 Add the extra virgin olive oil and swirl to mix together. Seal the bottle or jar and store in a cool place away from direct sunlight.

SPICES

Spices are the highly aromatic and scented parts of tropical plants – the seeds and fruit, bark, and root. The number of edible fragrant seeds is vast, and includes caraway, cardamom, coriander, cumin, fennel, peppercorns, poppy, star anise, sumac, and wattleseed. Barks include cinnamon and cassia, and roots include ginger, galangal, and sassafras, when dried and ground.

Spices can be used whole – often dry-roasted to enhance flavour – or ground. They play a huge part in giving all kinds of dishes another dimension. For example, they can be added to breads, cakes, and pastries; rubbed into meats and fish before cooking; braised with onions and potatoes for aromatic Indian dishes; and fried in coconut oil with shrimp paste to make heady Thai curries.

Bruising spices

Spices added whole to a dish are often bruised first so that their flavours will be released more easily. Those commonly bruised include fresh ginger, galangal, and lemon-grass (see left). To bruise, trim or peel the spice, then place on a board. Lay a heavy knife flat on the spice and, using the heel of your hand, press down to crush and break open – do not smash.

Grating spices

It is often easier and quicker to grate fresh root and rhizome spices, such as ginger (see right), galangal, wasabi, and horseradish, rather than to chop them finely. Peel them before grating. Once grated, fresh ginger flesh can be squeezed to extract the juice, which is used in many Asian dishes. Whole dried nutmegs are also grated, using a grater with very fine holes.

LEMON-GRASS & TOMATO ROAST SARDINES

Sardines fresh from a Portuguese or Moroccan port, served on fresh white bread with a juicy lemon wedge, is the food of memories. Replacing the lemon with lemon-grass and adding lightly acidic tomatoes is the fusion effect. The oiliness of the fish benefits from the hit of citrus.

3 lemon-grass sticks
4 garlic cloves, finely sliced
100ml (3½fl oz) olive oil
2 very ripe tomatoes, chopped into smallish chunks
few sprigs of thyme, chopped
8–12 sardines, about 125–150g (4½–5½oz) each, gutted and scaled
4 slices of good-quality, crusty white bread

1 Preheat the oven to 200°C (400°F, gas 6). Place a non-reactive baking dish, large enough to hold the sardines comfortably in 1 layer, in the oven to heat. Preheat the grill too.

2 Cut off the top half of each lemon-grass stalk and bruise them (see above). Put in the baking dish with half the garlic, half the oil, and the tomatoes. Roast for 12 minutes. Remove from the oven and mix well.

3 Trim the base off the other half of the lemon-grass sticks and peel off the 3 outer layers. Discard these or use to flavour soups or stock. Finely chop the peeled lemon-grass. Mix with the remaining garlic, the thyme, and some sea salt and pepper.

4 Lay the sardines on a board and stuff the stomach cavities with the chopped lemon-grass mixture. Brush on both sides with the remaining oil.

5 Put the sardines in the roasting dish. Return to the oven and roast for 5 minutes. Turn the sardines over and transfer to the hot grill. Grill for 2–4 minutes to colour the fish and finish cooking. They are cooked when the flesh is opaque and will pull off the bone easily.

6 Toast the bread (or use untoasted) and spread with the tomato mixture from the roasting dish. Top with the sardines and lemon-grass stems, and serve piping hot with extra salt and pepper. Make sure you chew on the lemon-grass stems as you eat the sardines.

Dry-roasting spices

The flavour of spices is greatly enhanced when they are roasted, which can be done in the oven or on the stovetop. The oven method will give a more even roasting and is good for large or irregular-shaped spices such as star anise, cinnamon, and cloves. Whichever method you use, keep an eye on the spices as their colour darkens and the aroma increases – burnt spice will just add bitterness to a dish. Once roasted, leave spices to cool before crushing or grinding to use in spice blends, rubs, and marinades.

To dry-roast in the oven, preheat the oven to 160°C (325°F, gas 3). Spread out the spices on a baking tray and roast until they are aromatic and lightly coloured. If dry-roasting a selection of different spices (as shown right), be aware that they may take different times – a cinnamon stick, snapped into a few pieces, benefits from about 8 minutes of roasting; cumin seeds need about 7 minutes and cloves just 4 minutes. Transfer to a plate to cool.

To dry-roast on the stovetop, heat a heavy frying pan over a moderate heat. Put the spices in the pan and cook, shaking the pan constantly to keep the spices moving, until they darken and their aroma increases. Transfer the spices to a bowl or plate to cool.

Frying spices in oil

This is a good method to use when you have both oil and small, whole spices, such as caraway, coriander, cumin, and sesame seeds, in a recipe. By frying the spices in the oil, their flavour gets trapped in the oil.

Heat a pan until quite hot. Add 2–3tbsp oil and then 1tbsp spice. The oil should not be too hot when you add the spices. Reduce the heat to moderately low and fry until the spices are lightly coloured. Immediately remove from the heat.

Crushing spices

As well as helping to release aroma, crushing spices in a mortar with a pestle (see right) allows more of their surface area to be exposed to the food they are flavouring. As a result, you will need to use less of a crushed spice than if you use it whole. Crushing also makes spices more digestible – biting into a whole clove in a cake is much less appealing than enjoying the flavour imparted by a finely crushed clove.

Grinding spices

At work, I frequently use a domestic coffee grinder for grinding spices, as do many other professional chefs. Others prefer special spice grinders. The effect of these machines is much the same as using a mortar and pestle to crush spices finely. However, when using a grinder it is harder to control the degree to which the spices are ground, and overheating from overgrinding can cause the essential oils to dissipate if the ground spices are not used quickly.

SPICE BLENDS

Spice blends come primarily, but not exclusively, from Asia and North Africa, where the spice trails wove their ways in days of old. These blends are generally used to "sprinkle on flavour" after a dish is cooked, although you can also stir them into soups, stews, and other dishes for a more subtle approach. You can buy ready-made spice blends, but making your own with freshly ground spices allows you to vary the blend according to the dish. Store spice blends in airtight containers and use within one month of making.

GARAM MASALA

This spice blend is one of the basics in any Indian kitchen, and variations on the mixture are endless. Usually added towards the end of the cooking process, it can also be sprinkled onto prime cuts of meat and fish to infuse them with spice flavour before cooking.

Makes enough to flavour up to 2kg (4½lb) of meat, fish, or lentil stew

1½tbsp green cardamom pods, lightly dry-roasted
1tbsp fennel seeds, lightly dry-roasted
1tbsp cumin seeds, lightly dry-roasted
1tbsp coriander seeds, lightly dry-roasted
1tbsp black or white peppercorns
¼ cinnamon stick, lightly dry-roasted
½tsp chili flakes
½tsp ground ginger
good pinch of grated nutmeg

Grind the cardamom pods, fennel, cumin, and coriander seeds, peppercorns, and cinnamon. Pass through a sieve. Mix with the remaining ingredients and store in an airtight container.

PISTACHIO DUKKA

This Egyptian spice blend has been served in antipodean restaurants and cafés for the past 10 years. It is now beginning to appear in restaurants in Europe and the United States alongside extra virgin olive oil as a dip for bread.

Serves 10 as a dip

4tbsp shelled pistachio nuts
4tbsp sesame seeds
2tbsp cumin seeds
1tbsp coriander seeds
1½tsp fine sea salt
1tsp freshly ground black pepper

1 Preheat the oven to 160°C (325°F, gas 3). Spread the pistachio nuts in a small baking tray and roast for 15 minutes, or until they are fragrant but still retain their green colour. Remove from the tray and allow to cool.

2 Lightly dry-roast the sesame, cumin, and coriander seeds in the oven (p79). Allow to cool, then roughly crush the coriander seeds.

3 Coarsely chop the pistachio nuts, then mix with the other ingredients. Store the dukka in an airtight container.

SPICE RUBS

The purpose of a spice rub is to impart flavour to the outside of food to be cooked – in contrast to a marinade, where you want the flavour to seep a little deeper into the food. Spice rubs work really well in dishes where the food is wrapped before cooking (for example, in banana leaves, foil, or a roasting bag). Rubs are equally good for small cuts of meat or fish just before they are cooked very briefly as they are for larger items, such as a leg of lamb or a whole duck to be left overnight before cooking.

SALMON WITH CAJUN BLACKENING SPICES

The spices for this rub are not dry-roasted first since the fierce heat used to sear the salmon will roast them during cooking. You don't want the spices to burn, but they should "eat" into the fish. I like to serve this with thick yogurt, lemon wedges, and a tomato and cucumber salad. The spice mix makes enough for 8 pieces of salmon fillet, so keep the excess for next time.

1tbsp ground cumin seeds	1tbsp dried thyme
1tbsp coriander seeds, crushed	1tsp dried oregano
1tbsp dried ground garlic	2tbsp fine salt
2tbsp paprika or pimenton (smoked Spanish paprika)	4 pieces of salmon fillet, about 170g (6oz) each, skinned
1tbsp coarsely ground white or black pepper	vegetable oil

1 Mix together all the spices, herbs, and salt. Using half of the mixture, rub into both sides of the pieces of salmon and lay them on a tray. Cover and leave at room temperature for up to 30 minutes.

2 Heat a heavy-based frying pan over high heat until very hot. Brush the pan with oil, then place the fillets in the pan. Leave to cook for 2 minutes without moving them. Turn the fish over, cover the pan, and cook for 2 more minutes. The spices will have blackened and the fish will be barely cooked inside. Transfer the salmon to warm plates and serve.

SPICE MARINADES

The purpose of a marinade is to add flavour as well as to help tenderize protein foods. Simply adding liquid such as yogurt or oil will turn a spice rub into a marinade. If based on yogurt, the marinade will tenderize tough meat and make fish and prime meat cuts firm yet delicate. Alternatively, fruits (papaya, pineapple, and kiwi fruit, for example), chilies, or citrus juices can contribute the tenderizing enzymes. A marinade can be used for basting during cooking, as the liquid in a braised dish or stew, and to make a sauce (if used to marinate raw meat it must be boiled first). If you want to brown food that has been marinated, drain and dry it well.

CUMIN, NIGELLA & PEPPER MARINADE

This yogurt-based spice marinade works very well with monkfish (as described here), making the flesh a bit firmer and adding wonderful flavour. You can also use the marinade for kebabs of boned shoulder or leg of lamb (leave these to marinate for 24 hours) and for chicken legs or pork chops. I like to serve the monkfish with chunks of icy cold watermelon, lemon wedges, and some thick plain yogurt.

4tbsp olive oil
1tbsp cumin seeds
1tbsp freshly ground black pepper
1½tbsp nigella seeds
1tsp salt
1tbsp dried mint
150ml (5fl oz) plain yogurt
4 monkfish tails, on the bone, about 200g (7oz) each, skinned
large handful of mint

1 Put 2tbsp of the oil in a small frying pan and add the cumin seeds and black pepper. Set the pan over moderate heat and cook until the seeds are fizzing and becoming aromatic. Add the nigella seeds and salt and count to 15, then tip the mixture into a large mixing bowl. Add the dried mint and stir to mix. Leave to cool, then mix in the yogurt.

2 Add the monkfish to the bowl and rub the marinade onto the flesh, mixing well. Cover the bowl with cling film and put into the refrigerator. Leave to marinate for 4–6 hours.

3 Preheat the oven to 200°C (400°F, gas 6) and put a ceramic baking dish in to warm. Remove the fish from the bowl and wipe off and discard excess marinade. Drizzle 1tbsp oil into the baking dish and add the fish. Roast for 15–18 minutes, or until the fish is cooked. To test, use a sharp knife to separate the flesh from the bone at the thickest end – it should come away easily.

4 Just before serving, strip the mint leaves from the stalks. Scatter the mint leaves over the monkfish, drizzle with the remaining 1tbsp oil, and serve immediately.

MACE & CHILI MARINADE

Lip-smacking, sweet, and spicy, this marinade works well with pork chops (as here), and with pork fillet, chicken, or duck legs, whether barbecued, grilled, or roasted. The chops are great with a potato salad and green beans.

100ml (3½fl oz) maple syrup	1tbsp fennel seeds, dry-roasted and coarsely ground
80g (2¾oz) tomato purée	
50g (1¾oz) unsalted butter	3 blades of mace, lightly dry-roasted and coarsely ground
1 small red onion, finely chopped	1½tsp sea salt
2 garlic cloves, finely chopped	4 pork chops, about 200g (7oz) each
2tsp chili flakes	100ml (3½fl oz) water

1 Place all the ingredients, except the pork and water, in a pan. Bring slowly to the boil, stirring. Reduce the heat and simmer, stirring frequently, for 12–15 minutes, or until thickened.

2 Transfer to a bowl and leave to cool completely. Then add the pork chops and rub the marinade into the meat. Cover the bowl with cling film and leave to marinate in the refrigerator overnight.

3 Preheat the grill to high. Wipe excess marinade from the chops (reserve the marinade), then grill for 6–8 minutes on each side. Or, roast in a preheated 200°C (400°F, gas 6) oven for 15–20 minutes. Meanwhile, place the marinade in a pan with the water and bring to the boil, stirring. Taste for seasoning. Pour this sauce over the chops before serving.

CHILIES

All chilies have a characteristic flavour and not just heat. A fresh green chili is an immature red chili – leave it long enough and it will turn red. I like the flavour of fresh green chilies when I'm making a refreshing crunchy salsa with, say, cucumber, apples, mint, or melon. Red chilies have a deeper, more mature flavour and work well with almost anything. When chilies are dried they develop different characteristics, and fresh and dried chilies are usually not interchangeable in a recipe.

As a rule of thumb, a large smooth chili will be far less hot than a small wrinkly one. But whatever the size, it is the seeds and ribs in a chili that contain the heat. If you are not used to cooking with chilies, start with half the quantity given in a recipe.

Seeding fresh chilies

To lessen the heat of a chili, cut it in half lengthways, then scrape out the seeds and ribs with a spoon or knife. An alkaloid in chilies, called capsaicin, can irritate your skin, so you might want to wear plastic or rubber gloves when preparing them. Otherwise, avoid putting your fingers to eyes or lips, and thoroughly wash your hands.

Roasting dried chilies

Dry-roasting chilies gives them a light smoky flavour. Heat a heavy-based frying pan over high heat, add the chilies, and roast until they start to darken in colour and blister; do not let them burn. Alternatively, spread the chilies on a baking tray and roast in a preheated 200°C (400°C, gas 6) oven for 5–10 minutes, or until they puff up.

Grinding dried chilies

Once dry-roasted, chilies can be soaked and the flesh sieved (p84) or they can be left to cool and then ground to a fine powder. You can also grind dried chilies without first dry-roasting them. Use a mortar and pestle for grinding or an electric spice or coffee grinder. Store the ground chili in an airtight jar in a cool, dark place.

SOAKING & SIEVING DRIED CHILIES

This process enables you to use dried chili flesh in a dressing, paste, or stew without the papery skins. If you do not want too fierce a heat, first break open the chilies and shake out the seeds.

1 Put the chilies in a bowl of warm, lightly salted water and set a small plate on top to keep them submerged. Soak for 15–30 minutes, depending on size, until they are malleable.

2 Drain the chilies and put them in a sieve. Using a ladle or the back of a spoon, press the flesh through the sieve into a bowl. Or, if the chilies are large enough, scrape the flesh from the skin. Discard the skin and seeds.

CHILI OIL

Drizzle this oil over a shellfish risotto or over grilled or roast meats or fish, or mix it into salad dressings, marinades, and salsas. The heat of the oil will depend on the chilies you use. It will keep up to 6 months.

Remove the stalks from 6 fresh, unblemished chilies, 20–30g (about 1oz) in total, and cut lengthways in half. Put the chilies and 150ml (5fl oz) light olive oil in a small pan over a moderate heat. When the mixture starts to bubble, stir it a little. Once the bubbling slows down, but before the chilies wilt completely and darken too much, remove from the heat and pour into a bowl. Leave to cool completely, then decant the oil and chilies into a clean jar or bottle and pour in another 150ml (5fl oz) oil. Leave for a few days before using. Keep in the refrigerator, or in a cool, dark place.

RED CURRY PASTE

This dense-tasting, sweetish paste is delicious spread over grilled meats or fried fish, but it is most useful when making a coconut-based curry. Use whatever chilies you prefer – the amount and type will determine the heat of the finished paste. It will keep in the refrigerator for 2 weeks.

Makes enough for 12 portions of curry	100g (3½oz) fresh ginger, thinly sliced
vegetable oil, for deep-frying	50g (1¾oz) galangal, thinly sliced
2 large red onions, sliced into 1cm (½in) thick rings	20 garlic cloves, quartered
2 red peppers, quartered and seeded	60g (2¼oz) tomato purée
5 moderately hot red chilies, halved lengthways	½tbsp salt

1 Heat oil for deep-frying to 160°C (325°F). Add the onions and fry, stirring occasionally, for 10–15 minutes, or until lightly blackened and shrivelled. Using a slotted spoon, remove the onions and drain on kitchen paper. Deep-fry the peppers for 7–8 minutes, then drain.

2 Add the chilies to the hot oil and deep-fry for 4–5 minutes, or until tinged black and shrivelled. Remove and drain. Deep-fry the ginger with the galangal for 5 minutes. Fry the garlic, which will cook quite quickly.

3 Put all the deep-fried ingredients in a food processor and process to a fine paste. Add the tomato purée and salt, and process again briefly to combine the ingredients.

4 Transfer the paste to a clean jar or plastic container and cover the surface with baking parchment. Leave to cool. The frying oil can be used to baste foods on the barbecue or to fry fish. Cool in the pan, then decant into a jar.

Tomato chili jam

This jam is indispensable in my kitchens at home and at work. It is great on toast with a fried egg on top, dolloped onto roast lamb or pork, used to glaze a fillet of fish under the grill, or in a sandwich of goat's cheese, rocket, and avocado. The chilies you use will affect the final taste – I prefer finger-sized serrano chilies. The jam will keep for 2 months.

Simmer until the jam is thick and glossy

Makes about 500g (1lb 2oz)

500g (1lb 2oz) very ripe tomatoes

2 thumbs of fresh ginger, roughly chopped

3tbsp nam pla (fish sauce)

4 fresh serrano or other red chilies, finely sliced

4 garlic cloves, finely sliced

300g (10½oz) caster sugar

100ml (3½fl oz) red wine or cider vinegar

Put half the tomatoes, the ginger, and fish sauce in a blender and purée until smooth.

(Although some people have an aversion to tomato seeds, they provide the pectin that makes this jam set, so I don't suggest passing the puréed tomatoes through a sieve.) Chop the remaining tomatoes into 1cm (½in) dice (you can peel them if you want, but I don't).

Put the puréed tomatoes, chopped tomatoes, and all the remaining ingredients into a deep pan and slowly bring to the boil, stirring frequently. Once the mixture boils, reduce the heat to a gentle simmer.

Skim off any foam that rises to the surface, then simmer for 30–40 minutes, stirring every few minutes to release the solids that will settle on the bottom of the pan. Be sure to scrape the sides of the pan from time to time so that the jam cooks evenly. The jam is ready when it thickens and become glossy.

Pour the jam into sterilized glass jars, seal, and label. Leave to cool to room temperature before storing in the refrigerator or a cold larder.

SALTY FLAVOURINGS

Salt has two major roles in the kitchen: to flavour food and to preserve it. Refrigeration and freezing have mostly replaced the role of salt as a preservative, although there are still many foods that depend almost entirely on salt for their production. Among them are capers, olives, and anchovies. These, with salt itself, are used to add savour and to heighten the flavour of other foods. In the oriental kitchen, several flavouring ingredients are used to add saltiness, including soy sauce, fish sauce (nam pla or nuoc nam), miso (a savoury paste made from soya beans), gomasio (toasted sesame seeds mixed with salt), and salted black beans.

Preparing salted anchovies

Salted anchovies are far superior to anchovies in brine. Rinse excess salt from the anchovies and pat them dry with kitchen paper. Using your thumbnail, split an anchovy open, then separate the flesh from the spine. The fillet should come off easily. Remove the second fillet in the same way. Pull off any remaining small bones.

Pitting olives

Pitting olives is a tedious job, but often an essential one. The simplest and quickest method is to squash the olives, 1 at a time, with a flat knife blade, then squeeze or pull out the pit. Alternatively, you can use a tool, such as a cherry pitter, that pushes a hole all the way through the olive and extracts the pit.

TAPENADE

Made from many of the salty products of the Mediterranean, tapenade has a surprisingly light taste. Use it as a crostini topping, dollop it onto grilled tuna and swordfish, or drizzle it over spring lamb with roast tomatoes. It will keep in the refrigerator for up to a week.

Makes 300g (10½oz)

180g (6¼oz) black olives, pitted and roughly chopped
1 salted anchovy, rinsed, filleted (see left), and roughly chopped
2tsp capers, lightly rinsed
1 garlic clove, finely chopped or crushed
few leaves of flat-leaf parsley, roughly chopped
80ml (2½fl oz) extra virgin olive oil

1 Put the olives, anchovy fillets, capers, garlic, and parsley into a mortar and pound with a pestle until amalgamated.

2 Slowly drizzle in the olive oil and pound to a smooth, thick paste. Alternatively, blitz all the ingredients together in a food processor, making sure not to overwork until too fine.

ANCHOVY BUTTER

I love this butter melted into pasta that has been tossed with broccoli. It's also great dolloped onto grilled fish or barbecued lamb chops, substituted for regular butter in a chicken sandwich, or spread on toast with very sweet tomatoes and chives. Store in the refrigerator for up to 2 weeks.

Makes 300g (10½oz)

5 salted anchovies, rinsed and filleted (see left)
200g (7oz) unsalted butter, at room temperature
2 spring onions, finely sliced
80ml (2½fl oz) olive oil

Put all the ingredients into a food processor and process for about 15 seconds to a paste, scraping down the sides of the processor bowl once or twice. Alternatively, finely chop the anchovy fillets and beat them into the butter together with the spring onions, then whisk in the olive oil. Use at room temperature.

CAPER DRESSING

Almost a runny salsa, this dressing is delicious spooned over grilled snapper or tuna, or lightly steamed asparagus. Make it just before you need it, otherwise the coriander leaves will discolour.

Serves 6 as a dressing

2tsp coriander seeds, lightly dry-roasted

small bunch of coriander

grated zest and juice of 1 large juicy orange

2tbsp small capers in brine, drained

150ml (5fl oz) extra virgin olive oil

2tbsp light soy sauce

1 Finely grind the coriander seeds in a mortar with a pestle. Remove the leaves from the coriander and set aside. Chop the coriander stalks, add to the mortar, and pound into the seeds. Add the orange zest and pound in, then add the capers and smash them roughly, keeping them chunky.

2 Mix in the olive oil, then the orange juice and soy sauce, and finally the coriander leaves. Leave the dressing to infuse for a few minutes before serving.

BLACK BEAN, LIME & CHILI DRESSING

Salted (or fermented) Chinese black beans have a delicious musty taste – full on the tongue and quite rich. In this chunky dressing, they add texture and colour contrast to the other ingredients, working as a foil for the acidity of the limes and the chilies (use more or less chili, according to your taste).

Spoon the dressing generously over fish such as salmon, mahi mahi, or swordfish, or on grilled chicken legs, duck breasts, or pork chops. The dressing can be kept in a covered jar at room temperature for up to a day.

Serves 6 as a dressing

1 small red onion, finely sliced or diced

grated zest and juice of 3 limes

½ fresh red chili, finely chopped

½ fresh green chili, finely chopped

50g (1¾oz) pale palm sugar, grated, or demerara sugar

2tsp nam pla (fish sauce)

3tbsp black beans, rinsed and roughly chopped

2tsp toasted sesame oil

150ml (5fl oz) groundnut or grapeseed oil

1 Put the onion, lime zest, and lime juice into a bowl and mix together. Leave for 20 minutes.

2 Add the chilies, palm sugar, and fish sauce. Stir to dissolve the sugar. Add the black beans and the sesame and groundnut or grapeseed oils and mix well. Leave the dressing to rest for 30 minutes before using.

CITRUS & SOUR FLAVOURINGS

Citrus and sour flavours play an important balancing role in cooking. In dishes of pork belly, duck, or sardines, for example, a little zing from citrus fruit or a sour hint from tamarind is a good way to offset the richness. These flavours are not commonly used in northern Europe, where vinegar traditionally provides the souring agent, but elsewhere in the world many types of citrus and sour flavours are considered essential – for example, tamarind, preserved lemons, and sumac in the Middle East; limes and ground dried mango in Southeast Asia and India; yuzu in China and Japan; and lemon myrtle and bush and finger limes in the Pacific and Australasia.

SALTED, SPICED, PRESERVED LEMONS

Traditionally used in Moroccan tagines, preserved lemon peel now flavours all kinds of dishes – from salads and dressings to stewed fruits and simple cakes. You need a sterilized preserving jar that will hold 10 lemons (they should be a little squashed). To use, take a lemon from the jar, rinse briefly, cut into 4, and scrape the flesh from the peel – the peel is the part you want. You can add the flesh to marinades and to chickpea or lentil soups – it will be salty and sour.

Makes 10 lemons

14 medium to large unwaxed, ripe lemons
200g (7oz) sea salt
1 cinnamon stick, snapped into 4
1tbsp fennel seeds, lightly dry-roasted
2 thumbs of fresh ginger, thinly sliced

1 Wash the 10 plumpest lemons in tepid water and dry thoroughly. Hold each lemon, pointed end up, on a board and cut lengthways into quarters, not cutting all the way through the base so the quarters stay connected.

2 Stuff each lemon with as much salt as it will hold, then put it into the jar. Sprinkle the spices in as you pack in the lemons. Add any remaining salt to the jar, then seal and leave in a cool place for 3 days.

3 Squeeze the juice from the remaining lemons. Press the lemons in the jar to compress them further, then pour the juice into the jar. The lemons should be completely covered (you may need extra juice). Seal the jar and leave for at least 8 weeks before using.

Dried limes

Usually added whole to stews and soups, dried limes give a sharp and bitter background flavour that works well with sweet spices. Dried limes can also be crushed and soaked to use in marinades or put under a roasting leg of lamb.

Dried mangoes

Dried unripe mango, in strips or ground into a brown powder, gives a tart, fruity background taste to vegetarian dishes. It is also good mixed into a chicken broth or used to flavour poached fish. It can be the tenderizer in a marinade, too.

Kaffir lime

The zest is added to salad dressings and fish cakes, the juice (what there is) adds an edge to sour dressings, and the leaf (which freezes well) is essential in many Thai and Malaysian dishes.

Pomegranate molasses

The flavour varies from sweet, with a hint of tartness and sourness, to very sour. Add to soda water for a cordial, drizzle over stone fruit and berries, or brush over roast chicken 10 minutes before the end of cooking.

Sumac

A coarse powder ground from berries, sumac has a sour taste. Use in spice mixtures, such as zatar, or sprinkle over cooked foods.

Tamarind

Available sour or sweet, tamarind can be bought in the pod; in jars of dark, sour, resinous paste; and in blocks of compressed pulp and seeds.

Yuzu

This citrus fruit has a sweet, pungent aroma and an agreeable sour taste. The grated zest is much used in Japanese cooking; the bottled salted juice is added to dressings, dips, and marinades.

CHOCOLATE

Its use in sweet dishes is well known, but chocolate can be added to savoury dishes too. One example is the moles of Mexico, famous for their complex flavours – a good mole is thickened with bread and nuts, flavoured with a startling array of spices, and finished with the richness of chocolate and the aroma of oranges. The recipe below is inspired by moles, but chocolate is used altogether differently.

BLACK BEAN, CHOCOLATE & PEANUT PURÉE

Serve this as a spread for breads or as a garnish for roast venison or duck. It will keep in the refrigerator for up to 2 days.

Serves 6–8 as a spread

120g (4¼oz) dried black beans, soaked overnight and drained

2 red onions, thinly sliced

150ml (5fl oz) olive oil

6 garlic cloves, chopped

1tsp pimenton (smoked paprika)

80ml (2¾fl oz) sherry vinegar

80g (2¾oz) shelled peanuts, roasted and roughly chopped

40g (1¼oz) dark chocolate (55–65 per cent cocoa solids), roughly chopped

2tbsp soy sauce

1 Put the soaked beans into a pan of cold water. Bring to the boil, skimming off any foam, then partly cover and simmer for about 1 hour, or until tender. When the beans are done, drain them in a colander.

2 Meanwhile, sauté the onions in half the olive oil until they are caramelized, stirring occasionally. Add the garlic and pimenton and cook for a few more minutes. Add the vinegar and peanuts and cook for another minute, stirring well.

3 Put the hot beans and onion mixture into a food processor with the chocolate, soy sauce, and remaining olive oil. Process to a chunky paste. Taste and add more soy sauce or salt, if needed. Cool.

VANILLA

The first time I had vanilla in anything other than a dessert was in 1996: it was teamed with duck and kumara (New Zealand's native sweet potato) in a samosa. Since then I have experimented using vanilla in lots of savoury dishes – for example, in an oil to drizzle over a prawn dish, stewed with cannellini beans to serve with duck, and, with saffron, for flavouring braised onions to serve with halibut.

EXTRACTING VANILLA SEEDS

Vanilla pods (the cured unripe fruit of a climbing orchid) are used whole or split open, or the seeds alone are used. After infusing a dish with a split vanilla pod, the seeds can be scraped out and added back – they look great in creamy desserts. Use the empty pod to flavour vodka, sugar syrups, and cordials if you don't want to use it in cooking. If a vanilla pod is kept whole, it can be rinsed, dried, and used again to flavour another dish.

1 Lay the vanilla pod on a chopping board and, using the tip of a sharp knife, cut the pod in half lengthways.

2 Using a teaspoon or the back of a small knife, scrape off the sticky seeds along the length of the pod, pressing firmly.

VANILLA EXTRACT

Pure vanilla extract is made by crushing the cured pods and extracting the vanillin (the chemical compound that gives vanilla its aroma and flavour) with alcohol. Cheaper vanilla essence is made from synthesized vanillin aldehyde.

EGGS & DAIRY
PRODUCE

Michael Romano

MICHAEL ROMANO

Of all our foodstuffs, the egg is perhaps the most versatile, and certainly one of the most nutritious. Used as an ingredient, the egg is prized for its ability to bind, lighten, emulsify, and enrich. Cooked and eaten on their own, eggs lend themselves to dozens of preparations. Egg yolks and whites have very diverse properties and are at times used separately to achieve different effects.

The protein and fat properties of egg yolks allow them to enrich, emulsify, or otherwise bind ingredients such as fats and liquids, which do not normally combine. Hollandaise and mayonnaise are sauces that owe their rich, creamy texture to that ability. Yolks are also used in cakes and some bread-baking and pasta-making; as the basis of certain sauces like sabayon; and in drinks like eggnog. As a wash they help baked foods brown and, when hard-boiled and sliced or chopped, they are used as a garnish. Egg whites can increase to about eight times their shell volume when air is beaten into them, and therefore help create the airy lightness of some cakes as well as giving us meringues and soufflés. Whites are also useful in the clarification of liquids, such as consommé and wine, because the albumin they contain can attract and entrap particulate matter.

Products from milk and cream Left to stand, unhomogenized milk separates into two layers – the thinner body of milk and the milk fat, or cream, at the top. Today, most cream is produced by centrifugal extraction, and is usually pasteurized or ultra-pasteurized, a heating process that extends its shelf life but compromises its flavour and ability to whip.

Yogurt is made by mixing milk with helpful bacteria to ferment and thicken it. Unlike cream, yogurt cannot be boiled and reduced. It is heated by tempering – a little hot liquid is added to bring the yogurt slowly to temperature before it is incorporated in a dish. However, if the dish subsequently boils during cooking, there is a chance that the yogurt will coagulate and separate from the sauce. Crème fraîche is a fermented, thickened cream with a tangy, bracing flavour. In France, it is produced from unpasteurized milk and thickens naturally. At home it can be made by adding soured cream or buttermilk to pasteurized double cream, but the flavour is not as good as that of the French original. Butter is cream's apotheosis. It is made by churning cream long enough to cause the fat to separate from the cream's liquid, or whey. Unsalted butter contains no added salt. It is, I think, the best butter to use in baking and pastry-making. Unsalted butter is more vulnerable to spoilage than salted butter – the salt in salted butter is there as a preservative.

Cheese Derived from various animal milks, most typically those of cows, goats, and sheep, cheese is an ancient product. Cheeses can be mild or pungent, soft or hard. They can weigh as little as 30g (1oz), or as much as 135kg (300lb), as do some Swiss cheeses. Most cheeses can be enjoyed the day they are made, and some are wonderful after years of attentive ageing.

How you store cheese depends to a great extent on the cheese type and its state when you buy it. The freshest cheeses, most of which are packed in food storage containers, should be kept tightly covered and refrigerated for no more than a week. Use a container also for storing whole young goat's cheeses or other small whole cheeses. Put these in the coldest part of your refrigerator. Soft-ripened and other soft-textured or creamy cheeses should be similarly stored, wrapped in cling film, but not for too long or rinds will become slimy and the interior hard. Firm cheeses are best stored in a plastic bag in the refrigerator door or the warmest part of the refrigerator.

Check stored cheese before eating for bad odours, cracking rinds, or discoloration, all of which indicate that the cheese should be discarded. Some cheese, however, can mould superficially without affecting its quality. If you notice mould on a semi-soft cheese, such as Emmental or Fontina, or a firmer cheese, cut it away together with some of the cheese surrounding it. However, throw away a mouldy soft-ripened cheese, such as Brie or Camembert.

BASIC EGG PREPARATION

Aside from cooking eggs whole, both in their shells (hard-boiled, soft-boiled, and coddled) and out (poached, fried, and au plat), most preparations that utilize eggs will require either beating yolks and whites together, or separating the yolk and white and beating them separately. Here are some notes on the best methods to use when performing these basic but essential tasks.

SEPARATING EGGS

Many recipes call for eggs that have been separated, which means they are divided into yolks and whites. It's a good idea to give the eggs a sniff test before you start – a bad egg will be obviously smelly. One bad egg will spoil all the rest.

1 Have 2 non-reactive bowls ready. Tap each egg in turn against a hard surface (the rim of the bowl is good for this) to break its shell. Insert your fingers in the break and halve the shell roughly along its "equator", keeping the egg's contents in one shell half.

2 While shifting the contents back and forth between the shell halves, allow as much white as possible to fall into one bowl. Finish by dropping the yolk into the second bowl and discarding the shells.

REMOVING ANY STRAY YOLK

For egg whites to be whisked until stiff, it's important that they be free from even the smallest speck of yolk. This is because yolks are fatty and fat inhibits air incorporation. If, when separating the eggs, some yolk has fallen into your whites, remove it either by scooping it out using a bit of broken shell, or by touching the yolk with the corner of a piece of damp kitchen paper (the yolk should adhere to the paper). In some cases too much yolk will have landed in the whites. If that happens, you'll need to discard the whites and start again.

BEATING WHOLE EGGS

Break the eggs into a non-reactive bowl. Beat with a fork, whisk, or mechanical or electric mixer for about 45 seconds, or until the yolks and whites are completely combined. Once beaten, the eggs are ready to be used to make an omelette (p102) or in any other recipe that calls for beaten eggs.

BEATING EGG YOLKS

Separate the eggs into 2 bowls. Beat the yolks with a whisk and a figure-of-8 motion. This breaks them up and gives them volume. Once lightly aerated, they're ready to receive other ingredients, such as oil (to make mayonnaise, for example) or sugar (for cakes and other desserts). In many cases, the ingredients to be beaten in with the yolks can be added right from the beginning, as is the case with zabaglione (see opposite).

CHILLED MOSCATO & PINEAPPLE ZABAGLIONE

This light and citrussy zabaglione differs from the traditional dessert in two ways. One is that instead of Marsala it uses Moscato d'Asti, the extraordinary Italian dessert wine. It is also chilled, which makes it very refreshing indeed. This is excellent on its own, or you can dollop it over fruit. Accompany the dessert with the Moscato d'Asti remaining in the bottle.

Serves 4–6

4 egg yolks
100g (3½oz) caster sugar
120ml (4fl oz) unsweetened pineapple juice concentrate, thawed if frozen
4tbsp Moscato d'Asti wine
240ml (8fl oz) double cream

1 In a large, metal mixing bowl, combine the egg yolks, sugar, pineapple concentrate, and wine. Beat with a balloon whisk to combine. Set the bowl over a saucepan one-third full of simmering water (the base of the bowl should not touch the water) and whisk constantly for about 10 minutes, or until the mixture has thickened and coats the back of a spoon.

2 Transfer the zabaglione to the bowl of an electric mixer and beat on low speed until cool. Refrigerate for at least 1 hour to chill the zabaglione thoroughly.

3 Just before serving, whip the cream in a bowl set over ice until soft peaks form. Fold it gently into the chilled zabaglione. Spoon into dessert glasses – over tropical fruit such as thinly sliced star fruit, sticks of pineapple, and mango chunks, or over berries – or serve it plain.

WHISKING EGG WHITES

To whisk egg whites, the type of bowl you use is of greater importance than it is for whole eggs or egg yolks. Avoid plastic bowls, which, despite washing, can retain a grease film that will inhibit the "mounting". Unlined copper bowls are best for turning out stable, voluminous whites, due to a positive reaction that occurs between the whites and the metal. If whisking egg whites in a glass or stainless steel bowl, you can help stabilize them by adding a pinch of cream of tartar.

I think that whites are best beaten with a balloon whisk, which should be large enough to keep a maximum amount of white moving and aerated as you work. A whisk gives you a bigger stroke than any other kind of beater, and therefore more volume. Here are more tips for success:

- Make sure the interior of the bowl is spotlessly clean and free of grease. Especially if using a copper bowl, you may want to wipe the interior with lemon juice or vinegar, then rinse and dry thoroughly.
- Whites will "mount" more easily if they're at room temperature.
- When separating the eggs, take care to prevent any yolk from falling into and contaminating the whites (p94).
- Use a large balloon whisk that is perfectly clean.
- Whisk just until the whites are stiff but not dry.
- Use stiffly whisked whites as soon as possible to preserve their volume.

1 Separate the eggs (p94). Begin whisking the whites slowly, using a small range of motion to break up their viscosity.

2 Continue to whisk steadily, using larger strokes, until the whites have lost their translucency and begin to foam. If you relax your shoulders and work from the wrist, the job will be much easier.

3 Now increase your speed and use an even larger range of motion, to incorporate as much air as possible. Continue to whisk until the whites have mounted to the required degree.

Whisking egg whites with an electric mixer

You can whisk egg whites using an electric mixer (but never a blender or food processor, which don't incorporate enough air). If using a stationary mixer with a whisk attachment, start on low speed and gradually increase it as the whites stiffen. Pay attention as this method leads more easily to overbeating than any other. Use the same speed progression with a hand-held mixer, but move the beaters through the whites for maximum aeration.

4 In most cases, the whites should be stiff but not dry. Test by lifting some of the whites out of the bowl; the peaks that form should be firm but glossy, with tips that droop gently.

OVERWHISKED EGG WHITES

If you overwhisk egg whites they will be stretched to capacity so they can't expand further in baking to aerate foods. Overwhisked whites are grainy and, because water leaches from them, will slide around in the bowl if you tilt it. If you have overwhisked whites they will have to be discarded.

FOLDING WHISKED EGG WHITES

This is the process by which stiffly whisked egg whites are incorporated into other, often heavier mixtures. The aim is to deflate the whites as little as possible as you fold, to retain maximum volume. Folding is done using a large rubber spatula, and the whites are added in two batches.

1 Gently drop half of the whisked egg whites onto the surface of the heavier mixture – never the reverse, which could deflate the whites. With your spatula cut down through the centre of the whites and gently bring some of the heavier mixture up and over them.

2 Turn the bowl, continuing the cut, lift, and sweep process just until no whites are visible. Drop the rest of the whites on top and fold in, this time working more delicately. At the end of the folding process no egg whites should be visible, unless the recipe directs you to leave some traces of white.

BITTERSWEET CHOCOLATE MOUSSE

Serves 4–6

300g (10½oz) bittersweet chocolate, broken into pieces

45g (1½oz) unsalted butter

5 eggs, separated

4tbsp caster sugar

240ml (8fl oz) double cream

1tsp vanilla extract

1 Combine the chocolate and butter in a bowl and set over a pan of simmering water to melt. Allow to cool slightly.

2 Put the egg yolks and 2tbsp of the sugar in another bowl and set over the pan of simmering water (the base of the bowl should not touch the water). Whisk until warm.

3 Transfer the egg yolk mixture to the bowl of an electric mixer and beat at high speed until fluffy and pale in colour. Fold the yolk mixture into the chocolate mixture.

4 In a clean bowl, whisk the egg whites with the remaining sugar until they hold firm peaks. Fold the egg whites, in 2 batches, into the chocolate mixture (see left).

5 In a bowl set over ice, whip the cream with the vanilla extract until it holds soft peaks, then fold into the chocolate mixture.

6 Transfer the mousse to individual serving cups or a large bowl. Cover and chill for at least 2 hours, or until set. To complete, just before serving sprinkle shavings of bittersweet chocolate on top, if you like.

BASIC EGG COOKING

Egg cookery, to my mind, is characterized by two concepts: diversity and simplicity. There are so many different ways to cook eggs, yet most remain quite simple in execution. One thing is for certain, however: all egg cooking requires attention because the threshold between done and overdone is quite narrow. Here is how to guarantee successful results.

BOILING EGGS

This cooking method is thought to be so simple it has become a standard for kitchen competence, as in: "He can't even boil an egg!" In fact, there are some guidelines worth following:

■ Despite the description, eggs must never be boiled, just simmered. This is because boiling can toughen whites and lead to overcooking.

■ The unsightly green ring around the yolk is caused by a reaction between the iron in the yolk and the sulphur in the egg's albumen. The main reason for a ring to appear is overcooking, although the use of older eggs can also result in a ring. You can help to prevent a ring from forming by putting just-cooked eggs immediately under cold running water to stop any further heat penetration.

■ Older eggs are easier to peel, because their lower acidity makes it harder for whites and shells to stick together.

■ Eggs straight from the refrigerator will take a few minutes longer to reach desired "doneness" than will those at room temperature.

soft-boiled egg

hard-boiled egg

1 Put the eggs in a pan that is large enough for them to remain in a single layer at the bottom. Cover them by at least 5cm (2in) with cold water. Bring the water to the boil over high heat, then immediately lower the heat so that the water simmers.

2 Soft-boiled eggs (see left), which have a set white and a runny yolk, need to be simmered for 2–3 minutes.

3 If you want hard-boiled eggs (see left below), when both the yolk and white will be set, continue to simmer, allowing about 10 minutes in total.

4 At the end of the cooking time, place the pan in the sink under the tap and run cold water into it to displace the hot water and stop the cooking process. Continue until the eggs are cool enough to handle.

5 To peel boiled eggs, crack the shell at the rounded end and, using the sides of your thumbs, push the shell and thin inner membrane away from the cooked egg, trying not to dig into the egg white too much.

BLUE SMOKE DEVILLED EGGS

These curry-flavoured stuffed eggs were developed at Blue Smoke, our barbecue and jazz restaurant in New York City.

Serves 5–6

10 eggs, hard-boiled (see left)
7tbsp mayonnaise, home-made or ready-made
1tsp Champagne or white wine vinegar
¼tsp dry mustard
2tsp Dijon mustard
¼tsp cayenne pepper
¼tsp curry powder

1 Peel the eggs. To enable the egg halves to stand upright, cut a small sliver from both ends of each egg. Halve the eggs widthways, making sure both halves are the same size.

2 Set the egg white cups aside and transfer the yolks to the bowl of a food processor. Add the mayonnaise, vinegar, mustards, cayenne pepper, and curry powder and process until smooth. Season to taste with salt and pepper.

3 Pipe the mixture into the egg white cups, making rosettes, or spoon it in neatly. Serve immediately, or cover lightly with cling film and keep in the refrigerator for up to 2 days.

CODDLING EGGS

A softly coddled egg is gently cooked to produce a result not dissimilar to soft-boiled – the differences being that for coddling, eggs are added to the boiling water and then cooked off the heat, so needing less active watching time. Perhaps it is the cook being coddled? It takes 30 minutes to hard-boil a coddled egg, so if that is the stage of cooking desired it is probably a much better idea to boil the egg instead.

1 Put enough water into a pan to cover the eggs by 4–5cm (1½–2in) when they are added. Bring to the boil. Using a large slotted spoon, gently lower the eggs into the boiling water one by one. Immediately remove from the heat and cover the pan.

2 Leave for 6 minutes for softly coddled eggs (ie just set white and a very runny yolk) or allow 8–10 minutes for more firmly cooked. To ensure that the egg yolk is centred in the white, at the beginning of the cooking time turn the eggs over gently in the pan several times using the slotted spoon. Stop the cooking process by running cold water over the eggs.

POACHING IN ADVANCE

To poach eggs ahead of time for later use, skip the salt water bath after cooking and instead plunge them into a bowl of plain chilled water to arrest the cooking. Then refrigerate the eggs in the water. When you're ready to serve them, transfer the eggs to a pan of simmering, salted water to heat through for 1 minute. Do not cook the eggs further.

POACHING EGGS

For poaching, choose the freshest eggs you can find because their whites will be thicker and less likely to disperse when cooking. To help the egg white coagulate rather than form streamers in the water, add white vinegar in the proportion of about 1tsp to 1 litre (1¾ pints) water. Do not add any salt because it discourages coagulation. Unless you are a poaching pro, you will probably want to do no more than 4 eggs at a time. For this amount, I use a large saucepan with about 1.5 litres (2¾ pints) of water.

In professional kitchens, when serving the eggs immediately we often plunge them into another pan of hot water, salted but without vinegar, to season them and remove any vinegary taste.

1 Bring a pan of water to a gentle boil and add a little vinegar (see above). Have ready another pan of simmering, salted water. One at a time, crack the eggs onto a small plate, without breaking the yolk, then slide carefully into the pan of vinegared water.

2 Using a basting motion, envelop the yolk with the white to "shape" the egg for 20 seconds, or until the white is just set. Repeat with the remaining eggs. Adjust the heat so the water is at a gentle boil. Poach for 3–5 minutes, or until the whites are completely set.

3 Using a slotted spoon, carefully lift the eggs from the water and dip them into the simmering, salted water for 30 seconds. Then place them on a clean tea towel to drain briefly. The eggs are now ready to be served – on toasted muffin halves, for example.

SCRAMBLING EGGS

There's more than one way to make great scrambled eggs. The method you choose depends on how you like your scrambled egg curds – large, small, or, in the French manner, totally blended to make a luscious cream.

If you like traditional scrambled eggs, what you're aiming for is what a friend of mine calls "concupiscent curds" – soft and billowing, no matter the size. To achieve these, keep the egg mass moving slowly and gently, and don't overcook. The last-minute addition of cream enriches the eggs deliciously and stops the cooking so that they stay creamy.

Serves 2

4 eggs

15–30g (½–1oz) butter

4tsp single or double cream

1 Beat the eggs well, then season them with salt and pepper. Heat a non-stick or well-seasoned frying pan over moderate heat, then add the butter and melt it. Pour in the beaten eggs. If you want large curds, allow the eggs to set for a bit before you start to scramble them.

Sprinkle scrambled eggs with some snipped chives and serve with buttered toast

SCRAMBLING EGGS: The French method

The French method produces eggs that are rich and super-creamy. It's a bit more laborious and time-consuming than the traditional method, but once you try it, you'll probably be hooked. The eggs are cooked in a double boiler, which should be placed over hot but not boiling water.

1 Beat the eggs well, then season with salt and pepper. For extra creaminess, add butter cut into pieces (30g/1oz butter for 3–4 eggs).

2 Melt about 15g (½oz) of butter in the top of a double boiler. Add the eggs and start stirring with a wooden spoon or whisk. Stir constantly for 10–15 minutes, or until the eggs have thickened into a creamy mass.

2 Using a wooden spoon or heat-resistant rubber spatula, pull the mass of setting egg to the centre of the pan so uncooked egg can come into contact with the hot pan. Continue this process, stirring slowly and gently, for about 2 minutes, breaking up the curds somewhat. For smaller, "tighter" curds don't wait as long to start scrambling and stir more vigorously.

3 Just before you think the eggs are done to your satisfaction, remove the pan from the heat and add the cream. Stir to mix the cream quickly into the eggs, then serve.

TIPS FOR SUCCESS WHEN SCRAMBLING EGGS

■ The eggs should be well beaten so that whites and yolks are completely combined.

■ Season with salt and pepper only after the eggs are beaten and you're ready to cook them because salt can thin them out, thus inhibiting a fluffy result.

■ Butter is the usual fat of choice for cooking eggs by the traditional method, although for various reasons some people prefer to use oil.

■ For the traditional method a non-stick pan is easiest to use, but if you choose not to your pan should be well seasoned to prevent the eggs from sticking. The pan should be preheated before butter is added – it should be hot enough to melt the butter within a few seconds, but not so hot that the butter browns before the eggs go in. I suggest that you experiment with this, starting with moderate heat and adjusting the heat as necessary.

■ For the French method the eggs are best made in a double boiler filled with hot water.

3 Add 1–2tbsp of single or double cream to the eggs to stop their cooking. Stir to mix, then turn them onto serving plates.

MAKING A CLASSIC FOLDED OMELETTE

A classic omelette is without a doubt one of the most glorious egg dishes. It isn't hard to make once you get the knack, which shouldn't take long at all. What you're aiming for is a soft, oval "egg pillow", firm on the outside and runny to almost moist within – like scrambled eggs encased in a thin cooked-egg layer.

■ A 3-egg omelette is easiest to manage; never use more than 6 eggs per omelette.

■ You'll need a non-stick or well-seasoned pan. The egg mass should not come more than 5mm (¼in) up the side of the pan.

■ The pan should be hot enough to begin setting the beaten eggs as soon as they're added, but not so hot that some of the egg mass fries or colours before the rest can cook.

■ You'll need to work quickly – an omelette takes less than 2 minutes to cook.

Serves 1

3 eggs

15–30g (½–1oz) butter

1 Beat the eggs, then season with salt and pepper. Melt the butter in a 15–20cm (6–8in) omelette or frying pan over moderately high heat. When the butter begins to foam, add the eggs. Shake the pan gently to distribute evenly.

2 Start stirring with a table fork, keeping the rounded side of the fork as parallel as possible to the pan's bottom while continuing to shake it. After 20–30 seconds, or as soon as the eggs are set but still soft, stop stirring.

3 With the help of the fork, fold the side of the omelette nearest you halfway over itself, as if folding a letter. Grasp the handle of the pan from underneath, with your palm facing upwards, and lift the pan to a 45° angle.

4 With your free hand, sharply tap the top of the handle closest to the pan, which will encourage the other side of the omelette to curl over the folded portion. Use the fork to fully "close the letter".

5 Bring the serving plate to the omelette, then tilt the pan so the omelette falls onto the plate, seam-side down. Serve immediately.

Adding a filling to a classic folded omelette

Fillings for classic folded omelettes may be savoury – grated cheese, cooked vegetables such as courgettes, mushrooms, artichokes, and asparagus, and mixtures such as sautéed chicken livers and onions – or sweet, such as jams or a variety of fruit compotes.

In volume you'll need about 240ml (8fl oz) of filling for a 3-egg omelette. If using a cooked filling, it should be hot. Before making the first fold (step 3), place the filling across the centre of the omelette, then fold as shown below to enclose the filling completely.

Distribute grated cheese and sautéed halved asparagus spears down the centre of the omelette before folding it

OTHER OMELETTES

In addition to the classic folded omelette, there are also thick, flat omelettes, which are cut into wedges for serving hot, warm, or at room temperature, and fluffy soufflé omelettes.

Flat omelettes

For unfolded omelettes, filling ingredients such as cheese, vegetables, and herbs are mixed with the beaten eggs at some point during the cooking process. The omelette is most often cooked in oil or a combination of oil and butter in a frying pan until set and browned on one side. Then the omelette is turned over to colour the other side, or transferred to the oven or grill for the final browning. In Italy flat omelettes are called frittatas (see the recipe for sweet onion frittata with balsamic vinegar on p104). They are known as tortillas in Spain, where they traditionally contain potatoes and onions, and as eggah in the Middle East.

Soufflé omelettes

Fluffy omelettes are made by separating the eggs, then whisking the whites until stiff and folding them into the yolks. They can be either sweet or savoury. In the former case, the yolks are beaten with sugar (4–5tbsp for 4 eggs, or to your taste) until light, and the whisked whites folded in. The cooked omelette is commonly sprinkled with icing sugar, or may be served with jam. For savoury soufflé omelettes, garnishes such as grated cheese, finely chopped herbs, or sautéed, thinly sliced mushrooms can either be mixed in with the yolks before folding in the whites, or sprinkled atop the cooked omelette. In both cases, cooking starts on the stovetop in a pan with melted butter and is finished in the oven or under the grill.

Egg white omelettes

A low-fat version of the classic folded omelette is made just with egg whites. You will need to use a non-stick pan, which eliminates the need for fat. To colour and enrich the omelette you could add baked mashed sweet potato or butternut squash, in the proportion of 1–2tbsp per egg white. Add the vegetable after the whites are beaten to mix them together.

SWEET ONION FRITTATA WITH BALSAMIC VINEGAR

This oniony frittata was inspired by a dish served at a trattoria that my partner Danny Meyer and I visited and loved. Located in Nonantola, in the heart of Emilia-Romagna's balsamic vinegar region, the Osteria di Rubbiara serves a small wedge of the frittata to accompany its famous chicken stewed in Lambrusco wine. Of course the frittata is excellent on its own, drizzled with a few precious drops of aged balsamico tradizionale.

Serves 4–6

2tbsp olive oil
4 large onions, about 1.1kg (2½lb) in total, thinly sliced
1tsp finely chopped garlic
2tsp finely chopped oregano
1¼tsp sea salt
⅛tsp freshly ground black pepper
2tbsp balsamic vinegar
2tbsp water
10 eggs
3tbsp freshly grated Parmesan (Parmigiano Reggiano)
2tbsp finely chopped parsley

1 Heat the olive oil in a 25cm (10in) non-stick frying pan over moderate heat. Add the onions, garlic, and oregano and season with half of the salt and pepper. Cook, stirring occasionally, for 25–30 minutes, or until the onions are tender and browned.

2 Add the balsamic vinegar and water and stir well to incorporate any browned bits. Continue cooking to reduce the liquid and coat the onions. (The onions can be prepared up to a day ahead to this point and kept, covered, in the refrigerator.)

3 Put the eggs in a large bowl and beat until combined and frothy. Add the Parmesan, parsley, and remaining salt and pepper. Pour the egg mixture into the pan and mix with the onions.

4 Over moderately high heat, stir while shaking the pan back and forth. The eggs will begin to form small curds. When the eggs are set but still somewhat soft on top, stop stirring and shaking the pan to allow the frittata to set.

5 Loosen the frittata from the pan with a rubber spatula and slide it onto a large dinner plate. Cover the frittata with another dinner plate and, holding them together, invert the plates.

6 Slide the frittata back into the pan and continue cooking over high heat for about 2 minutes to brown the other side. Carefully transfer the frittata to a large dinner plate. Cut into wedges and serve hot or at room temperature.

FRYING EGGS

Eggs can be fried over relatively high heat and the cooking can be accelerated by covering the pan. Doing that requires some vigilance to avoid overcooking the yolks, however. There is also the option of flipping the nearly set eggs over for a short time to create eggs "over easy", rather than leaving them unturned "sunny side up".

1 For 4 eggs, heat 15–30g (½–1oz) butter or lard, or 1–2tbsp oil, in a frying pan. Break each egg into a saucer, then slide it into the hot pan. Baste the egg with the hot fat and season with salt and pepper as it begins to set.

2 Cook until the egg white is set and the yolk runny or set, according to your preference. For a firm egg white cook with the pan covered.

FRIED EGGS & BACON

This is my favourite Sunday breakfast. For 2 servings, cook 6 rashers of good-quality smoked streaky bacon in a non-stick frying pan, then drain off most of the fat. Spread out the bacon rashers in a single layer. Slide 4 eggs into the pan on top of the bacon. Season the eggs as they start to set, then cover the pan and cook until they are done to your liking, basting them with the bacon fat occasionally. Sprinkle with tabasco or your favourite sauce for eggs, then serve with plenty of hot toast.

DEEP-FRYING EGGS

I learned this cooking method in France while working with three-star chef, Michel Guérard. Madame Guérard had a fondness for eggs cooked in this manner. It is quite different from what we think of as fried eggs and resembles a poached egg cooked in hot fat. The deep-frying produces a delicious caramelized taste and the eggs look great. Following this method, it's also easier to keep the yolks runny.

Be sure you have your utensils ready because the eggs cook very quickly. The wooden spoon for basting must be absolutely dry, otherwise the egg white will stick to it. To remove any moisture first dip the spoon briefly in the hot oil.

1 In a large heavy-bottomed saucepan, heat 750ml (1¼ pints) vegetable or olive oil over high heat until the oil reaches a temperature of about 190°C (375°F). Crack an egg into a small cup, without breaking the yolk, then transfer it to a ladle. Tilt the pan slightly, then gently lower in the ladle to slide the egg into the hot oil.

2 With a dry wooden spoon, gently and quickly baste the egg with the oil until the egg has taken on an oval shape and the yolk is completely concealed by the white. Continue with the process for 1 minute. The egg should be set and lightly coloured.

3 Using a slotted spoon, lift the egg from the oil and drain it on kitchen paper. Before eating, season the egg with salt and pepper.

CHEESE SOUFFLÉ

Surely one of the most sublime achievements of egg cookery is the soufflé. Fragrant, feather-light, and golden crowned, few dishes capture the diner's imagination like a perfect soufflé. Soufflés are remarkably versatile and can be served as first courses, light main courses, or spectacular desserts. And contrary to popular belief, a soufflé is not difficult to make – it simply requires focus and attention to detail to obtain great results.

55g (2oz) butter
1 small onion, finely chopped
2 whole cloves
1 small bay leaf
½tsp anchovy purée (optional)
¼tsp Aleppo pepper or paprika
3 tbsp plain flour
240ml (8fl oz) milk
5tbsp freshly grated Parmesan (Parmigiano Reggiano)
2tbsp finely diced Gruyère or Montasio cheese
3 egg yolks
4 egg whites

1 Preheat the oven to 180°C (350°F, gas 4). Using 15g (½oz) of the butter, coat a 15cm (6in) soufflé dish, or four 7.5cm (3in) individual dishes. Do this by brushing the soft, not melted, butter over the bottom of the dish in a circular motion, then up the sides. Chill to set the butter.

2 Melt the remaining butter in a heavy-bottomed saucepan and add the onion, cloves, bay leaf, anchovy (if using), and Aleppo pepper or paprika. Cook gently until the onion is softened but not at all coloured.

3 Stir in the flour and cook gently for 4–5 minutes. Slowly add the milk, using a small whisk to incorporate it into the butter and flour roux. Bring to a very slow simmer and cook the sauce, stirring often, for 10–15 minutes, or until it is thicker than double cream and smooth.

4 Strain the sauce into a bowl, pressing well on the solids. Discard the solids. Stir the cheeses into the hot sauce until completely melted and smooth, then mix in the egg yolks.

 ## FLAVOURING SOUFFLES

With all soufflés there are 3 basic elements: the flavour base, egg yolks to enrich and bind, and whisked egg whites to lighten. In the case of savoury soufflés the flavour base can be a béchamel or velouté sauce or a vegetable purée, either on its own or in combination with the sauce. Finely chopped meats such as ham or sweetbreads, chopped vegetables and mushrooms, and grated cheese are frequently used to flavour savoury soufflés. For a dessert soufflé the flavour base can be a crème pâtissière or simply a very reduced fruit compote enhanced, perhaps, by an eau-de-vie or liqueur. In all cases the important thing is to have the correct proportions and to combine the ingredients properly.

5 Whisk the egg whites until they hold soft peaks. Pile half of the whites on top of the cheese mixture and fold them in thoroughly using a rubber spatula (p97).

6 Spoon the remaining whites on top and fold them in more lightly and delicately. Pour the mixture into the prepared soufflé dish.

BAKING EGGS SUR LE PLAT

It has been said that French chefs will test the mettle of a new cook by requiring him or her to prepare this deceptively simple dish. The challenge lies in regulating both the cooking procedure and temperature so that the eggs are cooked to just the right point.

1 Preheat the oven to 200°C (400°F, gas 6). Put ½tbsp melted butter in a small enamelled cast-iron gratin dish. Season the bottom of the dish with salt and pepper (this prevents the salt from marring the appearance of the eggs).

2 Place the dish on moderate heat and slide in 2 eggs, without breaking the yolks. Cover the eggs with another ½tbsp melted butter.

3 Transfer the dish to the oven and bake for 6–8 minutes, or just until the whites are set and milky and the yolks have a shiny, glazed appearance. Serve the eggs immediately.

Once baked, take the souffle to the table immediately and serve

7 Run your thumb around the edge of the mixture to make a groove (this will cause the soufflé to rise with a high cap). Place in the centre of the oven and bake for 25–30 minutes, or until set, puffed, and browned.

 SUR LE PLAT EXTRAS

Although somewhat untraditional, I sometimes like to sprinkle the eggs in step 2 with some finely chopped herbs – tarragon and chives being among my favourites – just before cooking.

COOKING WITH CREAM

Things of particular excellence are often called the "cream" of their kind. And cream is an unsurpassed treat. It adds richness and incomparable flavour to a wide range of sweet and savoury dishes and mellows sauces of all kinds. Rich creams can be boiled and reduced and, unless there is too much fat or acidity in the sauce, they usually will not "break" (when fat and liquid separate).

WHIPPING CREAM

Only those creams with a fat content of at least 30 per cent will whip. As with whisking egg whites, your goal is to incorporate as much air as possible into the cream to make it stiffen. Most recipes calling for whipping cream ask for it to be whipped to the light or stiff stage.

■ Both whipping cream and double cream will almost double in volume when whipped. Single cream is not suitable for whipping.

■ Have your bowl and beater, as well as the cream, well chilled because fat droplets in the cream need to stay cold and firm to bond and create a stiff structure. Otherwise, your cream will go from liquid to butter while you keep trying to make it mount.

■ I find hand-whipping with a chilled balloon whisk best, but you can use an electric mixer.

■ To maintain the cold I beat over a bowl of ice.

■ Whipped cream can be stored for several hours in the refrigerator. It may exude liquid as it stands. If the cream has not been overwhipped, stir the liquid back in or pour it off.

1 Pour the chilled cream into a bowl set in a larger bowl of ice. Start whipping with a broad circular motion at a leisurely pace, about 2 strokes per second (or on low speed if using a mixer), until the cream begins to thicken.

2 Now whip a bit faster if you like (or at a moderate speed if using a mixer) for 2–3 minutes. At this point the cream will probably be softly or lightly whipped – it will barely hold its shape when lifted with your beater.

3 For stiffly whipped cream, which mounts sufficiently to make firm peaks, keep beating. At this point you can fold in other ingredients, such as sugar or vanilla extract.

OVERWHIPPING CREAM

If you whip cream beyond the stiff peak stage, it will develop a granular texture. If this happens, the cream can be whipped further until it completely separates into butter and whey, and the butter can then be used in cooking or desserts. Discard the whey.

Pumpkin & chocolate chip cheesecake with country cream

"Country cream", our name for a topping we use with lots of desserts, is a tangy and slightly richer alternative to whipped cream. It can also be frozen and scooped like ice cream (try it with a sprinkle of cinnamon). I serve it with a delicious, seasonal variation on the classic American cheesecake. If you choose to use fresh pumpkin for the cheesecake instead of canned, be sure to cook it down slowly and thoroughly after it has been peeled, boiled, and puréed, so that the water content is reduced.

Serves 6–8

For the crust

150g (5½oz) wholemeal or digestive biscuits, finely crushed

4tbsp icing sugar, sifted

85g (3oz) butter, melted

For the filling

450g (1lb) cream cheese, at room temperature

100g (3½oz) caster sugar

2 eggs

½tsp vanilla extract

125g (4½oz) canned pumpkin purée

1tsp ground cinnamon

½tsp freshly grated nutmeg

½tsp ground cloves

85g (3oz) bittersweet chocolate chips

For the country cream

115g (4oz) soured cream

125g (4½oz) mascarpone

125g (4½oz) plain whole-milk yogurt

100g (3½oz) caster sugar

2tsp vanilla extract

To prepare the crust, combine the crumbs, sugar, and butter in a large bowl and knead together until well blended. Press evenly over the bottom and sides of a 23cm (9in) springform cake tin. Chill until needed.

Preheat the oven to 180°C (350°F, gas 4). In the bowl of an electric mixer fitted with the paddle attachment, beat the cream cheese and sugar together until smooth. Add the eggs and vanilla extract and mix until well blended. Beat in the pumpkin purée and spices.

Remove the mixing bowl from the machine and fold in the chocolate chips with a rubber spatula. Pour the filling into the chilled crust.

Place in the oven and bake for 30–40 minutes. The centre of the cheesecake should feel somewhat firm to the touch. Leave to cool to room temperature, then refrigerate, covered, for at least 6 hours or overnight.

To make the country cream, place all the ingredients in a deep mixing bowl and set the bowl over a larger bowl filled with ice. Whisk together until the mixture will hold soft, smooth peaks and is the consistency of whipped double cream. (This makes 480ml/ 16fl oz of country cream. It lasts, covered, in the refrigerator for up to 3–4 days.)

To serve the cheesecake, remove the sides of the springform tin. Cut the cheesecake into portions and serve topped with the country cream. Alternatively, serve the cheesecake with plain whipped cream or with chocolate sauce or your favourite flavour of ice cream.

FISH & SHELLFISH

CHARLIE TROTTER

"When cooking seafood, always have a sensual touch." That is a note I once wrote to myself, and it truly embodies my thoughts about seafood. There is sheer hedonism in eating the unique creatures that reside in the waters of the Earth, with all their delicious textures and flavours. I encourage you to begin a journey of exploration with seafood unlike any you have made before. Try new species. Test new cooking methods. The possibilities are endless.

I work with a variety of purveyors to secure seafood from around the world, and my interest just keeps growing. As with fruits and vegetables, I'm only interested in working with seafood that is in season. This is so important, because it almost guarantees a wonderfully flavourful product. Many people are unaware that fish and shellfish are seasonal, but they certainly are. Everything on Earth has a season, and seafood is no exception.

Protecting fish stocks I certainly respect and appreciate the efforts of aquaculturists, as I have concerns about the overfishing of certain species. Overfishing denies all fish species a fighting chance of maintaining their populations. It is no longer simply the familiar scenario of nets raking the ocean and getting everything. Overfishing has gone beyond that. Some fishing fleets use sonar technology and satellites to direct them into the best areas, where they capture everything there is to be found. I cannot agree with that approach at all. Some parts of the world, such as Australia, have legislated against overfishing, allowing fish species time for regeneration to sustainable levels. That is what I would like to see in force everywhere.

While I'm not a great fan of fish farms, I do believe there is a place for them. Catfish, a "bottom feeder" from America's Deep South, is a wonderful example of a fish that, when produced with the necessary care and restrictions, is being farmed very successfully. I would love to see every fish farm producing fish of such high quality. My main concern with most farming is that the fish are raised in a restricted area, which makes them more prone to disease. They have to be given antibiotics, and most people would prefer the fish they eat to be antibiotic-free.

Storing and preparing fish and shellfish Purchase fresh fish as close to the day of cooking and serving as possible, since it is highly perishable. However, it can be kept for up to 24 hours, and following a few simple steps will ensure its quality and safety.

Whole fish should be stored whole on crushed ice in the refrigerator. Place crushed ice in a pan to catch drips should melting take place, and then place the fish on top. Cover the entire fish with more crushed ice and place in the refrigerator. Fillets should be placed in a plastic or metal container, which is then covered with cling film. Set this covered container on crushed ice in the refrigerator. Never store fillets in direct contact with crushed ice because contact with water will cause the fillets to break down. Shellfish, still in their original bags, should be stored in the refrigerator in a bowl covered with wet kitchen paper. Shellfish should never come in direct contact with ice or cold water. Frozen fish should be stored, in its packaging, in the freezer. Before using, let it thaw in the refrigerator for 24 hours. Never thaw fish by microwaving or by putting it into direct contact with water. Fish preparation is not as daunting as you might think. The basic techniques for whole fish are cleaning, scaling, gutting, and cutting or filleting, with slightly different methods used for flat fish and round fish. Of course you can buy fish already prepared, but it is unlikely to be as fresh as whole fish you deal with yourself, and you are able to control how it is done.

It is best to avoid handling shellfish until you are ready to prepare them for immediate cooking. When selecting molluscs, pay close attention to the shells. Fresh molluscs, such as mussels, should have hard, well-cupped shells; avoid those that are broken. Before preparing for cooking, gently tap each shell – if it does not close, the mollusc is dead and not safe for consumption.

PREPARING ROUND FISH

Round fish are those "fin fish" that are round in body shape and have eyes on both sides of their heads (the other type of fin fish are flat fish). There are both freshwater and saltwater varieties of round fish. Some of the more popular are salmon, sea bass, cod and haddock, and tuna. The techniques used to prepare a round fish will vary according to how you are going to cook it, but the most common are gutting, scaling, boning (if you intend to stuff the fish), cutting into steaks, and filleting.

GUTTING THROUGH THE STOMACH

Gutting a fish means to remove all the viscera (everything in the stomach cavity). While most of the fish you buy have already been gutted, there may be occasions when you will need to know how to do this yourself. The most common way of gutting fish is to remove the viscera through a cut into the stomach, but fish can also be gutted through the gills (see opposite). A pike is shown here.

BUYING FISH

It is easier to assess the quality of whole fish than that of steaks or fillets, so always try to buy fish whole and then ask the fishmonger to prepare it for you or do this yourself (following the instructions here and on the following pages).

■ When buying whole fish use your sense of smell to aid in determining quality. Sniff under the gills and in the stomach cavity – fish should not smell strong or fishy. The skin should be very smooth, not slimy, and eyes should not be cloudy.

■ For fillets and steaks, sniff the flesh – it should smell sweet and of the sea.

1 Hold the fish firmly on its side and, using a fish knife, small chef's knife, or kitchen scissors, make a shallow slit in the underside, cutting from the tail end to the head end.

2 Pull out the guts (viscera), then cut off the gills (see opposite), taking care as they can be sharp. Discard the guts and gills.

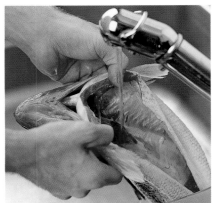

3 Rinse the cavity under cold running water to remove any remaining blood and guts. Pat the fish dry with kitchen paper. It can now be scaled (see opposite) and boned.

GUTTING THROUGH THE GILLS

This technique is often used for fish to be poached whole or cut into steaks, as well as for small flat fish because it keeps their natural shape. Before gutting this way, scale the fish and trim the fins (see right). A rainbow trout is shown here.

1 First, cut off the gills at the base of the head (the gills are sharp, so hook your index finger around them to pull them out).

2 Put your fingers into the hole left by the gills and pull out the viscera.

3 Using kitchen scissors, snip a small slit in the stomach at the ventral (anal) opening near the tail. Insert your fingers and pull out any remaining viscera.

SCALING & TRIMMING

While there are no hard and fast rules about whether or not to scale a fish, there are some general guidelines that should prove helpful. The first is that if you plan to eat the skin then it is best to scale the fish. If, on the other hand, you are going to remove the skin before serving the fish, then there is no need to scale it. A salmon is shown here.

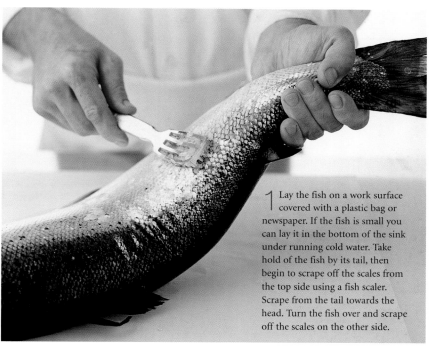

1 Lay the fish on a work surface covered with a plastic bag or newspaper. If the fish is small you can lay it in the bottom of the sink under running cold water. Take hold of the fish by its tail, then begin to scrape off the scales from the top side using a fish scaler. Scrape from the tail towards the head. Turn the fish over and scrape off the scales on the other side.

SCALING WITH A KNIFE

If you don't have a fish scaler, you can use a chef's knife to scale the fish. Scrape off the scales with the back (blunt) side of the knife blade.

2 Cut off the back (dorsal) fins and belly fins with kitchen scissors, then trim off the fins on either side of the head. If you like, trim the tail with the scissors to neaten it, perhaps cutting into a "V" shape.

BONING THROUGH THE STOMACH

To bone a whole fish in this way, it is first gutted through the stomach (p114) and then scaled and the fins trimmed (p115). Once boned, it can be stuffed for cooking, most commonly by baking. A sea bass is shown here.

1 Open up the fish. Loosen the ribcage (transverse bones) from the flesh on the top side by sliding a sharp knife along the ribcage. Turn the fish over and repeat to loosen the transverse bones from the flesh on that side.

2 Snip the backbone at head and tail ends using kitchen scissors. Then, starting at the tail, peel it away from the flesh. The transverse bones will come away with the backbone.

BONING FROM THE BACK

Boning a whole round fish from the back prepares it for stuffing and then baking or cooking en papillote. First scale the fish, then trim off the fins (p115). Do not gut the fish. Use a filleting knife or other sharp, flexible knife for boning. A black sea bass is shown here.

1 Cut down the back of the fish, cutting along one side of the backbone from head to tail. Continue cutting into the fish, keeping the knife close on top of the bones. When you reach the belly, don't cut through the skin.

2 Turn the fish over and cut down the back from tail to head along the other side of the backbone. Continue cutting as before, to cut away the flesh from that side of the backbone.

3 Using kitchen scissors, snip the backbone at the head and tail ends, then remove it. Pull out the guts (viscera) and discard. Rinse the cavity under cold running water and pat dry.

4 Pull out any pin bones (the line of tiny bones down each side of the fish) using large tweezers or small needle-nose pliers.

FILLETING

A round fish is typically cut into two fillets after it has been gutted. It is best to use a filleting knife because the blade is long and more flexible than that of a regular kitchen knife. Once filleted, the fish can be cooked by almost any method. However, it's important to note that if a fillet is small and very thin (such as the red mullet shown here), you will need to be very careful not to overcook it.

1 Depending on the fish you are preparing and whether you are going to leave the skin on the fillets, scale the fish (p115). Using a filleting knife, cut into the fish at the head end, just behind the gills, cutting with the knife at an angle just until you reach the backbone.

2 Starting near the gills, cut the fish down the length of the back, cutting along the top side of the backbone.

3 Working again from head to tail, continue cutting over the bone, keeping the knife flat and folding the fillet back as you cut. When the fillet has been freed, remove it.

4 Turn the fish over and repeat the process to remove the second fillet, this time cutting from the tail to the head.

SKINNING A FILLET

If you plan to skin fish fillets, there is no need to scale them or the whole fish from which the fillets are cut, unless you want to fry the skin later for use as a garnish. Round fish and flat fish fillets are skinned in the same way. A whole salmon fillet is shown here.

1 With the fillet skin-side down, insert a fish knife into the flesh near the tail end, turning the blade at a slight angle. Cut through the flesh just to the skin.

2 Turn the blade of the knife almost flat and take tight hold of the end of the skin. Holding the knife firmly in place, close to the skin, pull the skin away so as to cut off the fillet.

CUTTING STEAKS

Any large round fish can be cut into steaks, but those most commonly found in steak form are varieties of tuna, swordfish, and salmon. With the exception of halibut, flat fish are too thin to cut into steaks.

Fish steaks can be cooked in many ways, although thickness may determine the best method. For instance, a thinly cut steak of about 1cm (½in) is best quickly grilled, while a thicker steak of about 2.5cm (1in) will fare well on a barbecue. A salmon is shown here.

1 Gut the fish through the stomach. Scale it, then trim off the fins. Using a chef's knife, cut off the head just behind the gills.

2 Holding the fish firmly on its side, cut across to get steaks of the desired thickness.

PREPARING FLAT FISH

Flat fish, which with round fish comprise the family of "fin fish", are flat and oval-shaped, with eyes on only one side of the body. They typically have a coloured top side, which may be dark brown, black, or dark grey, and a white underside.

Common types of flat fish are halibut, plaice, turbot, and Dover sole. They can be cooked in a variety of ways, including grilling, steaming, sautéing, baking, and poaching. Flat fish make a very dramatic presentation when served whole.

GUTTING & TRIMMING

If you plan to serve a flat fish whole, this is the first part of the preparation you need to do (the second part is to remove the tough, dark skin, but not the white. Flat fish are normally gutted as a first step to ensure that there are no viscera to cut into when the fish is being trimmed. Then the fins are trimmed and the fish is scaled, if necessary. A plaice is shown in the photographs here.

1 With a chef's knife, make a small cut along the stomach so you can reach in to remove the guts (viscera) and any roe. Discard these.

2 Use kitchen scissors to trim away the fins. Leave about 5mm (¼in) of fin still attached to the fish to ensure that you don't cut into the fish body when trimming.

3 Scale the white side of the fish, if necessary (see below), then cut off the gills with scissors and discard them. Rinse the fish inside and out under cold running water.

SCALING FLAT FISH

If the skin on the white side of a flat fish feels rough to the touch, scale it after gutting the fish and trimming off the fins (see above).

Lay the fish on newspaper or a plastic bag. Using a special fish scaler or the back (blunt) side of a chef's knife, scrape off the scales, working from the tail towards the head.

There is no need to scale the dark side of a flat fish as this skin will be removed before serving.

GUTTING BY TAKING OFF THE HEAD

When you are planning to serve a flat fish whole but without the head, use this easier way to gut the fish. It can also be used to gut a fish prior to cutting it into fillets.

Trim the fins (see above), then, if necessary, scale the skin on the white side of the fish. Lay the fish dark-side up and make a V-shaped cut all the way around the head. Grasp the head gently but firmly and, with a quick twisting turn, pull the head away. The guts (viscera) and the gills should come out with the head. Rinse the cavity under cold running waterto remove any remaining blood and guts.

SKINNING & FILLETING A DOVER SOLE

Dover sole requires special handling, differing from the preparation of other flat fish. Most chefs prefer to skin Dover sole prior to filleting; however, if the sole is being prepared to cook whole, the skin is left on. Note that only the black skin is removed. The delicate white skin remains intact, even when the fish is cut into fillets.

1 Make a small cut through the skin at the tail end, cutting at an angle, to separate a flap of the dark skin from the flesh.

2 Using a towel, take hold of the freed flap of dark skin securely. Holding the tail end of the fish firmly with your other hand, pull the dark skin away from the fish. Fillet the fish to make 2 fillets.

GRIP THE SKIN

To get a good grip on the skin when pulling it from a fish, you can either grasp the flap of skin in a towel or dip your fingers in salt first. Pull off the skin sharply, parallel to the flesh and as quickly as possible.

FILLETING A SKATE WING

Skate is a type of ray fish. It is prized for its "wings", which are sometimes filleted to remove the meat from the gelatinous cartilage. Filleted skate wings are most commonly just lightly sautéed, although they are also delicious poached in a light court bouillon (p140).

1 Lay the skate wing on a board dark-side uppermost and with the thickest side nearest to you. Cut into the flesh on the thickest side until you reach the cartilage that is about halfway down.

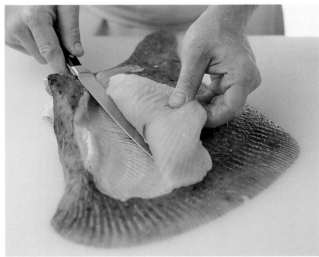

2 Turn the wing around. Turn the knife flat on the cartilage and cut the flesh away until you reach the outer edge of the wing. Cut along the edge and detach this fillet. Repeat on the other side. Remove the skin from the fillets as for round fish (p118).

PREPARING SHELLFISH

The shellfish family of seafood is made up of two primary categories: crustaceans and molluscs. Crustaceans, such as lobsters, prawns, and crabs, have an exterior skeleton, segmented bodies, and jointed limbs. Most molluscs have hard shells – univalves (eg abalone or ormer and conch) have a single shell and bivalves (eg scallops, clams, oysters, and mussels) have two shells. The third type of mollusc, cephalopods (eg octopuses and squid), don't have a hard outer shell.

Shellfish are usually cooked by boiling or steaming. Crustaceans may also be grilled and many molluscs are served raw.

CLEANING & DE-BEARDING MUSSELS

Mussels sold live usually have a fibrous attachment, called a "beard", on their shell. This beard needs to be removed and the shells thoroughly scrubbed prior to cooking. Mussels are most commonly steamed to open their shells, and a popular way to serve them is in a wine and chopped tomato liquid. They may also be shelled to grill or to stuff and bake. Unlike clams and oysters, mussels are almost never served raw.

1 Scrub the mussels under cold running water to remove all grit and sand. Scrape off any barnacles using a small, sharp knife.

2 Pinch the stringy dark "beard" between your forefinger and thumb and pull it away from the mussel shell.

MOLLUSC SAFETY

■ When buying oysters and clams, check that the shells are tightly closed. The exception is geoduck clams, which are usually slightly open; however, they should close when tapped lightly. Mussel shells may also gape open slightly; like geoduck clams, they should close immediately if tapped. If this does not happen, do not buy the molluscs or – if already purchased – discard them.

■ To prepare molluscs for cooking, first discard any with broken shells. Some, such as clams, tend to be sandy so it is a good idea to "purge" them. Put them in a large bowl of cold water with some cornmeal or polenta and leave to soak overnight in the refrigerator. The clams eat the meal and expel the sand.

■ After boiling or steaming molluscs such as clams and mussels, check all have opened; discard any that are closed. Discard oysters that smell "fishy" on opening. All seafood should smell fresh, sweet, and of the sea.

OPENING OYSTERS

For the technique of opening (shucking) oysters, "practice makes perfect". Use a thick towel or wear a special wire mesh glove to protect your hand from the sharp edges of the oyster shell. And try to hold the oyster flat as you work to prevent the delicious briny liquid from spilling out (if you are going to cook them, work over a pan to catch the liquid). If you intend to serve oysters raw on the half shell, scrub them well before opening.

1 Hold the oyster in a thick towel. Insert the tip of an oyster knife into the hinge and twist to open the oyster shell. Carefully cut the muscle, keeping the blade of the knife horizontal and close to the top shell, to release the oyster. Lift off the top shell.

2 Loosen the oyster from the bottom shell by gently sliding the knife underneath the oyster. Take care not to cut the oyster meat, nor to tip the shell and spill out the briny liquid.

OPENING CLAMS

There are two types of clams: hard shell (such as carpet-shell and venus) and soft shell (eg longneck steamers). All clams should be scrubbed well and, as they tend to be very sandy, they may need to be purged (p121). Then they can be opened to eat raw or cooked. Alternatively, they can be boiled or steamed to open the shells. Cockles can be prepared and cooked in the same way as clams.

1 Holding the clam in a thick towel to protect your fingers, work the tip of the knife between the top and bottom shells, then twist the knife upwards to force the shells apart.

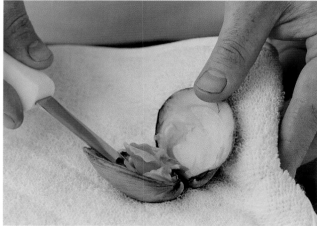

2 Slide the knife over the inside of the top shell to sever the muscle and release the clam, then do the same to release the clam from the bottom shell. Take care not to cut into the clam meat. If serving raw on the half shell, snap off the top shell. For soft-shell clams, remove the dark membrane from the clam meat before serving.

OPENING SCALLOPS

Although most home cooks will buy scallops already opened, you will sometimes find them in the shell. Scrub the shells clean before opening. The scallops can then be served raw, as part of sushi or sashimi meals, or cooked. The red or orange scallop roe (called the coral) can be sautéed and served alongside the scallop dish, or puréed and added to a sauce.

1 Holding the scallop firmly in your hand, flat shell uppermost, insert a long, thin, flexible knife in between the top and bottom shells, keeping the blade as close to the inside of the top shell as possible to avoid damaging the scallop meat inside. Slide the knife around the top shell to sever the muscle.

2 When the scallop meat has been freed from the top shell, remove the shell. Detach the scallop from the bottom shell with the help of the knife, again taking care not to cut into the scallop meat.

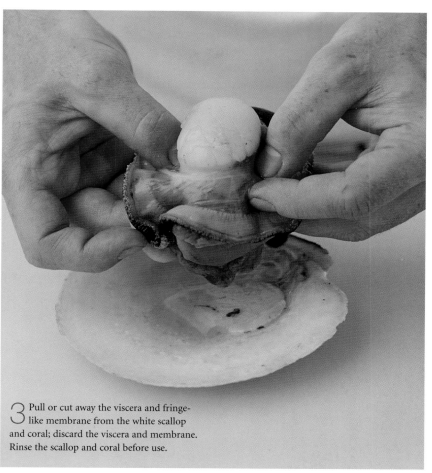

3 Pull or cut away the viscera and fringe-like membrane from the white scallop and coral; discard the viscera and membrane. Rinse the scallop and coral before use.

PREPARING ABALONE & WHELKS

Abalone, also called ormer or ear-shell, is a large mollusc consisting of a "foot" covered by a single shell. The foot, which is really a muscle that adheres it firmly to its rock, is the edible part. Harvesting abalone is difficult, so you rarely find it for sale alive in the shell.

To prepare abalone, you need to cut around the inside of the shell to free the foot, which then needs to be trimmed of any dark skin and fringe and viscera. The flesh of some abalone is tough so it must be tenderized by beating it with a meat pounder. Abalone is most often eaten raw. Alternatively, slice it thinly and sauté quickly – like squid and octopus, abalone should be cooked briefly or be given a long, slow simmering, as otherwise it will be tough.

Whelks are sea snails. After scrubbing and purging (p121), they are usually cooked in the shell, by simmering in salted water, stock, or court bouillon (p140), then pulled out with a small fork for eating. (Tiny winkles are prepared and cooked in the same way.)

Alternatively, you can simmer whelks just long enough to be able to remove them from their shells, then use them in soups or stews.

CLEANING LIVE LOBSTER

Here is how to clean and cut up a live lobster before cooking it. Reserve the tomalley (greenish liver) and any coral (the roe, which will be black) to use in a sauce, flavoured butter, or stuffing. The head, body, and legs can be used in a fish stock; they contain incredibly intense lobster flavour.

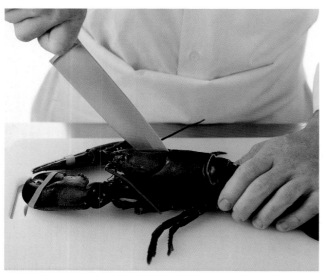

1 Leave the rubber bands in place around the claws. Lay the lobster flat on a chopping board and hold it firmly. Put the tip of a heavy chef's knife into the lobster's head, then cut straight down and split it in 2.

2 Remove the claws by twisting them off the lobster or, if necessary, by cutting them off with the chef's knife.

3 Take hold of the body and head section with one hand and the tail section with the other hand. Twist to separate them.

4 Spoon the tomalley and any coral from the head and tail sections and reserve. The tail section and claws are now ready for cooking.

TAKING THE MEAT FROM A COOKED LOBSTER

Rather than cut up a live lobster before cooking, you can cook the lobster whole and then take out the meat to use in a wide variety of dishes. To cook, simply plunge the lobster into a deep pot of boiling water and boil until the shell turns red. For a 450g (1lb) lobster this will take about 6 minutes.

1 Take firm hold of the tail section and twist sharply to separate it from the body and head section.

2 Turn the tail section over and, using kitchen scissors, cut down the centre of the flat underside of the shell.

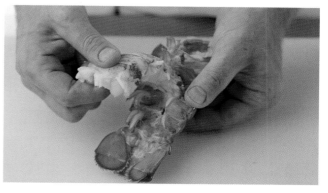

3 With your thumbs, press on both sides of the cut and pull open the tail shell. Remove the meat in one piece.

4 With lobster crackers or a small hammer, crack open the claw shells. Take care not to crush the meat inside.

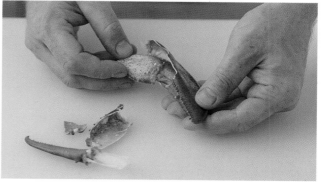

5 Remove the meat from the claws, in whole pieces if possible. Discard any membrane attached to the meat.

PICKING COOKED CRAYFISH

Crayfish are very similar to lobsters, just much smaller. After boiling them for 6–8 minutes in fish stock, court bouillon (p140), or seafood or crab boil – perhaps with some cayenne pepper added for a kick – leave them to cool, then serve. This is how to get at their sweet meat.

1 Break off the head section (suck out the delicious juices from the head, if you like).

2 Gently squeeze the tail to crack the shell, then remove the meat by pulling off the sides of the shell.

PREPARING PRAWNS

Prawns contain a small sand line, also known as the intestinal vein. Unless the prawns are small, this vein is usually removed before cooking (the process is called deveining). This is done because the vein can tend to be a bit gritty on the palate. You can devein prawns after peeling or while they are still in the shell.

Large prawns to be stuffed and then grilled or baked are first cut open or "butterflied".

Peeling & deveining

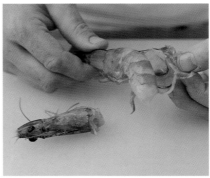

1 Pull off the head, then peel off the shell and legs with your fingers. Sometimes the last tail section is left on the prawn. Save heads and shells for use in stock, if you like.

Deveining without cutting

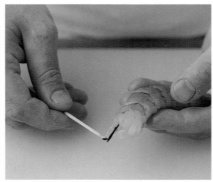

Peel the prawn or just pull off the head and leave the prawn in shell. Use a cocktail stick to "hook" the vein and remove it. Rinse the prawn under cold running water and pat dry.

PREPARING LANGOUSTINES

Also called scampi or Dublin Bay prawns, these are small members of the lobster family. Only the tail is eaten. Langoustines are prepared in the same way as prawns (although their shell is tougher).

2 Run a paring knife lightly along the back of the prawn to expose the dark intestinal vein. Remove the vein with the tip of the knife or your fingers. Rinse the prawn under cold running water and pat dry.

Butterflying

Peel the prawn. Make a cut along the back so that the prawn can be opened flat like a book. Do not cut all the way through. Remove the vein, then rinse the prawn under cold running water and pat dry.

Langoustines with green curry sauce & spring onions

Sweet, buttery langoustines contrast with the sharpness of green curry sauce, resulting in a unique flavour. The aroma of kaffir lime leaves adds exotic flair. If you don't have shellfish oil for garnishing, you can mix 2tsp of the juices from the langoustines with 1tbsp extra virgin olive oil.

For the green curry sauce

6 spring onions, chopped

2 fresh green chilies, seeded and chopped

2 garlic cloves, chopped

1tbsp finely chopped fresh ginger

1tbsp coriander seeds, dry-roasted (p79) and crushed

½tsp cracked black pepper

4 kaffir lime leaves, torn

2 lemon-grass stalks, chopped

100g (3½oz) basil, chopped

50g (1¾oz) coriander with stalks, chopped

3tbsp olive oil

grated zest and juice of 4 limes

4tbsp coconut milk

For the langoustines

2 shallots, finely chopped

2tbsp extra virgin olive oil

12 spring onions, cut in half

8 baby golden beetroots, peeled and quartered, or 2 medium golden beetroots, peeled and cut into 2.5cm (1in) pieces or wedges

8 raw langoustines, peeled

2 large handfuls of tiny lettuce leaves

To garnish

4tsp shellfish oil

4tsp finely shredded basil

To prepare the sauce, purée the spring onions, chilies, garlic, ginger, coriander seeds, cracked pepper, lime leaves, lemon-grass, herbs, olive oil, and lime zest and juice in a blender. Press the purée through a fine-mesh sieve into a small saucepan. Add the coconut milk and season to taste with salt and pepper. Set aside.

Before serving warm the sauce over moderately low heat for about 3 minutes until just hot (the sauce will darken).

To prepare the langoustines, heat a sauté pan over moderate heat. Add the shallots, olive oil, spring onions, and beetroot pieces. Cook for 2 minutes. Add the langoustines, increase the heat to high, and cook for 2–3 minutes on each side, or until just cooked through. Remove the langoustines from the pan and season to taste.

Add the lettuce leaves to the sauté pan and toss to quickly wilt the lettuce. Transfer the lettuce, beetroots, and spring onions to a bowl and season to taste with salt and pepper. Slice each langoustine into 2 pieces.

Cover the centre of each plate with a generous amount of the green curry sauce. Arrange some of the wilted lettuce, langoustines, and vegetables on top of the sauce. Drizzle the shellfish oil around the plate and top with the shredded basil and a grinding of pepper.

CLEANING A LIVE BLUE CRAB

The cleaning process described here will prepare
a hard-shell blue crab for cooking in a soup or
sauce. Alternatively, it can be done after the crab
has been boiled or steamed (skip step 1).

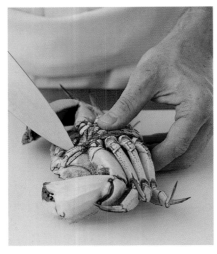

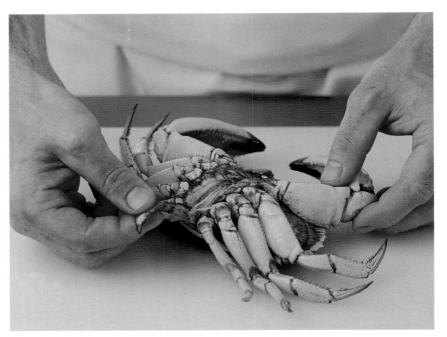

1 Hold the crab on its back on a chopping
board. Insert the tip of a chef's knife into the
crab, directly behind the eyes, and quickly bring
the knife blade down to the board.

2 Pull and twist off the small, folded tail flap (the apron) from the underside. Female crabs have
rounded aprons; male crabs have thin, pointed aprons.

3 Press down on the centre and leg section,
and pull off the top shell.

4 With kitchen scissors, snip off the gills
(dead man's fingers). Discard the spongy
sand bag that is located behind the eyes.

5 Cut the crab in half or into quarters. It is
now ready for cooking.

CLEANING A LIVE SOFT-SHELL CRAB

Soft-shell crabs are blue crabs that have moulted their hard shells. The most popular ways to cook soft-shell crabs are deep-frying and sautéing. The entire crab is eaten – the newly formed shell is crunchy and delicious.

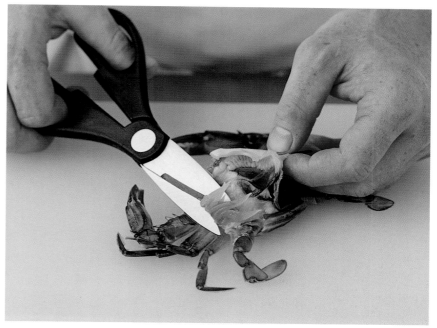

1 With kitchen scissors, cut across the front of the crab to remove the eyes and mouth.

2 Fold back the top shell so you can snip away the gills from both sides.

COOKING CRAB

A whole live crab is most commonly cooked by boiling, although it can also be steamed. The cooking time will vary according to the size of the crab. As a general guide, a 450g (1lb) blue crab will take 8–10 minutes to boil. Common European and Dungeness crabs will take longer – about 15–20 minutes for a 900g (2lb) crab. When cooked, the shell turns red.

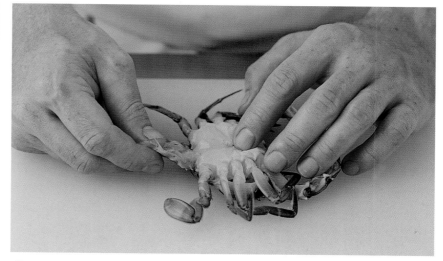

3 Turn the crab over. Unfold the tail flap (the apron) on this side and pull it off. This also removes the guts (viscera).

REMOVING THE MEAT FROM A COOKED CRAB

All large, meaty crabs have the essential parts of claws, legs, and body. Shown here is a common European crab, which contains soft brown meat as well as white meat. Dungeness crab is prepared in much the same way.

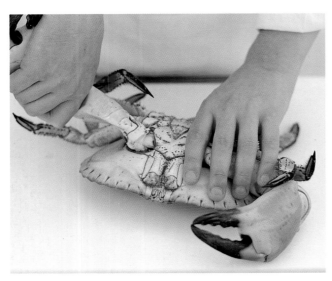

1 Set the crab on its back on a chopping board and firmly twist the claws and all the legs to break them from the body.

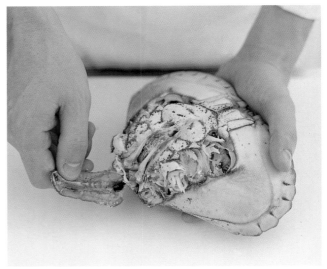

2 Lift up the triangular tail flap (the apron) on the underside of the body, then twist it off and discard.

5 Crack or cut the central body section into several large pieces. Dig out the white meat using a lobster pick or skewer, discarding small pieces of membrane. Reserve the white meat in a bowl.

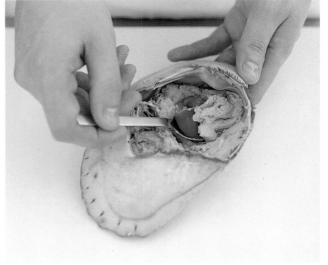

6 Spoon out the soft brown meat from the shell and reserve it to serve with the white meat (there is no brown meat in a Dungeness crab). Discard the head sac. If there is any roe, spoon this out too and reserve it.

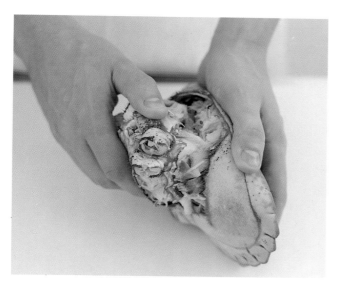

3 Crack the central section of the shell under the tail. Using your thumbs to start off, prise it apart, then lift off the shell. Remove any white meat from the shell using a teaspoon.

4 Pull off the gills (dead man's fingers) from the sides of the central body section and discard them. Also discard the intestines, which will either be on each side of the shell or be clinging to the body.

7 With poultry shears or the blunt side of a heavy knife, tap one side of the shell on each leg to crack it. Lift out the meat, in one piece if possible, using a lobster pick to help. Add to the white meat from the body.

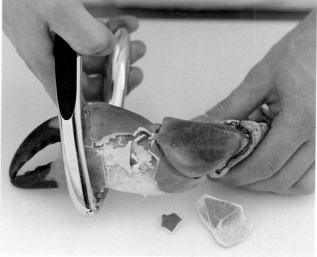

8 Crack the claws with special lobster crackers, a nutcracker, or a small hammer and extract the meat. Check all the white meat for bits of membrane and shell before serving.

COOKING SEAFOOD

Seafood is one of the most delicate foods to cook. There are many ways in which it can be prepared, including baking, grilling, poaching, and curing. Shellfish is often prepared by steaming or deep-frying. Whatever method is chosen, use the suggested cooking times only as a guide because seafood can be easily overcooked and the wonderful flavour and texture destroyed.

CURING

There are many methods of curing seafood, although most are used more for flavour than for storage of the fish. One of the most popular preparations is gravlax, where salmon is cured in a salt and sugar mixture (see right). Other curing techniques include escabeche, ceviche, salting, and smoking.

WAYS TO CURE

■ For escabeche, popular in South America and the Mediterranean, fish is pan-fried and then marinated with herbs, aromatic vegetables, and an acid such as lemon juice or vinegar.

■ Ceviche, a common technique in Mexico, involves marinating seafood in lime or lemon juice with herbs and aromatic vegetables.

■ Salting, primarily used for cod, is done by covering the fish in salt, which draws out the juices. It may then be dried to preserve it. The fish is always soaked before cooking. Salt cod is the main ingredient in the popular French dish, brandade.

■ Smoking is done in two ways. Hot smoking cooks the seafood so it is ready to eat; as it is only partially preserved it cannot be kept for more than a few days. Cold smoking uses already cured seafood and cool smoke so the seafood dries rather than cooks. You can smoke seafood on a barbecue, on the stovetop, or using a special smoker.

GRAVLAX

For this Swedish speciality, raw salmon is cured in a sweet salt mixture. Dill is the most common flavouring, although peppercorns or slices of orange or lemon are also sometimes used. The salmon is sliced paper-thin for serving.

Serves 8–10

4tbsp coarse sea salt
4tbsp granulated sugar
1½tbsp chopped dill
2tbsp black peppercorns, crushed
2tbsp Darjeeling tea leaves
2tbsp vodka (optional)
grated zest of 2 small lemons
1 salmon fillet, with skin, about 900g (2lb)
slices of lemon and orange to garnish (optional)

1 Make the cure by mixing together the salt, sugar, dill, peppercorns, tea leaves, optional vodka, and lemon zest. Spoon half of the cure onto a baking tray covered with muslin and spread out into an even layer.

2 Place the salmon fillet, skin-side down, on the cure. Sprinkle the remaining cure over the salmon to cover it evenly. Press the cure down onto the flesh of the fish.

3 Wrap the fish tightly in the muslin, then weigh it down with something such as a heavy pan or chopping board. Refrigerate for 48 hours, turning the fish over every 12 hours.

4 Unwrap the fish and quickly rinse off the cure under cold running water. Pat the fish dry with kitchen paper.

5 Lay the fillet out flat, flesh-side up, and slice very thinly on the diagonal, cutting away from the skin. Gently lift the slices off the skin and serve, garnished with slices of citrus if you like.

Open-face tomato tart with gravlax & caper vinaigrette

Gravlax is used in this preparation, but smoked salmon or anchovies would work nicely as well.
These tarts can also be made in bite-sized pieces and served as a canapé for a dinner party.

Makes 4

For the tart bases

1tbsp olive oil

1tbsp finely chopped garlic

4tbsp finely chopped shallots

225g (8oz) butter, cubed

280g (10oz) plain flour

225g (8oz) cream cheese

1 egg, beaten, for wash

For the filling

1tbsp plus 2tsp olive oil for the tomato oil

3 garlic cloves, thinly sliced

1 shallot, julienned

3 small tomatoes, cored and cut into eighths

1tbsp tomato purée

2tbsp drained capers

For the caper vinaigrette

2tbsp drained capers, halved

5tbsp extra virgin olive oil

1½tbsp freshly squeezed lemon juice

For the topping

340g (12oz) yellow grape tomatoes or red and yellow cherry tomatoes, cut into thin rings

175g (6oz) gravlax (p132)

2tbsp chopped flat-leaf parsley

To prepare the dough for the tart bases, heat the olive oil in a small pan and sauté the garlic and shallots for about 2 minutes, or until translucent. Cool to room temperature. Place the butter, flour, and cream cheese in an electric mixer with the shallot mixture. Mix on medium speed until blended into a dough. Form into a ball, wrap, and chill for 1 hour.

Preheat the oven to 180°C (350°F, gas 4). Divide the dough into 4 and roll out each piece into an 18cm (7in) circle. Place on a baking tray lined with baking parchment. Pinch or crimp the edges of the dough circles to create a slight rim. Brush with egg wash, then bake for about 15 minutes, or until golden brown. Cool while you make the filling and vinaigrette.

To prepare the filling, heat 1tbsp of the olive oil in a small pan and sauté the garlic and shallot for 1 minute. Add the tomatoes, tomato purée, and capers and cook over moderately low heat until all the liquid from the tomatoes has evaporated. Press 3tbsp of the filling through a sieve. Whisk the remaining 2tsp olive oil into the sieved pulp to make a tomato oil and set aside for the garnish. Season the remaining tomato filling and set aside.

To prepare the vinaigrette, whisk together the ingredients in a small bowl until emulsified.

Turn the oven up to 200°C (400°F, gas 6). Spread the tomato filling over the tart bases and arrange the tomato rings in a pinwheel shape over the filling. Put the tarts into the oven and bake for about 10 minutes, or until the tomatoes have softened. Remove the tarts from the oven and arrange the gravlax slices over the top.

To serve, place a tart in the centre of each plate. Sprinkle with the parsley and spoon the tomato oil around the plate. Drizzle the caper vinaigrette around the plate and finish with some sliced caper berries, if you like, and a grinding of black pepper.

BAKING

Most fish – either whole or in fillets or steaks – can be baked in the oven, as can shellfish such as clams and oysters. Baking is also sometimes used to finish cooking fish that has first been char-grilled (p145). In addition to the plain baking of fish, there are some special techniques. These include baking a stuffed whole fish, baking en papillote (p138), baking in salt, and baking in pastry. Baking fish in a wrapper – be it baking parchment or foil, banana leaves, salt, or puff pastry – seals in all the flavours and can be a dramatic table presentation.

BAKING TIPS

■ Whole fish that can be baked include sea bass, trout, hake, whiting, mackerel, and bream.
■ Fish fillets suitable for baking include skinless plaice, halibut, cod, sole, hake, salmon, orange roughy, mackerel, and sea bass.
■ Fat or oil-rich whole fish are ideal for baking as they remain beautifully moist. Lean whole fish need to be basted during cooking to prevent them from drying out in the heat of the oven.
■ When baking fish steaks and fillets, coat them with oil or butter to keep them moist. If the fish is lean, brush it with more oil or butter during baking. You can also add a topping such as chopped herbs, a breadcrumb mixture, slices of lemon, sliced mushrooms, or a sauce.
■ Bake fish at 180–200°C (350–400°F, gas 4–6). A whole fish will take about 10 minutes to each 2.5cm (1in) of thickness. Fish fillets need about 6 minutes per 1cm (½in) of thickness and fish steaks about 10 minutes per 2.5cm (1in) of thickness.

BAKED PLAICE FILLETS

For this simple method of baking fish fillets, brushing them with melted butter or oil will ensure they remain moist during the cooking process. Many other fish fillets can be cooked in the same way.

4 plaice fillets, about 115g (4oz) each, skinned
2tbsp chopped parsley or another herb
55g (2oz) melted butter or 4tbsp olive oil plus extra for the baking sheet
lemon slices to garnish

1 Preheat the oven to 180°C (350°F, gas 4). Place the fillets side by side on a buttered or oiled baking tray or in a baking dish. Season with salt and freshly ground black pepper and sprinkle with the chopped parsley. Brush the fish with the melted butter or oil.

2 Put into the oven and bake for up to 6 minutes, according to thickness. Test for doneness with the tip of a knife – the flesh should just pull apart but still look moist and opaque in the centre of the fillet.

3 If necessary, return to the oven to bake for another minute or so. When the fish is ready, remove it from the oven and transfer to hot plates. Garnish with lemon slices and serve.

BAKED WHOLE SEA BASS

This is a simple yet delicious way to bake a whole fish. Instead of sea bass you could use a whole salmon or trout.

30g (1oz) butter
1 shallot, finely chopped
150g (5½oz) morel mushrooms, cut into thirds
4tbsp chicken stock or water
1tbsp finely chopped thyme plus sprigs to garnish
1 whole sea bass, about 675g (1½lb), gutted, scaled, and boned through the stomach (p116)
2tbsp extra virgin olive oil
lemon wedges to garnish

1 Preheat the oven to 220°C (425°F, gas 7). Melt the butter in a sauté pan over moderate heat and sweat the shallot until translucent.

2 Add the mushrooms and cook, uncovered, for 1 minute. Add the stock, increase the heat to moderately high, and sauté for about 5 minutes, or until the mushrooms are tender. Stir in the chopped thyme and season with salt and pepper to taste.

3 Rub the fish all over, inside and out, with the olive oil, then sprinkle with salt and pepper. Spoon the mushroom stuffing into the cavity in the fish (see right).

4 Place the fish on an oiled or foil-lined baking tray. Bake for about 15 minutes, or until just cooked through. To test for doneness, gently lift one side of the cavity skin with a paring knife to check that the colour of the flesh has changed from dark and translucent to light and opaque. Transfer the fish to a serving plate.

Garnish with the thyme sprigs and lemon wedges before serving

SERVING WHOLE COOKED FISH

After cooking a whole fish – most commonly by baking, poaching, or braising – the easiest way to serve it is to transfer it from its baking dish or tin to a chopping board and prepare the fish for serving while still in the kitchen. After preparation, transfer the fish to a large heated platter to serve. Alternatively, you can lift the fish from its baking dish or tin directly onto the heated platter, and present it at the table for serving.

Serving whole round fish
Whole round fish, such as the red snapper shown here, are easily served using a fork, large spoon, and knife.

1 Carefully peel away the skin from the top of the fish, cutting it from the head and tail if these are left on. Scrape away any dark flesh and scrape off the bones that lie along the back of the fish.

2 Cut down the centre of the fish with the edge of the spoon, then lift off the top 2 fillets, one at a time. Snap the backbone at the head and tail ends and lift it out. Replace the top fillets to reshape the fish. If you have done the preparation in the kitchen, transfer to a hot platter.

Serving whole flat fish
For large flat fish such as Dover sole, as shown here, you can use a table knife and large spoon for serving at the table.

1 Place the fish on a hot serving platter. With the knife and spoon, push away the fin bones from both sides of the fish. With the edge of the spoon, cut along both sides of the backbone, just cutting through the flesh to the bone. Lift off the top 2 fillets, one at a time.

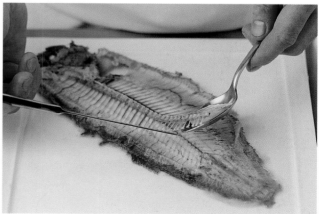

2 Lift out the backbone and set it aside to discard. You can replace the top fillets for an attractive presentation.

BAKED SALMON EN PAPILLOTE

This recipe demonstrates how to cook fish "in a parcel". While the traditional method uses baking parchment, other wraps such as foil and plantain and banana leaves also work well. Here, salmon is cooked en papillote, but many other types of seafood are suitable for this simple method, including halibut, cod, and scallops.

olive oil for brushing
8 baby turnips, cut in half
2 celery sticks, thinly sliced diagonally
115g (4oz) fennel, thinly sliced
8 baby carrots, cut in half
4tbsp snipped chives
4 pieces of salmon fillet, about 85g (3oz) each
sprigs of thyme

1 Preheat the oven to 220°C (425°F, gas 7). Cut out 4 large, heart-shaped pieces of baking parchment. The halves of each heart should be about twice the size of a piece of salmon. Brush one half of each heart with olive oil.

2 Divide the vegetables and chives into 4 portions. Place one portion in the centre of the oiled half of one paper heart. Season a piece of salmon with salt and pepper and set it on top. Add a few sprigs of thyme.

3 Fold over the other half of the heart. Crimp the open edges to seal them by making a series of small folds all around. Fill and seal the remaining parcels in the same way. Place the parcels on a baking tray.

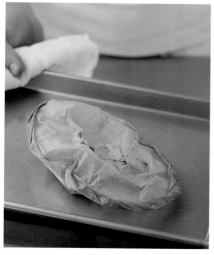

4 Bake for 5–7 minutes, or until the paper parcels are puffed up and lightly browned. To serve, cut open the parcels and transfer them to individual serving plates. Alternatively, put the sealed parcels on the plates and let each person open his or her own parcel.

MICROWAVING

Microwaving is a simple and very quick way to cook seafood, producing tender, moist results. It is also healthy, as it uses little or no fat – just a light brushing of oil, if wanted. Moisture can be added by brushing the seafood with stock or water before microwaving. For extra flavour, try using wine or citrus juice. You could also add some fresh herbs.

Most seafood can be microwaved, including fillets, steaks, fish nuggets, and even shellfish such as prawns and scallops. This method is not recommended for whole fish.

MICROWAVED SALMON STEAKS

All kinds of fish steaks and fillets can be cooked in this way. To give your fish a hint of flavour, brush it with a herb-flavoured oil before cooking. A mustard oil basting would also be delicious. Just remember not to use too much flavouring when preparing fish as its delicate sweet taste can easily be masked.

Serves 2

2 salmon steaks

olive oil for brushing

MICROWAVING TIPS

■ Fish and shellfish need to be in pieces of equal thickness to ensure that they cook evenly.
■ Even cooking is also helped by turning the dish several times. A rotating plate, found in many microwaves, does this automatically.
■ Another way to prevent uneven cooking is to microwave the fish with a little liquid. The steam that is created in the sealed environment helps to cook the fish evenly.
■ After microwaving, most fish should be allowed to stand for 1–2 minutes. Take care when removing the cover from your microwave container as the steam inside will be very hot.
■ The wattage times of microwave ovens vary significantly so it is important to follow your microwave owner's manual for guidelines.

1 Place the salmon steaks in a single layer in an oiled microwave-safe dish. Season with salt and pepper, then brush the steaks with olive oil. Cover the dish loosely with cling film.

2 Put the dish into the microwave to cook on full power. For salmon steaks about 2.5cm (1in) thick, the cooking time will be 2–3 minutes. The cooking time is the same for fillets that are about 3cm (1¼in) thick.

3 Remove the dish from the microwave and let it stand for 1–2 minutes. Then carefully remove the cling film, starting at one corner to let the steam escape. Serve the fish hot.

POACHING

Poaching is a luscious way to cook seafood. It uses a well-seasoned liquid and a very low, controlled heat. The classic method poaches seafood in fish fumet (a concentrated fish stock) and wine, and after cooking the liquid is used to make a sauce to serve with the fish. Court bouillon (see below) is also often used as the poaching liquid for seafood, but after cooking it is discarded. Another, lesser-known technique utilizes olive oil for slow poaching. Salmon is particularly wonderful poached in olive oil – it simply melts in the mouth.

POACHED SKATE WINGS

Skate is one of the best fish to poach in a court bouillon. Here, the wings are filleted and skinned before poaching, but they can also be cooked whole. Then, after poaching, the skin can be peeled away easily and the flesh lifted from the cartilage. Serve the skate hot or cold.

900g (2lb) skate wings, filleted (p120) and skinned (p118)

For the court bouillon

1 litre (1¾ pints) water

120ml (4fl oz) white wine vinegar or lemon juice

55g (2oz) sliced onion

2 bay leaves

12 sprigs of thyme

12 sprigs of parsley

1tbsp black peppercorns

1 To prepare the court bouillon, combine the water, vinegar or lemon juice, onion, bay leaves, thyme and parsley sprigs, and black peppercorns in a saucepan and bring to the boil. Reduce the heat and simmer for 10 minutes. Remove from the heat. Leave the court bouillon to cool until warm before using.

2 Cut the skate into 4 equal pieces. Place the pieces in a fish kettle or another pan in which they will fit comfortably. Ladle enough of the warm, not hot, court bouillon into the pan to cover the fish.

POACHING TIPS

■ Suitable fish for poaching include cod and halibut (whole or in steaks or thick fillets), whole trout, skate wings, whole sea bass, and salmon (whole or in steaks or thick fillets).

■ Poach fish for about 5–7 minutes to each 2.5cm (1in) of thickness, or until the internal temperature reaches 63°C (145°F).

■ Shellfish that are excellent poached include lobsters, crabs, prawns, and crayfish.

SERVING THE SKATE COLD

If you want to serve the skate cold, lift the pieces out of the court bouillon and place them in a shallow dish. Set this in an ice bath – a larger vessel such as a roasting tin filled with iced water – to cool down rapidly. Once cooled, cover the dish and keep the fish in the refrigerator until ready to serve.

3 Bring the court bouillon back to just below a simmer (70–82°C/160–180°F). Do not allow the liquid to get too hot or to boil.

4 Cook the skate just below a simmer for 10–15 minutes. Use a spoon and fork to test for doneness: the flesh should be flaky.

5 To serve the skate hot, lift it out of the court bouillon and arrange on a hot serving platter with some of the herbs and onion.

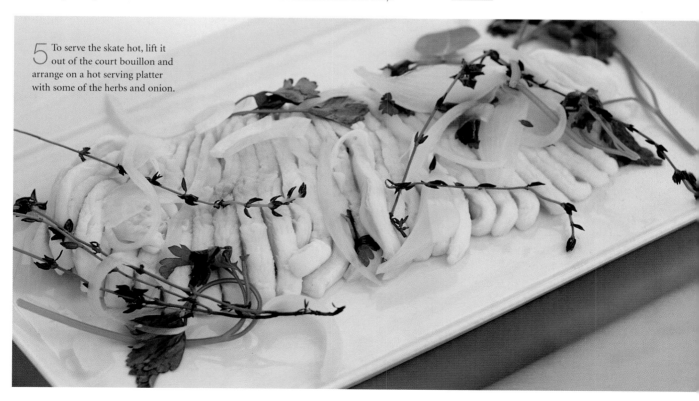

STEAMING

Steaming is a gentle way to prepare fish and shellfish. It is very close to poaching and braising except that the fish does not come into direct contact with any liquid. Therefore, the flavours are pure, and the fish retains its shape.

Any fish that is suitable for braising or poaching is also a great candidate for steaming. Some favourites include bass, all flatfish, john dory, mahimahi, and pompano. Shellfish that are good steamed include clams, mussels, prawns, lobster, and crab.

STEAMED CLAMS

Other molluscs, such as mussels, are also often cooked in this way.

Serves 2

240ml (8fl oz) white wine
1 tbsp chopped parsley
1 small garlic clove, finely chopped
squeeze of lemon juice
12 clams, scrubbed and purged (p121), if necessary

STEAMING TIPS

■ Steam whole fish and fish steaks and fillets on a rack set above the steaming liquid. For most shellfish a rack isn't needed.

■ Depending on the liquid used for steaming, it can be served with the seafood. For example, if prawns are steamed in beer, they can be served in the beer, with plenty of bread to soak it up. The liquid from steaming a fish can be incorporated into a sauce to serve over the fish.

■ Cooking time for fish is about 8 minutes per 2.5cm (1in) of thickness.

1 Combine the wine, parsley, garlic, and lemon juice in a large pan with a tight-fitting lid. Bring to a boil, then reduce the heat until the liquid is simmering.

2 Add the clams to the pan. Cover tightly and turn the heat back to high. Steam for 2–3 minutes, or until all or most of the clams have opened (discard any that remain closed). Transfer the clams to wide serving bowls, ladling the cooking liquid over them. Serve immediately.

BRAISING

Braising is a very gentle way to cook seafood in the oven, and produces wonderfully tender and moist results. Both whole fish and fish portions can be braised. Typically the liquid used for braising is water or fish stock, and you can add a variety of flavouring ingredients, including carrots, celery, and herbs such as thyme and parsley. The braising liquid is usually served with the seafood – simply strained or forming the base of a sauce.

BRAISED MONKFISH

Serves 6

450g (1lb) mixed carrots, celery, and onions
6 sprigs of rosemary
2 large monkfish fillets, about 450g (1lb) each, skinned
1 litre (1¾ pints) fish stock, heated to simmering

BRAISING TIPS

■ Any fish that is appropriate for baking is also fine for braising, but the method is particularly suitable for delicate-flavoured fish, such as cod, snapper, porgy, skate, salmon, monkfish, and sea bass.

■ Strong-flavoured oily fish, such as eel, should not be braised because their flavour would become even more concentrated.

■ Fish braising times in a 220°C (425°F) oven are about 8 minutes for each 2.5cm (1in) of thickness.

1 Preheat the oven to 220°C (425°F, gas 7). Roughly chop the vegetables and place in an oiled roasting tin that is deep enough to hold the fish and braising liquid. Add the herbs. Season the monkfish fillets, then lay them on top of the bed of vegetables and herbs.

2 Ladle enough simmering fish stock into the tin to come halfway up the fish. Cover the tin with a lid or foil and braise in the oven for 12–15 minutes, or until the fish is cooked – the flesh should be white through the centre.

Spoon the flavourful braising liquid over the fish when serving or use to make a sauce to serve alongside

GRILLING

Both grilling and barbecuing are dry-heat methods of cooking at high temperatures. It's therefore important to select the appropriate seafood for these methods and to ensure that you don't overcook it.

Fat, oil-rich fish such as salmon are best for grilling, although lean fish are good too, as long as you give them some kind of coating to keep them moist. Flouring and then dipping in oil is one idea; another is to dip the fish in oil and then coat it with breadcrumbs. Many shellfish are ideal for grilling, including langoustines, halved lobsters in shell, and scallops.

GRILLING TIPS

■ Cooking times will vary according to the thickness of the fish or shellfish. Allow about 4 minutes per side for a fillet that is 2.5cm (1in) thick, or a whole fish of this thickness. Thinner fillets about 1cm (½in) thick will require only 2 minutes of cooking per side.

■ The distance from the grill will also vary according to the thickness of the fish. Fillets and whole fish that are 2.5cm (1in) thick should be grilled 10–15cm (4–6in) from the heat; grill 1cm (½in) fillets at a distance of 5cm (2in).

■ Whole fish, fish steaks, and thick fish fillets will need to be turned over halfway through the cooking time and may need brushing with additional oil or melted butter. Very thin fillets don't need to be turned over because you can cook them through just by grilling on one side for 4–5 minutes.

■ If grilling fish fillets with the skin on, cook for only three-quarters of the suggested time.

GRILLED RED MULLET FILLETS

4 red mullet fillets, about 115g (4oz) each, scaled (p115)

melted butter or olive oil for brushing

1 Preheat the grill to high. Score the skin of the fish fillets with a sharp knife. Arrange the fillets, skin-side up, on the rack of the grill pan and brush them with melted butter or olive oil. Season with salt and pepper.

2 Place the pan 5cm (2in) from the heat and grill for 4–5 minutes, or until the fish fillets are cooked through. They do not need to be turned over during cooking. Test for doneness with the tip of a knife.

BARBECUING & CHAR-GRILLING

Barbecuing is a great way to cook fish and shellfish. The smoke imparts wonderful flavour – adding wood chips such as hickory or mesquite to the coals enhances this – as will marinating beforehand or basting with a marinade during cooking.

Seafood suitable for barbecuing include salmon and trout, cod and haddock, sea bass, mahimahi, tuna and swordfish, lobsters, tiger and king prawns, and baby octopus.

Using a hot ridged, cast-iron grill pan will produce similar results to cooking over hot coals, although it doesn't impart a smoky flavour. When food is cooked on a grill pan it is described as char-grilled or griddled.

CHAR-GRILLED SCALLOPS

Scallops are delicious cooked on a grill pan, as shown here, or barbecued over hot coals. The preparation (marinating and threading onto skewers) is the same for both methods.

175ml (6fl oz) extra virgin olive oil
1tbsp chopped parsley or coriander
12 large scallops

1 Mix together the oil, parsley or coriander, and salt and pepper to taste in a bowl. Put the scallops in a shallow dish. Spoon the oil mixture over them and turn to coat all sides. Marinate in the refrigerator for 2 hours.

2 Thread the scallops onto skewers. (If using wooden skewers, soak them in hot water for 30 minutes before using.) Heat a ridged, cast-iron grill pan until thoroughly hot.

BARBECUING TIPS

■ Be sure the barbecue rack is clean and hot before putting on the seafood to cook. This will prevent it from sticking.

■ Leave the skin on whole fish as this helps to hold it together (and also helps prevent it from sticking to the rack). If you are going to remove the skin before serving, there is no need to scale the fish.

■ Small whole fish are easy to barbecue, although they may fall apart. Putting them in a special wire basket will prevent this.

■ Fish steaks and fillets need to be at least 1cm (½in) thick so that they won't overcook.

■ For small pieces of seafood, such as cubes of fish, scallops, and prawns, thread them onto skewers. This will make it easier to turn them during cooking.

■ An interesting idea is to wrap fish in vine leaves before putting it on the barbecue.

■ To make attractive crisscross grill marks, re-position the seafood halfway through the cooking time on each side – lift it up and turn it 45°, then replace it on the barbecue (or grill pan).

3 Place the scallops on the hot pan and char-grill, turning them over once, for 2–3 minutes, or until they are done. When ready the scallops will have become opaque, but will still feel tender to the touch. Remove from the pan and serve immediately, on or off the skewers.

SHALLOW-FRYING

Shallow-frying is an excellent way to cook fish and shellfish. The seafood remains moist and succulent within a crisp, browned exterior. In general, lean fish are the best suited to shallow-frying, either whole or in steaks or fillets. Fat, oil-rich fish can be shallow-fried, but the quantity of oil or other fat used for cooking may need to be reduced.

Grapeseed and canola oils are the best ones to use when shallow-frying

or when sautéing (see below). Olive oil is good too, but you'll need to watch carefully as it has a lower smoke point than grapeseed and canola oils. If you want to use butter, mix it with oil or choose unsalted or clarified butter (p24) to avoid any burning of the fat at high heat.

To achieve a wonderful crisp crust, coat the seafood with flour, cornmeal or polenta, or breadcrumbs before putting it into the pan.

SHALLOW-FRIED RED MULLET

4 red mullet, gutted, scaled, trimmed, and head removed (p114)

cornmeal or polenta for coating

grapeseed oil for frying

lemon juice to finish

SAUTÉING SEAFOOD

Sautéing is very similar to shallow-frying. The main differences are the quantity of oil or other fat used (more for frying than sautéing), the heat (higher for sautéing), and the moving of the seafood in the pan (for sautéing the seafood is tossed and turned almost constantly, while for shallow-frying it is usually turned just once). Sautéing is not a good method to use for fragile fish, as the tossing in the pan will break the fish into pieces. However, it works very well for fish such as skate and for firm shellfish.

Finish with a squeeze of lemon juice before serving

1 Season the fish with salt and pepper, then coat it on both sides with cornmeal. Shake off the excess. Set a non-stick or cast-iron frying pan over moderately high heat and add a small amount of grapeseed oil (use just enough oil to coat the bottom of the pan).

2 Put the prepared fish into the hot oil, presentation side (the side that will be uppermost when serving) down. Shallow-fry for 2 minutes, or until the fish is golden brown on the presentation side.

3 Turn the fish using tongs and cook until the other side is golden brown. To test for doneness, insert a thin-bladed knife into the centre of the fish, then touch the tip of the knife to your thumb. If the knife is warm, the fish is ready. Drain briefly on kitchen paper.

DEEP-FRYING

Deep-frying is one of the most popular ways to cook seafood. Small, whole, lean fish; pieces of fish; and shellfish, such as prawns and shelled clams, oysters, and scallops, are all well suited to deep-frying. The seafood is usually coated with flour, crumbs, or batter before frying, which protects it from the heat of the oil as well as providing a crisp, tasty crust.

There are a number of fats and oils you can use when deep-frying. The most common are rendered animal fat (such as bacon and duck), and corn, groundnut, canola, and safflower oils. Take care not to put too much fat or oil in the pan – it should not be more than half full.

Frying times will vary according to the size of the fish and on the temperature of the oil (see right). As a general rule, however, fry fish for 7–9 minutes to each 2.5cm (1in) of thickness. Fry shellfish until they turn golden brown and float to the surface of the oil.

FRYING TEMPERATURES

When frying small, whole fish the oil should be at about 180°C (350°F). Shellfish and small pieces of fish should be fried at a slightly higher temperature, around 190°C (375°F).

DEEP-FRIED TIGER PRAWNS

oil for deep-frying

900g (2lb) raw tiger prawns, peeled and deveined

plain flour for coating

2 eggs, beaten with 2tbsp water

fresh breadcrumbs for coating

For serving

lemon wedges

tartare sauce

1 Heat oil for deep-frying in a wide pan to 190°C (375°F). Make sure the prawns are completely dry, then season them with salt and pepper. One at a time, dip them in flour to coat evenly. Shake off excess flour.

2 Next, dip the prawns in the egg wash (eggs beaten with water). Lift out of the egg wash and let excess drip off, back into the bowl.

3 Finally, dip the prawns into breadcrumbs to cover completely. Press to ensure the crumbs adhere, then shake off excess. As the prawns are prepared, lay them on a tray.

4 Add the prawns, in small batches, to the hot oil. Do not crowd the pan. Deep-fry, turning the prawns so they cook and colour evenly, for about 2 minutes, or until golden brown.

5 When the prawns are golden brown and crisp, remove with a slotted spoon to drain on kitchen paper, then serve immediately with lemon wedges and tartare sauce.

POULTRY & GAME BIRDS

SHAUN HILL

Intensive farming has transformed poultry from being an occasional treat, perhaps bought for a special event, to cheap and everyday meat. Today's poultry may seem to have little in common with the well-flavoured and well-nurtured products of before. But do not be disheartened – a good butcher will guide you to the best quality. Ignore terms such as "farm fresh", which means battery-farmed, or even "free range", which may mean only minimal access to daylight and guarantees nothing regarding the type and age of birds, or the quality of feed used. The term "organic" is usually a good sign, but having a trusted supplier to advise you is better still.

Buying poultry and game birds Most poultry is available year-round. Choose a large bird for a more developed flavour and a better ratio of meat to bone. The meat should look plump rather than bony and the skin should have no dry patches. With game birds there is quite a difference between young and old. Young birds are tender and suit roasting, whereas older specimens are tougher and need to be braised. A good game bird will be plump and heavy relative to its size.

Game birds are always seasonal. The first grouse appears in August, but the majority of game birds follow in late September and October. Of course it is possible to farm some birds all year round, but whether these still count as game is questionable. Wild birds are more strongly flavoured than their farmed counterparts and may have a tougher texture. Farmed birds are also much more expensive than wild ones, so experiment to find out which type you prefer.

Handling and storage Raw poultry carries high levels of bacteria and there are important guidelines in its safe preparation and storage. First, always scrub the board and knives you use to prepare poultry in hot, soapy water before using them again to carve the same bird once cooked. Commercial kitchens use different, colour-coded chopping boards to avoid any risk of cross-contamination. Second, store raw poultry at the bottom of the fridge as a precaution against juices from the raw meat dripping onto other food, especially foods that will not be cooked further. Cooked and cooled poultry should be stored in the upper part of the fridge to prevent contamination from raw meats. Poultry is best bought fresh and used immediately. Birds stored in the refrigerator dry out quickly because the meat has little or no fat covering. Game birds are generally smaller than poultry and are even more prone to drying out. However, covering or wrapping the meat in cling film is a good preventative measure. Birds kept for any length of time should be turned and rewrapped regularly. A light brushing with oil also inhibits drying, but the oil can flavour the finished result. Bland oils such as sunflower are better than olive oil unless you want the flavour of olive oil in the finished dish.

To enjoy frozen poultry at its best, buy fresh poultry, wrap it carefully, and freeze it yourself. Ready-frozen poultry rarely has any opportunity to develop flavour, and there is little point in buying frozen game either. Part of the pleasure in eating game is the fleeting nature of the hunting season, but game birds shot early in the season and frozen, then defrosted and cooked within a reasonably short time, say a month or two, still make first-rate meals.

Cooking poultry and game birds An important general rule for all cooking methods is to use the right size of container for cooking the bird. If it is a chicken to be poached, find a pan that allows the bird to be covered using the minimum of liquid, so that you end up with a smallish quantity of well-flavoured stock. If roasting, use a tray large enough to collect the cooking juices ready for use in a sauce or gravy, but not so large that fat and cooking juices spit over the oven wall.

When cooking, use the method that suits the bird best. Small, young birds are fine roasted, but older, larger ones may well be better braised or poached. Birds should be brought to room temperature before cooking, rather than taken straight from refrigerator to oven. Use cookery books only as a general guide for cooking times, and always test the meat for doneness before serving.

PREPARING A WHOLE BIRD

A fresh bird should have skin unblemished by dry patches, be plump relative to its size and weight, and should show no sign of bruising. Patches of dry skin indicate that the bird has been stored badly or frozen and it will need lots of extra butter or oil during cooking in compensation. Bruising is generally a problem with shot game birds such as mallard. Look out for red patches as these will turn dark and unsightly during cooking.

A traditional preparation of any whole bird involves sewing a piece of string through it so that it remains in a tight shape throughout cooking. However, this technique, known as trussing, has certain disadvantages. Heat will take longer to penetrate to the centre of a trussed bird and removing the string is a messy business.

Removing the wishbone is important if you want to make carving of the cooked bird or dissection into joints a great deal easier.

PARTS OF A BIRD

All poultry divides into two main parts, breast and legs. The winglets can be left attached to the breast or served separately as wished. Whether the breasts are halved or the legs further subdivided into thigh and drumstick will vary, but this will be a matter of portioning, cooking time, or convenience rather than any major separation of differing types of meat.

Leg meat, being darker and denser in texture than the paler, more delicate breast meat, will take longer to cook. Swift cooking processes like frying or roasting show the advantages of breast meat, while slow cooking processes like braising and poaching favour the leg meat. In reality a touch of compromise will produce uniformly acceptable results from the entire bird.

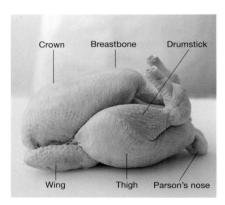

Whole chicken on its back

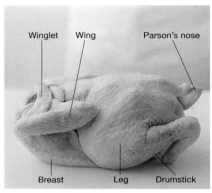

Whole chicken on its breast

REMOVING THE WISHBONE

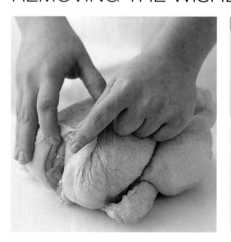

1 Lay the bird on its back and lift the flap of skin from around the bird's neck. Run your finger around the neck cavity and you will feel the wishbone just in from the edge.

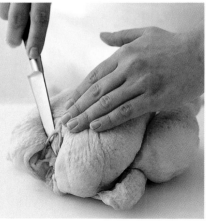

2 Using a small, sharp knife, scrape the flesh away from the wishbone so that it is exposed and clearly visible.

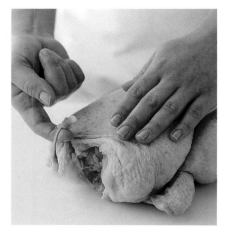

3 Run the blade of the knife just behind the bone, then use your fingers to lift and twist the wishbone free. Pull the skin back into place.

ROASTING

White poultry meat needs plenty of oil or butter while roasting or it will be dry. Only the duck family has enough natural fat to be roasted without help. In all poultry, the breasts tend to cook before the legs, so care is needed for both to be in perfect condition at the same time. This may mean turning the bird on its side or basting frequently.

Oven temperatures are important. A high initial temperature is needed to brown and caramelize the skin, but too much high heat will dry out the delicate breast meat. Possible solutions include covering the bird with buttered paper or foil halfway though cooking, turning the bird on its breast so that the back and legs take most of the heat, or reducing the oven temperature. However, few people roast a bird in isolation – potatoes, stuffings, and suchlike, all make demands on oven space and temperature levels. Try to take advantage of differing heat levels in the oven and move the roasting bird to a lower shelf.

White meats such as poultry are best cooked right through, but will not withstand prolonged cooking. When testing for doneness, insert a skewer into either the thigh or the thick end of the breast nearest the bone. If the juices run clear the bird is cooked. Any traces of blood and it is not.

Resting the cooked meat has two functions: it allows the heat from the outer part to gently finish cooking the centre; it also gives you a chance to decant any fat in the roasting tray, and allows juices to blend in with caramelized scraps from the roasting process and start producing the base for a sauce or gravy. The time needed to rest a bird will vary; a turkey will retain heat for 20 minutes, but a partridge may be ready in five. If you feel it has cooled too much, return the bird to the oven for a few moments before serving.

Lastly, there is the gravy. The pan residues contain concentrated flavour to make gravy taste of what has just been cooked and not some all-purpose commercial preparation. You can also tinker with the style of the finished dish by adding herbs such as tarragon or oregano or maybe some chopped garlic or lemon zest.

Roasting whole birds

Ovens vary so be guided in cooking times by testing the meat for doneness. For fan ovens, follow manufacturers' instructions.

TYPE OF BIRD	TIME (OVEN WEIGHT)	TEMPERATURE	POSITION OF BIRD
Chicken	45 minutes per 1kg (2 1/4lb) or 20 minutes per 450g (1lb)	First 15 minutes @ 220°C (425°F, gas 7); remainder of time @ 190°C (375°F, gas 5)	On back
Goose 2.25kg (5lb)	30 minutes per 1kg (2 1/4lb) or 15 minutes per 450g (1lb)	200°C (400°F, gas 6)	1 hour on back, 1 hour on front, 30 minutes on back
Turkey 2.25kg (5lb)	45 minutes per 1kg (2 1/4lb) or 20 minutes per 450g (1lb) plus 20 minutes	200°C (400°F, gas 6)	On back
Duck	50 minutes per 1kg (2 1/4lb) or 25 minutes per 450g (1lb)	180°C (350°F, gas 4)	On back
Wild duck	First 15 minutes @ temperature at right 1 hour @ temperature at right	220°C (425°F, gas 7) 190°C (375°F, gas 5)	On back
Quail	20–25 minutes	200°C (400°F, gas 6)	On back
Squab pigeon	15–20 minutes on each side	200°C (400°F, gas 6)	On sides
Woodcock	20 minutes	200°C (400°F, gas 6)	On back
Mallard crown	20 minutes	200°C (400°F, gas 6)	On back
Guinea fowl	40 minutes per 1kg (2 1/4lb) or 20 minutes per 450g (1lb)	200°C (400°F, gas 6)	On sides
Red legged partridge	25 minutes	200°C (400°F, gas 6)	On sides
Grey partridge	30 minutes	200°C (400°F, gas 6)	On sides

ROASTING CHICKEN

Taking the same level of care and concentration with a simple process such as roasting a chicken as with some complex culinary tour de force will produce surprisingly fine results. Indeed, if the basic roasting of the bird is sloppily executed, any fancy footwork with sauces and garnish will be a waste of effort, for the dish will never excel.

As with all cookery, the enemy is dryness and this can be avoided by paying attention to detail – the heat of the oven and the chicken's position in it, the amount of butter or oil, and, of course, the length of time allocated to cooking.

Larger chickens are generally better flavoured than small, so err on the side of generous and use any leftovers for sandwich fillings.

1 chicken, about 1.8kg (4lb), wishbone removed (p152)
2 tbsp olive oil
15g (½oz) butter
100ml (3½fl oz) water

1 Preheat the oven to 220°C (425°F, gas 7). Paint oil on the chicken, then rub on the butter and season. Place in a roasting pan that fits, pour in the water and put in the centre of the oven. After 15 minutes, reduce the heat to 190°C (375°F, gas 5) and roast for another 25 minutes.

2 At this point, baste the chicken with the juices in the pan and turn it over onto its breast, so that the heat – which is greater the higher you are in the oven – focuses on the thighs. Baste the chicken again, then continue roasting for another 25 minutes.

CHEF'S TIPS

■ Cooking times given here assume that the oven has been preheated and that a fresh, rather than defrosted, chicken is being cooked.
■ A whole lemon left in the central cavity of the bird will help keep the chicken moist and impart a subtle lemon scent.

4 Take the cooked chicken from the oven and tip any juices from its interior back into the pan. Put the chicken on a plate, cover loosely with foil, and let it rest for 10 minutes before carving. Meanwhile, make the gravy (p157).

3 Turn the chicken onto its back and test for doneness by inserting a skewer into the part least likely to be cooked through: the thigh or the thick end of the breast. If the juices run clear the bird is cooked. If there are traces of blood continue cooking and test again after 10 minutes.

STUFFING

A stuffing to accompany a roast bird can be cooked in two ways: either push it under the skin of the bird onto the breast, as with the watercress and apricot stuffing below, or wrap the stuffing in foil and place in the oven for the last 25 minutes of cooking, as with the sausage meat stuffing. The central cavity is not such a good spot as little heat penetrates the bird until it is quite well cooked.

Cooking stuffing separately

This stuffing is cooked in the oven for the last 25 minutes of roasting the bird, when the oven temperature has been reduced to 190°C (375°F, gas 5). Once the stuffing ingredients have been combined, roll the stuffing into a fat cigar shape, wrap it in buttered foil and secure the ends. When it is cooked, unwrap it, slice, and serve with the roast bird.

Sausage meat stuffing

25g (scant 1oz) butter

1 shallot, finely chopped

1 garlic clove, crushed

grated zest of ½ lemon

250g (8½oz) sausage meat

100g (3½oz) white breadcrumbs

50g (1¾oz) parsley, chopped

1 Heat the butter in a small pan and sweat the shallot, garlic, lemon zest, and some freshly ground black pepper; do not let it colour. Stir in all the remaining ingredients and add salt to taste.

2 Turn the stuffing onto a clean board and knead once or twice to incorporate all the components. Use as above.

Stuffing under the skin

If the stuffing is to be added to the bird, this is better done by placing it under the skin at the neck end rather than putting it in the central cavity. Stuffing placed inside this cavity does not start cooking until heat reaches it late in the roasting process, and imparts little to the bird's texture or taste, whereas stuffing placed under the skin will not only cook properly, but will help to protect the delicate breast meat during cooking and any butter or fat involved will help keep the meat moist as it melts or renders down.

2 Push the stuffing in under the skin onto the breast, then pull back the skin to cover it and tuck under the bird.

Watercress & apricot stuffing

This stuffing suits drier white poultry such as chicken or guinea fowl, as the apricots will lend moistness to the texture while the watercress gives a peppery contrast.

50g (1¾oz) dried apricots

3 slices white bread, processed into crumbs

50g (1¾oz) hazelnuts, skinned (p632)

1 small bunch of watercress, roughly chopped

Put the apricots into a small pan of water and bring to the boil. Drain and add to the breadcrumbs. Put the hazelnuts into a food processor and process for a few seconds, then add the chopped watercress and breadcrumbs. Process for a few seconds, then scrape the stuffing into a bowl. Use as above.

1 Lift the flap of skin from around the wishbone area, at the neck end, and draw this back until it exposes as much of the breast as necessary.

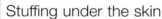

CARVING CHICKEN & OTHER SMALL BIRDS

All poultry with white flesh – that is chicken or turkey – is carved in the same way. Ducks, with their denser texture and elongated breasts, are slightly different and will be tackled later (p159). The point of carving is simple – to render the meat easy to eat. Next and secondary to this, you want it to look as presentable as possible. Thirdly, you want the least waste, with very little left on the bone or carcass.

The traditional shape of a carving knife is long and slim, tapering to a point at the top of the blade. This is fine, but not crucial. Sharpness is the essential quality and while a serrated knife or chopper will not do, a finely honed cook's knife will stand in very well. This is because there are two aspects to carving poultry, one of which is better tackled by the traditional carving knife. This is the slicing of the breast into thin

strips, especially on large birds such as turkey. The other aspect of poultry carving is the division of the bird into joints – thigh and drumstick, for example – and this is better done with the power given by the shape of a cook's knife than with the finesse of the carving knife. You can use both or either.

The choice of fork, too, is important (see opposite) and how you use it is a matter of choice.

1 Once the cooked bird has rested and any juices from it have been collected and added to the sauce or gravy, place the bird on its back on a clean chopping board. Hold the bird with a carving fork, then use a carving knife to cut the skin between the leg and the breast. Next, draw the knife down and cut close to the breast.

2 Lift the leg backwards to release the bone from the body and enable the cooked meat in crevices on the backbone to be taken off in one slice. Repeat the process for the other leg.

3 Hold the bird steady with the carving fork. Keeping the carving knife as close to the breastbone as possible, slice downwards and lengthways along one side of the bone to release the breast. Repeat on the other side.

PRESENTATION

■ The thicker the slices the longer they will retain their heat. Thin slices draped into a fan will need to be served straight away if that is your aesthetic preference.

■ It is a question of personal preference, but I would leave a little meat on the wing when carving chicken to make a more substantial portion.

4 You now have 2 legs and 2 breasts. In order to serve equal portions of both white and brown meat you divide these in half. Carve the breasts at a slight diagonal into equal and elegant pieces and put to one side.

5 Slice each leg through the joint to separate the thigh and drumstick. Place all the carved meat with the stuffing on a dish and serve with the gravy (see opposite).

MAKING GRAVY

Make the gravy in the roasting tray in which the chicken has just been cooked so that residues in the tray will dissolve into the gravy. If you wish, add some herbs or some chopped garlic or lemon zest. Use tomato passata, sparingly, rather than tomato purée in gravy – purée tends to overpower other ingredients.

1 Using a large spoon, skim off most of the fat from the pan juices. Put the pan on the hob over a gentle heat. Mix 1tbsp plain flour with 1tbsp of the chicken fat and whisk it into the remaining pan juices.

2 Add 300ml (10fl oz) water or stock and 1tbsp tomato passata, increase the heat and bring to the boil, whisking continuously.

3 Strain the gravy into a clean bowl and pour into a warmed serving jug.

CARVING FORKS: ANOTHER METHOD

The choice of carving fork is as important as the sharpness of the knife. Forks come in two styles. One is shaped like a tuning fork with two long, straight prongs and a short stem. This type of fork is good for prodding and jabbing things, but not for carving. You need the shape that has a long stem leading to short, curved prongs. When held in reverse – the curved edge downwards – these prongs will secure the meat completely without damaging it. Once the meat is held like this, you will have complete control over the carving and slicing.

ROASTING GOOSE

There is little point in buying a tiny goose to feed four. A 5kg (11lb) goose will feed six, or four with leftovers. The giblets and extra fat will be counted as part of the overall weight, so in fact your 5kg (11lb) goose will weigh more like 4kg (9lb) when you are putting it in the oven.

Prick the skin of goose (and duck), especially at the tail end where most fat lies, to ease its departure during cooking. Use a trivet or rack to lift the bird above the fat so that it roasts rather than fries, and add 1tbsp water in the roasting pan to keep the rendered fat in peak condition. The fat can then be set aside for reuse later.

Just as with duck, a fruity sauce or stuffing will work well with the rich meat – roast quinces perhaps or red cabbage braised with red wine and orange juice. The giblets (excluding the liver) should be cooked in advance to provide gravy. The wise cook will use the first harvest of goose fat from the bird during cooking to roast accompanying parsnips or potatoes.

Leftover cooked goose can be shredded and mixed in with a little of its fat and plenty of seasoning to make potted goose or rillettes.

1 Preheat the oven to 200°C (400°F, gas 6). Using a pointed skewer, prick the goose all over, but especially the fat gland underneath the wing, the parson's nose area, and along the sides of the breasts.

2 Cover the legs with foil and place the bird on its back on a rack in a large, deep roasting tray. Season the skin with salt and pepper. Add 1tbsp water to the tray and place the tray in the oven.

GIBLET STOCK FOR GRAVY

■ Bring the giblets to the boil with 1 diced carrot and 1 diced onion in 2 litres (3½ pints) water. Cover with a lid, then reduce the heat so that the stock simmers. Once the goose is out of the oven, drain the fat into a bowl then deglaze the roasting tin by straining then adding the giblet stock. Scrape in any caramelized residues and bring to the boil.

CARVING GOOSE & AYLESBURY DUCK

Goose and domesticated Aylesbury duck are carved more like chicken than Barbary duck and the wild duck family. The meat will be cooked through and should be tender, so splitting the bird into sections rather than cutting into strips is what is needed.

3 After 1 hour turn the goose onto its breast – do not tip the interior juices into the fat. Decant fat. Roast goose for 1 hour, then turn it over onto its back. Decant the fat, remove foil from the legs and cook for 30 minutes more.

4 Remove the goose from the oven and put onto a dish to rest for 15 minutes. Meanwhile, pour off the remaining fat and make the gravy (see opposite) using the giblet stock.

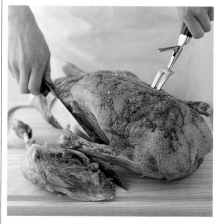

1 With the bird on its back, cut the skin between each leg and breast, lift the leg away from the body so that the thigh bone pops out and cut it away at the base. The leg can now be divided through the joint into drumstick and thigh.

2 Keeping the carving knife as close as possible to the body, slice downwards and lengthways along one side of the breastbone. Each breast will come off as a whole piece that may be subdivided into as many pieces as needed.

3 The larger the piece, the longer it will retain heat. If desired, carve each breast on the diagonal into slices.

ROASTING TURKEY

A 5kg (11lb) turkey will not only feed six
hungry diners, it will also delight/plague them
with leftovers. The timings are similar to goose:
1 hour on its back in an oven preheated to
200°C (400°F, gas 6), then 1 hour breast-side
down, and a final 30 minutes on its back again.
Just as with the goose, turkey legs should have a
protective foil wrapping for the first 2 hours of
cooking. If your oven is small in relation to the
size of the bird, you may be well advised to cover
the breasts with foil also.

There will not be any quantity of fat
rendering down and you will have to spread
oil and butter across the bird to keep it moist
and tender throughout cooking.

After it has cooked, rest the turkey for
15–20 minutes so that the meat settles, making
it easier to carve, and any cooking juices can
seep back into the roasting tray. Make gravy in
exactly the same way as for chicken (p157).

SERVING IDEAS

Cold roast turkey is as versatile as chicken and
lends itself to excellent salad treatments.
Try the following:
■ Sliced turkey brushed with olive oil, served on
a bed of cooked brown lentils and bacon in
mustard vinaigrette.
■ Cubed turkey and chestnut tossed in spiced
mayonnaise on crisp salad leaves.

CARVING TURKEY LEGS & BREAST

Separate the legs by cutting the skin between them and the main body. Press back each leg until it
disconnects, then cut away the upper edge from the main body. To remove each breast, keep the
carving knife very close to the carcass and slice downwards and lengthways along one side of the
breastbone to release the breast. The breast will come off in one piece.

Large leg

To carve the drumstick, hold it upright by the
bone and slice the meat downwards into strips.

Drumstick

For really large specimens, the bone can be cut
out of the thigh. Slice down along the thigh to
expose the bone, then cut underneath it and
remove. Slice the brown meat into strips.

Breast

Lay the breast, flat-side down, on the chopping board and slice with a sharp knife in the
way you would slice a loaf of bread.

Roast quail with salad leaves & walnut dressing

The contrasts of warm and cold and the use of a sweet and sour dressing add to the interest and complexity of this dish. This was a favourite item on the menu at Gidleigh Park for many years, either as a starter or light lunch. It also yielded quail carcasses for the owners' Siamese cats – which was almost as important.

4 quails, wishbones removed (p152)

1tbsp sunflower oil

2 streaky bacon rashers, cut into strips

1tbsp pine nuts

2tbsp walnut oil

1tsp sherry vinegar

a selection of salad leaves, such as frisée, radicchio, little gem, and corn salad

1tbsp snipped chives

50ml (1¾fl oz) chicken or veal stock or water

Preheat the oven to 200°C (400°F, gas 6). Smear the quails all over with the oil and season with salt and pepper. Brown the birds quickly on each side in a frying pan, then put them on their backs into a roasting tray. Roast in the oven for about 25 minutes, until cooked.

Meanwhile, grill the bacon until crisp and toast the pine nuts until browned.

Whisk together the walnut oil and vinegar and brush the salad leaves with half the dressing. Arrange the leaves on plates and scatter the hot bacon, pine nuts, and the chives around.

Lift the quails from the roasting tray and dismantle into legs and breasts. Discard the backs. Put the tray on the hob and pour in the stock or water and the remaining dressing. Stir to deglaze the pan, then bring just to the boil. Strain this around the quail and salad and serve immediately.

Dividing the quail into legs and breasts

SQUAB PIGEON WITH SPICES

Pigeons are called squabs in the United States. The name has recently been commandeered in Britain to cover pigeons reared and corn-fed for the table, to distinguish them from wood pigeons, which are wild with dark and gamey flesh. The farmed birds are pale-fleshed and tender, and also command higher prices.

There is in fact a long and honourable tradition of rearing pigeons for the table. They are very popular in North Africa and feature in the famous Moroccan sweet pastry dish bisteeya. In 11th century England, well-to-do Normans liked to keep a dovecote to provide meat for the household.

These small birds take longer to cook than you would think since the meat is firm-fleshed, so allow 35–40 minutes. The pan juices will make a fine sauce.

1 small red pepper, seeded, cored, and chopped
1 garlic clove
1tbsp chopped mint
8 sultanas, heated in 4tbsp sweet wine until plump
1tsp ground cinnamon
1tsp ground cumin
1tsp saffron threads
2tbsp olive oil
4 squab pigeons, wishbones removed (p152)
100ml (3½fl oz) white wine

CHEF'S VARIATIONS

■ An alternative way of dealing with pigeon is to roast the birds on their backs, then carve the legs off when the breasts are cooked, and return them to the oven to continue to cook through while the rest of the pigeon is resting.

■ The pan juices make a good addition to a rice pilaff (p312), made with plenty of interesting extras like cubes of aubergine and courgettes.

1 Put the pepper, garlic, mint, sultanas, and spices in a mortar and use the pestle to grind them together until almost pulp. Stir in the olive oil, then rub the mixture all over the pigeons. Wrap the birds in cling film and leave to marinate for 2 hours in a refrigerator.

2 Preheat the oven to 200°C (400°F, gas 6). The legs are tender enough to be cooked with the rest of the bird, but take longer to cook, so put the birds on their sides in the tray so that the legs take most of the direct heat. Roast for 15–20 minutes, then turn the birds over and cook for another 20 minutes until just done.

3 Stir the wine into the pan juices and heat through. Strain into a bowl, skim off the fat, and serve with the pigeons.

ROAST WOODCOCK

Woodcock and their smaller relatives, snipe, are among the last game birds to come on the market. They are distinctive in several ways. The flesh is dark and deeply flavoured and there is the bonus of the brains, which are delicate and delicious, if a rather unsightly spectacle to eat.

Neither bird has a spleen, so traditionally they were cooked without being gutted and the giblets, once cooked, were spread on toast. You are welcome to do this, but I find it a touch too visceral for good appetite. The head is skinned and left on during cooking, since the brains are a delicacy and are eaten in much the same way as a lollipop. No sauce other than pan juices made into gravy will be needed. The function of the toast is to sop up these juices. Some brown lentils braised with chopped bacon and red wine or a sprinkling of dried fruit in the gravy would act as counterpoint to the richness of the meat, but any hint of cream or creamy vegetable accompaniment will be unwelcome. Small roast potatoes could accompany.

| 4 woodcock, wishbones removed (p152) |
| 225g (8oz) unsalted butter |
| 4 slices French bread |

1 Preheat the oven to 200°C (400°F, gas 6). Make an incision at the base of the neck and peel back the skin over the top of the head. Wrap the head in foil to avoid overcooking. Spread the butter generously over the woodcock and place on their backs in a roasting tray. Roast for 20 minutes, basting with melted butter.

2 Take the birds out of the oven. If you haven't gutted the woodcock, use a spoon to do so now. Meanwhile, toast the bread.

3 Cut off the head and neck and split in half through the beak. Carve the birds into legs and breasts and arrange on the toast. Put the head on the side. Serve with the pan juices.

POACHING

Poaching is the slowest and most delicate cooking method. This makes it perfect for two quite differing kinds of meat: delicate kinds, like fish or chicken breast, or meat that is particularly dense or tough, like silverside of beef. Meat should never be boiled, but always poached. It must come to the boil and then simmer, otherwise the texture will be like boiled rags rather than the clean creaminess that the method can achieve.

The main reason to poach poultry rather than roast it is to obtain the cooking liquor. Most recipes that use the method depend heavily on this stock for the finished dish. And with those that

aren't as dependent on it, there will be the bonus of well-flavoured stock for whenever soup or some other sauce is to be made. Poached duck is superb, but you may have difficulty finding a pot large enough for the job. The steaming and poaching of game birds is usually confined to dishes like mousses and terrines.

Two items are essential to success with poaching – patience and a lidded pan. Patience, because any attempt to rush will provoke the hard boiling that dries out meat; a lidded pan because the steam rising will still cook anything protruding from the water as evaporation reduces the stock levels.

CHICKEN POT AU FEU WITH PARSLEY HOLLANDAISE

The quality of chicken needed for a poached dish is the same as that needed for a roast. Boiling fowl (older birds generally bred for egg production) are good only for flavouring stock.

The finished dish has three aspects – the broth, the cooked vegetables and meat, and the sauce that accompanies it. You eat the broth like any other soup, with a spoon, then ladle sauce onto the remainder. Two courses in one, in fact. So serve the dish in a deep plate and have soup spoons as well as knives and forks at the ready.

1 chicken, about 5kg (11lb), wishbone removed (p152)
12 small new potatoes, unpeeled
8 baby artichokes, outer leaves removed, cut into quarters, and brushed with lemon juice
8 baby carrots, trimmed
100g (3½oz) shelled broad beans, unskinned

For the hollandaise

3 egg yolks
4tsp white wine
100g (3½oz) unsalted butter, clarified (p24)
juice of ½ lemon
few drops of tabasco sauce
50g (1¾oz) parsley, finely chopped

1 Bring the water to the boil, then add a pinch of salt, the small potatoes, and the chicken. Bring the water back to a gentle simmer, cover the pan and poach for 30 minutes.

2 Add the artichokes and carrots and cook for 5 minutes, then add the broad beans and any other green vegetable you want to include – maybe cabbage strips or runner beans – and cook for a further 5 minutes.

3 To test the chicken for doneness, pierce the thigh to the bone – if the juices run clear it is done, if they are red it is not. Tip the bird slightly as you lift it out of the pan so that the hot stock in its cavity runs back into the pan.

4 To make the sauce, put the egg yolks and wine in a stainless steel bowl over hot water. Whisk until it forms a thick, ribbon-like consistency (a sabayon). Slowly whisk in the clarified butter. Add lemon juice, tabasco, and seasoning. Stir in the parsley.

5 Dismantle the chicken into serving pieces and place in deep bowls. Add the vegetables, pour over some of the cooking liquor, and serve with the parsley hollandaise sauce on the side.

CHEF'S TIPS

■ To calculate how much water is needed, place the raw chicken in the pan, then pour on enough cold water to just cover it. Remove the chicken and heat the water.

■ Take care when salting the water in which you are going to cook the chicken. If you scatter salt like a sumo wrestler starting a difficult bout, then you will end up with stock that tastes like the Dead Sea. A pinch will suffice. More can be added later if needed.

JOINTING

If you intend cooking the bird in any way other than whole, you will need to know how to dismantle it into its component joints. All poultry are formed in the same way so the difference between jointing a turkey and a partridge will be one of size rather than technique.

Ducks and geese are configured slightly differently, with long breasts and comparatively short legs. This affects carving, and the dark meat on wild ducks will affect the degree to which they are best cooked, but in essence they too are taken apart in the same way.

Cutting a bird into four pieces

1 Remove the wishbone (p152) from the bird, then cut down through the skin between the leg and the carcass.

2 Bend the leg back as far as you can. The tip of the leg bone, a ball and cup arrangement with the backbone, will pop free.

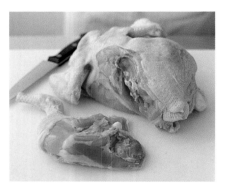

3 Cut the leg away from the backbone, then repeat the process with the other leg. Each leg may be divided into thigh and drumstick.

4 Pull the wing out to its fullest extent, then, using poultry shears, cut off the winglet at the second joint from the wing tip.

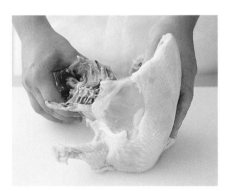

5 If a crown (the 2 breasts and wings on the bone) only is called for, snap the backbone at its halfway point.

6 Using poultry shears, remove the lower end of the backbone, which has no meat attached to it.

7 If the breasts are to be cooked on the bone, cut along the breastbone from neck to tail. Trim away any unwanted sections of backbone.

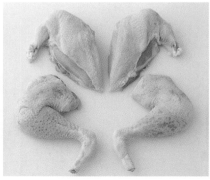

8 The chicken cut into 4 pieces. The legs take longer to cook than the breast so for some recipes you will need to cook them separately. For separate braising, or for boning and rolling.

Cutting a bird into eight pieces

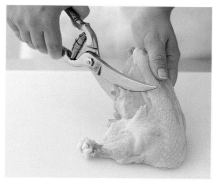

1 Using poultry shears, cut through the ribs two-thirds of the way along each breast and at an acute angle.

2 Each leg may be further divided. Locate the joint above the drumstick connecting it to the thigh and slice through to divide.

3 The chicken cut into 8 pieces. Many braising dishes call for the chicken to be divided into 4 or 8 pieces before cooking.

Dividing a crown

The crown consists of the main part of the bird, with the legs and the parson's nose removed, leaving the breasts and wings on the bone.

If the breasts are to be cooked on the bone, run the blade of a sharp knife downwards along the dividing bone at the top centre of the crown and chop the breastbone in 2 (see step 7, opposite).

If the breasts are to be cooked as fillets, cut the breasts away from the bone. Work from the thick, wing end downwards. The breastbone will act as a natural brake, so you can press firmly either side of the central bone and follow its contours (see below).

Cutting chicken wings

The wings can be separated from the breasts with a pair of kitchen scissors or a sharp knife (see right). Chicken wings have sweet and accessible meat and it is a shame not to use them as part of whatever dish is to be made with the chicken. Of course, if they are not used, they can otherwise be added to the carcass and used for making stock.

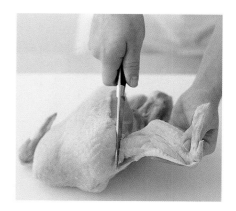

Detaching the breast section from the bone

1 Using poultry shears, cut away the ribs and the backbone. Work from the thickest (wing) end of the breast towards the narrowest part.

2 Using a sharp knife, separate the meat from the bone by following the contours of the breastbone, cutting the fillet neatly away.

3 Locate the small inner fillet on the underside of the breast and slice any connecting membrane to remove it.

FRYING

Only chicken is fried on a regular basis. The breadcrumbs that encase the meat are as much part of the attraction as the chicken itself – witness your high street take-away, not much free-range or organic there. The popularity, however, is undeniable and indeed properly fried chicken fillets in home-made crumbs are a great summer meal, especially when contrasted with a crisp salad and well-flavoured relish or dressing.

The best way to enjoy a portion of fried chicken is to bat out the leg or breast into a flat escalope, coat it in breadcrumbs, and fry it like Wiener schnitzel. The traditional Southern-fried chicken-type of dish is better if the chicken pieces are poached first and then cooled before being breadcrumbed. The flavour is enhanced in much the same way as a roast potato that has been parboiled ahead. Also, the chicken will need less time in the oil, be less greasy, and less prone to being undercooked at the centre, but will still have the crisp coating that makes the dish appetizing.

When frying in batches, clean the pan and renew the oil between each batch to prevent any loose crumbs from burning.

SOUTHERN-FRIED CHICKEN

If you forget the commercial versions and approach this method of treating chicken with care and respect, then there is a treat in store.

The meat is not poached in this recipe and the temperature of the cooking oil is crucial. If it is too hot, the coating will crisp before the inside of the meat is done. If the oil starts to smoke – a sure sign that it is too hot – add a little more oil to quickly reduce the overall temperature.

| 2 skinless, boneless chicken breasts |
| 2 skinless, boneless chicken thighs |
| 1tbsp Dijon mustard |
| 1tsp salt |
| 1tsp milled black pepper |
| pinch of cayenne pepper |
| 150ml (5fl oz) buttermilk |
| 4 back bacon rashers |
| 150g (5½oz) fresh white breadcrumbs |
| sunflower oil, for frying |

1 Using a sharp knife, slice each breast and thigh diagonally into 4 pieces.

2 Mix the mustard with the salt, pepper, and cayenne, then brush this mixture over the chicken pieces. Place the chicken in a bowl and spoon over the buttermilk. Turn the pieces gently so that they are all coated.

3 Pour oil into a pan to a depth of 1cm (½in) and heat, then fry the bacon until crisp. Lift out the rashers and when cool enough to handle, crumble or chop them into very small pieces. Mix these into the breadcrumbs, then gently coat each chicken piece with the mixture.

4 Add more oil to the pan so that it returns to a depth of 1cm (½in), heat gently and fry the chicken, turning once, for about 10 minutes, depending on the thickness of the pieces, until golden brown and cooked.

5 Your pan is unlikely to be wide enough to cook all the chicken at once. Either cook the meat in batches, keeping it warm in the oven between times, or use 2 pans. Sprinkle the chicken with salt and serve.

FRIED CHICKEN ESCALOPES

Boneless joints of chicken that are to be rolled in breadcrumbs and fried or brushed with oil and herbs and then grilled, should be flattened. Partly this is a tenderizing technique, and partly it helps the meat to cook evenly by obtaining a uniform thickness.

Chicken legs have more flavour than the breasts, but you may substitute all breast fillets if you are not confident about boning the chicken joints.

When frying, the oil should reach halfway up the escalope as it cooks. Cook the escalopes individually, keeping the cooked ones warm in the oven while you finish the job.

1 chicken, about 1.5kg (3lb 3oz), jointed into 8 pieces, boned and skinned
1 small white loaf, preferably 2 days old, crusts removed
1tbsp Dijon mustard
1tbsp chopped fresh herbs such as tarragon and parsley
2 eggs, beaten
sunflower oil, for frying

1 Remove any sinews from the chicken and place each fillet between 2 sheets of cling film, then tap the fillets with a rolling pin until they have increased in size by half and are an even thickness.

2 Dice the bread and process in a processor to crumbs, then put in a wide bowl. Season the escalopes with salt and pepper. Brush them with the mustard and sprinkle each with some of the chopped herbs.

3 Dip the escalopes into the beaten egg to coat on all sides.

4 Turn the escalopes in the breadcrumbs to coat well. Heat both pan and 1cm (½in) oil before adding the meat. Fry the escalopes in the oil for 4–5 minutes, until brown. Drain on paper and serve.

DEEP-FRYING

Deep-frying has more in common with boiling than it has with shallow or pan frying. The meat is completely immersed in liquid, in this case oil or fat, and cooked simultaneously from all sides. The temperatures reached by oils compared with water are much higher of course, so Maillard reactions – the caramelization of surface proteins that occurs in anything roasted or grilled – will take place, allowing the meat to be browned and crisped. The thicker

the piece of meat, the lower the temperature must be so that there is time for the heat to cook the centre of the joint at the same time as the outside turns golden. The oil is important. An unobtrusively flavoured oil is best, and one with a reasonably high flash point (the temperature at which the oil starts to burn and give colour). Oils such as olive, which have a low flash point, are unsuited to the task of deep-frying. Sunflower, groundnut and vegetable oils are ideal.

DEEP-FRIED CHICKEN

Chicken has to be cooked thoroughly. If you are frying chicken for a number of people, then do so in small, controllable batches, keeping the cooked chicken in a moderate oven while the remainder is frying.

115g (4oz) unsalted butter, softened

juice and grated zest of 1 lemon

2tbsp chopped tarragon

4 large skinless, boneless chicken breasts

1 large egg

115g (4oz) fresh white breadcrumbs

sunflower oil, for deep-frying

1 Cream the butter, lemon zest, and tarragon in a bowl. Add the lemon juice and season to taste with salt and pepper. Shape the butter into a rectangular block on a piece of foil, then wrap up and leave in the freezer to set solid.

2 Meanwhile, flatten each chicken breast into an escalope (p169). Place the chicken between 2 pieces of polythene or cling film before batting the meat out gently.

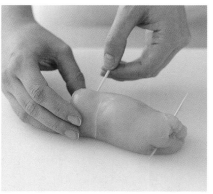

3 Cut the butter into 4 pieces. Place a piece in the centre of each escalope, ensuring that the butter is completely enclosed. Roll the fillet up tightly over the butter.

4 Secure the filled escalope at each end with a cocktail stick to secure.

5 Lightly beat the egg and dip the chicken in to coat on all sides, then roll the chicken in the breadcrumbs, pressing them in evenly and thoroughly. Leave the breadcrumbed parcels in the refrigerator until the coating has set.

6 Heat the oil in a deep-frying pan to 190°C (375°F) or test with a cube of bread. Do not let the oil get too hot, or the chicken will brown before it is cooked inside. Fry the chicken in several batches, without crowding the pan, for about 10 minutes, until golden brown.

7 Drain on kitchen paper and remove the cocktail sticks before serving.

STUFFING A BREAST FILLET

The essential point to ensure when stuffing a breast fillet is that the stuffing should remain safely in the centre of the fillet during cooking. The breadcrumbs should provide a good seal, but it helps if the stuffing is securely wrapped by the meat. Do not be tempted to be overly generous with the filling. The more stuffing inside there is, the higher the prospect of leakage during cooking. If there is any doubt in your mind, it is a good idea to coat the fillet a second time in the fresh breadcrumbs.

1 Cut a pocket about 4cm (1½in) deep in the side of the breast fillet with a sharp knife.

2 Press the stuffing deep into the pocket and roll back the meat. The crumb coating will seal everything in place.

BRAISING & POT-ROASTING

The defining characteristic of anything braised is that it should first be caramelized on the outside by frying or roasting, and then cooked slowly with liquid until it is completely tender. The purpose of this is to combine the concentrated flavour that the initial high temperatures give – Maillard reactions – with the slow cooking that will melt any tough or gelatinous parts. Maillard reactions are the browning of surface proteins and sugar. The process alters the character of the flavour of the meat (or vegetable) and is achieved only at a high temperature. Compare, for instance, the flavour of roast chicken with that of one poached – although both will be completely cooked, they will taste very different.

Importantly, cooking by braising gives you an opportunity to incorporate aromatic vegetables or herbs and spices to the dish as

it cooks, adding to its complexity and interest. There is also the bonus of the cooking liquor. As with a roast or grilled chicken dish, the timing of a braised chicken dish is important. Dark game birds, such as mallard, and butcher's meat, like pork or beef, improve with prolonged cooking and are no worse for an extra 30 minutes in the pan if your dinner timing has gone awry. But white poultry overcooks quickly and will turn to shreds if left too long. The same holds true for any white game, such as pheasant or partridge.

The notion of braising poultry generally implies cooking small joints rather than whole birds. Whole birds and larger joints are good braised, but for some reason they are referred to as pot-roasted when cooked by this method, although the process is exactly the same. Perhaps "pot roast" sounds grander than stew.

CHICKEN BRAISED IN RED WINE

Known in France as coq au vin, this is a staple of the French provincial culinary repertoire. It is the most celebrated, but regularly the worst-cooked dish of brasserie restaurants. Sometimes the chicken pieces are marinated overnight to deepen the effect of the red wine. This has the unwanted side effect, however, of drying out the meat and overpowering whatever flavour of chicken the poor bird may have to contribute.

It does not reheat well in the way of beef or lamb dishes that are prepared similarly, but if timed right it has a freshness and vitality that other braised meat dishes do not have.

55g (2oz) unsalted butter	
1 chicken, about 1.5kg (3lb 3oz), jointed into 8 pieces (p167)	
8 small onions	
100g (3½oz) unsmoked streaky bacon, cut into 2.5cm (1in) strips	
16 button mushrooms	
2 garlic cloves, crushed	
1tbsp plain flour	
1tbsp tomato passata	

250ml (8½fl oz) red wine	
1tbsp sugar	
500ml (17fl oz) chicken stock or water	
To serve	
1tbsp chopped parsley	
hot croûtons (p67)	

1 Heat half the butter in a heavy pan. Season the chicken with salt and pepper, add the pieces to the pan and cook, turning in the butter, until they have browned all over.

2 Add the onions and bacon and cook for about 10 minutes until coloured, then add the mushrooms and garlic and cook for a few minutes, turning them in the juices.

3 Stir the flour into the browned butter and juices and cook for a minute or 2. Add the tomato passata, red wine, and sugar, stir and bring to the boil. Add the stock or water and bring back to the boil.

Pour the sauce over the chicken and vegetables. Sprinkle with the parsley and serve with hot croûtons.

4 Turn down the heat so that the liquid barely simmers, then cover the pan and cook for 50 minutes or until the chicken is cooked.

5 Test for doneness, then lift out all the chicken pieces and vegetables onto a warmed serving dish.

6 Transfer batches of the cooking liquor and any trimmings left in it to a blender, add the remaining butter and blend. Amalgamate the batches of sauce and test for seasoning.

Chicken bourride

Bourride is a fish stew thickened with garlic mayonnaise. The treatment and its other major flavour combination of pepper, orange zest, and saffron suit chicken just as well. In fact, chicken survives the experience in considerably better shape than fish. The chicken may be cooked whole if preferred, but add 20 minutes' cooking time.

2 chickens, each 1.5kg (3lb 3oz), wishbones removed (p152, jointed into breasts, thighs, and drumsticks (p167)

olive oil, for frying

1tsp saffron threads

small pinch of ground cumin

zest of ½ orange

½ small red pepper, chopped

½ small red chili, chopped

500ml (17fl oz) water or chicken stock

8 small new potatoes, peeled

juice of ½ lemon

2 leeks, cut into strips

For the garlic mayonnaise

1tsp Dijon mustard

1tbsp white wine vinegar

2 egg yolks

50ml (1¾fl oz) sunflower oil

50ml (1¾fl oz) olive oil

4 garlic cloves, crushed

The sauce will be enhanced by any trimmings and the meat from the drumsticks

Two chickens call for a sizeable pot. If you do not have one, use a roasting tray covered tightly with kitchen foil. Preheat the oven to 190°C (375°F, gas 5). Season the chicken. Heat a little olive oil and seal the chicken until just coloured. Stir in the saffron, cumin, orange zest, pepper, and chili. Add the water or stock and potatoes. Bring to the boil, then reduce the heat to a bare simmer. Cover the pot and transfer to the lower shelf of the oven. Braise for about 25 minutes, until chicken and potatoes are cooked.

Whisk the mustard, vinegar, and egg yolks in a bowl, then slowly whisk in the sunflower and olive oils. Add the garlic and season to taste.

Lift the potatoes and chicken from the pot. Remove the meat from the drumsticks and put to one side. Remove the meat from the rest of the bird. Blend the drumstick meat and any fragments of meat or vegetables with the stock in a blender. While blending, add a spoonful of garlic mayonnaise and some lemon juice, then add more until the taste and texture suits you. Pour back over the chicken and potatoes.

Cook the leek strips in boiling, salted water for a few seconds, drain and scatter over the bourride.

GRILLING

Two processes are known as grilling. The chef's grill comprises bars that are heated from below and onto which food is then placed and cooked, an indoor barbecue, in fact. A salamander blasts heat from above, toasting and crisping food. In essence, they achieve the same thing – a caramelized seal on the food and fast cooking. They are both poor for slow cooking. The advantage of the barbecue-style grill is that the wood used will affect the flavour, a sort of small-scale smoking at the same time as the cooking, and there is an instant searing of whatever is cooking. The advantage of the salamander is that it can crisp delicate surfaces, brown gratin toppings, and deal effectively with poultry that is in a wet marinade.

In both cases the poultry must be brushed with butter or oil before cooking so that its surface can colour without drying. Use tender, fast-cooking cuts like breast fillet. Marinades will tenderize the meat and leave an oil coating to protect it during cooking.

Griddling is a method halfway between frying and grilling. The difference between it and frying is that the meat, rather than the griddle, is coated with oil. The difference between griddling and barbecue-style grilling is that there is no flavour from wood smoke, nor striped effect from the bars. A griddle's best use is for sealing at high temperature whatever is being cooked, which is then placed in a roasting pan and cooked in the oven at a less ferocious pace.

SPATCHCOCKING A BIRD FOR GRILLING

A spatchcocked bird has been flattened and transformed into something more two-dimensional, which can be grilled evenly. There is little point in the process otherwise. Once spatchcocked, the bird can be marinated in olive or some other oil mixed with, say, tarragon or oregano, then brushed with mustard and grilled. If you intend cooking it in an oven, it can be brushed with mustard after roasting, topped with a mixture of fresh breadcrumbs and herbs, then crisped under a conventional salamander-type grill.

Poussins (baby chickens) make ideal candidates for spatchcocking and then grilling. Other small birds, such as young guinea fowl, quail, and squab pigeon, can also be prepared in this way.

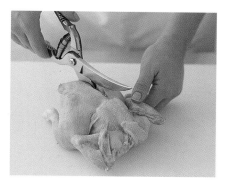

1 Turn the poussin upside down. Using poultry shears, cut along one side of the backbone, then cut along the other side and remove the backbone completely. Open out the bird and turn it over.

2 Using the heel of your hand or the flat side of a heavy knife, lightly crush the bird all over. This will tenderize the meat and ensure it will cook more evenly.

3 Using a sharp knife, cut a few slashes into the legs and thighs for the same reason.

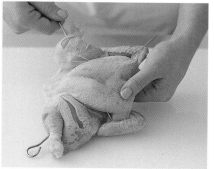

4 Push a skewer through the left leg to the right wing and another skewer through the right leg to the left wing.

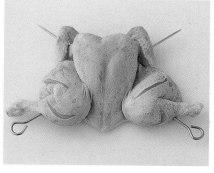

5 If wished, the spatchcocked bird can now be marinated before being grilled or it can be roasted in the oven.

GRILLED PHEASANT BREAST WITH BRAISED CHESTNUTS

Pheasant needs help if it is to be moist when grilled or roasted. The legs are a lost cause and are best braised whatever the dish. This can be an advantage, for any fast-cooking method like grilling or frying will produce good texture in tender breast joints, but not any pronounced pheasant flavour. So the legs can provide this. There is little point after all in using pheasant, rather than guinea fowl or chicken, if its distinctive flavour is not made use of.

4 young pheasants, wishbones removed (p152), jointed into breasts, thighs, and drumsticks (p167), breasts skinned, and skin reserved

20g (¾oz) butter

5 rashers streaky bacon, cut into 2.5cm (1in) lengths

6 small carrots, cut into 2.5cm (1in) lengths

12 shallots or pickling onions

1tsp grated nutmeg

1tsp ground cinnamon

100ml (3½ fl oz) white wine

1tbsp tomato passata

200ml (7fl oz) chicken stock

1tbsp brown lentils, soaked for 1 hour, then boiled until tender

8 peeled chestnuts (p481) or use unsweetened vacuum-packed chestnuts

4tbsp olive oil

1 Preheat the oven to 180°C (350°F, gas 4). Heat the butter in a heavy-based ovenproof pan and fry the thighs and drumsticks until browned. Add the bacon, vegetables, spices, and skin from the breasts.

CHEF'S TIPS

■ Pheasant legs – especially the drumsticks – have lots of little bones and gristle. These need careful removal before blending in the sauce.
■ Pheasant skin has little to recommend it, so it is removed from the breasts and added to the stock.
■ As an alternative, you could cook the legs over a low heat on the hob.

2 Season with salt and pepper, then stir in the wine, passata, and stock. Add the lentils and chestnuts. Bring to the boil, then reduce to a simmer, cover the pan and cook in the oven for about 1 hour until the legs are cooked.

4 Remove the vegetables, meat, and chestnuts from the pan. Discard the bones, skin, and gristle from the meat.

3 Meanwhile, bat out the pheasant breasts between 2 sheets of cling film to an even thickness. Season with salt and pepper and brush generously with olive oil ready for grilling.

5 Pour the remaining liquid, including the bacon and lentils, into a blender and add the meat from the legs. Blend, in batches if necessary, into a smooth sauce and pour back over the vegetables and chestnuts. Reheat.

6 Grill the breasts for a few minutes on each side, then serve on top of the braised chestnuts and vegetables.

Grilling times for specific birds

BIRD	TIME*
Chicken escalopes	7–10 minutes each side
Chicken joints	15 minutes each side
Kebab strips	5–6 minutes
Pheasant breasts	3–4 minutes each side
Poussin, spatchcocked	15 minutes each side
Quail, spatchcocked	12 minutes each side

*Turn meat regularly and baste if instructed by the recipe

MARINATING POULTRY

Marinades

Brush the marinade over chicken joints or other poultry. Leave for 1 hour, then cook the bird on a barbecue-style grill, brushing from time to time with the reserved marinade. Each marinade makes enough to coat one small chicken, jointed, or four breasts.

Sesame & chili marinade

Whisk together 100ml (3½fl oz) light sesame oil, 1 small seeded and finely chopped chili, 1tbsp soy sauce, and 1tbsp Asian citron juice (available from Japanese delicatessens as yuzu) to form an emulsion.

Orange & olive oil marinade

Whisk together 100ml (3½fl oz) olive oil, grated zest of 1 orange, 3 large crushed garlic cloves, 1tbsp chopped oregano, and milled black pepper to form an emulsion.

Cumin & cinnamon marinade

Whisk together 100ml (3½fl oz) olive oil, 1tbsp ground cumin, 1tsp ground paprika, 1tsp ground cinnamon, grated zest of 1 lime, 1 crushed garlic clove, ½ small seeded and finely chopped chili, and plenty of milled black pepper to form an emulsion.

DRY-MARINATING

A third type of marinade just about qualifies for inclusion. Dry-marinating, which involves no liquid, is an extension of the process of seasoning the poultry ahead of its cooking. The squab pigeon with spices recipe (p152) is an example of this. The spice mixture is left on the bird for an hour or so to penetrate the meat more than just skin-deep.

Marinating poultry serves one of two purposes. If the marinade has an acid component – such as red wine or vinegar – it will break down any tough proteins or connective tissue in the meat and, in theory at least, make it that much more tender to eat. This process has to be used with care when dealing with the delicate white meat of chicken or pheasant, for it can dominate their fragile quality, leaving you little but the taste of wine and peppercorns. Also, there is the danger of drying out the meat that contact with any non-oil or fat liquid brings. One hour is long enough for poultry to be left in this type of acid marinade.

The object of marinating for most types of poultry, and its second purpose, is to avoid any dryness in the meat and maybe to add some nuances of spicing to the finished dish. For this, you need a marinade that is oil-based. Added interest will be given to the meat by using aromatic ingredients such as grated orange zest, garlic, or chili, as well as whatever herbs and spices are appropriate to the dish.

Poultry can be left in this kind of oil-based marinade for longer – the coriander-marinated chicken kebabs opposite can be left in the seasoning for at least four hours, for example.

Coriander-marinated chicken kebabs

Versions of this dish are served as a main course across a large part of the Middle East and eastern Mediterranean. The method leaves the meat completely tender and the flavours nicely balanced between the acidity of the yogurt and the light sweetness of the chicken. The difference between the dish when made with good high-quality ingredients and one made with standard-issue ingredients is dramatic.

Small fingers of the marinated chicken also make a first-rate hot canapé – the lime and coriander tang will stimulate appetite without lending the bulk necessary to satisfy it.

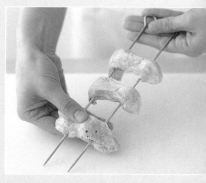

The skewers act as bones in keeping the meat stretched during cooking. Use at least 2, slightly apart, for best effect

4 skinless, boneless chicken breasts

100g (3½oz) Greek-style yogurt

1 scant tsp salt

juice of 1 lime

1tbsp chopped coriander leaves plus extra to garnish

1tsp milled black pepper

1tsp crushed coriander seeds

few drops of olive oil

Cut the chicken breasts into 2cm (¾in) strips from side to side rather than top to bottom. Mix the yogurt with the salt, lime, coriander leaves, and spices. Coat the chicken in this mixture and leave to marinate for 4 hours. The longer the chicken is left in the marinade the more effect it will have. Four hours is ideal if you still want some vestige of chicken taste coming through the spices.

Preheat a grill. Thread the chicken strips onto pairs of skewers, putting about 4 strips of chicken on each pair.

Sprinkle a few drops of olive oil on the kebabs and grill them for about 7 minutes on each side until they are done.

INDIAN COOKING

Atul Kochhar

ATUL KOCHHAR

Indian cuisine can be divided broadly into four main regions – north, south, east, and west – which are themselves subdivided into individual Indian states. All the states vary in the spices they grow and use, and the cooking techniques they employ. Tandoori chicken is a north Indian recipe. It is cooked in a tandoor, a charcoal-fired clay oven that gives food a characteristic finish and flavour. In this oven meats and vegetables are cooked skewered on iron spikes, and breads are baked by slapping them onto the oven's clay walls. It is common to serve the dish with bhajis, a type of savoury fritter also used as a snack or starter. The onion bhaji, from western India, is one of the most delicious examples, often served as a starter with mint chutney.

Cooking techniques India has more than 7,000km (4,350 miles) of warm water coasts, so seafood is an essential part of Indian gastronomy. The two seafood recipes in this chapter involve two different types of cooking – kadhai (Indian wok) and curry (poaching in a sauce). Kadhai cooking combines stir-frying and sautéing; curry cooking combines sautéing and poaching. Both methods employ their own set of spices. Kadhai spices are usually specific and are listed in recipes, whereas a curry's spice combinations vary according to regional differences and the main ingredients used. Bhuna is a sautéing technique that gives numerous Indian recipes a distinct flavour due to its heat treatment of spices. Fresh or dry spices are lightly toasted to release their essential oils, which then flavour lamb, chicken, prawns, and vegetables. The bhuna technique also varies from region to region in the spices and ingredients used. For example, yogurt is not always the cooking liquid used. Dum cooking, or slow cooking of food in its own steam, is an ancient method of Indian cooking first used in the city of Awadh (now Lucknow). In biriyani dishes made by this method, meat or vegetables are partly cooked and mixed with partly cooked rice, spices, and other flavourings. The food is oven-baked slowly at a low temperature in a sealed pot. Spices such as mace (the aril that surrounds the nutmeg) and green cardamom play a major role, and saffron, rosewater, cream, and yogurt are used liberally to enhance the dish. Tadka is a technique in which foods prepared with little or no spicing, such as lentils, are spiced just before they are served. This technique is also used to enhance preparations that are already spiced.

The spicing process In Indian cooking, spices are sizzled and made to release their flavours in hot oil. The oil becomes the carrier of the flavours and distributes them evenly through the dish. The temperature of the oil is critical. If too hot, the oil burns the spices, destroying the flavours and giving the preparation a burnt taste. If too cold, the oil fails to release the flavours from the spices, and the preparation becomes a poor or unworthy dish.

Spices are used in various forms – fresh and dried, whole and ground, and in coarse and fine pastes. Most notable are the whole and ground dried spices. Generally, whole spices are added to hot oil at the start of the preparation. Ground or powdered spices are used during or at the end of the preparation to complete the flavourings. Ground spices are rarely added directly to hot oil, since they burn readily and their flavours are spoilt.

Planning an Indian meal A traditional Indian meal may or may not have starters. These include fried snacks such as bhajis, a salad of cucumber, tomatoes, and onions, a lentil soup (rasam), or a tangy drink made with toasted cumin and mango powder. For the main course, a meat curry might be the main dish, with two vegetable accompaniments and a lentil preparation. Different spicing, cooking methods, ingredients, and textures are used to vary vegetable dishes; this is especially important for vegetarian meals. The main dish is served with an Indian bread such as a chapatti and either plain steamed rice or pilau rice. Pickles, chutneys, and poppadums are also served. Desserts vary from region to region but fresh fruits, kulfi, or rice pudding satisfy most palates.

MENU

- Tandoori murg

- Onion bhajis

- Raita

- Kadhai jhinga

- Paneer & baby corn
  with ginger

- Tadka dal

- Bhuna gosht

- Meen molee

TANDOORI MURG

The Indian culinary scene has been dominated for a long time by tandoori chicken dishes. This is a simple recipe that can be produced easily in household ovens or on a barbecue. Marinating (see opposite) helps to retain flavour in the meat during and after cooking. Birds are generally cooked without the skin because it is considered unhealthy.

1 chicken, about 1kg (2¼lb) skin removed

For the first marinade

1tsp salt

1tbsp ginger-garlic paste (see opposite)

1tsp red chili powder

2tbsp lemon juice

For the second marinade

250g (8½oz) Greek-style or thick yogurt

1tsp garam masala

100ml (3½fl oz) vegetable oil

½tsp cinnamon powder

½tsp red chili powder or paprika

1tsp salt

pinch of edible red food colouring (optional)

To serve

25g (scant 1oz) butter

2tbsp vegetable oil

1tbsp lime juice

1tsp chat masala (mixed spices)

1 Skin the chicken and, with a sharp knife, cut into 4 pieces (2 breasts and 2 legs). Pull the legs through the ball and socket joint, leaving some meat attached to the end of the bone for less shrinkage.

2 Cook the twice-marinated chicken pieces (see opposite) on a baking sheet in an oven preheated to 200°C (400°F, gas 6) or on barbecue grill bars for 10 minutes. Baste with half the butter and oil and cook for a further 15 minutes.

3 Remove the chicken from the oven or barbecue and baste with the remaining butter and oil mixture. Sprinkle over the lime juice and chat masala. Serve hot with a leafy salad and mint chutney.

RAITA

Lightly whisk 200g (7oz) Greek-style or thick yogurt. Stir in salt to taste, ½tsp toasted crushed cumin seeds, 1tbsp diced red onions, 1tbsp chopped mint leaves, and 1tbsp grated, peeled cucumber.

ONION BHAJIS

Bhaji, bhajia, and pakora are some of the common names of vegetable snacks that are deep-fried in a batter made from gram flour (ground chickpeas). Bhajis are best made just before serving.

3 onions, finely sliced

vegetable oil for deep-frying

For the batter

100g (3½oz) gram flour

¼tsp bicarbonate of soda

½tsp turmeric

1 green chili, finely chopped

1tbsp chopped coriander leaves

½tsp salt

5tbsp (40–50ml) water

The batter can be varied by using cornmeal or rice flour – if using cornmeal, use 100g (3½oz); if using rice flour, use 50g (1¾oz). Other vegetables such as cauliflower, cabbage, and carrot are also suitable for making crisp bhajis.

MARINATING

In Indian cooking, meats may be marinated twice: the first removes excess moisture; the second introduces flavours and spices.

1 With a sharp knife, make 3 or 4 deep incisions to the bone on each chicken piece without cutting across the flesh. This helps the marinade penetrate the meat and stops it from shrinking during the dry-heat cooking.

2 Mix all the ingredients in a bowl for the first marinade. Using gloves, coat the chicken with the marinade. Place the chicken in a sieve over the bowl and set aside for 20 minutes at room temperature to allow the juices to drain.

3 Mix together all the ingredients for the second marinade. Coat the chicken thoroughly and refrigerate for 2–3 hours.

GINGER-GARLIC PASTE

To prepare the ginger-garlic paste, blend equal quantities of peeled ginger and garlic with 10 per cent of their total weight in water using the blender of a mini-processor. The paste should be smooth and fine. Store in a sealed container in the refrigerator for up to a week. If you wish to keep the paste longer, add 5 per cent vegetable oil and 2 per cent lemon juice as you blend the paste. This makes it last longer and also lightens the colour of the paste. Alternatively, freeze this paste in ice-cube trays for future use.

MAKING ONION BHAJIS

In India, frying in a wok or deep-fryer is called "talna". If you are making fried foods such as bhajis in advance, reheat them in the oven or flash-fry in hot oil to regain their crispness.

1 Mix all the batter ingredients together and whisk well. The quantity of water is only a guide – the batter should be of dropping consistency.

2 Mix the onions in the batter with a spoon. Fill the wok with oil to a depth of 5–7.5cm (2–3in) or use a deep-fryer. Heat the oil to 160–180°C (325–350°F).

3 With 2 spoons, drop small portions of the onion-batter mixture into the hot oil and shape into patties. It should take 3–4 minutes to fry 12–15 bhajis. Remove to kitchen paper to soak up excess oil. Serve with raita.

COOKING BHAJIS

■ If the batter gets too thin, add extra gram flour to thicken it, though you may have to increase the spicing by a fraction to maintain the flavours.

■ Sometimes onion bhajis need to be fried twice if the onions are very watery. If this is the case, part-fry the onion bhajis, remove, and drain on kitchen paper. Press more kitchen paper on top to dry, then refry in hot oil until crisp. The patties will be flat.

KADHAI JHINGA

Kadhai is the Hindi name for a wok. This is a recipe for prawns cooked in tomatoes. Kadhai cooking is a style that has its own set of essential spices. Extremely fresh ingredients and quick cooking are the key to good kadhai dishes.

4tbsp vegetable oil

1tsp crushed garlic

1tbsp coriander seeds, pounded in a mortar

3 dried whole red chilies, roughly crushed

6 large tomatoes, roughly chopped

1tsp red chili powder

1tsp fenugreek leaf powder

1tsp finely chopped fresh ginger

1 green pepper, cut into julienne

20 large raw prawns, peeled and deveined (p126)

1½ tsp garam masala

2tbsp finely chopped coriander leaves

1 Heat 3tbsp of the oil in a wok or heavy-based pan. Add the garlic, pounded coriander seeds, and crushed chilies, stir, and cook for 1–2 minutes until the spices crackle and the garlic turns golden brown.

2 Add the tomatoes and a pinch of salt, cover with a lid, and cook for 8–10 minutes until the tomatoes are soft. Remove the lid, add the powdered spices, and cook for 3–5 minutes until the fat separates from the sauce.

3 Heat the remaining oil in another pan. Add the ginger and pepper, sauté for a minute, and add the prawns. Stir the prawns for 3–4 minutes, or until almost cooked.

4 Add the sauce to the prawns and cook for 2–3 minutes until the prawns are pink. Sprinkle with the garam masala and coriander leaves. Serve the dish in the wok or pan, with an Indian bread like chapatti, roti, or naan (p362).

Variations
Similar weights of boiled chickpeas, soft spring vegetables, fish, and chicken, cut into small pieces, can be cooked following this recipe.

PANEER & BABY CORN WITH GINGER

Foods cooked on a tawa, or griddle, are common in India and many of the preparations that adorn road-side cafés are cooked in this way.

600g (1lb 6oz) paneer cut into 2.5cm (1in) cubes

1.5 litres (2¾ pints) vegetable oil

1tsp ajwain seeds or thyme leaves

1tsp coriander seeds

2tbsp finely chopped fresh ginger

1tsp finely chopped green chili

2 onions, finely chopped

1tsp salt

1tbsp finely chopped red pepper

1tbsp finely chopped green pepper

2 tomatoes, finely chopped

1 tsp red chili powder

1tsp fenugreek leaf powder

1tsp garam masala

100g (3½oz) baby corn, sliced in half

To serve

2tbsp finely chopped coriander leaves

1tbsp fresh ginger julienne

1 spring onion, cut into thin strips

First deep-fry the paneer for 2–3 minutes in the vegetable oil (see opposite) and set aside for later combination with the freshly cooked tawa masala (see opposite).

TADKA DAL

This is an easy preparation of lentils highly seasoned with chili and garlic. The technique used to season the dish is called variously tadka, bhagar, or chowkna.

300g (10½oz) yellow split peas or lentils, preferably toor or chana
1tsp turmeric
1 litre (1¾ pints) water
1tbsp vegetable oil
1tsp butter or ghee
1tsp finely chopped garlic
1tsp red chili powder
2 tomatoes, chopped
1tsp salt
1tsp chopped coriander leaves
½ medium tomato, julienned, to garnish

1 In a heavy-based pan, bring the lentils to the boil with the turmeric and water. Simmer for 15–20 minutes until the lentils are cooked.

2 In a sauté pan heat the oil and butter and fry the garlic for about 2 minutes until it is light brown. Add the chili powder and sauté for 1 minute. Add the tomatoes and cook for 3–4 minutes.

3 Add the spiced tomato mixture and the salt to the cooked lentils and simmer for a further 5–7 minutes. Sprinkle with chopped coriander leaves and the julienned tomato, and serve hot.

DEEP-FRYING PANEER

Paneer, Indian cottage cheese, is very different from cottage cheese in Western countries. It is cooked as a vegetable and used on its own or in combination with true vegetables, either as the main course or as an accompaniment. Paneer has no taste of its own, so mixes easily with other flavoured ingredients while providing texture to the dish. The cheese should be deep-fried in hot oil to a light brown colour, then kept soft in lukewarm water until required.

MAKING THE TAWA MASALA

When making this accompaniment to the paneer, take care not to char the spices or onions over too high a heat or you will have to start again.

1 Heat a little oil in a frying pan. Add ajwain and coriander seeds, chopped ginger, and green chili. Sauté for 1 minute until the spices crackle then add onions and salt.

2 Cook for 3–5 minutes until the onions are translucent, add the peppers and tomatoes, and cook for a further 2 minutes until soft.

3 Add the powdered spices and cook until the fat leaves the masala. Add the paneer and baby corn to the simmering sauce, and cook for 3–5 minutes. Taste and adjust seasoning if necessary. Garnish with the chopped coriander, ginger julienne, and spring onion.

Variations

Most vegetables, such as diced blanched potatoes and carrots, or courgettes and peppers, are suitable for tawa cooking. Even meat, poultry, and seafood if cut small can be cooked by this method, using equivalent weights to the paneer.

MAKING BHUNA GOSHT

Bhuna literally means roasted, but for this type of preparation the term can also mean sautéed. The lamb is marinated in yogurt before being cooked in a spicy paste. Chili and turmeric are used in the marinade, but the dish's other spices are all cooked in oil to extract their flavours.

1 Add the salt to the yogurt in a stainless steel bowl, and stir in the chilli, turmeric, and lamb. Set aside for 15 minutes. Mix the poppy seeds and ginger and grind to a fine paste in a mortar.

2 In the mortar, grind the cloves, coriander powder, cinnamon sticks, cardamoms, and garlic to a fine paste. Heat the oil in a deep saucepan and sauté the onions for 5–7 minutes until light brown. Add the spices and sauté for 2–3 minutes.

3 Add the lamb and its marinade and cook uncovered on a low heat for about 30 minutes until tender. Stir in the butter.

MAKING COCONUT CURRY SAUCE

This coconut curry sauce is used opposite as the basis for a fish curry, but it serves equally well as a basis for chicken and vegetable curries. It has the strong flavourings of southern India.

1 Heat the coconut oil in a wide saucepan, fry 10 curry leaves until they are crisp, remove with a draining spoon, and place on kitchen paper. Set aside until required. Reheat the oil and sauté the onions, chilies, and garlic.

2 Add the remaining 10 curry leaves and cook for 3–5 minutes until the onion is translucent. Add the rest of the turmeric and salt, pour in the coconut milk, bring the sauce to a simmer, and simmer uncovered for 5 minutes.

 REHEATING

■ This recipe should be prepared close to serving but, if you have to hold the dish for a while, keep it warm (65°C/149°F), preferably with the fish separate from the sauce.

■ The sauce may thicken but can be thinned down with 3–4tbsp of warm water during reheating. Add the fish after the sauce has reheated.

BHUNA GOSHT

This lamb dish is commonly seen on the menus of Indian restaurants. It is easy to prepare this recipe.

1tsp salt or to taste
250g (8½oz) natural set yogurt
½tsp red chili powder
½tsp turmeric
500g (1lb 2oz) boneless lamb, cut into 1cm (½in) cubes
1½ tsp poppy seeds
2.5cm (1in) piece of fresh ginger
3 cloves
1tsp coriander powder
2 x 2.5cm (1in) sticks of cinnamon
3 green cardamoms
1 black cardamom
8 garlic cloves
3tbsp vegetable oil
2 onions, thinly sliced
1tbsp butter
To serve
1tsp garam masala
pinch of ginger julienne
1 tbsp chopped coriander leaves
10 cashew nuts, deep-fried

Prepare the bhuna gosht (see left). To serve, sprinkle garam masala, ginger julienne, and cashew nuts over the dish. Serve hot with Indian breads or rice.

MEEN MOLEE

Curry in India means a sauce preparation, so to use the word to describe a whole range of Indian foods is misleading. This fish curry is one of the simplest dishes that needs little advance planning. The sauce is made by simmering coconut milk and flavourings, and the fish is then poached in it. The sauce does not reduce much. In Indian cooking, fish, poultry, or meats are marinated with salt to draw out excessive moisture, so that during cooking flavours can be absorbed better.

4 small fillets of sea bass or sea bream (150g/5½oz each), skin on

1tsp salt

1tsp turmeric

2tbsp coconut oil

20 curry leaves

2 onions, finely sliced

6 whole green chilies, slit lengthways

3 garlic cloves, sliced into fine strips

400ml (14fl oz) coconut milk

small bunch of coriander, chopped

1 Score the fish fillets. Mix ½tsp salt and ½tsp turmeric, and gently rub the mixture into the fish. Leave the fish to marinate for at least 30 minutes, or until required.

2 Make the coconut curry sauce (see opposite) and add the fish fillets, skin-side up. Barely simmer the sauce for 3–5 minutes, uncovered, until the fish is just cooked. Garnish with the fried curry leaves and coriander, and serve.

Variations

Some chefs add black mustard seeds to this recipe. If liked, add 1tsp black mustard seeds before the onion. Let them splutter and then follow the recipe. The dish can be made with other seafood. Use the equivalent weight of prawns, lobster, scallops, whatever you prefer, and adjust the cooking time accordingly.

MEAT

MARCUS WAREING

The first step in ensuring success in meat cooking is to purchase meat of good quality from a professional butcher. When searching for a supplier in your local high street, look for premises that prepare carcasses on site – some butchers are little more than shops selling prepackaged meat, and their meat is less likely to be fresh. Ask the staff where they source their meat; a good butcher will know the farmer, the breed, and when the animal was slaughtered. Some supermarkets now encourage the sale of local meats by setting up specialist meat counters in their stores. This is a good service as long as trained staff are available to advise and assist you with your purchase. When purchasing ground meat or mince, always buy from a shop where it is minced on site. Farmers' markets are usually a source of good meat and you also have the opportunity to talk to the farmers about their animals and produce. In the United States alone there are 3,000 farmers' markets supporting 20,000 farmers. If you go further still and visit the farms themselves, you are able to assess the cleanliness and general appearance of the farm before buying. Some producers market their produce via mail order and the internet, although for the consumer these have the disadvantage of not allowing the meat to be viewed before purchase.

Selecting meat Good meat has little odour. With lamb and beef the fat should be slightly creamy, whereas pork fat should be white. Meat should not be unduly moist, and never slimy. The most tender cuts are from the loin and rump (where the muscles are less active), and these cuts are also the most expensive. However, lesser cuts of meat make equally stunning meals if cooked correctly. With the exception of offal, which should be eaten as soon as possible, all meat has to be hung for some time after slaughter. Meat cooked immediately after slaughter is quite acidic, due to the lactic acid present at the time of death. Lactic acid is present in all exercising muscle and gradually disperses after death. Rigor mortis also affects meat and can remain in a carcass for up to 30 hours. The optimum period of time for which meat should be hung varies according to the animal and the breed. Veal and pork can be hung for as little as a week, lamb for 1–3 weeks, and some beef for up to five weeks. Venison is normally hung for 1–3 weeks, rabbit requires just 4–5 days, and hare needs 7–10 days. The main reason for hanging meat is to maximize its tenderness, but remember that the longer the meat is hung, the "gamier" the taste will be.

Meat tends to be hung for a shorter period than in centuries past for a number of reasons. Modern breeding techniques produce animals with relatively tender flesh, so the meat requires less hanging time. Further, most westerners have lost their taste for the stronger flavours of well-hung meat. Hanging meat takes time and uses storage space, leading to expenses that make the meat business less financially attractive to producers and supermarkets. A further expense is incurred by the weight of the carcass actually falling slightly during hanging – in a market driven by price per kilo, lost weight equals lost earnings. Large producers therefore minimize meat hanging so that the produce can go into the food chain quickly, tying up their capital for as little time as possible.

Storing meat Raw meat carries bacteria and should be stored carefully to keep all your food safe from contamination. In warmer countries newly purchased meat should be carried home in an insulated bag to ensure that it does not become too warm. Before refrigeration, the meat should be removed from plastic packaging to prevent it from sweating. Place the meat at the bottom of the refrigerator, and never above cooked foods that could be contaminated by liquids dripping from the uncooked meat. Ideally the refrigerator should be maintained at the temperature of 4°C (39°F) and should not exceed 8°C (46°F). Meats placed in a meat safe or larder with a temperature of around 10°C (50°F) should be cooked within 48 hours.

ROASTING

One of the simplest of culinary techniques, roasting requires little more than basic skills in managing temperature and timing. It is also one of the least labour intensive – meat needs little or no attention during cooking, apart from occasional basting with fat.

Roasting time is calculated by the weight of the meat and the degree of doneness you require. For timing to be accurate, meat should be at room temperature before cooking or it will take longer to cook, and it will steam rather than roast. Take the meat out of the refrigerator at least 30–60 minutes before roasting, and wait until just before you put it in the oven before seasoning. Salt will draw the juices from raw meat if it is left to stand for any length of time, resulting in dry meat.

A meat thermometer is useful to gauge the internal temperature of meat accurately, but is not essential.

ROAST RIB OF BEEF

To begin with, the meat is seared in a hot oven for 15 minutes, then the temperature is reduced. This technique ensures a good, appetizing colour on the outside, and also helps prevent the juices "bleeding" and the meat becoming dry.

Serves 8–10

1 beef rib joint (with 4 bones), about 4.5kg (10lb) in total, chine bone removed

4tbsp olive or vegetable oil

2 large sprigs of thyme

Yorkshire puddings (see opposite) and gravy to serve

1 Preheat the oven to 220°C (425°F, gas 7). Weigh the beef and calculate the roasting time. Stand the beef, fat-side up, in a roasting pan and brush with the oil. Scatter with leaves from the thyme, season and place in the oven.

2 After 15 minutes, reduce the oven temperature to 180°C (350°F, gas 4) and continue roasting the beef for the rest of the calculated time, basting occasionally. For the most accurate results, test for doneness by using a meat thermometer.

RESTING MEAT

Letting the meat rest for 15–30 minutes after roasting allows the muscles to relax so the juices are retained within the meat and carving is easier. The meat will not go cold during this time – as long as it is not cut into, it will stay hot inside. This leaves plenty of time for you to make the Yorkshire puddings and gravy, and attend to any cooking of last-minute vegetables.

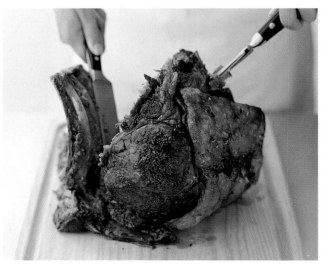

3 Transfer the meat to a carving board, cover loosely with foil and leave to rest in a warm place for 15–30 minutes before carving, during which time you can get the Yorkshire puddings in the oven and make the gravy.

4 To carve, stand the roast with the ends of the bones facing up. Steadying the meat with a carving fork on the fatty side, and using a sawing action with the knife, cut downwards between the bones and the meat to separate them.

YORKSHIRE PUDDINGS

250g (8½oz) plain white flour
2 eggs
250ml (8½fl oz) full-fat milk
250ml (8½fl oz) water
150ml (5fl oz) olive oil
pinch of salt

Mix all the ingredients in a food processor for 2–3 minutes. Leave to rest for a minimum of 3 hours. Preheat the oven to 200°C (400°F, gas 6). Put 1tbsp oil in each of 10 muffin tins and heat in the oven for 5 minutes or until very hot. Pulse in the food processor, pour into the tins and return to the oven. Bake for 25 minutes or until risen and golden. Tap on a heatproof surface and the puddings should lift out easily.

5 Discard the bones and put the chunk of meat, fat-side up, on the board. Cut downwards across the grain into thin slices, again using a sawing action with the knife.

Serve the slices of beef on warmed plates with gravy and Yorkshire puddings. Hand out mustard, horseradish and vegetables separately.

ROAST LEG OF LAMB WITH ROSEMARY & GARLIC

Studding a joint with rosemary and garlic has
a twofold effect – it imparts flavour to the meat,
and makes the roast look attractive when served.
This technique can be applied to any joint.

Serves 4–6

1 leg of lamb, bone in, about 2.5kg (5½lb)
12 sprigs of rosemary
6 garlic cloves
olive oil, for brushing

1 Preheat the oven to 220°C (425°F, gas 7).
Weigh the lamb and calculate the roasting
time. Make 12 incisions in the fat side
of the lamb with the tip of a small sharp knife.
Tear the tops off the rosemary and halve each
garlic clove lengthways. Insert the rosemary
and garlic into the slits in the meat.

2 Brush the meat with oil and season liberally.
Put the lamb in a roasting pan and roast in
the oven for 15 minutes until lightly browned.

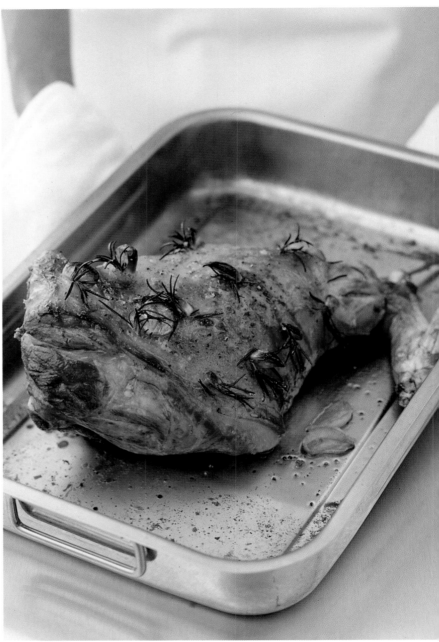

3 Reduce the temperature to 180°C (350°F, gas 4) and continue roasting for the rest of the
calculated time, basting occasionally. When the lamb is done, remove it from the oven and
transfer to a carving board. Cover loosely with foil and leave to rest in a warm place for 15–30 minutes.

4 Holding the roast upright by the bone, slice off the plump "lobe" of meat (the front of the thigh) by following along the bone with your knife. Now stand the roast on its cut surface and slice off the larger lobe of meat on the other side (the back of the thigh) by working your knife along the bone with a sawing action.

5 Remove the remaining meat from the bone so you have 3 chunks of boneless meat. Lay the chunks on their flat, cut sides, and carve thick slices downwards and against the grain, allowing 1 slice per person. The slices should be thick, almost like steaks. If they are too thin, they will be bloodless and the meat will be dry.

SLOW-ROAST SHOULDER OF PORK

There are 4 simple techniques to get crisp crackling: score the rind, rub it with salt and oil, roast at a high temperature for the first 15 minutes, and then do not baste the joint at all during roasting.

Serves 6–8

3.5kg (7¾lb) pork shoulder, boned, with rind left on
sea salt, for the rind
4tbsp vegetable oil
2 red onions, quartered lengthways
2 white onions, quartered lengthways
2 large lemons, quartered lengthways
2tbsp clear honey
2–3tbsp chopped sage
1 wineglass of dry white wine or cider
sage leaves to garnish

1 Preheat the oven to 220°C (425°F, gas 7). Score the rind widthways with a very sharp knife or a scalpel, keeping the lines parallel and close together. First work from the middle towards 1 edge, then turn the meat round and work from the middle towards the other edge. This is easier than scoring in a long line.

2 Massage the rind liberally with sea salt. Rub all over with a little oil, then stand the joint, rind-side up, on a trivet in a roasting pan and splash a little oil in the bottom of the pan. Roast the meat for 15 minutes, then reduce the temperature to 150°C (300°F, gas 2) and roast for another 2 hours, without basting.

3 Remove the pork and trivet from the pan, put the pan on the stove and sauté the onions and lemons in it for 10 minutes, until just caramelized. Drizzle with the honey and sprinkle with the sage, then push them to the outside of the pan and sit the pork in the middle.

4 Return to the oven for 1¼ hours, basting the onions and lemons occasionally but not the pork. The crackling will be crisp, and the meat will be tender when pierced through the middle with a thin metal skewer.

5 Transfer the meat to a carving board, cover loosely with foil and leave to rest in a warm place for 15–30 minutes. Transfer the onions and lemons to a dish with a slotted spoon, cover and keep warm.

6 Pour or skim off as much oily fat from the pan juices as possible. Place the pan on the stove and deglaze with the wine, scraping the pan bottom. Simmer until reduced by a third, then season and strain.

7 Steadying the meat with a carving fork, slice between the crackling and the meat so the crackling lifts off in 1 piece.

8 With scissors or a sharp knife, cut the crackling in half crossways to give short pieces that are easy to eat.

9 Carve the meat downwards and across the grain into thick slices, using a sawing action with a sharp knife.

Serve the meat and crackling on a platter with the onions, lemons, and sage as a garnish. Hand round the deglazed pan juices separately.

BAKING

When meat is baked in the oven it is covered, and so protected from direct heat. Coverings may be pastry, mashed or sliced potatoes, or thick layers of vegetables. This method suits lean prime cuts and cheaper tough cuts, both of which need protection to prevent them from drying out. For the meat to be a good, appetizing colour, it should always be seared or browned before covering and baking, but once this is done and the dish is in the oven it will need little or no further attention.

SHEPHERD'S PIE

Baking minced lamb under a plump pillow of rich and creamy potato purée transforms this humble cut of meat into a very special dish. This is no ordinary shepherd's pie.

6 small shallots
1 large carrot
2tbsp vegetable oil
50g (1¾oz) unsalted butter
1 bay leaf
1 sprig of fresh thyme
500g (1lb 2oz) minced lamb
1 tbsp tomato purée
dash of Worcestershire sauce
1 litre (1¾ pints) lamb or chicken stock
250g (8½oz) frozen peas
piccalilli to serve (see opposite – optional)

For the topping

500g (1lb 2oz) King Edward or Desirée potatoes, peeled and cut into large chunks
120ml (4fl oz) milk
125g (4½oz) butter
2 egg yolks

PIPING

I like piping the mashed potato because it gives a smoother, neater finish – but you can just spread it on with a palette knife if you prefer.

1 Dice the shallots and carrot as for a small mirepoix (p211). Heat the oil and butter in a frying pan over a moderate heat until foaming. Add the shallots, carrot, bay leaf and thyme and cook for 5 minutes, stirring occasionally.

2 Add the lamb and cook until it is all coloured, stirring and pressing with a fork to break up any lumps. Season, then stir in the tomato purée, Worcestershire sauce, and stock. Cook for 20 minutes or until reduced to a sauce-like consistency, adding the peas for the last 5 minutes.

3 Put the potatoes in a pan of cold water, bring to the boil and simmer for 20 minutes or until soft but not mushy. Drain and push through a drum sieve or potato ricer while still hot. Warm the milk and butter until the butter has melted, then mix into the potato with the egg yolks and seasoning.

4 Preheat the oven to 190°C (375°F, gas 5). Pour the meat mixture into an ovenproof dish and spread out evenly. Spoon the potato purée into a piping bag fitted with a large, plain nozzle and pipe the purée in straight lines on top.

5 Smooth the piped potato with a palette knife, then mark a pattern on top by drawing up the end of the knife at regular intervals. Bake in the oven for 30 minutes until the top of the shepherd's pie is golden brown.

Leave the pie to stand for 10 minutes, then serve straight from the dish.

PICCALILLI

Whenever my mother made shepherd's pie, she always put a jar of piccalilli on the table. Now I do the same, to continue the tradition.

Makes 2 large jars

12 pickling onions
1 head of cauliflower, cut into small florets
2 large gherkins, sliced
600ml (1 pint) white wine vinegar
300ml (10fl oz) malt vinegar
½tsp chopped fresh red chili
340g (12 oz) caster sugar
50g (1¾oz) English mustard powder
25g (scant 1oz) ground turmeric
4tbsp cornflour

1 Blanch the onions in boiling, salted water for 2 minutes, drain and refresh in cold water, then peel. Mix the onions in a bowl with the cauliflower and gherkins. Bring the vinegars to the boil with the chili. Cool, then strain. You can get to this stage the day before, and immerse the vegetables in salted water overnight.

2 Mix the sugar, mustard, turmeric, and cornflour to a paste with a little of the cold vinegar. Boil the remaining vinegar, whisk into the paste, and return to the pan. Boil for 3 minutes or until thickened.

3 Drain the vegetables, return them to the bowl and mix in the vinegar and seasoning. The piccalilli can be served when cold, or kept in a sealed jar in the refrigerator for up to 1 month.

PORK CHOPS WITH CARAMELIZED ONIONS

This is a dish for all sage and onion lovers. Pork chops are smothered in sweetly caramelized onions, which ooze into the meat during baking to give an exquisite flavour.

| 5tbsp olive oil |
| 85g (3oz) butter |
| 4 pork loin chops |
| 8 small onions, thinly sliced |
| 2 garlic cloves, sliced |
| leaves from 6 sprigs of thyme |
| leaves from 1 bunch of sage, roughly chopped |
| 1tsp dried sage |
| 4 bay leaves |

1 Preheat the oven to 180°C (350°F, gas 4). Heat 2tbsp of the oil and 25g (scant 1oz) of the butter a large heavy frying pan until just beginning to turn brown.

2 Place the chops in the pan and cook quickly over a medium-high heat, turning until well coloured. Transfer the chops to a roasting pan and season. Heat the remaining oil and another 25g (scant 1oz) of the butter in the frying pan and sauté the onions for 10–15 minutes until well coloured and almost caramelized.

3 Spread the onions over the chops and sprinkle with the garlic, thyme, and sage, then dot with small knobs of the remaining butter and put 1 bay leaf on each chop. Season well, cover with foil and bake for 45–60 minutes.

Transfer the chops and onions to warmed plates and keep warm while you boil the juices on the stove until reduced. Spoon the juices over the chops and serve immediately.

CHEF'S TIPS

■ This is my mother's recipe that I have adapted. My parents liked their chops well done, so my mother used to put the onions over the chops raw and bake them with the chops for 2–2½ hours in a low oven. I prefer my meat less well cooked, so I have caramelized the onions first to cut down on the baking time.

■ Use as many onions as you like – they break down during baking and mingle their juices with the butter and herbs to become so deliciously sweet and sticky that you can never have too many.

VENISON RAGOUT

I think of this as the French equivalent of Lancashire hotpot – a homely, comforting stew in which potatoes make the meat go further.

2tbsp olive oil
2 onions, finely chopped
1kg (2¼lb) diced haunch of venison
500ml (17fl oz) veal stock
250ml (8½fl oz) brown ale
1 garlic clove, chopped
2tbsp ground paprika
1tsp caraway seeds
500g (1lb 2oz) Russet or other red potatoes, peeled and cut into 5mm (¼in) cubes
3 tomatoes, skinned, seeded, and chopped
4tbsp chopped parsley

1 Heat the oil in a large flameproof casserole dish and sauté the onions over a low heat for 2–3 minutes until softened but not coloured. Remove with a slotted spoon and set aside.

2 Add half the meat and fry over a high heat until well browned. Remove and repeat with the remaining meat. Lower the heat to moderate and return the meat and the onions to the pan. Toss to mix. Add the stock, ale, garlic and spices, season well, and bring to the boil. Cover the pan, reduce the heat, and simmer for 2 hours.

3 Add the potatoes and tomatoes and simmer for a further hour until the venison is really tender. To serve, check the seasoning and sprinkle with the chopped parsley.

WILD BOAR

If you like the look of this stew, but not the gamey taste of venison, make it with wild boar, which is flavoursome but less strong. Boneless shoulder is a good cut for stewing, either sliced or diced.

BRAISING & STEWING

The connective tissue, fat and sinew that hold the muscles of meat together are broken down by either braising or stewing, rendering the meat tender and releasing gelatinous juices to create a rich, full-bodied gravy. Tougher, cheaper cuts respond well, and marinating before cooking adds flavour, with melt-in-the-mouth results.

The difference between braising and stewing is subtle. In a braise the meat is usually cut in large pieces (a whole joint is called a pot roast) and cooked in enough liquid to barely cover, whereas in a stew the pieces of meat are smaller and there is generally more liquid. There are two methods of starting the cooking. The meat can be seared in hot fat until coloured before the addition of vegetables and liquid, or the meat, vegetables and liquid can be put into the pan raw at the beginning. In either case, the subsequent cooking is always long and slow, either on top of the stove or in the oven. Cooking times are intended as a guide: the meat is ready when it is tender and moist, by which time the gravy should be glossy and rich.

IRISH STEW

A humble cut of meat combined with wholesome ingredients and the clever use of two types of potatoes creates a perfect dish to my mind. Floury potatoes break down to thicken the sauce, while waxy potatoes keep their shape and looks.

4 lamb neck fillets cut from 2 middle necks, bones reserved

675g (1½lb) carrots

1 onion

450g (1lb) floury potatoes, such as King Edward or Maris Piper

450g (1lb) waxy salad potatoes, such as Charlotte

1.2 litres (2 pints) hot lamb stock, made with reserved bones

leaves from 6 sprigs of thyme

chopped parsley to garnish

1 Cut the lamb fillets across the grain into large chunks, about 5cm (2in) thick. Cut the carrots into bite-sized pieces and thickly slice the onion. Cut both kinds of potato into 2.5cm (1in) chunks.

2 Put the meat into a saucepan and pour in the stock. Bring to the boil over a high heat, reduce to a simmer, and cook, uncovered, for 30 minutes.

3 During simmering, use a large scooping spoon to skim off the scummy impurities as they rise to the surface.

4 Remove the lamb and strain the stock through a fine sieve. Return the lamb and stock to the cleaned-out pan and bring to the boil. Reduce the heat, cover and simmer gently for 10 minutes. Add the onion, floury potatoes and carrots, cover and continue simmering for 10 minutes.

5 Add the thyme and waxy potatoes, cover and simmer for 15–20 minutes or until the lamb is very tender. The floury potatoes will break down to thicken the sauce; the waxy potatoes will retain their shape. Remove from the heat and leave to stand, covered, for about 15 minutes.

To serve, check the seasoning and sprinkle generously with chopped parsley

RABBIT WITH GARLIC & THYME

Rabbit is a tender meat that cooks quickly, so I have used a cartouche of greaseproof paper to prevent the cooking liquid evaporating during the short stewing time. However, if you are cooking a stew for a long time, you should use a tight lid rather than a cartouche. With a lid, moisture drips down inside the pan and creates extra liquid, which develops into a rich sauce over time.

4tbsp olive oil

6 rabbit legs

1 onion, thinly sliced

24 garlic cloves, peeled

15 sprigs of thyme

1 bay leaf

1tsp tomato purée

100ml (3½fl oz) dry white wine

6 ripe tomatoes, skinned, seeded, and chopped

600ml (1 pint) chicken stock

6 spring or salad onions, trimmed, with 5cm (2in) of the green stalk still attached

12 baby onions, peeled

55g (2oz) unsalted butter

6 thin slices of Parma or Bayonne ham

1 Heat 2tbsp oil in a wide heavy pan, add the rabbit, and brown on all sides over a medium-high heat. Season and lift out, then drain off the excess fat from the pan.

2 Reduce the heat under the pan, add another 2 tbsp oil and the onion, and cook for 5–6 minutes until softened, stirring occasionally. Add 23 of the garlic cloves and cook for 2 minutes before adding 5 of the thyme sprigs, the bay leaf, tomato purée, and wine.

3 Bring to the boil and simmer for 1 minute until reduced, then return the rabbit to the pan and add the tomatoes and stock. Stir well, cover with a cartouche (see opposite) and simmer for 35–45 minutes until the meat is tender. Remove from the heat.

4 Blanch both kinds of onions in boiling, salted water for 3–4 minutes, then drain. Melt half the butter in a pan and add the onions with 5 sprigs of thyme and the remaining garlic clove (pounded). Cover with buttered greaseproof paper and soften over a low heat for 4–5 minutes.

5 Grill the ham until crisp. Remove the rabbit and garlic from the liquid and keep warm. Pass the liquid through a coarse sieve into a clean pan. Add the onions, the remaining thyme leaves and butter, and bring to the boil.

6 Check the sauce for seasoning then pour over the rabbit and garlic in a warmed serving bowl. Surround with the grilled ham.

How to make a cartouche

It is as easy as child's play to make a cartouche – a disc of greaseproof paper that is cut to be the perfect fit for your pan. Use it instead of, or as well as, the pan lid. When placed in direct contact with the surface of the meat in the pan, it will prevent evaporation. If the meat is not covered by liquid, a cartouche will also help prevent it drying out.

1 Cut a large rectangle of greaseproof paper. Fold it lengthways in half, then fold again crossways in half.

2 With the closed corner as the point, fold the paper diagonally in half, then in half again to make a fan shape.

3 Holding the point over the centre of the pan, cut the paper about 2.5cm (1in) larger than the circumference, using the edge of the pan as a guide. Snip off the point and unfold the paper to reveal a disc with a hole in the middle.

4 Fit the cartouche in the pan so that it rests right on top of the meat and about 2.5cm (1in) up the sides of the pan.

HARE IN RED WINE

This is how I learnt to cook hare at Guy Savoy in Paris – it was served just as it is here, with pommes purées on the side. Now I make it to serve at home to friends – it makes a lovely, rustic winter dish. If you are going to make it, allow plenty of time. The hare needs to marinate for 24 hours and then gently braise for a further 8 hours.

Serves 4–6

| 1 hare, jointed |
| 1 litre (1¾ pints) chicken stock |
| 1 litre (1¾ pints) veal stock |
| 2 shallots, thinly sliced |
| **For the marinade** |
| 3 litres (5¼ pints) red wine |
| 2tbsp olive oil |
| 1 large carrot, finely diced |
| 1 large leek, finely diced |
| 1 onion, finely diced |
| 10 garlic cloves, crushed |
| 1 bouquet garni (p75) |

1 To make the marinade, boil the wine in a saucepan until reduced by half. Heat the oil in a frying pan, add the vegetables and garlic, and cook over a medium-high heat for 5–6 minutes until golden brown. Pour in the wine reduction and boil until reduced by half again, then remove from the heat and pour into a shallow non-metallic container. Add the bouquet garni and leave the marinade to cool.

2 Add the pieces of hare to the cold marinade and turn to coat. Cover tightly and marinate in the refrigerator for 24 hours, turning the pieces of hare occasionally during this time.

3 Transfer the hare and marinade to a large saucepan and pour in the stocks, ensuring that the meat is completely covered (add some water if not). Season, add the shallots, and bring slowly to the boil. Reduce the heat to very low, cover and braise for 8 hours.

BRAISED LAMB SHANKS

This is a superb dish for a family meal, particularly if you like succulent well-done meat that literally falls off the bone. It is simple to prepare as the vegetables are cooked with the meat and the gravy evolves naturally, cutting down on the number of pans that need washing up. When lamb shanks are braised, meat shrinkage is minimal, so a little goes a long way. I wish my mother had known this when feeding the 6 of us.

4 lamb shanks

2tbsp olive oil

1 carrot, cut into 1cm (½in) dice

1 onion, cut into 1cm (½in) dice

2 celery sticks, cut into 1cm (½in) dice

2–3 sprigs of thyme

2 bay leaves

2 garlic cloves, finely chopped

4tbsp tomato purée

750ml (1¼ pints) dry white wine

about 1 litre (1¾ pints) lamb stock or chicken stock

2tbsp very finely chopped rosemary

For the marinade

150ml (5fl oz) olive oil

1 whole head of garlic, smashed with skin on

4 large sprigs of rosemary

2 bay leaves

1 Put the lamb shanks and marinade ingredients in a bowl and turn until the meat is coated. Cover the bowl with cling film and marinate the shanks in the fridge for 24 hours, remembering to turn them occasionally.

2 Heat the oil in a large flameproof casserole dish and sweat the carrot, onion, and celery over a gentle heat for 5 minutes without browning. Add the thyme, bay leaves, garlic, tomato purée, and wine, bring to the boil and simmer until reduced by about half.

3 While the wine is simmering, heat a heavy frying pan over a medium-high heat and add the lamb shanks with their marinade. Season the meat and brown well on all sides. This should take 10–15 minutes. During this time, preheat the oven to 180°C (350°F, gas 4).

4 Transfer the lamb to the casserole dish, cover with stock and bring to the boil. Put on the lid and braise in the oven for 2 hours until the meat is tender. Remove the shanks and keep warm. Skim off excess fat, check seasoning, and boil until reduced to a sauce-like consistency.

Serve the lamb shanks with a generous amount of sauce and a sprinkling of chopped rosemary.

DAUBE OF PORK WITH APRICOTS

Braised dishes like this one are good made ahead and reheated before serving – not only is this convenient if you are working in the week, but the flavour improves with keeping. Start marinating the pork 2 days before you intend to serve it, then cook it the day before.

Serves 6

sunflower oil, for frying

1kg (2¼lb) boned lean pork shoulder, rind removed, cut into 7.5cm (3in) slices

12 dried apricots

300ml (10fl oz) dry white wine

200ml (7fl oz) orange juice

sugar (any kind), to taste

about 250ml (8½fl oz) veal stock

about 250ml (8½fl oz) brown chicken stock

For the marinade

375ml (12½fl oz) full-bodied red wine

250ml (8½fl oz) olive oil

3–4 plum tomatoes, halved lengthways

6 garlic cloves, crushed

1 carrot, sliced

2 celery sticks, chopped

1 leek, trimmed and sliced

1 onion, sliced

tiny pinch of cumin seeds

tiny pinch of fennel seeds

½ bunch of mint, chopped

a few sprigs of thyme

1 bay leaf

1 Heat a small amount of sunflower oil in a heavy roasting pan over a medium-high heat and fry the pork slices in a single layer until a rich dark brown on all sides. This should take 10–15 minutes.

2 Mix the marinade ingredients in a bowl with salt and pepper. Remove the pork from the heat, drain off excess fat, then spoon over the marinade. Cool, cover and marinate in the refrigerator for 24 hours. Boil the apricots, wine, orange juice, and a little sugar in a saucepan, remove from the heat and leave to rehydrate overnight.

3 Preheat the oven to 180°C (350°F, gas 4). Transfer the meat from the marinade to a flameproof casserole dish. Boil the marinade in a saucepan for 15 minutes, skimming off any foam. Add the stocks, bring to the boil, then pour into the casserole, making sure the meat is covered. Cover and braise in the oven for 2 hours.

4 Transfer the pork to a serving dish and keep warm. Pass the liquid through a fine sieve into a saucepan and reheat, boiling until reduced if it seems thin. Add the apricots and heat through, then check the seasoning.

Spoon the apricots and sauce over the pork and serve immediately

BRAISED OXTAIL

This braise is in the oven for a fairly long time, so the vegetables are not cut small or they will disintegrate into the sauce and make it cloudy. The opposite is true for the finely diced vegetable garnish at the end – it is only briefly blanched so the tiny pieces will retain their shapes.

2 oxtails, jointed into 8 (ask your butcher to do this or see step 1)
125g (4½oz) carrots
125g (4½oz) onions
125g (4½oz) celery sticks
125g (4½oz) leeks
3–4 tbsp olive oil or 50g (1¾oz) beef dripping
500g (1lb 2oz) tomatoes
8 sprigs of fresh thyme
2 bay leaves
4 garlic cloves, crushed
300ml (10fl oz) red wine
about 1 litre (1¾ pints) veal stock or chicken stock
For the vegetable garnish
1 carrot, finely diced
1 onion, finely diced
2 celery sticks, finely diced
½ small leek, finely diced
4 tomatoes, skinned, seeded, and finely diced
1 heaped tbsp chopped parsley

CHEF'S TIPS

■ The oxtail can be marinated in the wine and herbs for 48 hours before cooking to deepen its flavour.
■ If you have jointed the oxtail yourself, there will be tail ends. Cook them with the oxtail joints to enrich the sauce with their marrow, then discard them before sieving the sauce.

1 With a cleaver, chop each oxtail into 4 joints, not counting the tail ends. If you locate the space between each joint with your fingers first, you will find it easier to get a clean cut. Season well. Cut the carrots, onions, celery, and leeks into a medium mirepoix (see opposite).

2 Preheat the oven to 180°C (350°F, gas 4). Heat the oil in a large frying pan over a medium-high heat and brown the oxtail well. Let the pieces sit undisturbed until they are brown underneath before turning them. Remove with a slotted spoon and drain in a colander. In the same pan, brown the tail ends, then remove and drain.

3 Add the carrots, onions, celery and leeks, stir well with a spatula to collect the meat residue, then cook until the vegetables are browned. Stir in the tomatoes, thyme, bay leaves, and garlic and continue to cook for a few minutes more.

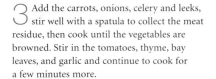

4 Put the oxtail in a flameproof casserole dish and top with the vegetables. Pour in the wine and boil over a high heat until nearly evaporated, then add enough stock to completely cover the meat. Bring to a simmer, cover with the pan lid and braise in the oven for 1½–2 hours until the meat is tender.

Serve the oxtail in warmed bowls, spooning the sauce over and around

5 Lift out the oxtail and keep warm. Pass the sauce through a sieve into a pan and skim off any fat and scum. Boil for 10 minutes until glossy, skimming often. Blanch the garnish vegetables (except the tomatoes) for 5 minutes, then drain and add to the sauce with the tomatoes and parsley. Simmer for 2 minutes.

MIREPOIX

This is a mixture of chopped celery, carrot, leek, and onion. The size of the vegetables varies from very large chunks to bite size according to the length of time the mirepoix is to be cooked – the longer the cooking, the larger the vegetable.

Large

Use in long-cooking stocks. Cut the celery, carrot, and leek into 5cm (2in) chunks. Cut the onion lengthways into quarters.

Medium

Use in braised dishes and stews. Cut the celery in half crossways, then lengthways. Gather the pieces together and cut crossways into 2cm (¾in) dice. Cut the carrot and leek into 5cm (2in) lengths, quarter lengthways and cut crossways into thirds. Halve the onion lengthways, then slice crossways into 2cm (¾in) pieces.

Small

Use for garnishing, keeping the cooking time short. Cut the celery, carrot, and leek into sticks. Stack the sticks and cut crossways into 5mm (¼in) dice. Finely dice the onion using the crosshatch method (p242).

BRAISED SHOULDER OF LAMB

In this classic example of French home cooking, the meat is braised while loosely covered with greaseproof paper. This allows for evaporation of the liquid, which concentrates the sauce at the same time as richly colouring the meat.

Serves 4–6

2 shoulders of baby lamb, bone in

olive oil for frying

24 baby onions, peeled

6 plum tomatoes, skinned, seeded, and chopped

3 garlic cloves, roughly chopped

1tsp cumin seeds

1 fresh chili, cut in half lengthways and seeded

3 sprigs of fresh rosemary

100ml (3½fl oz) Madeira

100ml (3½fl oz) port

200ml (7fl oz) fresh orange juice

500ml (17fl oz) chicken stock

To finish

olive oil, for frying

1 head of garlic, halved crossways

few sprigs of thyme

few bay leaves

1 Preheat the oven to 190°C (375°F, gas 5). Season the lamb well. Take a heavy frying pan large enough to hold a whole shoulder of lamb and place over a high heat. Add olive oil and brown the lamb well on all sides, basting often. Remove and brown the second shoulder, then lay them in a large roasting pan.

2 Put the onions and a little oil in a pan, sprinkle with salt and let the onions colour for 5 minutes. Add the tomatoes, garlic, cumin, chili, and rosemary, stir well and increase the heat. Add the Madeira and port and bring to the boil, then pour over the lamb and put the roasting pan on the stove over a medium-high heat.

3 Pour in the orange juice and stock and bring back to the boil, then cover the pan loosely with greaseproof paper and braise in the oven for 1–1¼ hours, turning the meat occasionally and stirring the vegetables and rosemary around gently at the same time. The lamb is done when the meat on the knuckle bone shrinks away.

4 Remove the lamb from the oven and leave until cold in the pan, then lift out the lamb and place in the refrigerator for 1 hour.

5 Lay the lamb skin-side down on a board. Using a heavy knife or a cleaver, cut each shoulder into 3 at the joints.

CHEF'S TIP

This is a beautiful way to cook a shoulder of young spring lamb, but older lamb can be cooked like this too – an extra-large roasting pan will be essential, or cook the shoulders in separate pans.

Braised shoulder of lamb is a warming and substantial family meal

6 Heat a few spoonfuls of olive oil in a frying pan until very hot and brown the pieces of lamb over a medium-high heat with the garlic, thyme and bay. At the end of frying, the lamb should be almost caramelized.

7 Meanwhile, strain the cooking liquid, reserving the vegetables but not the chili, and boil the liquid until reduced to a sauce-like consistency, skimming of excess fat. Return the vegetables to the sauce and heat through.

8 Serve a chunk of meat in the middle of each bowl with the sauce and vegetables spooned over and around. To get the most out of the meat at the end, pick up the bone as you would chicken – remember this is a homely meal.

BOILING & STEAMING

Boiling, simmering, and poaching are very similar techniques. The main difference is the slight variation in their temperatures: when water is boiling it is 100°C (212°F), whereas simmering water is 85–95°C (185–200°F), and water for poaching should be slightly lower at 77–82°C (170–180°F). In a professional kitchen we use a thermometer for absolutely accurate results, but at home you can judge the difference by eye – boiling liquid moves vigorously, simmering shows a little agitation, while poaching is more of a gentle murmuring.

With any of these three cooking methods, it is important to use the right one for each stage in a recipe. For example, meat may be boiled in the first stage, then the temperature is lowered to a simmer or a poach for the remainder of the cooking time – this is especially useful for tough cuts of meat that need long and low cooking to make them tender. If meat is boiled continuously and vigorously throughout cooking, it becomes stringy and tough.

Meat can also be steamed (ie cooked in the vapour produced by boiling water), but only indirectly. In direct steaming food is placed in a steamer or steaming basket above the water, which would make meat insipid, grey, and unappetizing, but with indirect steaming the food is sealed to protect it – a classic example of this is traditional steak and kidney pudding (p216), in which the meat is encased in suet pastry so that it cooks in its own juices to become rich and tender.

BOILING A HAM HOCK

Ham hocks are usually cooked in a lot less time than in my recipe here, but I have found that the gentler the heat and the longer they cook, the more juicy and tender the meat becomes. I use boiled ham for a variety of different things – sliced hot off the bone, it makes an inexpensive and homely meal served with fresh parsley sauce and boiled potatoes, while shredded ham is good in sandwiches and soups such as traditional pea and ham (for which I also use the strained ham stock).

2 ham hocks, each 1kg (2¼lb)
1 large onion
1 large carrot
1 large leek
2 celery sticks
10 sprigs of thyme
3 bay leaves
12 white peppercorns
handful of parsley stalks
about 2 litres (3½ pints) chicken stock

1 Put the ham hocks in a large bowl, cover with cold water and leave to soak in the refrigerator for 24 hours.

2 Remove the hocks, rinse in cold water, and put them in a large saucepan. Cover with cold water and bring to the boil, then simmer for 5 minutes until the scum rises to the surface. Drain and rinse, then return to the cleaned-out pan and add the remaining ingredients with enough stock to cover.

3 Bring to the boil, cover, and simmer over a very low heat for 2½ hours. To check if the ham is cooked, lift out the hocks and pull out the small bone that lies next to the knuckle bone – it should come away easily. To serve the ham hot, slice it thickly off the bone, stripping off the skin and fat first.

4 To shred the ham for use in sandwiches, soups, and terrines, leave the hocks in the stock until they are almost cool, then lift them out on to a board. Pull the meat away from the bones with your hands and shred it into chunky pieces, discarding all skin and fat.

Caramelized boiled bacon

Here I have taken a salty piece of bacon, boiled then pressed it overnight, then coated it in perfumed spices and a sweet and sour caramel – flavours that everyone loves. The presentation is pure Pétrus.

Serves 6

3 carrots

2 large onions

2 celery sticks

1 large leek

12 black peppercorns, lightly crushed

2 bay leaves

1 small bunch of fresh thyme

3kg (6½lb) slab of smoked streaky bacon, soaked in cold water overnight

For the spice mixture

10g (¼oz) ground cinnamon

10g (¼oz) ground star anise

10g (¼oz) ground coriander

For the sweet and sour caramel

100ml (3½fl oz) port

100ml (3½fl oz) clear honey

100ml (3½fl oz) rice wine vinegar

Cut the carrots, onions, celery and leek into a large mirepoix (p211) and put them in a very large saucepan with the peppercorns, bay leaves, and thyme. Drain the bacon and place in the pan, then fill the pan almost to the top with cold water. Bring to the boil, reduce the heat, and simmer uncovered for 2 hours or until the bacon is tender when pierced. During simmering, remove scum and top up the water to keep the bacon covered.

Remove the bacon, place in a shallow tray and place another tray on top. Put weights on the top tray to press the bacon down, leave until cold, then refrigerate overnight.

The next day, let the bacon come to room temperature. Strip off the skin and any dry meat underneath and around the sides, to reveal the pink flesh. Cut the bacon into 5 strips, each 4cm (1½in) wide, following the grain of the rashers. Square off the edges to make neat rectangles.

Mix the spices together and season the rashers (you will not need all of the mix at this stage).

Heat the caramel ingredients in a saucepan, pour half into a frying pan and bubble over a high heat until reduced by half. Put 1 bacon strip in the frying pan and let it sit undisturbed until it turns golden brown underneath, adding a little more caramel from the saucepan if it gets brown too quickly. Turn the bacon over and repeat, sprinkling with more spice mix as the sauce caramelizes. Repeat with the remaining strips. Cool the strips a little before slicing crossways against the grain.

At Pétrus we serve the bacon on red onion tartes Tatin and garnish with parsnips and baby carrots. We decorate the plate with Banyuls sauce, a classic red wine sauce made with Banyuls wine instead of Bordeaux.

STEAK & KIDNEY PUDDING

This was on the menu at The Savoy when I worked there. It was made in large pots of 8–10 portions, which were wheeled around the restaurant on trolleys.

1 quantity of suet pastry (see below)

For the filling

400g (14oz) chuck or best braising steak

125g (4½oz) trimmed veal or ox kidney

1 onion, thinly sliced

leaves from 6 sprigs of fresh thyme

1 garlic clove, finely chopped

3–4tbsp seasoned plain flour

Worcestershire sauce to taste

1 egg yolk, beaten

Guinness gravy (see opposite) to serve

1 Divide the suet pastry in half and roll each piece into a rectangle about 3mm (⅛in) thick. Leave to rest for 10 minutes, then cut out four 18cm (7in) discs and four 7.5cm (3in) discs. Leave the discs to rest for 10 minutes on a floured tray, then cover with cling film and chill in the refrigerator.

SUET PASTRY

300g (10½oz) self-raising flour
150g (5½oz) shredded beef suet

Make the pastry by sifting the flour and a pinch of salt into a large bowl. Add the suet and some black pepper and mix until evenly blended, then add a few drops of cold water and mix in with your hands. Continue adding water a few drops at a time until the mixture comes together as a dough – it should not be too sticky. Knead until you have a smooth elastic dough that leaves the bowl clean.

2 Chop the steak and kidney into small cubes (save the trimmings for the gravy), mix in a bowl with the onion, thyme, and garlic, then toss in enough seasoned flour to coat evenly.

3 Stretch out 3 layers of cling film and use to line 4 wetted dariole moulds, letting it overhang generously. Line each mould with a large pastry disc, pushing it in around the bottom edge and pressing it against the sides so that it forms a smooth layer and protrudes 1cm (½in) above the rim. Discard the trimmings.

5 Brush inside each pastry rim with egg yolk, put a small disc on top, and press and pinch to seal to the pastry lining. Trim the edges with scissors and brush with more egg yolk. Now roll the pastry over towards the middle to make a border, and press down to seal.

6 Wrap each mould in a double thickness of cling film, pulling it very tight to exclude all air. This will prevent water getting into the puddings and making the pastry soggy, and it will also stop the flavours of the filling ingredients leaching out.

Guinness gravy

steak and kidney trimmings (see opposite)

3–4 shallots, finely chopped

3 garlic cloves, crushed

1 sprig of thyme

1 bay leaf

10 white peppercorns, crushed

660ml (1 pint) Guinness

500ml (17fl oz) red wine

1 litre (1¾ pints) chicken stock

1 litre (1¾ pints) veal stock

good pinch of sugar

Put the meat trimmings in a saucepan with the shallots, garlic, herbs, peppercorns and some sea salt. Sweat down over a low heat for about 10 minutes, then increase the heat and cook until caramelized. Add the Guinness and boil to reduce by three-quarters, then add the wine and reduce in the same way. Repeat with the 2 stocks until the gravy has the consistency you like. Strain the gravy, then taste and add sugar and a seasoning of salt and pepper.

4 Divide the filling between the moulds and pour in enough cold water to come three-quarters of the way up each one. Sprinkle with a few drops of Worcestershire sauce.

Serve the puddings plain, or as presented here. Stand each one on a bed of wilted spinach, surround with blanched diced carrot, swede, and celery, and top with an oyster. Spoon the gravy over and garnish with rosemary sprigs.

7 Stand the puddings in the top of a steamer over boiling water, cover with the lid and steam for 2½ hours, topping up the water as necessary. To unmould, unwrap the cling film and open it out at the top, then turn the puddings out upside down on plates and gently ease the film off the sides.

BEEF STROGANOFF

Stroganoff was one of the first things I learnt to cook at catering college. The raw ingredients were cooked in front of guests in the dining room, and the meat was flambéed with brandy.

1tbsp olive oil
50g (1¾oz) unsalted butter
2 large onions, thinly sliced
250g (8½oz) small button mushrooms, thinly sliced
1kg (2¼lb) fillet steak, in one piece (see below)
2tbsp chopped curly parsley
120ml (4fl oz) double cream

CUTTING FILLET STEAK

To get even-sized pieces of meat, it is best to cut it yourself. Cut the fillet crossways into 7.5cm (3in) pieces, then cut each piece into slices against the grain, about 7.5cm (3in) square and 2.5cm (1in) thick. Lay the slices flat and cut the squares into 7.5x2.5cm (3x1in) strips.

1 Heat the oil and half the butter in a large frying pan over a medium-high heat and fry the onions until translucent. Add the mushrooms and fry for 2–3 minutes until beginning to soften. Remove the onions and mushrooms from the pan with a slotted spoon.

2 Add the rest of the butter to the pan and heat until beginning to foam. Add the steak and sauté quickly over a high heat for 3–4 minutes until browned on all sides.

3 Return the onions and mushrooms to the pan, and stir and shake to mix with the meat. Sprinkle with the parsley, pour in the cream, and cook for a further minute. Season well before serving.

Stroganoff is a great
dish to serve straight
from the pan

GRILLING

Prime, tender cuts of meat are suitable for grilling, which is either cooking under the grill, on the grid of a barbecue, or on a ridged cast-iron grill pan on top of the stove. All three of these methods are fast ways of cooking and the heat is intense, so care needs to be taken that the meat does not dry out, particularly as prime cuts are mostly lean. Marinating before grilling is a sure way to safeguard against dryness, coupled with basting during cooking.

CHAR-GRILLING STEAKS

A ridged cast-iron grill pan mimics a barbecue by imprinting charred lines on the meat. The technique shown here with sirloin steaks can be applied to the grill or barbecue, as you prefer. The cooking time is for rare steaks – if you like yours cooked more, add a minimum of 2 minutes.

1 Heat the grill pan over a high heat until very hot. Brush steaks on both sides with a little groundnut oil and season with salt and pepper.

2 Put the steaks on the pan, arranging them diagonally across the ridges. Cook for 1 minute, then turn them at a 45° angle and cook for another 1–2 minutes. Now turn the steaks over and repeat on the other side. Remove the steaks from the pan and leave to rest in a warm place for a few minutes before serving.

GUIDELINES FOR GOOD GRILLING

■ Ensure the grill or pan is hot before starting to cook. Barbecue coals should be ash grey.
■ Always oil the meat before cooking, not the pan, grid, or rack. This will help prevent smoking.
■ Season meat just before cooking, or immediately after. If meat is salted and left for any length of time before cooking the juices will be drawn out and the meat will be dry.

■ When cooking on a char-grill pan or the barbecue, allow time for the meat to brown underneath before turning it over. If moved too soon, it will stick.
■ Use tongs to turn the meat. A fork will pierce the flesh and cause the juices to flow.
■ When cooking meat for an extended time under the grill, lower the rack or pan away from the heat source rather than lowering the temperature of the grill.

ENTRECÔTE STEAKS BORDELAISE

This is a very rich dish for real meat lovers. With its beefy flavour, the melt-in-the-mouth marrow provides an extra element of indulgence, and it goes really well with the red wine sauce.

4 sirloin (entrecôte) steaks, 340g (12oz) each, trimmed of fat

1tbsp groundnut oil

50g (1¾oz) butter

340g (12oz) fresh ceps, cleaned (p249) and sliced lengthways

225g (8oz) marrow bone (see opposite)

2tbsp chopped flat-leaf parsley

For the Bordelaise sauce

115g (4oz) butter

8 shallots, finely chopped

6 garlic cloves, lightly crushed

300ml (10fl oz) red Bordeaux wine

1 bouquet garni (p75)

24 white peppercorns, crushed

6 sprigs of fresh thyme

1 sprig of fresh rosemary

175ml (6fl oz) veal stock

175ml (6fl oz) chicken stock

1 Make the sauce by melting half the butter in a large pan, adding the shallots and garlic, and cooking over a low heat for 5 minutes, turning often. Add the wine, bouquet garni, peppercorns, thyme, and rosemary, bring to the boil, and reduce to a syrupy consistency.

2 Pour in the stocks and simmer gently for 40 minutes over a low heat, skimming constantly. Remove the bouquet garni and herb stalks, leaving in the shallots, garlic, thyme, and rosemary leaves. Finish the sauce by whisking in the remaining butter.

3 Char-grill the steaks 2 at a time (see left). While the steaks are resting, heat the oil and butter in a frying pan and sauté the ceps until golden brown. Sprinkle with sea salt and drain on kitchen paper.

4 Slice each steak diagonally against the grain into 4 or 5 thick slices, using a gentle sawing action with the knife.

To serve, arrange the steak slices on warmed plates and top with the marrow. Ladle over the sauce, garnish with the ceps, and sprinkle with the parsley.

PREPARING MARROW

Dig pieces of the marrow out of the bone with a spoon into a small saucepan of cold water. Bring to the boil, remove the marrow, and set aside to cool.

SPIT ROASTING

A cross between grilling and conventional roasting, spit roasting uses either a rotisserie attachment in the oven, in which case the heat source is the grill above the meat, or an electrically operated spit on the barbecue, where the heat comes from the coals below. Both of these modern techniques mimic the original method of roasting meat on a spit over an open fire. Suitable joints are loin of pork, tunnel-boned leg of lamb, and boned and rolled rib eye of beef. With these, there is little shrinkage, and the fat responds well to the direct heat.

BRINING PORK FOR SPIT ROASTING

Soaking fresh pork in a brine of salt, sugar, spices, and herbs gives the meat a "cured" flavour and a brighter pink colour, as well as having a tenderizing effect. Brining is not an essential technique before spit roasting, but I think of it like soaking in a warm bath – it enables the muscles to relax. The more the meat relaxes the more tender it will be. It will also be easier to carve.

2.5kg (5½lb) pork loin, boned, with rind scored (p198)

For the brine

100g (3½oz) granulated sugar
100g (3½oz) coarse sea salt
20 black peppercorns
10 juniper berries
4 star anise
2tbsp fennel seeds
20 coriander seeds
10 sprigs of rosemary
10 sprigs of thyme
5 bay leaves
1 litre (1¾ pints) boiling water
about 4 litres (7¾ pints) cold water

3 Pour in the boiling water and stir until the sugar and salt have dissolved, then pour in the cold water.

4 Put the pork in the brine. If it is not covered, pour in more cold water until it is. Cover and keep in the refrigerator for 48 hours.

5 Remove the pork from the brine and dry it well. Allow the meat to come to room temperature before cooking. Retain brine for basting.

1 Form the pork into a sausage shape by rolling and pressing it together with your hands, then tie at regular intervals with kitchen string. Do not tie too tightly.

2 Put all the dry ingredients for the brine in a stainless steel pan or stockpot that is large enough to take the pork.

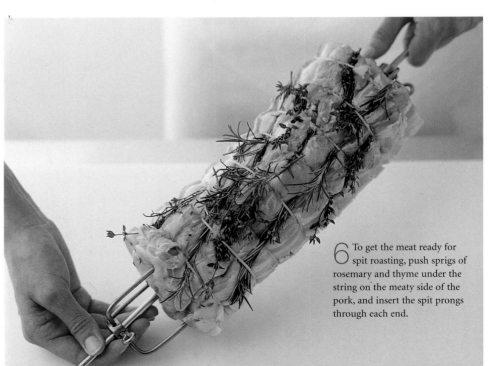

6 To get the meat ready for spit roasting, push sprigs of rosemary and thyme under the string on the meaty side of the pork, and insert the spit prongs through each end.

SPIT-ROASTED BRINE-CURED PORK

Once spit roasting is under way, the fat on the pork begins to melt and self baste the joint as it turns round. Do not worry if the herbs start to singe – this all adds to the flavour.

Serves 6–8

I brine-cured pork loin (see opposite)
5 sprigs of rosemary
5 sprigs of thyme
fresh bay leaves to garnish

1 Prepare the pork for spit roasting with sprigs of rosemary and thyme (see step 6, opposite).

2 Preheat the grill or get the barbecue ready for cooking. Spit roast the pork, with a drip tray underneath, for 2 hours. Baste often with the reserved brine to keep the meat moist and prevent burning.

3 When the roast is cooked, leave it to rest in a warm place for 15–30 minutes before removing the string and serving.

CHEF'S TIP

Serve roast vegetables with the pork. Chop 8 carrots and 1 large leek and mix in a roasting pan with 4 red onions, quartered, 3 heads of garlic, and a few sprigs of rosemary and thyme. Coat with pork juices and roast in an oven at 200°C (400°F, gas 6) for 1 hour. Before serving, press the garlic out of its skin and mix with the rest of the vegetables.

Succulent spit-roasted pork is served garnished with fresh bay leaves and carved into medium-thick slices

CHINESE COOKING

KEN HOM

Chinese cookery is a sophisticated cuisine involving a number of cooking methods that are relatively uncommon in the West. Several different techniques may be used in the preparation of a single dish, but most of them can be easily mastered with a little practice. When planning a meal, it is more challenging to select dishes that use a range of techniques. Limit yourself to one stir-fried dish per meal until you have become accustomed to this method of cooking.

Meticulous preparation The initial preparation of foods is probably more important and more time-consuming in Chinese cookery than in any other cuisine. Although many dishes are cooked rapidly, this presupposes that every ingredient has been properly prepared beforehand – usually chopped into smallish, well-shaped pieces to ensure even and quick cooking. Food can then be cooked in the minimum time to preserve its natural texture and taste.

Careful cutting also enhances the visual appeal of a dish. This is why most Chinese cooks are so specific about cutting techniques, particularly where vegetables are concerned. The Chinese use a cleaver for cutting, wielding it with skill and dexterity. Of course, a sharp knife can be used instead. Chinese meals traditionally consist of a soup; a rice, noodle, or bread dish; a vegetable dish; and at least two other dishes, which may be mainly meat, fish, or chicken. The meal may be preceded by and concluded with tea, but soup – really a broth – will be the only beverage during the meal itself. Soup is drunk not as a first course but throughout the meal. The exception to this is a banquet, when soup, if it is served at all, comes at the end of the meal or as a palate cleanser at several points during the dinner. On such occasions, wine, spirits, beer, or fruit juice will be drunk with the food. At banquets (which are really elaborate dinner parties), there may be as many as 8–12 courses. Dishes are served one at a time so that the individual qualities of each dish can be properly savoured. Rice will not be served except at the end of the meal, when fried rice might be offered. At ordinary meals, all the dishes comprising the meal are served together, including the soup. The food is placed in the centre of the table. Everyone has their own rice bowl, into which they put a generous amount of steamed rice. Then, using chopsticks, they each help themselves to a little of one dish, transferring this to their rice bowls. Once this has been eaten together with some of the rice, they will have a chopstick-full of another dish. Eating is a communal affair, and each diner takes care to see that everyone at the table receives a fair share of each dish.

Creating Chinese meals When devising a Chinese meal, aim for a good mix of textures, flavours, colours, and shapes. Apart from a staple, such as steamed rice, choose a variety of meat, poultry, and fish. It is better to serve one meat and one fish dish rather than two meat dishes, even if the meats are different. It also will be a better-balanced meal (and easier to prepare) if you use a variety of cooking methods. Serve a stir-fried dish with a braised, steamed, or cold dish. It is a good idea to select one or two things that can be prepared in advance.

You do not need any special crockery or cutlery to enjoy Chinese food, although I think it tastes decidedly better when it is eaten with chopsticks, rather than a fork. Knives are unnecessary since Chinese food is always cut into bite-sized pieces before it is served. Each person will need a rice bowl, a soup bowl, a teacup if you are serving tea, and a small plate for any bones and such. A small dish or saucer each will be needed if you serve dipping sauces. Soup or cereal bowls will do for the rice and soup. Chopsticks are usually set to the right of the rice bowl. A spoon – metal or china – will be needed for soup and as an adjunct to chopsticks for noodles. The Chinese help themselves (and others) to food using their own chopsticks. Some people provide separate serving chopsticks but these are often abandoned in the enthusiasm of communal eating.

MENU

- Steamed fish with spring onions & ginger

- Stir-fried broccoli

- Red-braised chiu chow duck

- Sichuan green beans

- Steeped chicken with Cantonese-style sauce

SLICING

Food is cut into fine slices on a chopping board. Slicing meat across the grain cuts its fibres and makes it more tender.

When using a cleaver, keep your index finger over the top of the blade for greater control. Hold the food with your other hand, using your knuckles to guide the cutting edge and turning your fingers under for safety.

STIR-FRYING

Stir-frying depends upon having all the ingredients prepared, measured, and immediately to hand, and upon having a good source of fierce heat. Properly executed, stir-fried foods can be cooked in minutes in very little oil so they retain their natural flavours and textures. Use a steep-sided wok or pan for stir-frying. Groundnut oil is best; corn and sunflower oil will do, but not olive oil.

1 Heat the wok or pan and add the groundnut oil, spreading it evenly with a spatula. When the oil is very hot, add any flavourings, such as garlic, ginger, chili, or spring onions, and quickly toss.

2 Add the recipe's ingredients and toss them across the wok or pan, moving the food from the centre to the sides. When stir-frying meat, rest each side for just a few seconds before continuing to stir.

3 Some stir-fried foods, such as this broccoli dish, benefit from the addition of a little water before the wok or pan is covered. This late steaming, combined with the earlier frying, perfects the dish.

SHREDDING

The shredding process is like the French julienne technique, in which food is cut into thin, fine, matchstick-like shreds.

Pile slices of food on top of each other and cut into fine strips. Some foods shred better if stiffened in the freezer for about 20 minutes.

STEAMING

Along with stir-frying and deep-frying, steaming is the most widely used Chinese cooking technique. Steaming works with a gentle, moist heat. It is an excellent method for bringing out subtle flavours and so is particularly appropriate for fish. The Chinese use bamboo steamers in woks, but a large roasting pan or pot is just as good. It is important that the simmering water never makes contact with the food.

1 Place a bamboo steamer or a metal or wooden rack into a wok holding 5cm (2in) water. Bring the water to a simmer.

2 Put the food to be steamed onto a heatproof plate and place it on the rack. Cover the steamer or wok tightly with a lid.

3 Occasionally check the water level and replenish if needed. Remove any water from the plate when the food is cooked.

STEAMED FISH WITH SPRING ONIONS AND GINGER

Steaming fish is a favourite Chinese cookery tradition. It is a simple, gentle technique that preserves the pure flavours of the fish while keeping it both moist and tender.

450g (1lb) firm white fish fillets, such as cod or sole, or a 900g (2lb) whole fish, such as sole or turbot

1tsp coarse sea salt or plain salt

1–1½tbsp finely shredded fresh ginger

3tbsp finely shredded spring onions

1tbsp light soy sauce

1tbsp dark soy sauce

1tbsp groundnut oil

2tsp toasted sesame oil

handful of coriander sprigs

1 Pat the fish fillets or whole fish dry with kitchen paper. Rub both sides evenly with the salt, and the inside as well if you are steaming a whole fish.

2 Put the fish onto a heatproof plate and scatter the ginger evenly over the top.

3 Put the plate of fish into the steamer. Cover tightly and gently steam the fish until it is just cooked. Fillets take about 5–8 minutes to cook, depending on thickness. Whole fish take 10–14 minutes.

4 Remove the plate of cooked fish, pour off any excess liquid that may have accumulated on it, and scatter the spring onions on the fish together with the light and dark soy sauces. Set aside.

5 Now heat the groundnut and sesame oils together in a small saucepan. When they are hot – almost smoking – pour this mixture on top of the fish.

6 Scatter with the coriander and serve at once.

STIR-FRIED BROCCOLI

Stir-frying is one of the most appealing ways to prepare broccoli. The secret to success with this simple dish is the late addition of water to round off the cooking process with 4–5 minutes of steaming.

450g (1lb) broccoli

1–1½ tbsp groundnut oil

4 garlic cloves, peeled and lightly crushed

1tsp salt

½tsp freshly ground black pepper

6tbsp water

2tsp toasted sesame oil

1 Separate the broccoli into small florets and peel and slice the stems. Heat a wok or frying pan over high heat until it is hot. Add the groundnut oil and, when it is almost smoking, add the garlic, salt, and pepper.

2 Stir-fry for 30 seconds or until the garlic is lightly browned. Add the broccoli and stir-fry for 2 minutes. Add the water, cover tightly with a lid, and cook over high heat for 4–5 minutes.

3 Stir in the sesame oil and stir-fry for 30 seconds, then serve.

RED-BRAISED CHIU CHOW DUCK

Throughout China and Southeast Asia – and in Chinatowns all over the world – you will see this red-braised duck hanging from hooks in the windows of food shops and restaurants. It is easy to make at home and can be served warm or at room temperature. Rock sugar, which has a richer, more subtle flavour than granulated sugar, gives a lustrous glaze to red-cooked dishes such as this. You can find rock sugar in Chinese shops.

1 duck, 1.6–1.8kg (3½–4lb), preferably organic, fresh or frozen and thawed

1.2 litres (2 pints) groundnut oil

For the sauce

1.2 litres (2 pints) chicken stock

1.2 litres (2 pints) dark soy sauce

300ml (10fl oz) light soy sauce

450ml (15fl oz) Shaoxing rice wine or dry sherry, or 210ml (7½fl oz) dry sherry mixed with 210ml (7½fl oz) chicken stock

100g (3½oz) rock sugar (or granulated sugar)

5 star anise

3 pieces of cassia or cinnamon sticks

2tbsp fennel seeds

1tbsp cumin seeds

coriander sprigs to garnish

1 Using a cleaver, chop the duck in half lengthways. Dry the halves well with kitchen paper.

2 Heat the oil in a wok or large frying pan until it is almost smoking. Add the duck halves, skin-side down. Turn the heat down to medium and deep-fry slowly for 15–20 minutes, or until the skin is lightly browned. Do not turn the pieces over, but baste the duck with the hot oil as it fries. Drain the duck on kitchen paper.

3 Mix together all the sauce ingredients in a large pot or wok and bring to the boil. Add the duck halves. Turn the heat down so the sauce is gently simmering and cover the pot or wok. Braise the duck for 1 hour, or until it is tender and cooked through, occasionally skimming off fat from the surface of the sauce.

4 When the duck is cooked, skim off any remaining surface fat, then remove the duck pieces with a slotted spoon. Allow them to cool slightly before chopping them into smaller serving-size pieces.

5 Arrange the pieces of duck on a warm platter, garnish with coriander, and serve. Alternatively, leave the duck to cool to room temperature before serving.

SICHUAN GREEN BEANS

Chinese asparagus or long beans are traditionally used in this tasty dish from western China, but green beans are equally good.

600ml (1 pint) groundnut oil
450g (1lb) green beans
2tbsp chopped garlic
1tbsp finely chopped fresh ginger
3tbsp finely chopped spring onions, white part only
1½tbsp chili bean sauce
1tbsp whole yellow bean sauce
2tbsp Shaoxing rice wine or dry sherry
1tbsp dark soy sauce
2tsp granulated sugar
1tbsp water
2tsp chili oil

1 Heat a wok or large frying pan over high heat and add the oil. When it is very hot and slightly smoking, add half the green beans and deep-fry for 3–4 minutes, or until they are slightly wrinkled. Remove with a slotted spoon to drain. Deep-fry the remaining beans and drain. Set aside.

2 Pour off the oil from the wok and reserve. Clean the wok, then return about 1tbsp of the oil and heat it. Add the garlic, ginger, and spring onions and stir-fry for about 30 seconds.

3 Add the rest of the flavouring ingredients and stir-fry for another 30 seconds.

4 Return the green beans to the wok and stir until they are thoroughly coated with the spicy mixture. Serve as soon as the beans are heated through.

CHOPPING

This term denotes completely cutting through food, and is usually applied to whole birds or cooked food with bones.

1 Using a heavy-duty cleaver or knife, chop with a straight, sharp, downward motion.

2 To chop through bones, hit with the blade, then strike with your hand or a mallet on the back edge of the cleaver or knife.

DEEP-FRYING

In China a wok is used for deep-frying, one of the most important techniques in Chinese cooking. The trick is to regulate the heat of the oil so that the surface of the food does not brown so fast that the food is uncooked inside. Fresh, clean oil gives the best results.

1 To prevent splattering, dry food thoroughly with kitchen paper before adding to hot oil. If the food is in a marinade, drain it well. When using a batter, dip in the food, then hold it up so excess batter can drip off.

2 Wait for the oil to get hot enough before adding the food. At the right temperature, the oil should give off a haze and almost produce little wisps of smoke. You can test by dropping in a small piece of food. If it bubbles all over, the oil is sufficiently hot. During frying, adjust the heat as necessary to prevent the oil from smoking or overheating.

3 Do not turn large pieces, but instead baste them with the hot oil as they fry.

4 Using tongs or a slotted spoon, remove the fried food from the hot oil and drain it on kitchen paper. Serve as soon as possible.

RED-BRAISING

Used for tougher cuts of meat, poultry, and certain vegetables, this cooking method gives food a reddish-brown colour. The food is usually browned first, then simmered in a dark liquid based on soy sauce, and flavoured with strong seasonings and spices. The braising sauce can be saved and frozen, then reused many times, becoming richer in flavour.

1 Combine the sauce ingredients in a wok or large pot and bring to the boil. Add the browned food, reduce the heat, and cover the wok.

2 Simmer gently until cooked. If necessary, skim off any fat from the surface of the sauce.

3 Remove the red-braised food. Once the sauce is cool, skim off fat, then save for future use.

STEEPING

In steeping, foods are immersed in liquid (usually stock but sometimes Shaoxing yellow rice wine) and simmered for a short time, then removed from the heat. The heat remaining in the liquid finishes off the cooking process. Delicate foods with a subtle taste lend themselves best to steeping; chicken is the most used, but fish, seafood, and even very thin slices of meat can also be steeped.

1 Place the food (in this case a whole chicken) in a large pot and immerse in stock or water.

2 Bring to the boil, then cover tightly and simmer for a short time, about 20 minutes. Remove from the heat and leave tightly covered for 1 hour to complete the cooking.

3 Remove the food from the pot and plunge into a bowl of ice-filled water to cool thoroughly.

4 Lift the food from the iced water and drain well.

5 Prepare the food according to the recipe and serve.

CANTONESE-STYLE SAUCE

The pure, simple flavours of steeped chicken call for a pungent counterpoint in the dipping sauce. Spring onions and fresh ginger, jolted to a full fragrance by a quick dousing of hot groundnut oil, offer the perfect flavour combination.

4tbsp finely chopped spring onions, white part only

2tsp finely chopped fresh ginger

2tsp salt

2tbsp groundnut oil

1 Place the spring onions, ginger, and salt in a bowl and mix well.

2 Heat a wok until it is hot, add the groundnut oil and spread it around the wok's base.

3 When the oil is very hot and slightly smoking, pour it on the ingredients in the bowl and mix well. Pour the sauce into a bowl and serve.

STEEPED CHICKEN

This is a classic Cantonese chicken dish that my mother often made. The gentlest possible heat is used so that the chicken remains extremely moist and flavourful with a satiny, almost velvet-like, texture. It is not difficult to make. When finished, save the cooking liquid for cooking rice or as a base for chicken stock.

1 chicken, 1.6–1.8kg (3½–4lb), preferably organic

1tbsp salt

chicken stock or water to cover

6 whole spring onions

6 slices of fresh ginger

freshly ground black pepper, to taste

1 Rub the chicken all over with the salt, aiming to achieve an even covering.

2 Place the chicken in a large pot, cover with chicken stock or water and bring to the boil. Add the spring onions, ginger slices, and a few grinds of black pepper. Cover the pot tightly and reduce the heat to simmer for 20 minutes.

3 Remove from the heat and leave the chicken in the pot, still tightly covered, for 1 hour.

4 Lift the chicken from the stock and immediately plunge it into a large bowl of iced water to cool the chicken thoroughly.

5 Remove the chicken, drain well, and pat dry with kitchen paper. Discard the water in which it was cooling.

6 Place the chicken on a chopping board, cut into bite-sized pieces, arranging these on a platter. Serve the chicken pieces with Cantonese-style dipping sauce (see opposite) on the side.

VEGETABLES

CHARLIE TROTTER

I have long been an advocate of small farms and organic farming, as much from the standpoint of flavour as that of politics. Just as foods are absolutely at their best at the height of their season, they also taste better when they are naturally raised. You can't fudge it with the seasons – tomatoes are available for only six weeks, not 12 months of the year. Farmers who embrace sustainable agriculture and grow natural, organic produce are forced to go by the rules of nature.

Traditional varieties Many organic farmers produce varieties of vegetables that have never been hybridized to extend their growing season, withstand frost, or "improve" their qualities in other ways. Many of these traditional varieties are astonishing in their appearance and flavour. For example, most people think that tomatoes are available year round and come in only one colour: red. Little do they know that there are 80–90 seasonal varieties of tomato native to the North America, such as Purple Cherokee, Yellow Taxi, Tiger Stripe, and Sunburst, and European varieties such as the Russian Black Prince and the Italian Principe Borghese. Some are meaty, some have very thin skin; others are high in acid, or so sweet you can eat them as a dessert. There are also various traditional strands of sweetcorn, squashes, and lettuce, amongst many others.

Traditional varieties tend not to be available in large supermarkets, but increasingly small farmers are bringing their wares to farmers' markets. Food doesn't get any fresher, coming straight from the ground or right off the tree. Serve meat or fish with farmers' market vegetables, perhaps braised cabbage or caramelized onions, and you will find that the flavours just explode. It won't be long before you will be experimenting and having fun with all the delicious vegetables now to be found. Always buy vegetables in season, when they are of the highest quality, have the best flavour, and typically cost less than when purchased out of season. Look for bright, vibrant colours, and avoid yellowing, especially in cauliflower and leafy greens – these should be young and tender. Ensure that members of the cabbage and root families are firm and unblemished, and that beans are firm and bright with no blemishes or soft spots. Corn-on-the-cob should be freshly picked, with small firm kernels; there should be no sign of mould, or brown silks overlaying the kernels.

Storing vegetables Most fresh vegetables, including winter squashes and members of the onion family, should ideally be kept in a larder at 10–18°C (50–65°F). If you don't have a larder, keep the vegetables in a cool, dry place with ample ventilation. Other vegetables should be stored in the refrigerator, which is colder and has a higher humidity than a larder. Cover or wrap different vegetable types and store them separately. Keep greens and other delicate vegetables away from tomatoes, which release ethylene gas that causes green vegetables to wilt. Keep potatoes in the larder because fridge temperatures break down their texture and flavour.

Vegetables are ideally purchased in season when they are fully ripe, but tomatoes, and some fruits, are ripened in the home. Store unripe tomatoes at room temperature. The ethylene gas produced by tomatoes is a ripening agent, and placing a ripe tomato with unripe ones in a box or brown paper bag helps to speed up the ripening of all the unripe ones.

Preparing vegetables Some vegetables are peeled to remove their tough skin. Peeling also serves to remove skin that might contain traces of pesticides and other chemicals that cannot be removed by washing. Otherwise, before washing, you can spray them using a spray bottle containing one part lemon juice to five parts water. This mixture will aid the removal of wax, surface contaminants, and moisture-resistant chemicals, some of which are otherwise stored in the body.

Delay the washing, peeling, and cutting of vegetables until just before cooking, as exposure to air and moisture causes vegetables to deteriorate and lose their vitamins. Discolouration can be minimized by immersing the vegetables in water to which lemon juice or vinegar has been added.

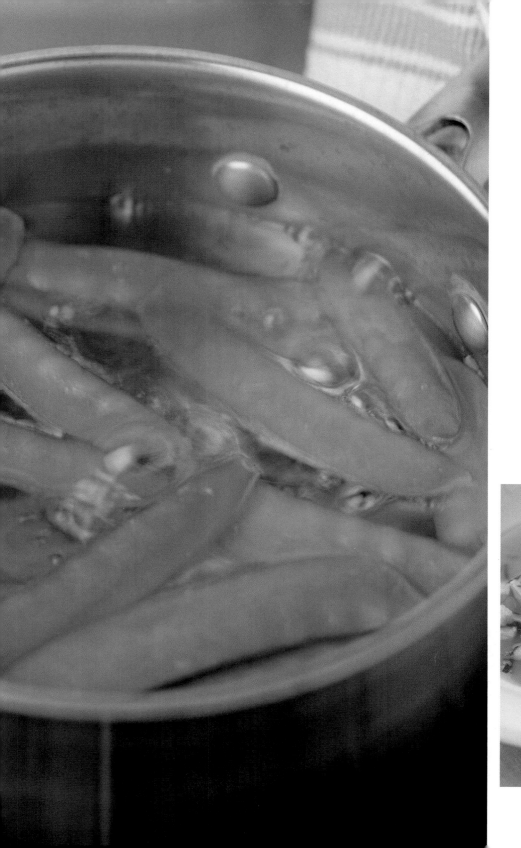

LEAFY VEGETABLES

Vegetables in this family are often used in salads. The most common of these is lettuce, but there is also a wonderful variety of other salad leaves, in all shapes, sizes, and colours.

Heartier leafy greens – such as kale, spinach, dandelion, Swiss chard leaves, spring greens, and sorrel – are usually richly coloured. They range in flavour from piquant to peppery, and even bitter.

TRIMMING, WASHING & DRYING SALAD LEAVES

Greens intended for a salad need to be trimmed and broken or cut into manageable pieces. Leaves that typically have the rib cut out include large cos, frisée, and radicchio. After thorough washing, the leaves must be dried well to prevent the salad dressing from being diluted. This method of washing and drying is also suitable for leafy greens such as spinach and sorrel.

1 Trim off the ends of the leaves, discarding any that are discoloured. If leaves are tough, separate them and cut out the rib from each one. Break or cut the leaves to the desired size.

2 Gather the salad greens loosely and hold under running water or immerse in cool water. Shake or swirl gently to loosen dirt.

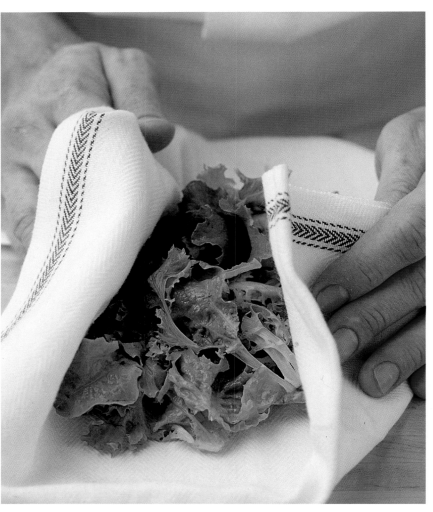

3 Drain the leaves in a colander, then pat dry in a clean tea towel or with kitchen paper. Alternatively, use a salad spinner to dry the leaves.

Dressing a salad

The most basic form of a salad is lettuce tossed in vinaigrette (p51). But there is an incredible variety of greens available for salads today. And you don't have to limit yourself just to greens – many roots and tubers, peppers, and other vegetables also make wonderful bases for salads. For complexity, add cooked meat, fish, cheese, nuts, and fruit. Have fun mixing vegetables such as roast beetroot with goat's cheese and balsamic vinegar, or fennel with oranges.

Another interesting way to prepare salads is to heat the greens slightly before tossing with the other elements. Composed salads are lovely too, with elements placed separately on the plate.

When making a green salad:
■ Add just enough dressing to give the leaves a light coating.
■ Gently toss and turn over the leaves – use salad servers or your clean hands.
■ Serve without delay: if a dressed salad waits to be served, the leaves will wilt.

TRIMMING & SLICING HEARTY GREENS

Leafy green vegetables such as spinach may be young and tender enough to eat raw in a salad, but most hearty greens – such as Swiss chard, kale, spring greens, and the leaves of vegetables such as turnips and beetroot – are cooked, most commonly by boiling, steaming, or sautéing.

Hearty greens are most often trimmed to remove the central rib and then sliced into strips (called a chiffonade). With mature leaves, the rib is cut out; with more tender leaves, such as spinach and sorrel, you can just pull off the stalk and rib (see below). This method of slicing into a chiffonade is also suitable for hearty spring greens (which are shown in the photographs) as well as for salad leaves.

1 Discard all limp or discoloured leaves. Using a chef's knife, quickly slash each leaf on either side of the rib. Remove and discard it.

2 Rinse in water as described for salad leaves (see opposite) and pat dry in a tea towel or with kitchen paper.

3 Grab a handful of leaves and roll loosely into a bunch. Cut across the roll into strips of the desired width.

 ## PREPARING SPINACH

Spinach tends to trap a lot of soil, so the leaves need thorough washing.
■ Immerse the spinach in several changes of cold water to clean it. After draining in a colander, pat dry in a tea towel or with kitchen paper.
■ Fold each leaf in half and pull off the central rib and stalk (see right). The spinach is now ready to eat raw or to cook.

CABBAGE FAMILY

The most common way to prepare tight, round heads of cabbage is to quarter them and cut out the hard central core, then to shred coarsely or finely. They can then be used raw in a salad or coleslaw or cooked by boiling or steaming, sautéing, or braising. Whole heads of cabbage and rolled leaves may also be stuffed and baked. Loose-leaf heads, such as Chinese cabbages and Chinese leaves, are prepared more like hearty greens (p239).

Both broccoli and cauliflower have tightly packed heads of buds or florets. The usual method of preparing broccoli and cauliflower is to trim the stalk and separate the florets, although heads are also sometimes cooked whole. Cooking methods include boiling and steaming, sautéing, stir-frying (blanch first), microwaving, and baking or simmering in a sauce. Florets can also be served raw as part of a selection of vegetable crudités.

CORING & SHREDDING CABBAGE

1 Holding the head of cabbage firmly on the board, use a chef's knife to cut it lengthways in half, cutting straight through the stalk end.

2 Cut each cabbage half lengthways in half again, cutting through the stalk end, then cut out the hard core centre from each quarter.

SPEEDY SHREDDING

Cabbage can be quickly shredded by hand with a chef's knife (see right). For the most efficient action and control, keep the point of the knife on the board as you raise and lower the handle; guide the knife blade with the knuckles of your other hand. Alternatively, you can use the shredding disc on a food processor, which will cut cabbage very quickly into the finest slices.

3 Take one cabbage quarter and place it cut-side down on the board. Cut across the cabbage, creating shreds of the desired thickness.

OUR FAVOURITE COLESLAW

Coleslaw is a true American classic. While this recipe is traditional, you can easily change it. For an exotic twist, add 1tbsp chopped Thai chili and substitute 120ml (4fl oz) of a Thai-style vinaigrette for the soured cream and mayonnaise.

Serves 4–6

115g (4oz) soured cream

2tbsp mayonnaise

4tbsp cider vinegar

2tbsp caster sugar

250g (8½oz) finely shredded green cabbage

115g (4oz) grated carrots

1 Combine the soured cream, mayonnaise, vinegar, sugar, and salt and pepper to taste in a bowl. Stir until evenly mixed.

2 Add the cabbage and carrots and toss to coat evenly. Cover and keep refrigerated until ready to serve.

TRIMMING BROCCOLI & CUTTING FLORETS

1 Lay the head of broccoli flat on the board. With a chef's knife, cut off the thick portion of the stalk, cutting just below the floret stalks.

2 Remove the florets by sliding the knife between their stalks to separate them. Rinse the florets in cold water and drain in a colander.

TRIMMING CAULIFLOWER & CUTTING FLORETS

1 Lay the head of cauliflower on its side on the board. With a chef's knife, cut off the end of the stalk. Pull or cut off any leaves.

2 Turn the head core-side up and use a paring knife to carefully cut the florets from the central stalk. Rinse the florets in cold water and drain in a colander.

ONION FAMILY

Sometimes cooked as a vegetable – by baking, roasting, or braising – or added raw to a salad, onions and shallots are most often used as a seasoning in a cooked dish. They are peeled and diced or sliced in the same way, then usually sweated so they soften without colouring – if cooked too rapidly or at too high a temperature they can become dark brown and bitter.

Used primarily as a flavouring, the pungency of garlic depends on how it is prepared. When left whole – in a head or individual cloves – and roasted or boiled, it tastes mild and sweet; when chopped the flavour is stronger. The more finely garlic is chopped, the more pungent it will become.

Although occasionally used raw in salads, leeks are most often cooked, whether whole or cut up, by boiling, braising, or baking in a sauce or in a vegetable mixture.

PEELING & DICING ONIONS

1 Using a chef's knife, cut the onion lengthways in half. Peel off the skin, leaving the root on to keep the onion halves together.

2 Lay one half flat-side down. Make 2 or 3 slices into it horizontally, cutting up to but not through the root end.

3 Cut the onion half vertically now, slicing down through the layers, again cutting up to but not through the root end.

SLICING ONIONS

Onions may be sliced into half moons or rings of varying thicknesses.

■ To slice half moons, cut the onion in half and peel it (see step 1 above). Lay each half cut-side down on the board and slice across (not lengthways).

■ For rings, peel the onion, keeping it whole. Hold it firmly on the board and slice across into rings. Discard the root and stalk ends.

4 Cut across the vertical slices to get an even dice. Discard the root end.

PEELING & CHOPPING GARLIC

WASHING LEEKS & CUTTING INTO JULIENNE

This mildest member of the onion family often collects soil between its many layers, so needs to be thoroughly washed before use.

1 Lay a garlic clove flat on the chopping board and place the side of the blade of a chef's knife on it. Lightly strike the blade to break the garlic skin. Peel off the skin.

2 Chop the garlic roughly, then sprinkle it with a little salt (this prevents the garlic from sticking to the knife). Continue chopping it until it is very fine. To make a paste, press and smash the garlic on the board as you chop.

1 With a chef's knife, trim off the root end and some of the dark green leaf top. Cut the leek in half lengthways and fan it open, holding the white end.

2 Rinse under cold running water to remove the soil from between the layers. Gently shake the leek to remove excess water, then pat dry with kitchen paper.

3 For julienne, cut off all the green part. Cut the white part across into sections of the required length. Lay a section flat-side down and slice into fine strips about 3mm (⅛in) thick.

SQUASH FAMILY

Squashes come in all shapes, colours, and sizes. Hard-skinned winter squashes, such as pumpkin, butternut, acorn, turban, and spaghetti squash, are always cooked, most often by boiling or steaming (and often then puréed) or by baking or roasting. Halves may also be stuffed and baked. In addition to courgettes, soft-skinned summer squashes include vegetable marrow, pattypan, and chayote. Summer squashes can be cooked whole or cut up, by steaming, baking, sautéing or frying, and grilling.

HALVING, SEEDING & PEELING WINTER SQUASHES

The skin of winter squashes are thick and hard, and the seeds are fully developed. Because of this, winter squashes are always peeled (either before or after cooking) and the seeds and central fibres are removed. Use a sharp, heavy knife for cutting. Butternut squash is shown in these photographs.

1 Hold the squash firmly on the board, then cut in half, cutting from the stalk end directly through the core end.

2 Use a spoon or a small ice cream scoop to remove the seeds and fibres from each squash half. Discard the seeds and fibres.

3 Cut the squash into sections. If removing the skin before cooking, peel the sections using a vegetable peeler or knife.

GRATING SUMMER SQUASHES

Soft-skinned summer squashes can be eaten peel and all. However, as their flesh is tender and moist they can become mushy if overcooked. Draining or squeezing out excess moisture before cooking can help to prevent this. This preparation technique is suitable for summer squashes such as courgettes (shown here) as well as for cucumber.

1 If you like, peel the courgette. Grasp the courgette firmly and grate the flesh on the side of the grater with large holes.

2 Wrap the grated courgette in a piece of muslin and squeeze to remove excess moisture. Discard all the liquid.

CUTTING BATONNETS

This method of cutting batonnets is also suitable for other slim vegetables, such as carrots, parsnips, and salsify. A courgette is shown here.

1 Cut off both ends of the courgette, then cut it in half lengthways. Cut each half again to make slices 5mm (¼in) thick.

2 Lay each slice of courgette flat on the board and cut across it to make sticks or batonnets about 5mm (¼in) wide.

ROOT & TUBER FAMILY

Vegetables that grow underground include carrots, turnips, potatoes, parsnips, swede, beetroot, salsify, celeriac, radishes, and Jerusalem artichokes. Some, such as radishes, are usually eaten raw; others, such as carrots, may be eaten raw or cooked. But it is more common to cook roots and tubers by boiling or steaming – often to make a purée – sous vide, or by baking or roasting, en papillote, sautéing, or frying. Many are also delicious thinly sliced and deep-fried. Most roots and tubers are peeled, before or after cooking.

TURNING

Called "tourner" in French, this is a common preparation technique for vegetables in the root and tuber family, such as carrots (shown here), turnips, and potatoes, as well as for summer squashes. The vegetable is shaved into classic seven-sided football shapes.

1 Peel the vegetables, if necessary, then cut into pieces that are 5cm (2in) long.

2 Holding one vegetable piece between thumb and forefinger, start shaving off the sides of the piece to curve them.

3 Continue cutting while turning the vegetable piece in your hand, to create a football shape with 7 curved sides.

SHOOTS & STALKS FAMILY

Vegetables in this family include young shoots (asparagus), leaf stalks (celery and fennel), and flower heads atop stalks (globe artichokes). Asparagus is rarely eaten raw, unless it is very young and slim, whereas celery and fennel may be used raw or cooked. Even when young, globe artichokes are always cooked before eating, either whole or trimmed down to the fleshy bottom or heart.

TRIMMING GLOBE ARTICHOKES TO SERVE WHOLE

Whole globe artichokes are cooked by boiling or steaming. The hairy "choke" in the centre can be scooped out after cooking or before eating. When cut and exposed to the air, artichokes will quickly discolour. To prevent them from browning prior to cooking, drop them into a bowl of water acidulated with lemon juice or rub all the cut surfaces with lemon.

2 Use a chef's knife to cut off the stalk flush with the base so that the artichoke will sit upright on a flat bottom.

1 Holding the stalk, cut the tough tips from the artichoke leaves with sturdy kitchen scissors.

3 Cut off the pointed top. The artichoke is now ready to be cooked.

PREPARING ARTICHOKE BOTTOMS

When all the leaves are removed from a globe artichoke, what is left is the fleshy, cup-shaped bottom or heart, which is completely edible apart from the central hairy "choke". The bottom can be cut up for cooking or left whole. If it is to be served whole, it will be easier to remove the choke after cooking. As you work, keep rubbing the exposed flesh of the artichoke with lemon juice to prevent browning.

1 Pull away or cut off all of the large leaves from the artichoke. Then cut off the stalk flush with the base.

2 Cut off the remaining soft "cone" of leaves in the middle, cutting across just above the choke (you will see the hairy fibres).

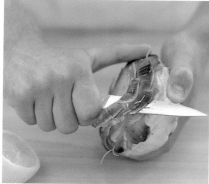

3 Neaten the bottom with a paring knife, trimming off all the remaining leaves and trimming the base so it is slightly flattened.

4 If cutting up the artichoke for cooking, scoop out the choke with a small spoon. Take care to remove all of the hairy fibres.

5 Rub the exposed surface of the hollow generously with lemon juice. The artichoke bottom is now ready to be cut up for cooking.

PREPARING ASPARAGUS

Asparagus needs little preparation, apart from trimming off the ends of the stalks. However, if the spears are larger you may want to peel them. Cook asparagus by boiling or steaming, or try roasting or char-grilling them.

1 With a chef's knife, cut the hard ends from the asparagus spears.

2 Holding the tip of a spear gently, use a vegetable peeler to peel off a thin layer of skin from the stalk, rotating to peel all sides.

 STRINGING CELERY

The thick, outer sticks of celery have long, stringy fibres that are best removed. Separate the sticks from the bunch and wash. Then, using a vegetable peeler, peel off a thin layer from each stick to remove the strings. Florence or bulb fennel and cardoons also have strings that are usually removed in the same way.

PODS & SEEDS

There are three types of peas and beans: those where the unripe seeds are eaten in the pod (eg green beans, mangetouts, and sugar snap peas); those where the seeds are mature and removed from the pod to be eaten fresh (eg peas and broad beans); and those where the podded mature seeds are dried before eating (eg pulses such as haricot beans, kidney beans, and black-eyed beans). The fresh types are usually cooked by boiling or steaming, although they may also be braised, sautéed, or stir-fried.

Although not in the same botanical family as peas and beans, sweetcorn is treated in the same way in the kitchen.

REMOVING STRINGS

Mangetouts (shown below) and some green beans, such as runner beans, have tough strings along one or both sides of the pod that need to be stripped off before cooking.

Carefully tear off the tip, which will be attached to the string, then pull it along the side to remove the string. With mangetouts, the flat side has the string. If you are preparing beans that have a tough string on the other side too, carefully tear off the tail of the bean in that direction and pull off the attached string.

CUTTING OFF SWEETCORN KERNELS

After removing the husks and silk from corn-on-the-cob, it can be boiled whole. Alternatively, the kernels can be cut off to be boiled or steamed, sautéed, or simmered or baked in a sauce or soup.

1 Pull off the husks and all of the silk from the corn-on-the-cob.

2 Hold the corn upright on a chopping board and, using a chef's knife, slice straight down the sides to cut off the kernels.

3 Hold the cob upright in a bowl, at a slight angle, and scrape down the length of the cob with the knife to extract the rest of the corn "milk".

MUSHROOMS

Mushrooms, both cultivated and wild, and truffles make up this vegetable family. Before cooking, most fresh fungi need only to be cleaned to remove earth or sand – only a few varieties of wild mushrooms need to be peeled. If the stalks are woody, trim the ends or cut them off completely. When they are cooked – sautéing and stewing are the most popular methods – fresh mushrooms produce a lot of liquid, which may need to be drained off or boiled to evaporate. Mushrooms preserved by drying – which intensifies their flavour – need to be soaked before use. Once reconstituted, they can be treated like fresh mushrooms.

REHYDRATING DRIED MUSHROOMS

1 Place the dried mushrooms (either cultivated or wild) in a bowl of hot water. Allow to soak for at least 15 minutes to rehydrate them.

2 Use a slotted spoon to remove the mushrooms from the soaking liquid. If you are going to use the soaking liquid in the dish with the mushrooms, strain the liquid through muslin or a coffee filter paper to remove all of the sand and grit.

CLEANING FRESH MUSHROOMS

Use wet kitchen paper to clean all soil from fresh mushrooms, wiping it off gently. If the mushrooms are sandy, you may need to plunge them into cold water and shake them around to loosen the sand (this is most likely to be needed with species that have deep gills). However, do not leave cultivated fresh mushrooms to soak because they quickly absorb moisture and become bloated.

PREPARING WILD MUSHROOMS & TRUFFLES

Fresh wild mushrooms need thorough cleaning and may need to be soaked for up to 5 minutes to loosen grit in their gills or indentations. Some species have a thick skin, which should be peeled off.

Fresh truffles usually only need to be brushed gently to remove any loose dirt, but if they contain a lot of grit and dirt they may need to be rinsed. Once the truffle is clean, peel off the rough skin (reserve the skin and use for flavouring).

FRUIT VEGETABLES

Tomatoes, aubergines, peppers, chilies, tomatillos, and avocados, which are fruits according to botanists, are treated as vegetables in the kitchen. With the exception of tomatillos, all are ideal for stuffing with a savoury mixture (see p263).

Aubergines are never used raw, while avocados are rarely cooked; tomatoes and peppers are extremely versatile and can be used either raw or cooked. Popular cooking methods include baking, grilling, and sautéing.

HALVING & STONING AVOCADO

Once avocado flesh has been removed from the skin, it can be added to salads, or mashed or puréed to use in uncooked soups and dips such as guacamole (see opposite). It may also be cooked lightly and briefly. Take care, though, because if it is heated for too long avocado will quickly lose its flavour.

PREVENTING BROWNING

The flesh of avocado will discolour quickly when exposed to the air, so serve it promptly or rub or toss it with lemon or lime juice.

1 Using a chef's knife, slice into the avocado, cutting all the way around the stone.

2 Twist the cut halves gently in opposite directions to separate them.

3 Strike the stone with the knife blade to pierce it firmly. Lift up the knife to remove the stone from the avocado half.

4 Use a wooden spoon to pry the stone off the knife. Discard the stone.

5 Holding an avocado half in your hand, gently scoop out the flesh with the help of a rubber spatula. Repeat with the other half.

PEELING & DICING AVOCADO

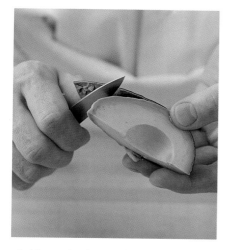

1 After cutting the avocado in half and removing the stone (see opposite), cut the half into quarters and remove the peel.

2 Cut the avocado flesh into neat slices. To dice the flesh, slice thinly and then cut across the slices to make dice.

EASY GUACAMOLE

Makes about 500ml (17fl oz)

3 small avocados

1 ripe but firm tomato, skinned, seeded, and chopped

1 small jalapeño or other green chili, seeded and finely chopped

½ small onion, chopped

25g (scant 1oz) coriander, chopped

2tbsp fresh lemon or lime juice

pinch of salt

1 Scoop the flesh from the avocados. Mash the flesh until smooth with a few slight lumps. Lightly stir in the rest of the ingredients without overmixing.

2 Use immediately or cover by pressing cling film directly onto the guacamole (not on top of the bowl) to prevent browning, and store in the refrigerator. Serve as a dip for tortilla chips or raw vegetables, or with tacos.

ROASTING, PEELING & SLICING PEPPERS

Red, yellow, and green peppers can have thick skins, which some people find indigestible. Roasting the peppers makes the skin easier to remove. It also imparts a delicious, slightly smoky taste and enhances the sweetness of the pepper flesh. The same roasting and peeling method can be used for chilies as well as for tomatoes and even garlic.

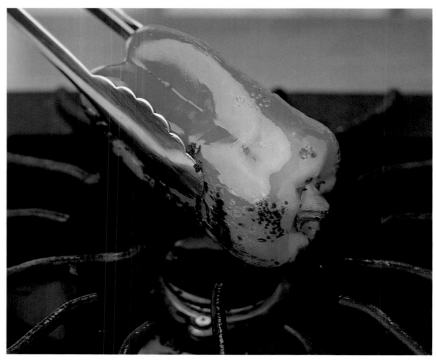

GRILLING

You can also char peppers under the grill. Place them on a baking tray, about 10cm (4in) from the heat, and grill for about 5 minutes, or until the skin blisters and blackens. Turn the peppers over and char the other side in the same way.

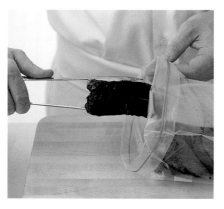

1 Using long-handled tongs, hold each pepper over an open flame to char it on all sides. (Alternatively, char under the grill; see box right.)

2 Put into a plastic bag and seal tightly. Set aside to allow steam to loosen the skin.

3 Using your fingers, peel away the charred skin from the pepper.

4 Pull off the stalk, taking the core with it, and remove all the seeds from inside.

5 Tear the peeled pepper into sections. Lay them flat and cut lengthways into strips.

SKINNING, SEEDING & CHOPPING TOMATOES

When tomatoes are used in a soup or sauce that is not sieved, they are often skinned and seeded first. This skinning method is also used for fruit such as peaches and plums, and for chestnuts.

1 With the tip of a paring knife, cut around the core of the tomato to remove it.

2 Score an "X" in the skin on the base of the tomato. Immerse it in a pan of boiling water.

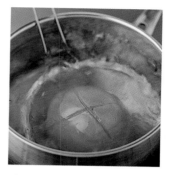

3 Leave the tomato in the boiling water for about 20 seconds, or until the skin splits.

4 Lift the tomato out of the pan and immediately submerge it in a bowl of iced water to cool.

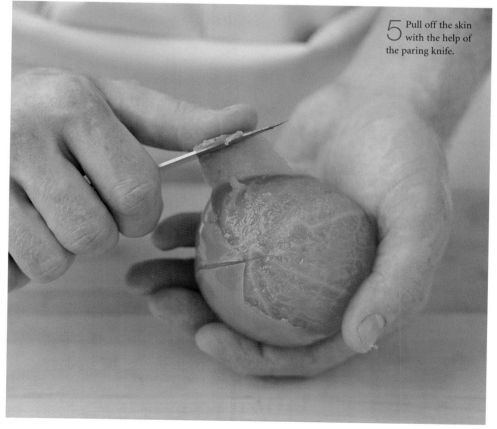

5 Pull off the skin with the help of the paring knife.

6 Cut the tomato in half and gently squeeze out the seeds.

7 Place each half cut-side down and cut into strips. Cut across the strips to make dice.

RAW

There is no better way to celebrate the pure, clean flavours and textures of vegetables than with the RAW approach. It is an intriguing style of vegetable preparation that includes such techniques as soaking and sprouting nuts and pulses, and marinating vegetables in order to break down their undesirable starchy complexity.

The overall concept of RAW is that nothing is ever heated over 48°C (118°F) because above that temperature enzymes in food are destroyed and food begins to lose its nutritional value. Leaving food in its natural – or RAW – state helps to retain most of the nutrients, as well as offering incredible flavour and texture.

Many people are adopting a 100 per cent RAW food regime as a way of life. While this is not what I'm proposing, I encourage you to try some of the RAW approach to explore flavours and textures.

DEHYDRATING TOMATOES

Tomatoes are one of the best vegetables to dry for using in RAW preparations. You can also use this technique to dry mushrooms, fruit such as pears and apples, and even squashes.

1 Using a serrated knife, cut the tomatoes into very thin slices – about 3mm (⅛in) thick.

2 Lay the slices in one layer on a dehydrator shelf. Lightly brush them with olive oil.

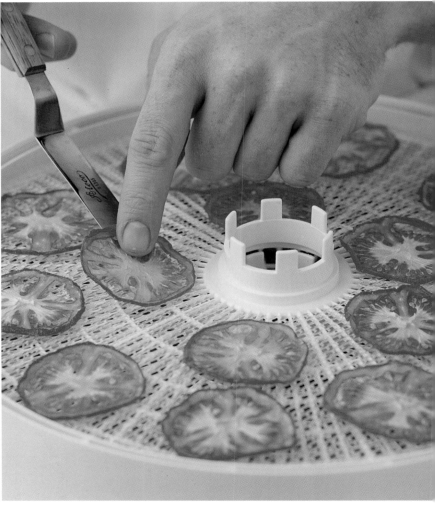

3 Dehydrate the tomatoes at 40°C (105°F) for 6–8 hours, or until dry. Remove the tomatoes from the dehydrator and allow to cool. Store in an airtight container until ready to use.

Chilled clear cucumber soup with watermelon, apple & jicama

This cucumber soup is so light and refreshing it could almost work as a summer beverage. Tart apple and sweet watermelon contrast deliciously. Togarashi powder is ground small, hot, red Japanese chilies.

2 cucumbers

2tbsp plain yogurt

1tsp freshly squeezed lemon juice

½tsp togarashi powder

4tbsp cucumber julienne, 2.5cm (1in) long

4tbsp green apple julienne, 2.5cm (1in) long

8tsp watermelon batonnets, seeds removed

4tbsp diced avocado

8tsp diced jicama

8tsp diced tomatillo

8 slices of dehydrated tomato (see opposite), julienned

4tsp snipped dill

4tsp green herb oil (p77)

Cut one of the cucumbers into eight 2.5cm (1in) pieces. Using a round cutter or a paring knife, remove the skin. Hollow out the inside of each cucumber piece using a spoon or melon ball scoop to make a cup. Put the scooped-out pulp in a blender.

Peel and chop the second cucumber and add to the blender with 1tsp salt. Purée until smooth. Pour the cucumber purée into a sieve lined with 3 layers of muslin and set in a bowl. Leave in the refrigerator until all of the liquid has strained through. Season this cucumber broth with salt if necessary and keep refrigerated until needed.

Combine the yogurt, lemon juice, and togarashi in a small bowl. Add the julienned cucumber and apple and toss to mix.

To assemble, set 2 cucumber cups in the centre of each wide serving bowl. Fill the cups with the cucumber and apple mixture. Place the watermelon, avocado, jicama, tomatillo, and tomato around the cups. Ladle the cucumber broth into each bowl and sprinkle with the dill. Drizzle 1tsp herb oil over each serving and finish with freshly ground pepper.

Scoop out the pulp to make cucumber cups

BOILING

Almost all vegetables can be boiled. It is important, however, to note some differences when boiling vegetables of different colour or texture. As a general rule, all tough-textured, starchy root vegetables, such as potatoes, turnips, and celeriac, should be started in cold water in order to ensure even cooking, whereas green vegetables should be added to boiling water. To ensure even cooking, cut or trim all vegetables to a uniform size.

When boiling vegetables with bright colours – red (eg beetroot), white (eg turnips), yellow (eg squashes), and orange (eg carrots) – cover the pan during boiling in order to retain acids that help hold the colour fast. However, never cover green vegetables when they are boiling, as they will lose their colour.

Root vegetables should be fast-boiled (at 100°C/212°F), whereas all other vegetables should be simmered more slowly.

BOILING GREEN VEGETABLES

This cooking method is suitable for green vegetables such as broccoli florets, brussels sprouts, shredded green cabbage, green beans, peas, broad beans, sugar snap peas, mangetouts (as shown in the photographs), and asparagus spears.

1 Salt the water or other cooking liquid and bring it to the boil. Add the vegetables to the boiling water in small batches to minimize temperature reduction.

2 Bring the water back to the boil, then reduce the heat and gently simmer the vegetables until cooked (see right and the chart opposite for approximate timings).

3 Drain in a colander. If needed, refresh the vegetables by rinsing under cold running water (for delicate vegetables, immerse them in iced water). This stops the cooking and sets the colour. Drain again well, then serve.

DEGREES OF COOKING

Vegetables can be boiled for varying lengths of time, according to how they are to be used or served, as well as how well done you prefer them to be. These terms are commonly used when boiling vegetables.
■ Blanch: to immerse in boiling water for a very short time, usually no more than a minute. This is followed by a quick refresh or cool down in iced water. A vegetable is blanched to set colour, to loosen skin so that it can be removed more easily, or to eliminate strong flavour.

■ Parboil: to partially cook. A vegetable is parboiled to prepare it for other finishing (by braising or stewing, grilling or char-grilling, sautéing, baking en papillote, roasting, etc).
■ Al dente: literally "to the tooth", to cook until just firm or crisp yet tender. This degree of cooking suits green vegetables such as green beans and mangetouts as well as courgettes.
■ Fully done: to cook until tender. Root vegetables and potatoes are always cooked until fully done.

STEAMING

Steaming vegetables results in a pure, clean flavour like no other. In addition, the end result is a vegetable that is firmer and more crisp than one that was boiled. This is primarily because the vegetable has had no contact with the liquid in the pan, just with steam. Any vegetable that can be boiled can be steamed.

It's a good idea to cut larger root vegetables into small pieces for steaming. Smaller vegetables can be left whole.

In general, the amount of liquid you use for steaming should be about the same as the amount of vegetables. You can add seasonings to the liquid (for example, herbs and citrus zest), which will impart flavour to the vegetables. Be sure that there is adequate room for steam circulation around them so that they cook evenly.

STEAMING BROCCOLI

Follow this method of steaming for all kinds of vegetables. You can use a steamer (as shown here) or stacking Chinese bamboo steamers.

1 Put water into the bottom of a steamer and bring to the boil. Place the broccoli on the steamer rack, spreading the florets out in a single layer. Cover the steamer.

2 Steam the broccoli until cooked (test by pricking the thickest part – here the stalk of a floret – with the tip of a paring knife). Remove from the steamer and serve immediately.

Boiling & steaming vegetables

This chart suggests times for boiling and steaming vegetables. Some people like vegetables to be fully done while others prefer some to be cooked al dente, so a range of timings is given. The range also covers differences that may result from the vegetable's age, size, or variety. Whether you start in cold or boiling water (see opposite), time the cooking from the moment the water reaches or returns to the boil. Then cover the pan if this is indicated. For perfect results, test for doneness with the point of a sharp knife or a fork.

VEGETABLE	BOILING			STEAMING
	Times (in minutes)	Cold/ boiling start	Cook covered?	Times (in minutes)
Artichoke bottoms	20–30	cold start	no	15–20
Artichokes, whole	20–40	cold start	no	25–35
artichokes, baby	15–18	cold start	no	15–20
Asparagus	3–4	boiling start	no	4–10
Beans, green	2–8	boiling start	no	5–12
Beetroot, whole	30–60	cold start	yes	30–60
Broccoli florets	2–3	boiling start	no	5–10
Brussels sprouts	5–12	boiling start	no	10–15
Cabbage, quartered	5–15	boiling start	no	6–15
Cabbage, shredded	3–5	boiling start	no	5–10
Carrots, baby	3–4	boiling start	yes	10
Carrots, sliced/diced	5–10	boiling start	yes	8–10
Cauliflower florets	2–3	boiling start	no	5–8
Cauliflower, whole	10–15	boiling start	no	15–20
Celeriac, cubed/wedges	8–10	cold start	no	8–10
Corn-on-the-cob	3–4	boiling start	no	6–10
Greens, hearty, sliced	5–7	boiling start	no	10–12
Leeks, whole/halved	10–15	boiling start	no	12–15
Mangetouts	2–3	boiling start	no	5–10
Peas, fresh	3–5	boiling start	no	5–10
Potatoes, boiling/new	10–25	cold start	no	15–35
Potatoes, floury, cubed	15–20	cold start	no	15–35
Spinach	1–2	boiling start	no	3–4
Squashes, summer, sliced	5–8	boiling start	no	5–10
Squashes, winter, pieces	12–15	boiling start	yes	15–30
Swede, thickly sliced	8–12	cold start	yes	10–15
Sweet potatoes, cubed	15–35	cold start	yes	30–45
Turnip, thickly sliced/cubes	8–12	cold start	yes	10–15

COOKING EN PAPILLOTE

This is a delicate way to cook vegetables quickly while retaining much of their texture, flavour, and aromas. The vegetables are wrapped in a parcel ("papillote" is French for parcel) and cooked in the oven. However, they are really steamed, not baked.

Tender vegetables are the best suited for cooking en papillote because they do not need long baking. Always consider sweating or parboiling potatoes and other roots and tubers first, to ensure even cooking and to speed up the process.

BABY CARROTS & TURNIPS EN PAPILLOTE

Cooking in individual paper parcels turns otherwise humble vegetables, such as carrots and turnips, into something special.

225g (8oz) baby carrots, peeled and green ends trimmed

225g (8oz) baby turnips, halved or cut into wedges, according to size

extra virgin olive oil for brushing

sprigs of thyme

sprigs of rosemary

1 Preheat the oven to 230°C (450°F, gas 8). Drop the baby carrots and turnips into a pan of boiling salted water and parboil for 3 minutes. Drain and refresh in iced water.

2 Cut out 4 large, heart-shaped pieces of baking parchment and brush them with extra virgin olive oil. Divide the carrots and turnips into 4 portions.

COOKING EN PAPILLOTE

This is done primarily in baking parchment or foil, which is cut into a heart shape and then folded around the food to be cooked and its flavourings to seal them in completely. During cooking the ingredients produce steam, which causes the parcel to puff up. The result is very juicy and full of flavour. The same effect can be achieved by wrapping food in banana leaves, vine leaves, and sweetcorn husks.

3 For each parcel, place the vegetables on one side of a heart and season with salt and pepper. Add thyme and rosemary sprigs. Fold the other half of the heart over the vegetables.

4 Starting at the top of the heart, crimp all around the edge to seal the 2 open sides of the halves together, ensuring that the crimps overlap each other.

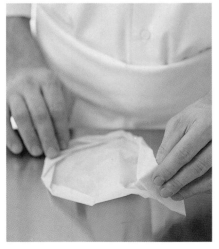

5 When you reach the bottom, fold the point under to hold all the crimping in place.

6 Place the parcels on a baking tray and bake for 5–8 minutes, or until the paper puffs.

Open the packages for serving, or let each person open his or her own

MICROWAVING

Microwave cooking is a form of steaming – the microwaves agitate water molecules, which in turn create steam. The water is either found naturally in the food or is added to the dish. Any vegetable that can be steamed can be successfully microwaved.

MICROWAVED BABY ARTICHOKES

1 Place the artichokes in a microwave-safe dish. Add enough water to cover the bottom of the dish plus some sprigs of rosemary.

2 Cover the dish with cling film that has been punctured for ventilation of steam, or cover with a lid. Microwave until cooked. Remove from the microwave and leave to stand for a few minutes. Then remove the cover and serve.

MICROWAVE TIPS

■ Cooking times will vary according to the wattage of your microwave, as well as the freshness of the vegetable you are cooking, the type of vegetable, the quantity, and how it is prepared. Consult your owner's manual for guidelines.

■ Be sure to allow vegetables to stand for a few minutes after they are removed from the microwave. This will complete the cooking.

■ Take care when uncovering the dish as steam trapped inside will be very hot. If you have used cling film, make a large cut in it before removing.

BAKING & ROASTING

These are both dry-heat methods of cooking wherein the food is surrounded by hot air, usually in an oven although sometimes on a spit over an open fire. The term roasting is usually applied to meats and poultry, while baking typically is used for breads, pastries, and fish. In reality, though, there is little difference in the techniques.

Both baking and roasting concentrate the flavours of vegetables and also often produce a delicious browned, caramelized exterior.

Thick-skinned vegetables, such as potatoes, turnips, winter and summer squashes, beetroot, aubergines, and peppers, are well suited to baking or roasting. Also try roasting mushrooms. The vegetables may be baked or roasted in their skins or peeled.

Potatoes and other roots and tubers cut in pieces are often parboiled before roasting. Many vegetables are baked or roasted as a first step when making a purée (p262).

BAKED BEETROOT

Potatoes are often baked in their skins, with or without wrapping in foil, but this cooking method is excellent for many other roots and tubers. Here, beetroots are baked in foil. Turnips, swede, and salsify are also excellent baked like this. For even cooking, choose vegetables of equal size. Once they are baked, peel the vegetables or serve in their skins.

4 beetroots, preferably the size of a cricket ball

olive oil for drizzling

1 Preheat the oven to 200°C (400°F, gas 6). Trim all but 2.5cm (1in) from the stalk of each beetroot, then wash thoroughly and dry well. Drizzle some olive oil over the beetroots and rub it on evenly, then sprinkle them with coarse sea salt. Wrap individually in foil.

2 Place in a shallow roasting tin. Bake in the middle of the oven for about 45 minutes, or until tender. Test with a fork: it should come out easily. Remove from the oven and set aside until cool enough to handle.

3 When the beetroots have cooled, peel away the skins using a paring knife (wear disposable gloves to prevent your hands from being stained with the beetroot juice).

4 Slice the beetroots and season with salt and pepper to taste. Serve warm or cool.

ROAST BUTTERNUT SQUASH

Butternut squash is particularly good cooked this way, as are other winter squashes such as pumpkin, acorn, turban, and kabocha. More vegetables to roast like this include potatoes, turnips, parsnips, and swede.

You can add extra flavour by tossing the buttered squash with chopped fresh herbs, such as rosemary, oregano, or thyme, before roasting. Or, for a sweet touch, try mixing a bit of brown sugar into the melted butter or oil.

675g (1½lb) butternut squash, halved, seeded, and peeled (p244)

3tbsp melted butter or olive oil

1 Preheat the oven to 200°C (400°F, gas 6). Cut the butternut squash into 2.5cm (1in) uniform-sized cubes. Put onto a foil-lined roasting tin. Drizzle over the melted butter or oil and toss until the cubes are evenly coated.

Timings for baking & roasting vegetables

Cook at 180–190°C (350–375°F, gas 4–5), unless a hot oven (200–220°C/400–425°F, gas 6–7) is noted. The size of the vegetables will affect the cooking times suggested.

SOME SUITABLE VEGETABLES	APPROXIMATE COOKING TIMES
Asparagus	8–10 mins (hot oven)
Aubergine, halved	25–35 mins
Beetroot (in skin)	45 mins (hot oven)
Cabbage, quartered and sliced (in sauce)	45–60 mins
Carrots, baby	45–60 mins
Chicory (in sauce)	20–30 mins
Corn-on-the-cob (in husk)	20–30 mins
Mushrooms, whole	15–20 mins
Parsnip pieces	30 mins (blanch first)
Potatoes, baking (in skin)	50–60 mins
Potato pieces	30 mins (blanch first)
Sweet potatoes (in skin)	45–60 mins
Winter squashes, cubed	45 mins (hot oven)
Winter squashes, halved	45–60 mins

2 Season the cubes of squash with salt to taste, then spread them out in a single layer. Put into the oven and roast for approximately 45 minutes, or until tender (test them with a fork or the tip of a knife). Serve the squash hot.

ROAST GARLIC

Preheat the oven to 180°C (350°F, gas 4). Cut the tops off 4 garlic bulbs. Put them in a small saucepan and cover with 750ml (1¼ pints) of milk. Bring to a simmer, then cook on low heat for about 10 minutes (cooking in milk helps to sweeten the garlic and preserve the colour). Drain. Set the bulbs upright in an ovenproof dish. Add 120ml (4fl oz) olive oil and cover. Roast for 1–1½ hours, or until the bulbs are soft. Leave to cool in the oil, then squeeze the soft cloves out of the skins. The garlic can be kept in the fridge (in the oil) for up to 3 days.

POTATO GRATIN

One of the most popular ways to bake vegetables is in a gratin. Baking is done uncovered so that an appetizing and flavourful crust can form.

Serves 6

butter for the tin

900g (2lb) waxy new potatoes, peeled and thinly sliced

200g (7oz) Parmesan or other well-flavoured cheese, freshly grated

500ml (17fl oz) double cream

1 Preheat the oven to 180°C (350°F, gas 4). Butter a 20cm (8in) square baking tin. Arrange a layer of potato slices on the bottom of the tin. Season with salt and pepper and sprinkle with some of the cheese. Continue the layering until all the potatoes are in the tin, finishing with the last of the cheese on top.

2 Pour the double cream evenly over the surface. Bake the gratin for 1½ hours, or until the potatoes are tender (test with a skewer) and the top is golden brown and crisp. Serve the gratin immediately.

PURÉEING

Cooked vegetable purées can be served as they are or used as a component of another recipe. They can also be mixed with other ingredients to make soufflés and terrines. Try experimenting with different combinations for purées, such as fennel with apple.

The most common way to cook vegetables for a purée is to boil, bake, or steam them. In some cases, a microwave can be used. The vegetables can be peeled before or after cooking. Most tubers and root vegetables can be boiled in water. In the case of vegetables such as celeriac, turnips, and parsnips, however, they are better cooked in milk, to retain their colour as well as to add a hint of sweetness. Green vegetables should only be cooked until just tender, as overcooking will cause them to discolour. All other vegetables should be cooked until very tender, almost falling apart.

Puréeing with a ricer, sieve, or food mill will remove any fibres and skin at the same time. If you use a blender or food processor to purée vegetables that are fibrous, you will then have to pass the purée through a sieve to remove the fibres and skin.

USING A FOOD MILL

1 Cook the vegetables (celeriac is shown here), then drain well. Transfer to a food mill set over a bowl and turn the handle to work the vegetables through the screen to make a purée.

2 Season the purée with salt and pepper to taste. It is now ready to serve (reheat if necessary) or to use in another recipe.

USING A SIEVE

If a cooked vegetable is fibrous (such as celeriac, shown here), first purée it in a blender or food processor, then transfer to a fine-mesh sieve set over a bowl. Use a rubber spatula to press the purée through the sieve to remove the fibres. The resulting purée will be very smooth.

STUFFING

This is a great way to present vegetables as a main course or as a side dish. Most vegetables are appropriate for stuffing, although the method will vary based on the vegetable's texture. Common stuffing ingredients are seafood, meat, cheese, rice, and crumbs.

Peppers, onions, winter and summer squashes, and tomatoes are all ideal for stuffing, and are usually baked. Other stuffed vegetables, such as courgette flowers, are cooked on the stovetop. In most cases the stuffing should include part of the vegetable being stuffed (ie a stuffed onion should include some onion in the stuffing) to bind the flavours together.

Stuffing a raw vegetable produces more integrated flavours in the finished dish; however, stuffing a partially cooked vegetable, such as a tomato, allows for easier control of flavour and texture. You can also stuff vegetables that are completely cooked. For example, roast squash can be stuffed with a cooked filling and then simply warmed through in the oven before serving.

PEPPERS WITH WILD RICE STUFFING

4 green peppers

85g (3oz) wild rice, boiled and then drained

115g (4oz) sun-dried tomatoes, julienned

75g (2½oz) roasted, peeled, and diced green pepper (p252)

100g (3½oz) cooked, diced aubergine

2tbsp snipped chives

2tsp extra virgin olive oil

1tsp fresh lemon juice

A HANDY TOOL

A melon ball cutter is a great tool for removing cores and flesh when preparing vegetables for stuffing, especially tomatoes, onions, and courgettes.

1 Preheat the oven to 190°C (375°F, gas 5). Cut around the stalk of each pepper and pull it off, taking the core with it. Rinse inside to remove all the seeds, then blot the peppers dry with kitchen paper.

2 Mix together all the remaining ingredients with seasoning to taste. Spoon this stuffing into the peppers. Stand them upright in an oiled baking tin and cover with foil. Bake for about 1 hour, or until piping hot and very tender.

SAUTÉING

For this quick method, vegetables are cooked in a small amount of fat in a shallow pan on the stovetop. The heat is very high and the vegetables are kept moving in the pan. Sautéing is similar to shallow-frying (p268), the differences being the amount of fat used and the fact that you don't "toss" the items when shallow-frying.

Vegetables suitable for sautéing include tender leafy greens, onions, summer squashes, and mushrooms. Take care not to crowd the pan so that all the vegetables cook quickly and evenly.

Sometimes sautéing is used as a finishing step for vegetables that have been parboiled, for example potatoes and other roots and tubers. Sautéed vegetables may also be finished by glazing (see opposite). For this, a small amount of sugar and butter are added at the end of cooking. The sugar caramelizes, coating the vegetable with a sweet glaze.

If you like, once the vegetables have been removed, a sauce can be made in the pan to capture all of the flavour.

SAUTÉING FIRM VEGETABLES

1 Set a sauté pan on high heat. When the pan is hot, add a small amount of clarified butter or oil (just enough to cover the bottom).

2 As soon as the fat is heated, add the vegetables to the pan (courgette batonnets are shown here). Constantly turn and toss the vegetables in the pan so that they cook evenly.

3 When the vegetables are browned and tender, remove from the heat and serve.

SAUTÉING LEAFY GREEN VEGETABLES

Leafy vegetables such as spinach (shown here) must be completely dry before cooking, otherwise the hot fat in the pan will spit. Heat a small amount of butter in a sauté pan, then add the vegetables. If you like, add a smashed garlic clove, too, to enhance the flavour. Turn and toss until the leaves are wilted and tender, then season and serve immediately.

GLAZED SAUTÉED CARROTS

Here, baby carrots are finished with a delicious butter and sugar glaze. You can glaze other sautéed vegetables, such as baby turnips and cubes of winter squash, in the same way.

20 small baby carrots or 225g (8oz) peeled, sliced carrots, parboiled for 3 minutes and drained

45–55g (1½–2oz) butter

1½–2tsp granulated sugar

1 Put the carrots in a hot sauté pan with the butter and sugar (use the smaller amounts of butter and sugar for baby carrots).

2 Turn and toss the carrots until they are tender and coated in a delicious butter and sugar glaze. Serve immediately.

Timings for sautéing vegetables

The size of the vegetables will affect the cooking times indicated in the chart.

SOME SUITABLE VEGETABLES	APPROXIMATE COOKING TIMES
Asparagus	3–4 mins
Cabbage, shredded	5–7 mins
Mangetouts	3–6 mins
Mushrooms	3–5 mins
Onions, sliced	3–5 mins
Peppers, sliced	3–6 mins
Porcini mushrooms, fresh	5–7 mins
Radicchio	3–5 mins
Shallots, whole (glazed)	10–15 mins
Spinach	3–5 mins
Sweetcorn kernels, fresh	3–5 mins
Winter squash pieces	3–5 mins

FATS FOR SAUTÉING & FRYING

It is important to know which fats are good for sautéing. The oils I like to use are canola, safflower, grapeseed, groundnut, corn, and olive. All of these suit shallow-frying and deep-frying. Butter – whole or clarified (p24) – and rendered animal fat, such as bacon and duck fat, are also great for sautéing and shallow-frying, but not for deep-frying.

When using olive oil for sautéing, take care that it doesn't overheat. Olive oil has a lower smoke point than other oils, so you can't get it as hot.

BRAISING & STEWING

The results of braising and stewing are amazing. For both of these methods, vegetables are gently simmered in a small amount of stock or other liquid (often flavoured with a mirepoix or with other vegetables) for an extended period of time. Cooking can be done on the stovetop or in the oven.

A key difference between braising and stewing is that braising uses much less liquid. Also, in some braising recipes the flavouring agents are not sweated or browned before the vegetables are added. Fat is always used to start braising or stewing vegetables, as it imparts flavour and texture to the finished dish.

BRAISED RED CABBAGE

2tbsp rendered bacon fat

115g (4oz) roughly chopped mirepoix of carrot, onion, and celery

200g (7oz) finely shredded red cabbage

1tbsp sherry vinegar, or to taste

2tbsp granulated sugar, or to taste

1 Heat the bacon fat in a heavy-based pan, add the mirepoix, and cook over low heat to soften and release flavour without letting the vegetables brown. Add the red cabbage and stir to mix with the fat and mirepoix.

2 Pour in enough water to partially cover the vegetables. Add the sherry vinegar and sugar. Bring to the boil, then cover and simmer for about 1 hour, or until the cabbage is tender.

3 Remove from the heat. Lift out and discard the mirepoix, then season the cabbage with salt and pepper to taste. Serve hot.

Timings for braising & stewing vegetables

Oven cooking is typically at 180°C (350°F, gas 4). On the stovetop the pan is always covered and heat is very low.

SOME SUITABLE VEGETABLES	APPROXIMATE COOKING TIMES
Artichokes, baby	30–45 mins
Brussels sprouts	30–40 mins
Cabbage, shredded	20–60 mins
Chicory	15–20 mins
Fennel	20–30 mins
Greens, hearty	30–45 mins
Leeks	20–30 mins
Okra	30–60 mins
Potatoes, new	20–30 mins
Radicchio	40–45 mins
Summer squashes, sliced	8–15 mins

MIREPOIX

A mirepoix is a mixture of aromatic vegetables – usually carrots, onions, and celery – used as a flavouring agent. I prefer to have a mirepoix in larger chunks so that more flavour is released during the sweating process, and I always remove it at the end of cooking. However, the mirepoix can be cut into small dice and left in the finished dish. It is really a matter of personal preference.

Curry & kaffir lime-braised vegetables with basmati rice

Sweet curry and kaffir lime leaves are a perfect combination, and when used with hot chilies, ginger, and lemon-grass to flavour root vegetables braised in coconut milk, the result is stunning.

1tbsp grapeseed oil

3 carrots, turned in 2.5cm (1in) pieces (p245)

3 parsnips, turned in 2.5cm (1in) pieces

1 swede, turned in 2.5cm (1in) pieces

20 button onions, peeled

16 waxy new potatoes, cut into 2.5cm (1in) pieces

8 garlic cloves, smashed

2 red Thai chilies, finely chopped

15cm (6in) piece of lemon-grass, chopped

2tbsp finely chopped fresh ginger

1 onion, chopped

2tbsp Madras curry powder

3 kaffir lime leaves, torn

500ml (17fl oz) vegetable stock or water

240ml (8fl oz) unsweetened coconut milk

To garnish

175g (6oz) basmati rice, cooked and hot

25g (scant 1oz) flaked almonds

1tbsp blackcurrants

1 kaffir lime leaf, finely shredded

Preheat the oven to 150°C (300°F, gas 2). Heat the grapeseed oil in a roasting tin over high heat. Add the carrots, parsnips, swede, button onions, and potatoes to the tin, together with the garlic, chilies, lemon-grass, ginger, and chopped onion. Reduce the heat to moderate and cook for 4–5 minutes, or until fragrant.

Add the curry powder, kaffir lime leaves, stock, and coconut milk and stir to blend everything together. Cover the tin tightly and transfer to the oven. Braise for about 2 hours, or until the vegetables are very tender. Season with salt and pepper to taste.

To serve, place the rice and vegetables in the centre of 4 wide, shallow bowls. Ladle the braising liquid from the vegetables into each bowl and garnish with the flaked almonds, blackcurrants, and shredded kaffir lime leaf.

SHALLOW-FRYING

This high-heat method of cooking vegetables on the stovetop is very similar to sautéing, except that you use more fat and turn the vegetables less often. Most vegetables are coated with crumbs or a batter to protect them from the heat of the fat, although simply dredging in flour is sufficient for some. Any of these coatings will create a nice golden crust.

Vegetables that are dense and tough-textured, such as root vegetables, should be parboiled first in order to ensure thorough cooking and to shorten the frying time.

Vegetable oils – such as groundnut, canola, grapeseed, and corn – and clarified butter (p24) can be used for shallow-frying, as well as rendered animal fats such as bacon or duck fat.

SHALLOW-FRIED CAULIFLOWER

900g (2lb) cauliflower, cut into florets

plain flour for dredging

grapeseed oil for cooking

1 Season the cauliflower florets with salt and pepper, then dredge them in flour, shaking off any additional excess flour.

2 Set a frying pan over moderately high heat. Add 1cm (½in) grapeseed oil. When the oil is hot, add the cauliflower florets and let them brown, then turn them over and cook until tender and browned on the other side. Cooking time is about 5 minutes in total.

3 Remove the cauliflower florets from the pan and drain briefly on kitchen paper. Serve immediately.

Timings for shallow-frying vegetables

The size of the vegetables will affect the cooking times indicated in the chart.

SOME SUITABLE VEGETABLES	APPROXIMATE COOKING TIMES
Artichokes, quartered (floured)	5–6 mins
Aubergine, sliced (floured)	5–10 mins
Parsnip pieces (parboil first)	8–10 mins
Potato, baking, pieces (parboil first)	5–10 mins
Potato, new, whole (parboil first)	8–15 mins
Sweet potato pieces (parboil first)	5–10 mins

DEEP-FRYING

This technique can produce many textures, from wafer-thin crisps to crunchy-on-the-outside/soft-on-the-inside croquettes. Most vegetables are suitable for deep-frying, although those with a higher starch content (such as potatoes and other roots and tubers) work particularly well. Some vegetables require a coating such as a batter to protect them from the heat of the fat. The aims of deep-frying are: minimum fat absorption, golden colour, crisp surface, no off flavours from the oil, and minimum loss of moisture.

SWEET POTATO CRISPS

oil for deep-frying

900g (2lb) sweet potatoes

1 Preheat the oil (or deep-fryer) to 160°C (325°F). Meanwhile, peel and thinly slice the sweet potatoes using a mandolin or knife. When the oil is hot, add a batch of the sliced sweet potatoes, using a spider or frying basket to lower them into the oil.

2 Fry for about 2 minutes, or until crisp and golden brown on both sides. Lift the sweet potato crisps out of the oil and drain briefly on kitchen paper. Keep hot in the oven, uncovered, until all the crisps are fried.

TESTING OIL TEMPERATURE

If you don't have a thermometer to test the temperature of oil for deep-frying, you can use this method instead. Heat the oil for about 8 minutes, then drop in a small piece of whatever it is you plan to fry. If it floats to the top, the oil is at the right temperature for frying. If not, continue heating the oil, testing it again at 1-minute intervals.

Timings for deep-frying vegetables

The oil temperature for deep-frying vegetables is usually 180–190°C (350–375°F).

SOME SUITABLE VEGETABLES	APPROXIMATE COOKING TIMES
Artichokes, baby (floured)	5–7 mins
Asparagus (in batter)	3–4 mins
Broccoli florets (in batter)	3–4 mins
Cauliflower florets (in batter)	3–4 mins
Onion rings (floured or in batter)	2–3 mins
Peppers, sliced (in batter)	3–4 mins
Potatoes, very thinly sliced (crisps)	2 mins
Summer squashes, sliced (in batter)	2–3 mins
Sweet potatoes, very thinly sliced (crisps)	2 mins

Sprinkle the crisps with salt before serving

GRILLING & BARBECUING

Grilling and barbecuing are both easy, healthy ways to cook vegetables. Most are suitable for these cooking methods, although vegetables that are dense or starchy, such as carrots, fennel, potatoes, and beetroot, may need to be parboiled first to ensure that they cook through without overbrowning or burning.

To add flavour, you can marinate vegetables prior to cooking, or a marinade or baste can be brushed onto the vegetables during the cooking process. This will also keep the vegetables moist, as well as promoting an appetizing browning.

When barbecuing over charcoal or char-grilling in a ridged, cast-iron grill pan, you can make attractive cross-stitch grill marks on the vegetables. To do this, turn the vegetables 90° as soon as they have the first set of charred marks. Then, after flipping the vegetables over, repeat the process on the other side.

BARBECUING

Vegetables cooked on a charcoal fire have a delicious smokiness. You can add an even more intense smoky flavour by putting hickory or other woodchips that have been soaked in water directly onto the hot coals.

If you have marinated the vegetables, avoid flare-ups by draining off excess marinade before you put the vegetables on the barbecue.

GRILLING

When cooking under the grill, the temperature can be controlled by the heat as well as the placement of the rack and its distance from the heat. To grill vegetables, and to char skins of peppers and chilies prior to peeling, put the rack 7.5–10cm (3–4in) below the grill.

CHAR-GRILLING

Also called griddling, this direct-heat method uses a heavy cast-iron grill pan on the stovetop. If the pan has a ridged bottom, you can achieve the same appearance and texture as a barbecue, but without the smoky flavour.

It is important that the grill pan be heated thoroughly before you put the vegetables on to cook – it can take up to 10 minutes to heat the pan. If the pan is well seasoned, you will only need to brush a little oil onto the vegetables to prevent them from sticking to the pan and to keep them moist.

CHAR-GRILLED COURGETTES

900g (2lb) courgettes, cut into slices 5mm (¼in) thick

good-quality plain or flavoured oil for brushing

1 Thoroughly heat the grill pan. Thread the courgette slices vertically onto skewers. (If using wooden skewers, first soak them in warm water for 20 minutes.) Brush the courgette slices with oil, then lay them on the hot pan.

2 Char-grill the courgettes, turning them over as necessary, for 4–5 minutes, or until just tender but still crisp. If desired, mark them with cross-stitch grill marks (see above).

 TIPS FOR SUCCESS

■ When preparing vegetables for grilling or barbecuing, be sure to cut them into uniform-sized pieces so that they will cook evenly.

■ If vegetables are in small pieces, thread them onto skewers to make turning easy.

■ If marinating vegetables before cooking, do not leave in the marinade for more than 20 minutes. If marinated longer than this they will absorb too much moisture and begin to break down.

■ For a simple marinade or baste, mix a good-quality olive oil with chopped herbs of your choice, such as rosemary, sage, oregano, or thyme.

PICKLING

These days, pickling is much more about flavour than it is about preserving in a spiced vinegar – pickling is used to give vegetables a pronounced sweet-sour taste. The simplest way to pickle is to prepare a brine and add either cooked or raw vegetables. A typical brine is made with one part salt to eight parts water, but many other ingredients are added to help flavour the pickled vegetables, such as sugar, spices, herbs, and chilies.

The most popular vegetable for pickling is cucumber, but many others – including okra, mushrooms, garlic, chilies, beetroot, cauliflower florets, carrots, and globe artichokes – can also be successfully pickled. Vegetables that have a firmer texture tend to hold up best when pickled.

As with any preserving, it is important to use sterilized jars and lids for this quick-pickling method.

QUICK-PICKLED CUCUMBERS

2 cucumbers

240ml (8fl oz) water

120ml (4fl oz) rice vinegar

5tbsp granulated sugar

2tbsp pickling salt

1 whole clove

1tsp mustard seed

1tsp black peppercorns

2 fresh Thai chilies

2 bay leaves

2 sprigs of thyme

1 Prepare the cucumbers for pickling by quartering them lengthways. If necessary, trim them so they'll fit in the jar. Combine all the remaining ingredients in a saucepan and bring to the boil. Stir to dissolve the sugar.

2 Put the cucumbers in a non-reactive jar or container and cover with the hot brine. Cover the jar and cool to room temperature. Keep in the refrigerator for at least 12 hours before serving. The pickled cucumbers can be kept, refrigerated, for up to 1 week.

PASTA & DUMPLINGS

MICHAEL ROMANO

"Pasta" is Italian for paste, or dough, and consists of a starch in the form of flour mixed with a liquid, frequently water. Pasta is made from starches. Perhaps most common is durum wheat (*Triticum turgidum* var. *durum*), a hard wheat with a high proportion of gluten content among the proteins; this is mostly used coarsely ground in the form of semolina. Hard wheat (*Triticum aestivum*) is used to make flour for fresh pasta and is sometimes blended with durum wheat. Emmer (*Triticum dicoccum*), or farro in Italian, is an ancient form of wheat made into flour for dried pasta. Wholemeal flour, milled with the bran and germ intact, is used in Venetian cooking to form bigoli, a type of fresh, thick spaghetti. Flour from buckwheat is used in Lombardy to make pizzoccheri, a rectangular-shaped pasta. Buckwheat flour is also made into dumplings and Japanese soba noodles.

Throughout Asia, barley, rice, millet, mung beans, seaweed, tapioca, soya beans, and oats are used to fashion different types of pasta. Also utilized are potato starch, cornflour, cornmeal (polenta), legumes, and dried vegetables, such as artichokes and Jerusalem artichokes. The processed seeds of amaranth and quinoa, two highly nutritious plants known and widely used by pre-Columbian peoples, are also still used to make pasta today.

Pasta varieties To make commercial dried pasta, water is used almost exclusively. In parts of Italy whole eggs, or egg yolks only, or a combination of both, are used for fresh pasta. Some dried pastas use dried eggs or egg yolks instead of fresh. Cheese is used for pasta in Sicily, and flour and ricotta cheese are used to make the dough for gnocchi and cavatelli. Some recipes call for olive oil, white wine, or milk to be added to the flour for pasta dough. There is also a whole category of pastas that are flavoured and coloured by being made with puréed spinach, green chard, beetroot, mushrooms, or tomatoes. Squid ink is also used to make a distinctive black-coloured fresh pasta.

In fresh pasta-making, some or all of the water used in the basic recipe is replaced with eggs and/or egg yolks, with the possible additions of white wine, oil, and other flavouring liquids. The starch used is bread wheat, which is less hard than durum wheat. Fresh pasta is typically associated with the Italian regions of Emilia-Romagna – and its capital, the great gastronomic city of Bologna – and Piedmont, famous also for its intense wines and fragrant white truffles.

Every day, millions of people eat dried pasta, moulded into hundreds of different shapes, in every part of the world. However, many people associate "fresh" with wholesomeness and better health, and view fresh pasta as better, or more special, than dried. This is simply not true. Dried pasta can be a product of very high quality. Indeed, some argue that dried pasta is more desirable than fresh, because durum wheat semolina retains more of its nutritious elements than the white flour used in fresh pasta. Today, one can even find Italian dried pasta made from organically grown wheat.

Dumplings Always made of some sort of cereal or starchy vegetable, dumplings consist of a kind of bread dough to which some seasonings or herbs are added. The cooking process involves simmering and/or steaming in a flavoured liquid, such as a broth or stew, to allow the proteins in the starch (or eggs) to expand, lighten, and set. Often, something is enclosed inside the ball or oblong of dough, such as meat or fruit. In southern Germany and Austria, eggs, butter, cheese, liver, milk, and other embellishments are added. In that part of the world, dumplings go by such names as Knödel, Nockerl, and Spätzle, according to their size and shape.

The "dumplings" of Italian and Asian cuisine lie somewhat apart from the English and central European models. Gnocchi, for example, can be considered a type of fresh pasta, with a fairly well-defined shape, while in China, throughout central Asia, and in Russia, many types of stuffed "dumplings", such as wonton, mantu, mantou, shao mai, and pel'meni, more closely resemble the "ravioli" pasta prototype than that of the dumpling.

MAKING FRESH PASTA

Preparing fresh pasta from scratch definitely ranks among the most pleasurable and satisfying tasks in the kitchen. Like any other worthwhile endeavour, it takes patience and practice, but to my mind there are few things that repay a little effort with such generous and delicious rewards.

There are two methods of making fresh pasta – by hand or in a food processor. While the latter is quicker, the former has the benefit of giving the pasta-maker, over time, a truer sense of the texture and feel of the dough, a sense of how much flour the eggs can absorb, and – ultimately – a more tender pasta. Remember, however, that "tender" does not mean flaccid: fresh pasta, if it is worked correctly during the stretching process, should have texture and "tooth" when it is cooked.

Once the pasta dough is made, there are again two methods you can use to stretch the dough. The hand method, using a long, dowel-like rolling pin, which is usually not more than 4cm (1½in) in diameter, is by far the more demanding skill. This rolling pin, by the way, is much recommended over the thicker style with a ball-bearing mechanism. Using the latter is like driving an automatic transmission car, as opposed to a sporty gear shift. With the plain,

cylindrical pin you can feel the dough as it stretches. I urge everyone to attempt hand-stretching the pasta dough, simply because it is so satisfying.

The alternative is a good-quality pasta machine, either hand-cranked or electric, which also produces an excellent result. To my taste, the hand-stretched pasta is a bit more porous, lighter, and more capable of absorbing sauce, while machine-stretching results in a denser, somewhat slicker, smoother strand.

Preferences for work surfaces vary, with wood, stone (marble or other), and stainless steel being the most popular choices.

Making fresh pasta entails four distinct steps:

■ The first step is the actual formation of the dough from the basic ingredients, which for home-made pasta are usually flour and eggs with a little salt, plus sometimes olive oil, white wine, or milk. Other flavourings and colourings may also be added.

■ The second step is the kneading of the dough to develop its "body". This enables it to be stretched thin.

■ The third step is creating "la sfoglia", which is what Italians call the thinly stretched sheet of dough (pasta-makers are "sfogline").

■ The final step is to cut the sfoglia into the desired shapes.

MAKING PASTA DOUGH BY HAND

Do keep in mind that in Italy – and, in fact, wherever people are familiar with making fresh pasta – the amounts given in a recipe are approximate. One speaks of making "an egg" of pasta per person, as opposed to a definite amount of flour. The eggs will absorb as much flour as they want. In certain parts of Italy, such as Emilia-Romagna, salt is omitted from the dough. I like to include it in the recipe.

It is better to have a dough that is a bit too wet than too dry as it is much easier to work in a bit more flour than it is to add more moisture. If you do find yourself needing to add some moisture, do it by wetting your hands and then working the dough, rather than by adding water directly to the dough.

Makes enough pasta to serve 4 as a starter or 2 as a main dish, depending on shape and thickness of cut

| 165g (scant 6oz) "00" flour or strong white flour |
| ½tsp salt |
| 2 eggs |

1 Prepare a clean, well-lit work surface, at least 60cm (2ft) deep and 92cm (3ft) wide, and have to hand your rolling pin, a pastry scraper, a fork, and a fine-mesh sieve. Pour the flour and salt onto the work surface and form a well large enough to hold the eggs. Crack the eggs into the well and beat lightly with the fork.

2 Keeping one hand at the ready on the outside of the well, in case some egg should escape, begin drawing in small amounts of flour from the inside bottom of the well and mixing to incorporate the flour into the eggs. Gently stir the eggs all the while, and continue pulling in small amounts of flour.

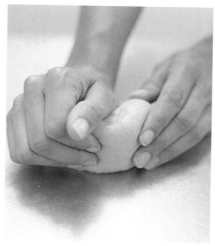

3 When the egg and flour mixture is thick enough not to run, push all the remaining flour into the centre and gently mix to form a dough. When the dough has stiffened somewhat and will no longer absorb flour, move it to a corner of the work surface. Scrape the work surface clean, and wash and dry your hands.

4 Place the scraped-away flour and bits of dough in the sieve and sift the clean flour onto a corner of the surface. Discard the pieces of dough in the sieve. Place the dough on the clean surface and knead until it holds together well. If it seems very sticky, sprinkle with a bit of the sifted flour, but do not let it get too dry.

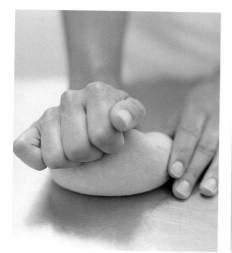

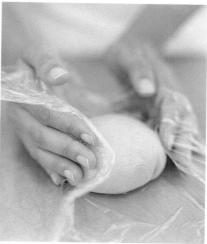

5 Continue to knead with a steady, firm motion, giving a quarter-turn with one hand while you press downwards and forwards with the heel of the other hand. Do this without rushing or exerting too much force, which will tire you out, but with a very steady, rhythmic motion, perhaps timed to your breathing.

6 Knead for 5–8 minutes, or until the dough feels very smooth and elastic. Wrap the dough in cling film and set aside at room temperature for at least 30 minutes, or up to 2 hours, before stretching it. This will give it time to soften enough to be stretched.

USING A MACHINE

A food processor is quick, but be careful not to overheat the dough by too much processing.

1 Combine the flour and salt in the bowl of a food processor and pulse a few times to aerate. With the machine running, add the beaten eggs (or eggs mixed with flavouring ingredients – see below) through the feed tube and process until the dough begins to form a ball. If it is too dry to do this, add water 1tsp at a time and continue to process.

2 Turn the dough onto a clean, unfloured surface and form it into a ball. Knead for 5–8 minutes (see step 5, left), or until the dough feels smooth and elastic. Wrap and set aside for at least 30 minutes before stretching.

FLAVOURING & COLOURING PASTA DOUGH

Mix one of the following with the eggs, then continue making the dough by hand or in a machine.

■ For spinach pasta (see below), use 85g (3oz) cooked, finely chopped or puréed, and well-drained spinach. Finely chopped spinach will give you a pasta that is speckled green, purée a more uniform green.

■ For pasta rossa, add 2tbsp tomato purée – ideally Sicilian sun-dried tomato purée.

■ For lemon and pepper pasta, add the grated zest of 2 small lemons, 1tsp coarsely ground black pepper, and 2tbsp freshly grated Parmesan (Parmigiano Reggiano).

■ For mushroom and herb pasta, rehydrate and purée 30g (1oz) dried porcini, then add with 1tbsp finely chopped rosemary.

STRETCHING PASTA DOUGH BY HAND

Stretching the dough by hand, using a rolling pin, is the part of the pasta-making process that requires the most skill – and patience. It is not all that difficult to master, however, and once you have the knack and the rhythm, you will find that it is definitely the most satisfying part. Remember that it is important to work quickly because if the dough is allowed to dry out and become stiff, it will no longer stretch.

When beginning to roll out the dough, apply pressure only in the outward direction, not on the return of the pin, and remember to think of this motion as pushing the dough out and away from you, rather than pressing it into the work surface. If the dough feels sticky at any time during the stretching process, sprinkle it with a small amount of flour.

If you are intending to use the dough for stuffed pasta, you can either stuff and cut each sheet as it is done, or cover each stretched sheet with a slightly damp tea towel and then stuff them all at the same time.

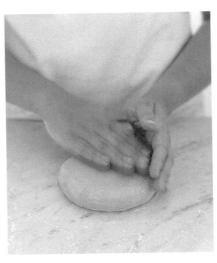

1 Unwrap the dough and cut it in half or into thirds or even quarters, depending on how skilled you are at stretching. Re-wrap all but one piece of the dough. Form the dough into a ball and flatten it slightly with your hands to create a disc. Sprinkle the work surface lightly with flour and place the dough in front of you.

2 Begin gently rolling the dough outward from a point about one-third of the way into the disc. Do not use too much pressure, and give the dough a quarter turn each time you complete an outward motion. Continue this process until you have formed a round piece of dough of equal thickness – about 3mm (⅛in).

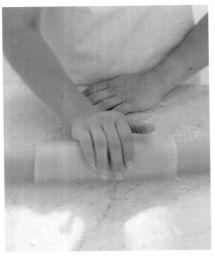

5 Continue, adding a bit more of the dough each time, until you have rolled up and unfurled the entire round. Roll all the dough onto the rolling pin and turn the pin around (not over) so that each hand is now grasping the other end, then unroll the dough again.

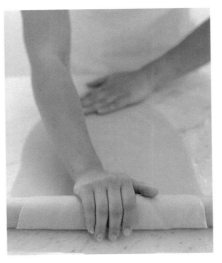

6 Begin the process once more, starting on the opposite end to where you last began. Keep repeating the curling, stretching, and unfurling process until the dough reaches the desired thickness (for stuffed pasta, roll as thinly as possible; for cut pasta roll to about 1mm).

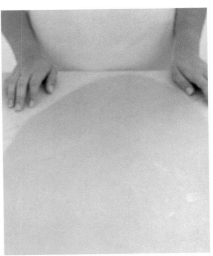

7 At the end of this process, you will have a very elongated oval shape of thinly rolled dough – the sfoglia – which I find easier to achieve and to work with than a perfect circle.

3 Place the rolling pin on the top edge of the dough round. Curl the dough over the pin and roll up about one-quarter of the dough using a light pressure. Anchor the dough on the table with your other hand. Using a somewhat staccato forwards-and-back rolling-and-pushing motion, quickly unfurl the dough from the pin.

4 Repeat the curling of the dough edge over the pin, but this time roll up a bit more of the dough than the last time, say one-third. Once again, anchor the dough with your other hand and give it the same forwards-and-back unfurling motion. These movements should be quick, but smooth and even.

CUTTING PASTA DOUGH BY HAND

Before cutting, you can trim the dough that results from hand-stretching. I prefer not to as it causes waste and lowers yield. Also, part of the hand-made process is the irregularity of lengths and shapes. It is generally just fine to use your eye to measure the widths of the various shapes and noodles. Flour the work surface and use a sharp chef's knife for cutting.

Square or rectangular shapes

Cut the dough to the required size: 12cm (5in) squares for fazzoletti or 12x15cm (5x6in) rectangles for lasagne or cannelloni.

Noodles

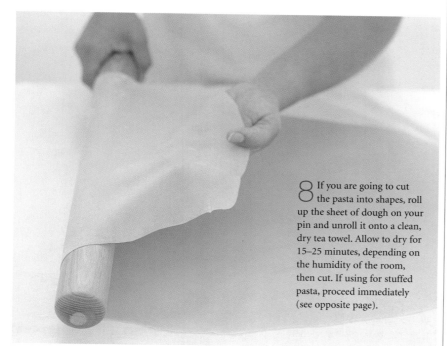

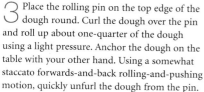

8 If you are going to cut the pasta into shapes, roll up the sheet of dough on your pin and unroll it onto a clean, dry tea towel. Allow to dry for 15–25 minutes, depending on the humidity of the room, then cut. If using for stuffed pasta, proceed immediately (see opposite page).

Fold the dough into thirds, like a letter. Place it with the folds at the top and bottom, then cut lengthways into strips: 5mm (¼in) wide for fettuccine and 1cm (½in) wide for pappardelle.

STRETCHING & CUTTING PASTA DOUGH WITH A MACHINE

You can use either a hand-cranked or electric pasta machine. I have included a little trick to make the work easier – pressing the ends of the strip of dough together to make a continuous loop. This technique works well for a large amount of dough, which when stretched becomes tricky to keep removing from and feeding back into the rollers. To start, set up the machine on the work surface and lightly flour the surface in front of the machine. During the initial folding and stretching process, drag the dough strip through the flour every now and then.

1 Cut the pasta dough into quarters; wrap 3 of the pieces in cling film and set aside. Flatten the remaining piece of dough into a rough circle and pass it through the widest setting on the machine. Decrease the setting a notch and pass the dough through once again. Decrease another notch and pass the dough through once more.

2 Fold the strip of dough into thirds and flatten it with your fingers. Return the machine to its widest setting. Turn the dough so that an unfolded end is against the rollers, then pass it through the machine. Repeat this folding and stretching process 5 or 6 times, or until the dough feels silky and elastic.

3 Now begin rolling the dough through the machine on decreasing settings until you reach the desired thickness. For cut pastas, this will usually be one notch before the finest setting; for stuffed pastas it will be all the way to the finest setting. To try my trick, pause 3 or 4 notches before the final setting.

5 Roll the loop through the machine several times to even it out, then continue rolling as you click down the settings to reach the desired thickness. Cut the dough with a paring knife and finish unrolling it from the machine.

6 If you are intending to use the dough for stuffed pasta, proceed immediately, without allowing the sheet to dry.
If you are going to cut the pasta into shapes, lay it flat on a clean, dry tea towel on the work surface and dry for 15–25 minutes, depending on the humidity of the room.

COOKING FRESH OR DRIED PASTA

In spite of its being a simple procedure, there seems to be a lot of erroneous information about the cooking of pasta. Here are my tips.
■ Do be sure to have an abundant amount of rapidly boiling water in the pan – in the order of 4 litres (7 pints) for 350–450g (12–16oz) fresh or dried pasta. There is nothing worse than cooking pasta in insufficient water that is not at a rapid boil.
■ Season the boiling water with 2tbsp salt – preferably sea salt – per 4 litres (7 pints). It is not possible to "season up" undersalted pasta once it is cooked; the salt will not penetrate.
■ Do not add oil to the water because this will only make the pasta slippery and less able to absorb the sauce. The reason people add oil is to prevent the pasta shapes from sticking together. This is better accomplished by stirring the pasta once it has been added to the pan.

■ It is sometimes a good idea, especially if your burners are not too strong, to cover the pan after you have added the pasta. This will help the water return to the boil more quickly. Once it has started boiling again, remove the lid and continue cooking uncovered.
■ While the pasta is cooking, be sure you have everything to hand, ready to go, so that the pasta can be quickly drained and sauced, then served immediately.
■ After draining the pasta, do not run cold water over it to stop the cooking – you will wash away all the starch and seasoning.
■ To sauce pasta, I recommend tossing it in the pan with the sauce to coat the pasta evenly and help it soak up the flavours. Make sure that the frying pan or saucepan in which you are making the sauce is large enough eventually to hold all the cooked pasta, too.

1 Be sure the water is at a rapid boil, then add the salt and plunge the pasta into the pan. Stir immediately to prevent the pasta from clumping together. When the water comes back to the boil, cook until the pasta is done (see below), continuing to stir occasionally.

2 Drain the pasta by pouring it into a large colander. Always reserve a small amount of the cooking water – it comes in very handy in many recipes to thin out and season the sauce. Do this by immediately placing the colander over the pan you cooked the pasta in.

4 Pass about half of the pasta strip through the rollers and stop. Press the edge of the other half onto the top surface of the machine in front of the rollers, then bring up and connect the edge of the extended half to it, pressing with your fingers to form a continuous loop of dough. Be sure that the edges line up accurately.

7 Use the cutters provided with the pasta machine to cut the pasta shape you desire, such as fettuccine or tagliarini (as shown above). Feed the strip of dough carefully into the machine so it falls straight onto the cutters. For square or rectangular shapes, cut it by hand.

HOW DO YOU KNOW WHEN PASTA IS COOKED?

When I was growing up, I remember hearing about the notion of testing the doneness of pasta by tossing a strand against the wall: if the pasta stuck, so the story went, it was done. I can assure you that I've never tried this system and it is entirely unnecessary. Follow the timing suggested on the packet of pasta and – most importantly – taste a strand or piece of pasta at several points during the duration of the cooking.

Dried pasta is cooked until it is "al dente", which means it should offer a slight resistance to the tooth when you bite into it. Also, if you break open a strand or piece of the cooked pasta, you should see a small white dot at the centre. Fresh pasta is cooked slightly beyond al dente – until it is tender. When cooked, the pasta will have lost its raw taste and it will be tender to the bite while retaining some body.

SERVING FRESH PASTA

Following are two of my favourite pasta recipes. Fazzoletti, which are large, flat pasta squares whimsically named for their resemblance to a silk handkerchief, can be folded, casually draped, or laid flat on a plate. At Union Square Café, we sauce the fazzoletti with a delicious courgette and marjoram purée.

Fettuccine with sweetcorn has long been a late-summer pasta staple at USC. For the sauce, we've borrowed from traditional corn chowder recipes, steeping the cobs with white wine and cream to lend a richly complex sweetcorn flavour. The addition of pancetta, Gorgonzola, and sun-dried tomatoes completes the dish.

FAZZOLETTI WITH COURGETTE & MARJORAM SAUCE

Serves 12 as a starter or 6 as a main course

1 quantity of fresh pasta dough made with 2 eggs (p276)

4 litres (7 pints) boiling water with 2tbsp sea salt for cooking

For the sauce

2tbsp extra virgin olive oil

1 garlic clove, sliced

340g (12oz) courgettes, quartered lengthways and thinly sliced

½tsp chopped marjoram

85g (3oz) skinned, seeded, and diced tomato

120ml (4fl oz) chicken stock, or more as needed

To finish

140g (5oz) plain flour for the baking trays

55g (2oz) butter

5tbsp water

fresh shavings of Parmesan (Parmigiano Reggiano)

1 To make the sauce, put the oil and garlic in a large, straight-sided frying pan. Cook over low heat for 2–3 minutes, or until the garlic is soft but not browned. Raise the heat to high and add the courgettes, marjoram, tomato, and some salt and pepper. Cook, stirring occasionally, until the courgettes have softened somewhat. Add the stock and cook for a further 4–5 minutes.

2 Transfer the courgette mixture to a food processor and pulse until smooth, but not too finely puréed. Return the purée to the pan and warm it through over moderate heat, stirring constantly. Adjust the consistency to taste (by adding more stock or water if it seems too thick) and check the seasoning. Set aside.

3 Dust 2 baking trays with the flour. Stretch the pasta dough to not quite paper-thin if you are doing it by hand, or to within one notch of the finest setting if using a machine. Dry, then cut into twelve 12cm (5in) squares (fazzoletti). Place in a single layer on the floured trays.

4 Combine the butter, water, ½tsp salt, and a pinch of pepper in a very large frying pan. Bring to the boil to melt the butter, then swirl the ingredients to mix. Remove from the heat.

5 Cook the fazzoletti in the boiling salted water for 2 minutes, or until tender. Return the courgette and marjoram sauce to a simmer.

Drain the fazzoletti and immediately add them to the butter mixture in the frying pan. Return it to moderate heat and toss the fazzoletti gently to coat with butter.

6 Spoon the courgette sauce onto the serving plates and spread the sauce to cover the bottom. Using tongs, place a fazzoletto (or 2, if serving as a main course) on top of each pool of sauce, draping the pasta so that it looks like a handkerchief. Sprinkle with Parmesan shavings and freshly ground black pepper, then serve.

FETTUCCINE WITH SWEETCORN & GORGONZOLA CREAM

Although this sauce has been designed to be served with freshly made fettuccine, you will also be satisfied if you use 450g (1lb) good-quality dried egg fettuccine.

Serves 6 as a starter or 3–4 as a main course

For the pasta

250g (8½oz) "00" flour or strong flour

½tsp salt

3 eggs

4 litres (7 pints) boiling water with 2tbsp sea salt for cooking

For the sauce

2 large corn-on-the-cob

1tbsp olive oil

75g (2½oz) pancetta, diced

55g (2oz) shallots, sliced

1tbsp coarsely chopped garlic

120ml (4fl oz) white wine

480ml (16fl oz) double cream

2 heaped tbsp crumbled Gorgonzola

1tsp sea salt

⅛tsp freshly ground black pepper

55g (2oz) spring onions, sliced diagonally (both white and green)

15g (½oz) basil leaves, sliced

12 oil-packed sun-dried tomatoes

1 Make the pasta dough following the master recipe (p276), but using the ingredients listed here. Stretch the dough to almost paper-thin if you are doing it by hand, or to within 1–2 notches of the finest setting if using a machine. Dry, then cut into fettuccine, which are long strands about 5mm (¼in) wide.

2 Cut the sweetcorn kernels off the cobs (p248); set aside. Cut the cobs into 5cm (2in) sections.

3 Combine the oil and pancetta in a large, straight-sided frying pan and cook over moderately high

heat for about 5 minutes to crisp the pancetta and render the fat. Remove the pancetta with a slotted spoon and set aside. Discard all but 1tbsp fat from the pan.

4 Reduce the heat to moderate. Add the shallots, garlic, and pieces of corn cob to the pan and

cook for about 3 minutes, or until the shallots are softened but not browned. Pour in the wine and reduce until almost dry. Add the cream and simmer very gently for 5 minutes. Remove from the heat, cover, and steep for 15 minutes.

5 Strain the sauce through a fine-mesh sieve into another frying pan or a saucepan that will be large enough to hold the cooked pasta, too. Place over moderate heat and gently whisk in the cheese in small pieces. Season with the salt and pepper. Add the sweetcorn kernels, pancetta, spring onions, and basil. Cut the tomatoes in half lengthways and stir in. Bring the sauce to a simmer, then remove from the heat, cover, and set aside.

6 Cook the fettuccine in the boiling salted water for 30–60 seconds, or until it is tender, then drain it in a colander. Add the pasta to the sauce.

7 Toss until all the strands of pasta are well coated with the sauce. Transfer to bowls and serve.

MAKING DUMPLINGS

In differentiating between pasta and dumplings, the distinguishing factor would appear to be shape, rather than ingredients. With pasta the dough is shaped or cut into a precise, well-defined form, whereas dumplings are generally left in a rather homely, irregular shape. For Spätzle, mainly seen in Alsace, Switzerland, Germany, and Austria, a batter-like dough is pressed into squiggly dumplings. Matzo balls and potato gnocchi are both shaped by hand, one into balls and the other into ridged ovals.

MAKING SPÄTZLE

Spätzle are quite simple to prepare: the dough is passed through a press directly into boiling salted water to create tiny, irregular dumplings. If you don't have a special Spätzle press, you can use a colander with 5mm (¼in) holes and press the dough through with a rubber spatula (as shown here). After boiling, Spätzle can be tossed with a sauce or sautéed.

Serves 4 as a starter

220g (scant 8oz) strong flour	5tbsp milk
2 eggs	5tbsp hot water
a scraping of freshly grated nutmeg	1tbsp olive oil and 30g (1oz) butter, if sautéing

1 Sift the flour into a large bowl. Form a well in the centre and break in the eggs. Add a pinch of salt and the nutmeg. Stirring with your hand, begin mixing the eggs and flour together. Slowly pour in the milk, still stirring with your hand. Stir in the hot water.

2 Beat the mixture lightly with your hand for 30 seconds. The mixture should be the consistency of a very wet, soft dough. Leave it to relax for at least 30 minutes in a cool place. Meanwhile, bring a large pan of salted water to the boil. Set a Spätzle press or colander on top.

3 Put the dough into the press or colander and begin pushing it through the holes. Cook in batches to avoid overcrowding the pan. As soon as the water resumes boiling, boil for 30 seconds. With a slotted spoon, transfer the cooked Spätzle to an ice-water bath, then drain well.

4 When all the Spätzle have been cooked and drained, reheat them in a sauce, or sauté them: heat the oil and butter in a large frying pan. When sizzling, add the Spätzle and sauté until they are golden brown and slightly crisp. Serve hot as a side dish.

RED CHARD SPÄTZLE

I really enjoy the earthy taste of red chard in combination with sautéed Spätzle. You could even include the chard stalks as well as the leaves – thinly slice and sauté the stalks separately, then add them with the leaves. Feel free to substitute green chard or spinach for the red chard.

Serves 4 as a starter

1 quantity of Spätzle (see above)
1tbsp olive oil
30g (1oz) butter
340g (12oz) red Swiss chard leaves, cut into large pieces

Sauté the Spätzle in the oil and butter (see above) until they begin to turn golden brown. Add the chard leaves and continue cooking until the leaves are wilted. Season to taste with salt and pepper, then serve immediately.

MATZO BALLS

Matzo balls – called kneidlach in Yiddish – are a type of dumpling made with a thick matzo meal batter. The dumplings are usually served in a rich chicken broth. Quantities to make 16 matzo balls are given in the recipe, right.

1 Put the eggs in a bowl and stir with a fork just to combine the white and yolks. Stir in the water or seltzer, the schmaltz, and some salt and pepper. Gradually add the matzo meal, stirring all the while to eliminate lumps. Refrigerate the batter for at least 1 hour.

2 With moistened hands, form the matzo balls, using about 2oz (55g) of batter for each one. As they are shaped, drop the balls, a couple at a time, into a large pot of boiling salted water. When the water returns to a boil, reduce the heat so it is simmering, then cover and cook for 30 minutes. Lift out with a slotted spoon, tasting one ball to be sure it is cooked through. Serve in rich chicken broth.

SUSAN FRIEDLAND'S MATZO BALL SOUP

This recipe for traditional matzo ball soup comes from my friend Susan Friedland, cookbook author and editor. The recipe for the broth makes twice the amount you need, but given the time and labour involved I think this is a good thing. Half of the broth can be frozen – it is useful to have on hand. If you want to serve the soup as a main course for 5–6, add the chicken meat to the broth.

Serves 8 as a starter

For the rich chicken broth

2 boiling fowl, 2.7–3.6kg (6–8lb) each, including neck and giblets but not the liver

5–6 litres (4¼–5¼ pints) water

4 large onions, halved

6 carrots, cut into large chunks

10 black peppercorns, crushed

15 sprigs of parsley

dill and parsley to garnish

For the matzo balls

4 eggs

120ml (4fl oz) water or seltzer

6tbsp melted schmaltz (chicken fat)

115g (4oz) matzo meal

1 First make the broth. Remove the fat from the cavities of the boiling fowl. Place one in a stockpot with the water and half of the vegetables. The ingredients should barely be covered with water. Bring to the boil and skim off the foam, then adjust the heat so that only a couple of bubbles appear on the surface.

2 Add the peppercorns and parsley sprigs, partly cover the pan, and simmer for about 2 hours, or until the chicken is tender but not falling apart, skimming occasionally.

3 Remove the chicken to a large platter. When it is cool enough to handle, take the meat from the bones (reserve for serving or for other use). Put the bones and skin back in the broth. Simmer, partly covered, for about 1 hour, then strain into a bowl. Leave to cool, then refrigerate overnight.

4 Remove the fat that has hardened on the surface of the broth. Pour into the cleaned pot and add the second chicken, the remaining vegetables, and more water if necessary to cover. Repeat the cooking process, then strain and refrigerate. Reheat for serving.

5 Make the matzo balls (see left). Place 2 matzo balls in each soup bowl, add some of the reserved meat if liked, and ladle in hot chicken broth. Garnish and serve.

POTATO GNOCCHI

Potato gnocchi can be exquisitely delicate or quite leaden, depending on the handling and care they are given. The secret is to use a light touch and not over-handle or over-work the potatoes once they have been riced.

If not cooking the gnocchi the day you make them, freeze in a single layer, covered. They can be stored in the freezer for up to one week. Cook from frozen (they'll take a little longer to float to the surface).

Serves 6 as a starter or 4 as a main course

600g (1¼lb) floury potatoes, unpeeled, cooked in boiling salted water until tender, then drained

5tbsp freshly grated Parmesan (Parmigiano Reggiano)

1 egg

½tsp sea salt

¼tsp freshly ground black pepper

175g (6oz) "00" flour or strong flour, or more as needed

4 litres (7 pints) boiling water and 2tbsp sea salt for cooking

1 Peel the warm potatoes, then pass through a ricer or food mill onto a large baking tray in an even layer. Chill for 15 minutes, or until cool. Mound the potatoes on a clean work surface and form a well in the centre.

2 Add the Parmesan, egg, salt, and pepper to the well. With your fingertips, combine these ingredients with the potato, stirring to form a rough dough. Sprinkle the flour over the potato mixture and combine gently.

3 Knead the dough, using a downward press-and-quarter-turn motion, for 8–10 minutes, or until smooth, elastic, and uniform in colour. Form into a 20cm (8in) roll and cut crossways into 4 pieces. Cover with cling film.

4 Clean the work surface and your hands. Take one piece of dough and roll it back and forth on the surface while applying a gentle downward pressure, to form a cylinder 46–50cm (18–20in) long and as thick as your forefinger. Lightly dust with flour. Repeat with the remaining pieces of dough.

5 Cut the cylinders into 3cm (1¼in) pieces. Form each into the traditional gnocchi crescent shape: hold a fork backside up in one hand; with the thumb of your other hand press the dough against the back of the fork, forming an indentation, while simultaneously rolling it down over the prongs.

6 Lay the gnocchi on several baking trays in a single layer so that they don't stick together. Cover with cling film and keep refrigerated until ready to cook.

7 Cook the gnocchi, in batches, in the boiling salted water. As soon as they float to the surface, remove them with a slotted spoon and drain in a colander. Spread out in one layer on baking trays or add directly to the sauce (in a large pan). When all the gnocchi are cooked, reheat them gently in the sauce for serving.

Porcini gnocchi with prosciutto & parmigiano cream

Each year, with the arrival of the first autumn chill, I bring our porcini gnocchi back to the menu. Our guests tell us how much they look forward to the return of this popular dish, so delicate but richly flavoured.

**Serves 8 as a starter or
4–6 as a main course**

For the gnocchi

480ml (16fl oz) boiling water

30g (1oz) dried porcini mushrooms

ingredients for potato gnocchi (see opposite)

For the parmigiano cream

45g (1½oz) butter

1 small red onion, sliced

2tbsp finely chopped garlic

140g (5oz) shiitake mushrooms, stalks removed and reserved, caps sliced

15g (½oz) parsley stalks

240ml (8fl oz) dry white wine

480ml (16fl oz) double cream

55g (2oz) Parma ham, cut into thin strips 2.5cm (1in) long

115g (4oz) red or green Swiss chard leaves or spinach, chopped

4tbsp freshly grated Parmesan (Parmigiano Reggiano)

2tbsp chopped parsley

Pour the boiling water over the porcini and soak for about 15 minutes, or until rehydrated. Lift them out with a slotted spoon and set aside. Strain the liquid through a coffee filter to remove any grit. Reserve 240ml (8fl oz) of the liquid for the sauce. Squeeze the mushrooms with your hands until very dry, then purée to a smooth paste in a food processor.

Make the gnocchi dough following the master recipe (see opposite), adding the porcini purée with the Parmesan and egg. Shape the gnocchi, then lay them in a single layer on baking trays. Cover and refrigerate until ready to cook.

For the sauce, melt half the butter in a large, non-reactive saucepan over moderate heat. Add the onions, garlic, mushroom stalks, and parsley stalks. Cook for about 4 minutes, or until softened but not browned. Add the wine and reserved porcini liquid. Bring to the boil, then reduce to about one-third of the original volume. Add the cream and reduce again until the sauce coats the back of a spoon. Strain into a bowl and set aside.

In the cleaned saucepan, heat the remaining butter over moderately high heat until it is just beginning to brown. Add the shiitake mushroom caps and sauté for 2–3 minutes. Return the cream sauce to the pan together with the Parma ham, Swiss chard, and half of the Parmesan. Cook over moderate heat for 3–4 minutes. Season with ½tsp sea salt and ⅛tsp pepper. Keep the sauce warm.

Cook the porcini gnocchi, in batches, as in the master recipe. When all are cooked and drained, reheat them gently in the cream sauce over moderate heat. Spoon into warm bowls, sprinkle with the chopped parsley and remaining Parmesan, and serve.

ASIAN NOODLES & DUMPLINGS

CHRISTINE MANFIELD

For the peoples of Asia, noodles and dumplings rival bread and rice as sources of energy, starch, and dietary fibre. From China to Indonesia, dishes are made with noodles or dumplings as their starting point. On Asian streets, noodles and dumplings dispensed from small carts, hole-in-the-wall counters, and restaurants sustain millions of locals daily, from sunrise to well into the night.

The variety of noodles Noodle types vary across the Asian continent. Those from northern China are tougher, made from wheat or barley and water; further south, wheat noodles become more pliant with the use of egg; and in the wetter climes of Southeast Asia the soft-textured rice noodle is more common. The Vietnamese and Cambodians have perfected the gorgeously soft and sensuous rice noodle; the Japanese are experts with soba and udon; and the Koreans have the unique dang myun, a translucent cellophane vermicelli made with vegetable starch, and a more textured version of the soba, naeng myun. In Malaysia and Singapore, where noodles were introduced by the Chinese, wheat, egg, and rice noodles weave their way into everything from soups to stir-fries.

In China, noodles are served on birthdays; symbolizing long life, they are considered as important as birthday cakes. Usually the e-fu or long-life noodle is used, and the noodles are never cut as this would suggest shortening one's life. Another noodle, from China's Shandong province, is the la mian, or dragon's whisker. A work of art in itself, this noodle is hand-drawn and hand-thrown from a length of dough by specially trained master chefs.

Within the Taoist tradition of yin yang, flavours and textures come together to create perfect harmony and balance – cold with hot, crunchy with soft, wet with dry, smooth with crisp. Noodles, whether steamed, boiled, braised, deep-fried, or stir-fried, make a vital contribution. When many dishes are to be shared at the table, the cook needs special knowledge of all the ingredients and skill in their assembly to achieve a true balance of yin and yang.

Dim sum and dumplings Dumplings have a slightly different role in the lives of Asians. The ritual of taking dim sum, traditionally served with jasmine tea, is practised in the late morning and lunchtime in Chinese restaurants all over the world. Minuscule dumplings and pastry pillows are paraded before the customer – ingenious morsels with delicious centres, created daily by an army of cooks, and devoured within seconds. Vying for attention are deep-fried or boiled spring rolls or wontons, melt-in-the-mouth fried taro pastries called wu gok, and steamed har gau – translucent pastries with luscious prawn, pork, or scallop centres. There are steamed siu mai, with their minced pork, prawn, and water-chestnut filling; jai gau, glutinous rice wrappers stuffed with green leafy vegetables and ginger; and wondrous pot sticker dumplings, Chinese jiaozi or Japanese gyoza, consisting of a special dough made with boiling water and usually filled with minced pork. Other components are the sublime duck pancakes – wafer-thin sheets cooked in a hot pan, steamed, then wrapped around crisp Peking duck, cucumber sticks, and spring onions, seasoned with a hoisin or plum sauce.

The Vietnamese make a spring roll using rice-paper sheets for a light, crisp texture. The same rice-paper sheets are used to make cold rolls filled with prawns, crab, pork, or vegetables, with fresh rice vermicelli usually added to enhance the soft textures. Malaysia has given us the popiah, another version of the fresh roll in which the pastry sheets are made paper-thin, in the same way as you would a crêpe, then filled with vegetables or minced pork and chili.

Dumplings can be made from glutinous rice flour, potato or water chestnut flour, eggs, wheat flour, duck fat, lard, rice paper, mung beans, or even green vegetable leaves, like pandanus or banana. Whatever the wrapper or pastry used to encase the filling, it should be paper-thin with the texture and consistency of a floating cloud. It is important to consider the ratio of wrapper to filling, since the wrapper is there simply to hold the filling in place and shape, not to dominate the finished dumpling.

EGG NOODLES

Manufactured dried egg noodles produce good results, but there is a particular pleasure in making your own from fresh ingredients.

Serves 6

250g (8½oz) bread flour

3 large eggs

1tbsp olive oil

pinch of sea salt

rice flour for dusting

1 Blend all the ingredients except the rice flour in a food processor until the dough forms into a ball. Wrap the dough in cling film and refrigerate for 1 hour.

2 Cut the dough into 4 pieces, then flatten each by hand or with a rolling pin. Pass each piece through the rollers of a pasta machine (dusting it each time with rice flour to prevent sticking). Work gradually through the settings until you reach the finest one. Hang the sheets over a broom handle or back of a chair to dry for 10 minutes. This makes the dough easier to cut.

3 Pass the dough through your pasta machine's spaghetti cutters. Hang the noodles over a broom handle or back of a chair for 30 minutes or until ready to cook.

4 Bring a large saucepan of water to a rolling boil, then add the noodles and allow the water to return to the boil. Cook for 2 minutes, then remove the noodles from the heat with a sieve and drain.

5 If not eating immediately, stop the cooking by running cold water over the noodles, then drain and toss lightly with a little oil to prevent sticking. To reheat, immerse the noodles in boiling water for 10 seconds, then drain.

BOILING NOODLES

All noodles, whether fresh or dried, need to be softened in hot or boiling water before use. Most are boiled for a few minutes. The exceptions are those noodles that would fall apart if boiled. To prepare fresh rice noodles, for instance, simply pour boiling water over them and immediately drain. Fine dried cellophane (bean thread) noodles just need to be soaked in hot water.

1 To boil egg, wheat, or buckwheat noodles, bring a large saucepan of water to a rolling boil. Add the noodles and allow the water to return to the boil, then cook for 2 minutes, or until the noodles are softened and pliable.

2 Drain the noodles in a sieve. Refresh under cold running water to stop them cooking further, then drain again. Toss lightly with a little oil to prevent sticking. Use immediately or set aside. To reheat for serving, immerse noodles in boiling water for 10 seconds, then drain.

UDON NOODLE SOUP

The thick, slippery Japanese udon noodle is ideal for soup and braising and takes on big robust flavours with ease. It is used in this hearty broth, which is perfect during cold weather. Serve with chopsticks for the noodles and a spoon for the liquid.

1 knob of fresh ginger plus 2 slices of fresh ginger, shredded

1tbsp water

4tbsp shiro (white) miso paste

3tbsp mirin

2½tbsp sake

5tbsp light soy sauce

100g (3½oz) dried udon noodles, boiled for 4–5 minutes, then drained

200g (7oz) salmon fillet, finely sliced

85g (3oz) fresh firm tofu, diced

8 shiitake mushrooms, sliced and sautéed until soft

4 spring onions, finely sliced

1tbsp snipped chives

For the dashi stock

2 litres (3½ pints) still mineral or spring water

3cm (1¼in) piece of dried konbu

50g (1¾oz) dried bonito flakes

1 To make the dashi stock, place the water and konbu in a large pan and bring slowly to the boil over a low heat. Once simmering, stir in the bonito flakes, then remove from the heat and leave to infuse for 30 minutes. Strain the stock through a fine mesh sieve. Discard the solids.

2 Meanwhile, process the knob of ginger and the water in a blender to a paste, then press through a fine sieve to extract the juice. You need 1tbsp (keep the rest in a jar, refrigerated).

3 Return the stock to the pan and bring to simmering point. Whisk in the miso, then season the soup with the mirin, sake, soy sauce, and ginger juice. Bring back to simmering point. Taste and adjust the flavourings, if necessary.

4 To serve the soup, divide the noodles, salmon, tofu, mushrooms, spring onions, and shredded ginger equally among 4 bowls. Ladle in the hot soup and stir with a chopstick. Sprinkle over the chives and serve immediately.

Black pepper chicken tea, noodles & watercress

The chicken tea is made in the same way as consommé, providing a clear soup in which to float the solid ingredients. Enoki mushrooms are available in most supermarkets, but if you cannot find cloud ear fungus, leave it out – there is no substitute. In the restaurant, I like to serve the soup in a cup on a saucer.

For the chicken tea

1 head of garlic

4tsp vegetable oil

1 onion, chopped

1 large, fresh red chili, sliced

1tsp chopped fresh ginger

½tsp black peppercorns, freshly cracked

1tsp Sichuan peppercorns, freshly cracked

3tbsp Shaoxing rice wine or dry sherry

2 kaffir lime leaves, shredded

2 spring onions, chopped

1.5 litres (2¾ pints) chicken stock

3tbsp light Chinese soy sauce

2tbsp fish sauce

1tbsp freshly squeezed lime juice, strained

To serve

120g (4½oz) cooked fresh egg noodles, made with 2tsp freshly ground and sifted black pepper added to the basic recipe (p291)

300g (10½oz) chicken breasts, cooked, boned, and meat finely shredded

100g (3½oz) enoki mushrooms, trimmed

4 fresh cloud ear fungi, finely shredded

8 chives, finely snipped

8tbsp tiny watercress leaves

2tbsp chopped coriander

To make the tea, preheat the oven to 180°C (350°F, gas 4). Wrap the garlic in foil and roast for 30 minutes, or until soft. Cool, then squeeze from the skins and slice thickly.

Heat the oil in a heavy-based saucepan or cast-iron stockpot and fry the onion, chili, and ginger until soft and starting to colour. Stir in the black and Sichuan peppercorns, then deglaze the pan with the rice wine. When the wine comes to the boil, remove from the heat.

Add the roasted garlic, lime leaves, spring onions, chicken stock, and soy sauce. Slowly bring to the boil over a gentle heat, then simmer for 1 hour, skimming the surface regularly with a slotted spoon. Do not allow to boil or the tea will become cloudy.

Strain the tea through a muslin-lined sieve to ensure it is clear and free of sediment, pressing to extract the liquid. Discard the solids. Allow the tea to cool, then refrigerate.

Remove any fat from the top of the chilled tea, then strain again through a musin-lined sieve into a clean saucepan, avoiding any sediment. Bring the tea to a simmer. Stir in the fish sauce and lime juice and cook for 3 minutes. Taste and adjust the seasoning.

Divide the serving ingredients among 4 cups or bowls, then ladle in the hot tea. Swirl with a chopstick to combine, and serve.

HONEY & SESAME BEEF WITH RICE STICKS

Once they have been softened in hot water, rice noodles are ideal for braising or stir-frying in a sauce. You can also use fine egg noodles, boiled until soft and pliable. For a milder flavour, remove the chili seeds.

2 large garlic cloves, crushed

2tbsp light soy sauce

1tbsp fish sauce

1tsp toasted sesame oil

2tbsp light honey

1tsp freshly ground black pepper

3 fresh, green bird's eye chilies, very finely chopped

3tbsp vegetable oil

300g (10½oz) beef fillet, thinly sliced

200g (7oz) dried rice sticks, softened in hot water, then drained

2tsp white sesame seeds, lightly dry-roasted (p79)

bunch of watercress leaves or sprigs

½ bunch (a large handful) of garlic chives, snipped into 2.5cm (1in) lengths

1 In a bowl, mix the garlic, soy sauce, fish sauce, sesame oil, honey, pepper, and chilies with half the oil. Add the beef slices, mix well, and marinate for 10 minutes.

2 Heat a large wok and add 2tsp oil. Add half the beef with half its marinade. Toss over high heat to sear and cook quickly, separating the strips with chopsticks. Remove from the wok. Cook the remaining beef, using the rest of the oil.

3 Return all the seared beef to the wok with its juices and any remaining marinade. Add the rice sticks and stir and toss to coat them with the sauce in the wok. Add the sesame seeds, watercress, and garlic chives and toss through to mix, then serve immediately.

SESAME CHICKEN & NOODLE SALAD

This recipe is a variation on the classic bang bang chicken. It uses thick and substantial Shanghai noodles. You can substitute thick-cut rice noodles or rice sticks, but the texture and taste will be slightly different.

200g (7oz) fresh Shanghai noodles, boiled for 2–3 minutes, or until softened, then drained and refreshed

300g (10½oz) chicken breasts, cooked, boned, and meat shredded

1 cucumber, finely sliced

100g (3½oz) bean sprouts

1tbsp white sesame seeds, dry-roasted (p79)

4 spring onions, finely sliced

For the sesame dressing

3tbsp Chinese toasted sesame paste

¼tsp Sichuan peppercorns, dry-roasted and ground

4 garlic cloves

2tsp chopped fresh ginger

1 small, fresh green chili, chopped

1tsp chili paste or sambal

2tbsp vegetable oil

2tbsp light soy sauce

1tbsp fish sauce

1tbsp Shaoxing rice wine or dry sherry

1tbsp Chinese black vinegar

1tbsp caster sugar

100ml (3½fl oz) chicken stock

Arrange the noodles on a serving plate. Mix the other ingredients together and place on top. Process the dressing ingredients in a blender until smooth. Spoon the dressing over the salad and serve.

SOMEN NOODLES WITH CLAMS & MUSSELS

This simple stir-fry is full of delicate, silky textures and fresh sea flavours. Instead of clams and mussels, you can use scallops or other molluscs – fresh abalone, steamed until softened and finely sliced, is fabulous.

1kg (2¼lb) mussels

1kg (2¼lb) clams

4tbsp vegetable oil

6 spring onions, cut into 1cm (½in) lengths

12 garlic cloves, crushed

4 large dried chilies, crushed

3tbsp Shaoxing rice wine

200ml (7fl oz) fish stock

3tbsp mirin

2tbsp Chinese black vinegar

2tbsp fish sauce

200g (7oz) dried somen noodles, boiled for 2 minutes, then drained

6 Chinese cabbage leaves, shredded

large handful of Thai basil leaves

1 Steam the mussels and clams open, separately, in a covered pan over high heat; discard any that remain closed. Plunge into iced water, then remove from shells. Reserve clam and mussel juices.

2 Heat the oil in a wok and stir-fry the spring onions, garlic, and chilies briefly until softened. Add the rice wine and swirl to deglaze, then add the stock, mirin, vinegar, fish sauce, and reserved juices. Bring to the boil. Taste and adjust the seasoning, if necessary.

3 Add the clams and mussels to the wok together with the noodles and cabbage. Stir over high heat for 1 minute, or until warmed through. Add the Thai basil leaves and toss to mix, then ladle into deep bowls to serve.

NOODLE-WRAPPED TIGER PRAWNS

Thin egg noodles wrapped around big juicy prawns – or scallops or chunks of white fish – and then deep-fried until crisp make a perfect party snack. Serve with a sweet chili dipping sauce.

16 raw tiger prawns in shell

2tsp fish sauce

½tsp ground chili (hot chili powder)

250g (8½oz) fresh thin egg noodles, boiled for 2 minutes, or until softened, then drained and refreshed

vegetable oil for deep-frying

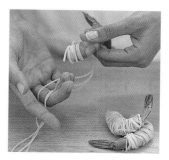

1 Peel the prawns, leaving the last tail section intact, then devein them. Season the prawns with the fish sauce and ground chili.

2 Divide the noodles into 16 bundles. Lay out each bundle of noodles in lengths and wrap around a prawn.

3 Heat the vegetable oil in a large wok or deep-fryer to 180°C (350°F). Fry the prawns, a few at a time, for 3 minutes, or until they are pink and the noodles are crisp and golden.

4 Remove with a slotted spoon and drain on kitchen paper. Serve freshly fried, with sweet chili sauce for dipping.

THAI COOKING

DAVID THOMPSON

Thailand has produced one of the world's great cuisines. Developing over centuries from a rustic base, firmly rooted in the land, Thai cuisine came to reflect the sophistication and complexity of Thai society. In the palaces of the wealthy, elaborate methods prevailed – time, labour, and costs were barely considered and days could be spent preparing dishes. By contrast, peasant food was always robust, but never coarse or tasteless. Refined or basic, Thai food is always eaten with rice. Curries, soups, salads, relishes, or stir-fries are merely savoury accompaniments to this essential grain. Poorer households tend to consume more rice, and the accompanying dishes are usually spicier.

Agricultural self-sufficiency Rice growing has sculpted the countryside. Small rivers and canals irrigate the fields and provide fresh fish, eels, frogs, and semi-aquatic greens. Slender jasmine rice is the preferred choice in the central plains and the south, while glutinous or sticky rice is consumed in the north and northeast. Groves of fruit trees ring the fields, which pass into forests where small game, wild herbs, and vegetables are gathered. Each house or compound has a small garden where vegetables and fruits such as garlic, chilies, kaffir limes, coriander, and basil are grown; and chickens, pigs, and ducks are raised. In Thailand diet was always determined by availability – and to a large degree still is – since most Thais continue to live in the countryside, growing their own produce or purchasing food from traditional markets. What is constantly surprising is the quality and variety of ingredients to be found in even the dustiest of village markets.

Thailand is a geographically diverse country. In the northern forests, along the Mekong River, game, wild vegetables, and herbs abound. Away from the wilder areas, freshwater fish and pork may be found. Coconuts do not grow this far north, so pork fat – or now, more healthily, vegetable oil – is the cooking medium used instead of coconut cream. The remote northeast is poor and arid; here, sticky rice is preferred, and foods are whatever can be found: catfish, buffalo, vegetables – even insects are collected for the pot. Since the farmers are impoverished and food scarce, the cooking of this region is highly seasoned with chilies and often with fermented fish, eaten whole or in a pungent sauce. The central plains are cultivated with long-grain rice, and there is less wild food to be found. The Thai food most westerners are familiar with comes from this region. The south is monsoonal and here the diet depends on the sea. Fish and seafood are avidly consumed. Gapi, fermented shrimp paste, flavours most dishes, ample coconut cream enriches them, and hot chilies make them memorable. Equipment determines culinary technique no matter what the cuisine. Perhaps most indispensable in the Thai kitchen is the mortar and pestle, used in making relishes, curry pastes, and sauces. Knife work – chopping, fine slicing, and shredding – ensures that pungent ingredients are evenly distributed in the dish and do not overwhelm the palate.

Distinctive flavours Thai seasoning is a varying balance of four elements: salty, hot, sour, and sweet. The degree and sequence of the seasonings depends on the dish's style and region of origin. Northern food is primarily salty and not overly hot. Southern food is salty, sour, and hot, using chilies, sugar, and tamarind. The northeast is spicy and salty; the central plains combine all four seasonings. Textures also play an important part in Thai cooking. Chilies sensitize the palate, heightening awareness of inherent textures in fruits and vegetables. The Thais also coax increased texture out of ingredients in their dish selections; for example, deep-fried shallots offer a crunchy contrast to soft stewed sweet pork and its spicy relish accompaniment.

When planning a meal, Thais avoid repeating the style of dishes, techniques used, and seasonings – this is because repetition indicates a lack of consideration on the part of the cook. A balanced meal comprises rice, a curry, a soup, a relish, a salad, and a stir-fried, deep-fried, or grilled dish, all working in concert with each other in their textures and seasonings.

MENU

- Spicy relish of prawns & pea
  aubergines with sweet pork

- Stir-fried Siamese watercress
  with yellow beans, garlic
  & chilies

- Snake gourd, egg
  & crab soup

- Green curry of beef with corn
  & Thai basil

SPICY RELISH OF PRAWNS & PEA AUBERGINES
with sweet pork

This spicy relish (nahm prik) should be thick, hot, salty, sour, and slightly sweet. Serve with raw cucumbers, green tomatoes, white turmeric or chicory, blanched green beans, and sweet pork. You can buy the aubergines in oriental shops.

For the spicy relish

2 coriander roots, soaked in water for 5–10 minutes, scraped clean with a knife and chopped

4 garlic cloves, chopped

9 whole bird's eye chilies, or to taste, chopped

1 rounded tbsp ground dried shrimp

6 raw prawns, blanched in simmering water until cooked, refreshed, peeled, and deveined

1 rounded tsp prawn tomalley (optional) (see opposite)

½tsp roasted shrimp paste (gapi)

few tbsp chicken stock, or as needed

1tbsp palm sugar, or more to taste

tamarind water, made by dissolving 1tbsp tamarind pulp in 2tbsp water and sieving

1½tbsp lime juice

1tbsp Asian citron (som sa) or mandarin juice (optional)

1tbsp fish sauce (nahm pla)

2tbsp pickled pea aubergines (makreua puang)

3 sour fuzzy aubergines (maeuk), scraped and finely sliced (optional)

2tbsp green mango, julienned

pinch of Asian citron or mandarin zest, julienned (optional)

For the sweet pork

200g (7oz) pork belly

chicken stock or water as needed

1 pandanus (bai dtoei horm) leaf

250g (8½oz) palm sugar

3tbsp fish sauce or soy sauce

1 point of star anise (optional)

1 small piece dried orange peel

To serve

3 deep-fried shallots, about 30g (1oz), see opposite

white pepper, finely ground

few whole coriander leaves

1 Prepare the spicy relish (see opposite).

2 Place the pork in a saucepan and cover with cold water and add a pinch of salt. Bring to the boil then simmer for 1 minute, uncovered, to remove excess blood and impurities. Drain.

3 Place in the pan again, cover with water or chicken stock, a pinch of salt, and the pandanus leaf and simmer, covered, for 20–30 minutes, until a skewer comes away clean from the meat. Drain and cool.

4 Cut the pork into 1–2cm (½–¾in) cubes. In a heavy saucepan, melt the sugar with a pinch of salt in enough chicken stock or water to cover. Add the pork. Season with fish or soy sauce and simmer, uncovered, for about 40 minutes, until the sauce is thick and the pork is a rich amber. Moisten with more water, if needed.

5 Present the pork sprinkled with the deep-fried shallots, white pepper, and coriander leaves, and serve with the spicy relish.

PRAWN TOMALLEY

This seasoned prawn paste lasts for several weeks in the refrigerator. It can be used to flavour soups, curries, salad dressings, or even fried rice. It should taste sweet, prawny, and salty in equal measure.

1 coriander root, soaked in water for 5–10 minutes, scraped clean with a knife, and chopped

2 garlic cloves, chopped

5 whole white peppercorns

6 prawn heads

1tbsp vegetable oil

1–2tbsp granulated sugar, or to taste

1tbsp fish sauce (nahm pla)

1 In a mortar with a pestle, pound the coriander root with a pinch of salt, the garlic, and white peppercorns to make a fine paste. Squeeze the prawn heads over a bowl to extract about 2–3tbsp tomalley.

2 Heat the oil in a small wok or pan. Add the garlic paste and fry until golden, stirring often. Add the tomalley and simmer, uncovered, until it changes colour. Season with sugar and fish sauce and simmer for another minute or so.

POUNDING THE SPICY RELISH

This nahm prik can be served with deep-fried battered breadfruit, fresh betel leaves (see photograph opposite), or grilled fish – traditionally a small mackerel, but any oily fish such as sardines, herrings, or bonito can be used.

1 In a mortar with a pestle, pound the coriander roots and garlic into a paste with a good pinch of salt. Add the chilies and continue to pound until quite fine. Add the dried shrimp, blanched prawns, the tomalley, if using, and the shrimp paste. Continue to pound until puréed.

2 Moisten with the stock. Season with the sugar, tamarind water, lime juice, and, if using, the mandarin juice. Carefully add fish sauce to taste. Do not add too much as there is already a lot of salt present. Mix in the aubergines, green mango, and, if using, the Asian citron or mandarin zest.

DEEP-FRYING SHALLOTS

Deep-fried shallots are an important garnish in Thai cooking. Although you can buy them, it is much better to fry your own. They can burn easily, so fry at least 100g (3½oz) shallots at a time in order to control their cooking, and take care when adding the shallots to the wok, as the oil will bubble up. 200g (7oz) fresh red shallots yields 100g (3½oz) deep-fried shallots, for which you need 300ml (10fl oz) vegetable oil.

1 Peel the shallots and cut lengthways into thin slices. Heat the oil in a wok until fairly hot, then turn up the heat and add the shallots. When the oil has recovered its heat and the shallots are frying, turn down slightly. Deep-fry, stirring constantly, until the shallots begin to colour.

2 After about 5 minutes, when the shallots are golden, have lost their onion-like aroma, and begin to smell enticingly nutty, drain and spread out on kitchen paper to cool. The shallots will become crisp, retaining surprisingly little oil. They keep for 2 days in an airtight container.

STIR-FRIED SIAMESE WATERCRESS
with yellow beans, garlic & chili

If you cannot find Siamese watercress, use any other Asian green, such as gai lan or choy sum or, at a pinch, spinach.

2 garlic cloves

2–3tbsp vegetable oil

200g (7oz) Siamese watercress (pak bung) or similar

3tbsp yellow bean sauce (dtow jiaw)

1 long red chili, crushed (optional)

pinch of granulated sugar

2tbsp chicken stock

2tbsp light soy sauce

Using a mortar and pestle, crush the garlic with a pinch of salt. Heat a wok, add the oil and, when hot, add the watercress, crushed garlic and salt, yellow bean sauce, chili, if using, and sugar. When the watercress has wilted, add the stock and season with the soy sauce. Serve.

SNAKE GOURD, EGG & CRAB SOUP

This cooling soup is a perfect complement to any spicy dish. The best gourd to use is called a snake gourd because it is long, ribbed, and curvaceous.

1tbsp chopped garlic

1tbsp vegetable oil

1 litre (1¾ pints) Thai chicken stock (see opposite)

1–2tbsp light soy sauce

pinch of granulated sugar

1 snake gourd (boap nguu) or cucumber, about 150g (5½oz), prepared (see opposite)

1 egg, lightly beaten

1tbsp cooked fresh crab meat

1tbsp coriander leaves

pinch of ground white pepper

1 Make a coarse paste by pounding the garlic with a pinch of salt in a mortar with a pestle. Heat the oil in a large pan and fry the garlic paste until golden. Drain off the excess oil, then pour in the stock and season with the soy sauce and sugar. Bring to the boil, add the gourd or cucumber, and simmer, uncovered, for a few minutes, skimming often.

2 When the gourd is tender, add the egg and continue to simmer until it is just scrambled. Remove from the heat and transfer to a tureen. Add the crab meat and serve the dish sprinkled with the coriander leaves and white pepper.

THAI CHICKEN STOCK

This stock can be made with chicken bones or with a whole chicken. Vegetables provide flavouring, but using too many can overwhelm the chicken flavour.

Makes 2–3 litres (3½–5¼ pints)

1kg (2¼lb) chicken bones or a whole chicken without giblets removed
pinch of shredded fresh ginger
pinch of crushed garlic
200g (7oz) trimmings from vegetables such as spring onions, cabbage, or coriander stalks
small piece of peeled mooli
6 shiitake mushroom stalks (optional)

1 If using bones, rinse them well with water. Place in a large saucepan and add enough cold water to cover them fully, adding a pinch of salt. Bring to the boil, uncovered, to blanch. Refresh the bones under cold water for a few minutes; return them to the pan.

2 Cover the bones in the pan, or the whole chicken if used, with water plus a pinch of salt and bring to the boil. Simmer, uncovered, for 20 minutes, then add all the flavourings and vegetables. Cook, uncovered, for 2 hours. Strain and reserve the stock. Meat from the chicken can be used separately.

PREPARING SNAKE GOURD OR CUCUMBER

1 Using a potato peeler, peel the skin from the gourd or cucumber, and trim off the ends as you do so.

2 With a sharp chef's knife, cut the gourd into diagonal slices about 2.5cm (1in) thick.

COOKING RICE

To serve 4 people, fill a measuring jug with long-grain, preferably jasmine, rice up to the 600ml (1 pint) mark and use about 600ml (1 pint) water. Do not add salt because the other dishes have enough seasoning. Once cooked, the rice will stay warm in the covered pan for 30 minutes. The aroma can be enhanced by pushing a pandanus leaf into the cooked rice, which is then left to rest for a few minutes before serving.

1 Place the rice in a bowl of water. Wash it by combing your hands through the grains and rubbing your palms together to remove any husks or grit. Drain. Repeat 2–3 times until the water is clear.

2 Drain the rice and transfer to a large saucepan. Cover with cold water to the first joint of an index finger above the rice. Cover and bring rapidly to the boil. Turn the heat right down and cook for 10 minutes. Do not stir. Remove from the heat and rest the rice, covered, for another 10 minutes.

GREEN CURRY PASTE

Curry paste made by hand in the traditional way has a vibrancy of flavour that commercial products cannot hope to achieve.

1tbsp chopped Thai bird's eye chilies

1tbsp chopped long green chilies, seeded

1tbsp chopped galangal (khaa)

3tbsp chopped lemon grass (dtakrai)

1tsp kaffir lime (bai makrut) zest

1tbsp chopped coriander root

1tsp chopped red turmeric (kamin leuang)

1tsp chopped wild ginger (grachai) (optional)

3tbsp chopped red shallots

2tbsp chopped garlic

1tsp roasted shrimp paste (gapi)

¼tbsp whole white peppercorns

¼tbsp coriander seeds, dry-roasted

pinch of cumin seeds, dry-roasted

2–3 blades toasted mace or a good pinch of freshly grated nutmeg (optional)

1 Place a good pinch of salt in a mortar to act as an abrasive. Place each item in the mortar, one at a time in the order given, and pound with a pestle to make a fine paste. Stop when you have added and pounded in the shrimp paste.

2 Grind the peppercorns, coriander, cumin seeds, and mace. Sieve before mixing into the paste. Put the finished paste into a sterilized jar; cover with greaseproof paper, waxed side down, or with cling film. The paste will last for a week or two if refrigerated.

PREPARING A COCONUT

When buying a coconut, choose one that feels heavy for its size. There will be more flesh in the coconut and so it will yield more cream. Normally, one good coconut yields about 200–220ml (7–7½fl oz) cream. Shake the coconut. If there is water inside, the flesh is less likely to be fermented. Coconut water, when fresh, is the most thirst-quenching of liquids. However, it sours very quickly and is sometimes used to ferment vegetables or make vinegar.

1 Hold the coconut in a tea towel or cloth over a bowl with its eyes towards your thumb or little finger. Turning the nut, wallop it three or four times until it is cleaved in half. The bowl beneath it should catch all the coconut water.

2 Taking each coconut half in turn, score the flesh or cut it into segments. This makes it easier to prise the flesh away from the shell with a blunt knife.

3 Using a cleaver or sharp knife, peel away and discard the brown inner skin. Roughly chop the flesh with the cleaver.

4 Blend the flesh in a food processor with 500ml (17fl oz) warm water until it is shredded.

COCONUT CREAM

Fresh coconut cream is incomparably luscious, with a complexity and depth of flavour that justify the labour required to produce it.

1 Extract the coconut cream and milk by squeezing the blended mixture through 2 layers of muslin or a very clean tea towel into a glass, china, or plastic bowl (metal taints the cream). Leave it to separate for at least 20 minutes. The cream is the thicker, opaque liquid that separates and floats on top of the thinner liquid, which is the milk.

2 Spoon off the cream into a separate bowl. Both the cream and the milk are best used within a few hours. They can be refrigerated, but harden and become difficult to use. Coconut cream can begin to sour after a few hours and certainly within a day. Thai cooks bring the cream to the boil to delay its souring, although this does destroy some of its wonderful flavour.

CRACKED CREAM

Curries fried in coconut cream often call for the cream to be "cracked" or separated. The cream is simmered until most of the water evaporates.

Pour the cream into a wok or saucepan and simmer until the cream separates into thin oil and milk solids (the cracked cream). Once separated, cracked cream lasts for a few weeks refrigerated. The oil can be used for deep-frying.

GREEN CURRY OF BEEF with corn & Thai basil

Green curries are hot, salty, and just a little sweet from the rich coconut cream used in the cooking. Kaffir lime leaves, cut chilies, and Thai basil leaves are customary garnishes.

3tbsp cracked coconut cream (above)

3tbsp green curry paste (see opposite)

100g (3½oz) beef rump, with some fat attached, sliced into 5mm (¼in) pieces

2tbsp fish sauce (nahm pla), or to taste

200ml (7fl oz) coconut milk or chicken stock

50g (1¾oz) baby corn, cut in half lengthwise

2 large kaffir lime (bai makrut) leaves, torn

3 young green or red chilies, diagonally cut from the centre and seeded

handful of fresh Thai basil (bai horapha) leaves

pinch of shredded wild ginger (grachai) (optional)

pinch of shredded white turmeric (kamin kao) (optional)

1 Heat the cracked coconut cream in a wok or large saucepan. Add the curry paste and fry over a medium heat for 5–10 minutes, stirring regularly until the cream is cooked and fragrant.

2 Add the beef and simmer in the cream and paste, uncovered, for a minute or so before seasoning with the fish sauce. Moisten with the coconut milk or stock. Bring to the boil, add the corn and simmer, uncovered, for a few minutes, until tender.

3 Add the remaining ingredients and simmer for a few seconds. Rest off the heat for a minute before serving.

GRAINS & PULSES

PAUL GAYLER

Cereal grains have sustained humanity for centuries. In temperate climates, wheat, barley, rye, and oats are the staple grains, while rice, maize (corn), and millet grow in the tropics and subtropics. Grains are favoured because they are economical and filling, and most of the world's population eat locally grown grains. Only in richer countries has meat overtaken cereals as the primary food. Grains require some preparation before cooking. It is advisable to rinse them several times under cold running water to remove surface dust. Many milled rices have food additives tossed into the flour and added to the grains, so these should be washed under running water. Grains can be cooked dry, without presoaking, except for whole wheat, barley, brown and basmati rice, and rye.

Cooking grains To cook grains, all you need to know is how much water (or stock) to add to the quantity you are boiling, and how long you need to cook them. In addition to boiling, grains may also be steamed quite successfully. One tip I picked up in Asia is that if you run a little oil around the pan before cooking the grain, it not only prevents the grains from sticking but also makes the pan easier to clean afterwards. Whole grains tend to take longer to cook than processed grains. Some require stirring as they cool, but most do not. Some recipes call for the grain to be lightly fried in oil before water is added for boiling. Called toasting, this process is one of the steps in making pilaff rice and it enhances the flavour of grains dramatically.

The legume family Pulses, which include beans, peas, and lentils, are also known as legumes. The lentil was reputedly the first plant ever to be domesticated by humans. Most pulses thrive in warm climates, but some grow better in temperate regions. They can be eaten fresh or dried and are found in many varieties, colours, flavours, and textures.

Today, the availability of pulses has never been better, ranging from deep maroon kidney beans and pale green limas to speckled borlotti and black beans. Europeans treat pulses with reverence, but the English-speaking world has made only limited use of them. This may change with greater awareness of their value as a vegetarian source of protein and a complex carbohydrate – the body digests them slowly, ensuring a steady supply of energy.

All pulses, apart from soya beans, have a very similar content of protein, carbohydrate, vitamins, and minerals, especially iron. Pulses provide protein in their own right, but eating them with grains or nuts also ensures a rich intake of essential amino acids. Except for soya, pulses are low in fat and packed with fibre, which helps to prevent fluctuations in blood-sugar levels. Recent research indicates that the fibre in pulses helps to lower blood cholesterol, and thereby heart disease. A bean-rich diet can also benefit diabetes sufferers by helping to control their blood-glucose levels, appetite, and weight. Some people avoid beans because they can cause intestinal gas. This problem mostly arises when people follow a low-fibre eating pattern, then switch to a diet rich in beans. While the gases can produce discomfort, they are not harmful and the problem lessens as the body adjusts to the diet. However, it is not safe to eat raw or undercooked beans, especially red kidney beans and soya beans, because their skins contain toxins. These beans are perfectly safe after thorough cooking.

Storing grains and pulses While dried grains and pulses last well if stored carefully, it is preferable to buy smaller quantities as you need them and so keep storage periods to a minimum. Buy from shops with a rapid and regular turnover. Grains should not be kept longer than six months because their oils can turn rancid. Pulses become tough with age and take longer to cook.

Decant all grains and pulses into airtight containers away from the light, preferably in a cool, dark cupboard, ideally at around 21°C (70°F). Never mix a new batch with an old one, since they may need different cooking times. Keeping grains and pulses in glass jars is fine as long as they are used rapidly and are not exposed to light, which impairs their flavour and nutrients.

RICE

There are over 2,000 varieties of rice, grown in more than 110 countries, and every culture has its own repertoire of rice dishes, from the paellas of Spain, the nasi goreng of Indonesia, and the congees served for breakfast throughout Asia to the famous pilavs of the Balkans and Middle East, and the risottos of Italy. Rice can generally be divided into two types – long-grain (which tends to stay separate when cooked) and round or short-grain (which sticks together, making it ideal for risottos and rice pudding).

Washing/rinsing

Packaged rice sold in the West is rigorously checked and thoroughly cleaned, so if you "wash" it (ie rinse it) all you are doing is washing away nutrients. In Asian countries, however, rice is normally washed several times before cooking to help keep the grains separate.

Soaking

With the exception of basmati, and sometimes wild rice (to reduce the cooking time), rice does not need to be soaked before use. Some people suggest soaking long-grain brown rice before cooking to make it softer; this will not shorten the cooking time. Follow recipe instructions, and soak rice only if directed to do so.

Toasting

When boiling or steaming rice, it can first be lightly toasted (ie fried) in oil or butter for 1–2 minutes before the water or other liquid is added. This greatly enhances the flavour.

Steaming

Steamed rice is cooked in a hot vapour, rather than directly in liquid, which significantly reduces the loss of nutrients. The rice in the upper section of a steamer cooks in the steam produced by the water or stock boiling in the lower section. A well-fitting lid is essential to keep the steam in, as is careful timing, since steamed rice is tasteless if even slightly overcooked. Rice can also be steamed very successfully in a pressure cooker.

Using leftover cooked rice

Once cooled, cooked rice can be kept in an airtight container in the refrigerator for up to 24 hours. It is great for rice salads and to use in stir-fries and soups.

When rice is reheated it tastes as good as it did when first prepared. Either reheat it in a tightly covered bowl in the microwave (see opposite) or put the rice in a saucepan with 2tbsp water or stock, cover, and heat gently for 4–5 minutes. Fluff with a fork before serving.

THE ABSORPTION METHOD

This way of cooking rice is the most common method used throughout Asia. A pan with a tight-fitting lid is essential, and it is important to measure the water or stock accurately. You can cook the rice on the stovetop (as shown here) or in the oven, which is in fact the basic pilaff method (p312).

Brown rice (long-grain or basmati) can be cooked by this method, although it will need more liquid, or it can be boiled (see opposite). Whichever method is used, brown rice will take up to double the cooking time of white rice.

| 450g (1lb) long-grain white rice |
| 600ml (1 pint) water or stock |

1 Put the rice and water or stock into a large saucepan. Bring to the boil over moderate heat. Stir once, then simmer, uncovered, for 10–12 minutes, or until all liquid is absorbed.

2 Remove from heat. Cover the pan with a tea towel and a tight-fitting lid. Return to a very low heat and leave undisturbed for 10 minutes.

3 Remove the pan from the heat and leave for 5 minutes with the towel and lid still in place, then uncover and serve.

TIPS FOR PERFECT RICE

■ Always buy good-quality rice.
■ Use a heavy-bottomed pan with a tight-fitting lid. Be sure the pan is big enough (rice will triple in volume).
■ To add extra flavour, use stock instead of water.
■ Do not add salt to the cooking water – it can cause the rice grains to rupture.

■ When cooking by the absorption method or boiling, never stir, prod, or even taste rice during the cooking process. Rice grains are delicate and can easily split, releasing their starch and becoming sticky.
■ As soon as it is cooked, remove rice from the pan. If left in the pan it will become overcooked.

BOILING RICE

The usual way to boil rice is in twice its volume of liquid for 10–20 minutes, until all the water has been absorbed. But I have never been happy with the results, so I now cook rice in five to six times its volume of water at a rolling boil for 12–15 minutes. I believe the extra water used helps to dilute the starch from the rice during cooking and results in light, distinct grains. Never stir rice when boiling because it ruptures the cells in the grain, making it sticky.

3 litres (5¼ pints) water

450g (1lb) long-grain white rice

1 Pour the water into a large saucepan and bring to a rolling boil. Add the rice and return to the boil. Reduce to a simmer and cook for 12–15 minutes, or until tender but still firm.

2 Pour the rice and water into a colander, cover with a cloth, and leave for 10 minutes. Fluff up with a fork and serve.

OTHER WAYS TO COOK RICE

Electric rice cooker

This will cook glutinous rice, Japanese sushi rice, and brown rice very successfully and conveniently. Use the absorption method, opposite, with the same precise ratio of water to rice, and follow the manufacturer's instructions for timings. When the rice is cooked the cooker will switch off automatically and keep the rice hot until needed. Although rice cookers can be expensive, it is important to buy a good-quality model; thermostats on cheaper models are not always accurate and you can end up with a sticky mass.

Microwave oven

You can cook good rice in a microwave, although, contrary to popular belief, you don't save any time by doing so. Use the absorption method ratio of water to rice, and choose a bowl large enough to ensure that the water doesn't boil over (I add a little oil to the water, which helps to prevent this). Microwave, covered, for 5 minutes on full power, then on half power for 15 minutes. Do not stir during cooking. Cooked rice reheats well in a microwave, on full power for about 2 minutes plus 2–3 minutes standing time.

Preparation & cooking times for rice

The following chart gives basic guidelines for cooking rice. Wherever possible, it is advisable to check packet instructions, especially for oriental varieties of rice.

TYPE OF RICE	BEST FOR	SPECIAL PREPARATION	BEST COOKING METHODS AND APPROX COOKING TIMES
LONG-GRAIN White and brown	pilaffs, salads, stuffings, stir-fries	can be toasted	absorption: 20 mins (white), 30–40 mins (brown); steam: 20 mins (white), 30–35 mins (brown)
Basmati (white and brown)	Indian pilaus, spicy Indian dishes	soak for 30 mins; can be toasted	absorption: 20–25 mins; boil: 20 mins (white), 40 mins (brown)
SHORT-GRAIN Risotto (arborio, carnaroli, vialone nano)	classic risottos	can be toasted	risotto: 20–25 mins
Paella (Valencia, calaspara, granza)	paella, other Spanish rice dishes	can be toasted	paella: 20–25 mins
Pudding	rice pudding, sweet dishes		absorption (oven): 1–1¼ hours
ORIENTAL Chinese black	sweet and savoury dishes, stuffings	soak overnight	boil: 30–40 mins
Glutinous (sticky)	sweet and savoury dishes, rice dumplings	soak for 4 hours minimum	absorption (rice cooker): 20 mins; steam: 15–20 mins
Jasmine (Thai fragrant)	spicy Thai dishes, congees, stir-fries	wash	absorption (rice cooker): 25 mins; boil: 20–25 mins
Sushi	sushi, sweet dishes	wash	absorption (rice cooker): 20 mins; boil: 20–25 mins
SPECIALIST Red or Camargue, Himalayan red	stuffings, salads, pilaffs, stir-fries	soak for 1 hour; can be toasted	boil: 40–60 mins
Wild	stuffings, pilaffs, salads		boil: 40–60 mins

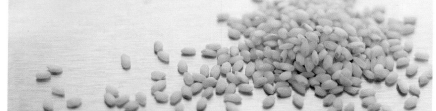

BASIC PILAFF

Pilaff rice is cooked in different ways throughout the world, but what all the methods have in common is that the rice is not stirred during cooking so that the grains remain separate. The basic recipe here is cooked in the oven, which is indicative of the classic French style, although pilaffs are also often cooked on the stovetop, as in Indian-style pilaus. For a Turkish pilav, the rice is first cooked with onions and other vegetables, topped with stock, and simmered for 30 minutes. It is then covered with a cloth and left to steam, off the heat, for 10 minutes, which results in a softer, fluffier pilaff.

50g (1¾oz) unsalted butter or 2tbsp olive oil

1 small onion, finely chopped

180g (6½oz) long-grain rice

375ml (12½fl oz) well-flavoured chicken or vegetable stock

PILAFF ADDITIONS

Try these to vary the basic recipe:
■ Add 100g (3½oz) finely diced vegetables, such as peppers, aubergines, or mushrooms, and cook with the onion.
■ Infuse the boiling stock with a pinch of saffron threads for 2–3 minutes before adding to the rice.
■ Add 2tsp ground spice, such as cumin, cardamom, or cinnamon, to the softened onion and cook for a further 2 minutes before adding the rice.
■ Flavour with tomato by adding 1tbsp tomato purée or a 400g (14oz) can of chopped tomatoes, drained, to the onions before stirring in the rice.
■ Fold 100g (3½oz) spiced cooked lentils into the cooked rice and add 1tsp garam masala and 2tbsp chopped coriander with the salt and pepper.
■ Stir 2tbsp chopped herbs into the finished pilaff.

1 Preheat the oven to 160°C (325°F, gas 3). Heat half the butter or oil in a flameproof casserole. Add the onion and cook over moderate heat for 5 minutes, or until softened. Add the rice and stir with a wooden spoon to coat the grains well with the fat and onions.

2 Bring the stock to the boil in a separate pan. Add to the rice, stir once, and return to the boil. Cover with a tight-fitting lid, place in the oven, and cook for 18–20 minutes, or until the rice is tender and all liquid has been absorbed.

3 Fork in the remaining butter or oil, season to taste with salt and pepper, and serve.

PAELLA

The traditional Spanish dish paella takes its name from the pan in which it is cooked. The pan is, in fact, key to a good paella – it needs to be large and shallow with a flat base to ensure the rice cooks in a thin, even layer. Rice for paella is never washed first as it is the starchy coating that keeps the grains separate during cooking. Nor is it stirred, as this would break up the grains. When the paella is ready, the pan is brought to table and people help themselves.

1.4 litres (2½ pints) fish stock

2 good pinches of saffron threads

3 garlic cloves, crushed

90ml (3fl oz) olive oil

50g (1¾oz) chorizo sausage, thinly sliced (optional)

2 small bay leaves

1 onion, finely chopped

2 red peppers, halved, seeded, and cut into long strips

300g (10½oz) monkfish fillet, cut into 2.5cm (1in) chunks

250g (8½oz) small squid, cleaned and cut into pieces, including tentacles

6 tomatoes, skinned and chopped

1tsp paprika

450g (1lb) Valencian paella rice or risotto rice

200g (7oz) fresh clams, scrubbed

12 raw tiger prawns, heads removed but tails left on and deveined

8 raw langoustines

250g (8½oz) fresh mussels, scrubbed

50g (1¾oz) cooked French beans, cut into 2.5cm (1in) lengths

50g (1¾oz) cooked peas

lemon wedges, to serve

1 Pour the fish stock into a saucepan, add the saffron and one-third of the garlic, and bring to the boil. Simmer for 5 minutes. Meanwhile, heat half the oil in a paella pan, large frying pan, or wok. Add the chorizo, if using, the remaining garlic, and the bay leaves and cook over a gentle heat for 1 minute. Add the onion and peppers and cook for 5 minutes. Add the monkfish and sauté for 2–3 minutes, or until sealed all over.

2 Increase the heat, add the squid, and fry for 2–3 minutes, or until golden. Stir in the tomatoes, paprika, and remaining oil, and fry for 4–5 minutes (this tomato mixture is known as a sofrito).

3 Scatter in the rice to distribute it evenly over the ingredients in the pan. Pour over the hot stock, then add the clams, tiger prawns, langoustines, and mussels.

4 Reduce the heat and cook gently for 15–20 minutes, or until the rice is tender but still slightly firm (it may be necessary to add a little more stock or water). Shake the pan occasionally; do not stir.

5 The rice will form a golden crust on the bottom (called a soccarat). When all the liquid has been absorbed, add the beans and peas, and fold in gently. Discard any mussels that have not opened.

Serve hot, garnished with lemon wedges

BASIC RISOTTO

Risotto, a dish from northern Italy, is simple food at its best. The basic recipe is made by gradually stirring hot stock into rice and softened onions until all the stock has been absorbed and the risotto is creamy with firm (al dente), separate rice grains. It is easy to prepare, the secrets being the choice of rice, the quality of the stock, and constant stirring. A basic risotto can be embellished with fish, shellfish, meat, chicken, or vegetables.

900ml (1½ pints) chicken or vegetable stock
1tbsp olive oil
75g (2½oz) unsalted butter
1 onion or 2 shallots, finely chopped
275g (10oz) risotto rice – vialone nano, arborio, or carnaroli
75ml (2½fl oz) dry white wine
50g (1¾oz) Parmesan, freshly grated

HOW TO EXCEL

■ Choose a wide, heavy-bottomed saucepan that will be large enough to accommodate the rice, and all the other ingredients.

■ Only ever use risotto rice. The medium-short, stubby grains absorb liquid and swell up while retaining their individual shape.

■ Always use a good, well-flavoured stock – chicken, fish, or vegetable, depending on the type of risotto.

■ Keep the stock at a gentle simmer, and the rice at a lively simmer.

■ Stir constantly throughout the cooking process to release the starch in the rice and give the risotto the desired creamy texture.

1 Heat the stock in a saucepan to a gentle simmer. Meanwhile, heat the oil and half the butter in a wide, heavy pan. Add the onion and cook for 5 minutes, or until softened. Add the rice and stir to coat the grains well with the fat.

2 Add the wine and boil, stirring, until absorbed. Add a ladleful of simmering stock and stir until absorbed. Continue adding stock by the ladleful, stirring, until the rice is tender but retains a bite. This will take 20–25 minutes in all.

3 Stir in the remaining butter and the Parmesan. Season to taste and remove from the heat. Cover the pan and leave the risotto to rest for 2 minutes before serving.

A basic risotto – creamy, but with separate grains of rice

Supplì al telefono

This is one of my favourite vegetarian dishes – moist, basil-flavoured risotto cakes filled with mozzarella and tomatoes. The dish gets its name because, when you cut into the cakes, the melting mozzarella forms strings that look like telephone wires. A light supper dish for four with a crisp green salad, supplì can also be served as a starter for eight.

Place some tomatoes and 2 cubes of mozzarella in the pocket of each risotto ball

Makes 8

½ quantity basic risotto (see opposite), chilled

4tbsp pesto sauce (p42)

75g (2½oz) oven-dried or sun-blushed tomatoes, chopped

225g (8oz) buffalo mozzarella, cut into 16 small cubes

75g (2½oz) fresh white breadcrumbs

75ml (2½fl oz) olive oil

Put the chilled risotto into a bowl and mix in the pesto with a fork. Divide the risotto into 8 equal-sized balls. For each supplì, cup a ball in your hand and use your fingers to make a pocket about 1cm (½in) deep in the centre. Place some tomatoes and 2 cubes of mozzarella in the pocket. Mould the rice over the filling to enclose it completely, then shape the ball into a small cake.

Put the breadcrumbs into a shallow bowl and roll the cakes in them until well coated all over.

Heat the olive oil in a large frying pan over a moderate heat. Add the supplì and fry for 4–5 minutes on each side, or until golden brown and crisp. Drain on kitchen paper, then serve.

EGG FRIED RICE

When making any fried rice dish, it is important that the oil be hot before the rice is added. This will ensure the rice turns out crisp and light in texture rather than soggy and heavy. Cook the rice in advance and thoroughly cool before using.

2tbsp vegetable oil

400g (14oz) cold, steamed or boiled basmati or other long-grain rice

50g (1¾oz) cooked ham, diced

100g (3½oz) cooked peas

75g (2½oz) bean sprouts

⅓ iceberg lettuce, shredded

pinch of salt

2 large eggs, beaten

4 spring onions, chopped (optional)

1 Heat a wok or heavy frying pan over high heat. Add the oil and swirl it round to coat the pan. When the oil is very hot, add the rice and stir-fry for 1 minute.

2 Add the ham, peas, bean sprouts, lettuce, and salt to the wok, and continue stir-frying over high heat for 1 minute.

3 Make a well in the ingredients and pour in the eggs. Stir in quickly, then cook for 2–3 minutes. Transfer to a dish, sprinkle with spring onions, if using, and serve.

NASI GORENG

This is a well-loved Indonesian fried rice dish. Boil 300g (10½oz) basmati rice; cool. Blend 1 chopped onion, 2 crushed garlic cloves, 1tsp dried shrimp paste, 1 seeded and chopped red chili, the juice of 1 lime, and 4tbsp tomato ketchup to a paste (called a sambal). Heat 4tbsp vegetable oil in a wok or large frying pan. Add 1 thinly sliced onion and 1 seeded and shredded red chili and stir-fry for 2–3 minutes. Stir in the sambal and cook for 2 minutes. Increase the heat to high, and add the rice and a pinch of salt. Stir well. Add 200g (7oz) thinly sliced, cooked chicken breast, 150g (5½oz) peeled, cooked prawns, 75g (2½oz) shredded Chinese white cabbage, 2tbsp soy sauce, and 2tbsp peanuts. Stir-fry until hot, then serve, topped with fried egg, deep-fried shallots, and shredded cucumber.

CONGEE

Often eaten for breakfast throughout the Far East, congee is rice poached until the grains swell and burst to form a kind of porridge. It can be made plain, simply with water, or using an aromatic broth and the addition of various meats and fish or eggs. When enlivened with garlic, spring onions, and coriander leaves, it is delicious. My only reservation is the time of its serving – in the West we are not quite ready for such a heavy start to the day. For those like me, I suggest serving congee for lunch or dinner, or as an evening snack.

For the base broth and rice

1 litre (1¾ pints) chicken stock

100g (3½oz) coriander roots or stalks, lightly smashed with the back of a knife

200g (7oz) jasmine or white glutinous rice, rinsed under running water for 5 minutes

For the flavourings

2tbsp groundnut oil

2 garlic cloves, thinly sliced

5cm (2in) piece of fresh ginger, peeled and thinly shredded

1tbsp light soy sauce

1tbsp nam pla (fish sauce)

6 spring onions, finely shredded

sprigs of coriander, to garnish

1 Put the stock and coriander roots in a large pan. Bring to the boil, then reduce the heat and simmer, uncovered, for 30 minutes. Strain into a clean pan, return to the heat, and bring to a simmer. Add the rice and simmer gently, uncovered, for 1–1½ hours, or until the grains are swollen and almost disintegrating.

2 Meanwhile, heat the oil in a small pan. Add the garlic and ginger. Cook for 1 minute, or until golden and crisp. Stir into the rice.

3 Stir in the soy and fish sauces. Spoon into individual soup bowls, sprinkle over the spring onions, and top with coriander sprigs.

CHICKEN DUMPLINGS

To make congee more substantial and interesting, add these little dumplings.

100g (3½oz) skinless, boneless chicken, minced

4tbsp chopped coriander

2 garlic cloves, crushed

1tbsp nam pla (fish sauce)

Put all the ingredients into a bowl and season with ground white pepper. Using a teaspoon, form the mixture into small dumplings and drop into the strained stock, before the rice is added. Simmer for 8–10 minutes, then remove with a slotted spoon and keep warm while you make the congee. When serving the congee, place the dumplings on top.

RICE PAPER WRAPS

Delicate, thin rice paper sheets (banh trang) are used in Vietnam and Thailand to wrap all kinds of interesting fillings – fish, meat, or vegetable. Served uncooked, steamed, or fried, they make great pre-dinner snacks or appetizers. The wrappers are sold dried at oriental food stores and need to be moistened before use. Prepare and fill one wrapper at a time.

1 Immerse the wrapper in a bowl filled with lukewarm water and leave for 30 seconds. Remove and place on a flat work surface.

2 Place the filling in the centre of the wrapper. Fold the bottom half up over the filling.

3 Fold in the sides, then roll over to enclose the filling and make a square packet. Repeat to moisten and fill the remaining wrappers.

STEAMED SEAFOOD WRAPS

Makes 12

12 rice paper wrappers	1tbsp soy sauce
banana leaves or foil	3tbsp chopped coriander
2 spring onions, shredded	1tbsp caster sugar
2 red chilies, seeded and shredded	1 small red chili, seeded and chopped
For the seafood filling	1tbsp chopped mint
225g (8oz) fresh white crab meat	
75g (2½oz) peeled cooked prawns, chopped	
5 water chestnuts, chopped	
50g (1¾oz) bean sprouts	
4 spring onions, chopped	
2.5cm (1in) piece of fresh ginger, peeled and finely chopped	
1tbsp soy sauce	
1tbsp nam pla (fish sauce)	
For the dipping sauce	
2tbsp rice wine vinegar	
1tbsp chopped pickled ginger	
4tbsp vegetable oil	

1 Mix the ingredients for the filling in a bowl. Place 2tbsp filling on a moistened rice paper wrapper and fold into a square packet (see left). Repeat to make 12 packets.

2 Line a bamboo steamer with banana leaves or foil and brush with a little oil. Lay the prepared packets seam-side down on the leaves, spaced well apart. Cover, set over a pan of boiling water, and steam for 5–6 minutes.

3 Meanwhile, put all the sauce ingredients in a bowl and whisk to mix. Transfer the wraps to a plate, garnish with the spring onions and chili, and serve with the dipping sauce.

CORN (MAIZE)

Corn originates from Central and South America where it was the staple grain of the Incas, Mayas, and Aztecs. There are several types of corn, and yellow, blue, red, and black varieties. In the kitchen, corn is used as hominy (dried and hulled whole or coarsely ground grains), cornmeal (also called maize meal or polenta), masa harina (a flour made from ground, cooked corn kernels), and cornflour (a fine starch). Other types of corn yield sweetcorn or corn on the cob, which is eaten as a vegetable, and popping corn.

BUTTERMILK CORNBREAD

I always serve cornbread when I cook brunch, and often add other ingredients to the batter, such as 3 crushed garlic cloves or diced chilies, or 150g (5½oz) grated jalapeño jack cheese or Cheddar, crumbled fried bacon, sautéed diced mixed peppers, or roasted sweetcorn kernels. You can also pour the batter into greased muffin tins and bake for 15–18 minutes.

150g (5½oz) plain flour
150g (5½oz) fine cornmeal (polenta)
4tsp baking powder
pinch of salt
50g (1¾oz) caster sugar
2 eggs, beaten
250ml (8½fl oz) buttermilk or full-fat milk
2tbsp melted unsalted butter

1 Preheat the oven to 190°C (375°F, gas 5). Combine the flour, cornmeal, baking powder, salt, and sugar in a bowl, and make a well in the centre. Pour in the eggs, buttermilk, and butter, and mix well to form a smooth batter.

2 Pour the batter into a lightly greased 20cm (8in) square cake tin. Place in the oven and bake for 25–30 minutes, or until golden and firm to the touch. Allow the cornbread to cool a little in the tin, then turn out and cut into small squares. Serve warm.

MAKING SOFT POLENTA

Made from cornmeal, polenta is a staple food in northern Italy. Long associated with Italian peasant cooking, it now enjoys gourmet status and an international reputation. Whether served soft, or allowed to set and then grilled, char-grilled, or fried, it is great with stews to sop up the juices, with grilled or roast meats, or topped with cooked vegetables. Soft polenta can also be baked with a savoury topping.

Instant or pre-cooked polenta can be cooked in just 5–8 minutes, but is not as good in quality as the traditional variety.

If polenta becomes lumpy during cooking, pour it into a blender and process until smooth, then return to the pan and continue to cook.

1.5 litres (2¾ pints) water
½tbsp coarse sea salt
300g (10½oz) polenta (cornmeal)
150g (5½oz) unsalted butter
100g (3½oz) Parmesan, freshly grated

1 Pour the water and salt into a large heavy-based saucepan and bring to the boil. Gradually rain in the polenta, whisking continuously and rapidly to ensure that no lumps form and the mixture is smooth.

2 Reduce the heat to its lowest setting and cook for 40–45 minutes, or until thick and creamy and coming away from the pan. Whisk occasionally to prevent a skin from forming. Stir in the butter and cheese, and season well.

SOFT POLENTA IDEAS

You can enhance the basic soft polenta with many flavourings. Here are some to try.
■ Add 1tsp saffron to the water with the salt.
■ Stir in 2tbsp tapenade or 100ml (3½fl oz) pesto sauce with the butter, cheese, and seasoning.
■ Add 150ml (5fl oz) red pepper purée or 150g (5½oz) cooked ratatouille to the finished polenta.
■ Pour the soft polenta into a greased baking dish and top with a mixture of 300g (10½oz) browned minced pork seasoned with 1 crushed garlic clove, 2tsp finely chopped rosemary, and 1tbsp freshly grated Parmesan. Bake at 180°C (350°F, gas 4) for 15 minutes.

For a superb vegetarian dish, top the soft polenta with sautéed wild mushrooms garnished with parsley

GRILLING POLENTA

1 Make soft polenta as opposite, but omit the butter and cheese. Pour onto an oiled baking tray and spread out evenly with a wet spatula to a 1–2cm (½–¾in) thickness. Leave to cool and set. (It can be kept in the refrigerator for up to 4 days.)

2 When ready to use, turn the set sheet of polenta out of the tray onto a board. Using a knife or pastry cutters, cut the polenta into triangles, rectangles, squares, or other shapes.

3 Brush the polenta shapes with olive oil, then char-grill on a hot, ridged grill pan, or grill under a medium heat, for 3–5 minutes on each side, or until golden brown and crisp.

GRILLED POLENTA IDEAS

■ Use grilled polenta as a pizza base: top with sliced tomatoes and mozzarella, and basil leaves. Bake in a preheated 200°C (400°F, gas 6) oven for 18–20 minutes, or until lightly browned.

■ Arrange slices or triangles of set polenta on top of a cooked meat or vegetable stew (p204 and 266), drizzle with olive oil, and bake for 15–18 minutes, or until golden and crisp.

■ Cut set polenta into small squares, coat in beaten egg and breadcrumbs, and deep-fry in hot oil for 1–2 minutes, or until golden.

■ Make a polenta-style lasagne. Layer slices of set polenta with 100g (3½oz) freshly grated Parmesan or pecorino, 1kg (2¼lb) spinach, cooked and drained, and 600ml (1 pint) tomato sauce (p40). Finish with another 50g (1¾oz) grated cheese, then bake in a preheated 200°C (400°F, gas 6) oven for 20–25 minutes, or until bubbling and golden brown on top.

Types & uses of other grains

TYPE OF GRAIN	WHOLEGRAIN	REFINED GRAIN	FLAKES	FLOUR OR MEAL
Barley	(pot barley) as brown rice, pilaffs, soups, stews	(pearl barley) soups, casseroles, salads	muesli, porridge	breads, bakes, thickening soups and casseroles
Buckwheat	(also called kasha) as brown rice		breakfast cereal	blinis, pasta, soba noodles
Millet	as brown rice, stuffing vegetables		casseroles, soups, stews	soups, salads, as rice - in pilaffs and risottos, stuffings for poultry and vegetables
Oats	(groats) as brown rice		(rolled oats) muesli, porridge, in baking	breads, oatcakes, in baking
Quinoa	as brown rice			breads
Rye	as brown rice	(cracked rye) breads	muesli	breads
Wheat	(berries) as brown rice	(cracked wheat, bulgur, couscous) salads, stuffings	muesli, savoury crumbles	breads, cakes, biscuits, other baking

WHEAT

The most universally grown grain, wheat is also the most important of all the food grains. It is ground into flour for bread-making and into semolina for gnocchi, pasta, and puddings. In its other forms – "berries" (the whole grain), flakes, bulgur, cracked wheat, and couscous – it needs only minimum preparation for use in pilaffs, salads, stuffings, crumble toppings, and breakfast cereal. The pleasant, earthy flavour works well with a wide range of foods, most particularly fruit, vegetables, and nuts.

BULGUR: Tabbouleh

Sold under various names (bulgar, burghul, pourgouri), bulgur is made by boiling wheat grains until they crack. As a result, it only needs to be rehydrated, by soaking or simmering. Cracked wheat, with which bulgur is often confused, is not pre-cooked.

Bulgur is a staple throughout the Middle East, where it is often combined with pounded lamb to make kibbeh. It is also the main ingredient in the Lebanese salad tabbouleh, which is often served as a mezze (appetizer) with lettuce leaves: a large spoonful of tabbouleh is rolled in a leaf and eaten with the fingers.

75g (2½oz) bulgur, picked over to remove any grit
1 large bunch of flat-leaf parsley, stalks removed and leaves coarsely chopped
4 tomatoes, skinned and chopped
6 spring onions, chopped
4tbsp chopped fresh mint or 1tsp dried
½tsp mixed spice
juice of 2 lemons
4tbsp olive oil
2 lettuces, separated into leaves

1 Put the bulgur in a sieve and rinse well, then tip it into a bowl. Cover with hot water and leave to soak for 25 minutes. Drain well in the sieve and pat dry in a cloth. Put the bulgur into a clean bowl.

2 Add the parsley to the bulgur together with the tomatoes, spring onions, mint, mixed spice, lemon juice, and olive oil. Mix well, and season with salt and pepper to taste. Spoon the tabbouleh into a wide serving bowl and garnish with the lettuce leaves.

Tabbouleh –
a classic
Lebanese salad

BULGUR PILAFF

A bulgur pilaff is made in the same way as a rice pilaff (p312). Simply substitute bulgur for rice, or combine equal quantities of white basmati rice and bulgur. Either way, cook for about 20 minutes, or until tender to the bite.

Summer fruit tabbouleh

This unusual dessert – a variation of the classic tabbouleh – is light, fruity, and refreshing in warm weather. The choice of fruit can be varied depending on what is best in season.

75g (2½oz) bulgur, picked over to remove any grit

150g (5½oz) blueberries

150g (5½oz) raspberries

100g (3½oz) strawberries, halved

100g (3½oz) pineapple flesh, chopped

1 mango, peeled and chopped

150g (5½oz) watermelon, chopped

100g (3½oz) redcurrants

For the syrup

75g (2½oz) granulated sugar

150ml (5fl oz) water

4 passion fruits

small bunch of mint, stalks removed

juice of 2 limes

Put the bulgur in a sieve and rinse well, then tip it into a bowl. Cover with hot water and leave to soak for 25 minutes. Drain well in the sieve and pat dry in a cloth. Put the bulgur into a large bowl. Add the fruit and fold together gently. Set aside in a cool place.

To make the syrup, put the sugar and water into a small pan and slowly bring to the boil. Cook to dissolve the sugar. Cut the passion fruits in half and, using a teaspoon, scoop out the seeds and juice. Add to the boiling syrup together with the fruit shells. Simmer gently for 10 minutes, uncovered. Remove from the heat, discard the shells, and leave to cool.

Finely chop half the mint leaves. Stir into the cold syrup with the lime juice. Pour over the bulgur and fruit and mix well. Cover and chill for 1 hour. Scatter the whole mint leaves over the tabbouleh before serving.

COUSCOUS

Couscous is a mixture of fine and coarse semolina, the finer flour binding itself around the coarser grain to form the couscous granules. Traditional couscous takes a long time to cook by steaming, whereas instant or quick-cooking couscous – the type most commonly available these days in supermarkets and Middle Eastern shops – has already been cooked and so cuts down on preparation time dramatically. Instant couscous only needs to be rehydrated with boiling water or a brief steaming.

Couscous can simply be enriched with oil or butter, but is also great when combined with other ingredients in salads and stuffings.

300g (10½oz) instant couscous

400ml (14fl oz) boiling water

1tbsp olive oil or 50g (1¾oz) unsalted butter, cut into cubes

1tsp salt

Rehydrating instant couscous

1 Place the couscous in a large bowl and pour over the boiling water. Cover with cling film and leave to stand for 5 minutes. Remove the cling film and fluff up the couscous grains with a fork, then cover the bowl again and leave for 5 more minutes.

2 Remove the cling film. Add the olive oil or butter and the salt, and fluff up the grains with a fork until they are light and separate. The couscous is now ready to serve.

Steaming instant couscous to serve hot

ADDING HERBS & SPICES

Couscous combines well with many flavourings and which you use depends largely on what you intend to serve with the couscous. Add 1tsp spice, such as ground coriander, ground cumin, or saffron, before you soak or steam the couscous. Or, stir in 1tbsp chopped herbs, such as coriander, dill, parsley, or mint, once the couscous is cooked.

Place the couscous in a bowl, sprinkle with boiling water, cover, and leave for 10 minutes.

Break up any lumps with your fingers, then transfer the couscous to a muslin-lined steamer basket set over boiling water. Cover and steam for 15–20 minutes, or until the grains are tender.

Add olive oil or unsalted butter and salt as above, and fluff up the grains with a fork.

Roast baby chicken with couscous stuffing

This is one of my favourite chicken dishes, equally delicious served hot or cold. The fruity couscous stuffing keeps the bird wonderfully moist.

4 baby chickens (poussins), 400–450g (14–16oz) each

For the marinade

3tbsp chopped coriander

3tbsp chopped flat-leaf parsley

1tbsp cumin seeds

1tsp smoked sweet paprika

1tsp ground turmeric

100ml (3½fl oz) olive oil

juice of ½ lemon

1tbsp harissa

For the stuffing

good pinch of saffron threads

300ml (10fl oz) boiling water

200g (7oz) instant couscous

75g (2½oz) dried fruits, such as apricots, prunes, and figs, chopped

50g (1¾oz) raisins, soaked in water until plump

25g (scant 1oz) pine nuts, toasted

2tbsp chopped coriander

Mix the ingredients for the marinade in a large, shallow dish. Place the chickens in the dish and coat generously with the marinade. Leave at cool room temperature for 2–3 hours, turning the birds occasionally.

Meanwhile, mix the saffron and boiling water in a jug, then use to rehydrate the couscous by soaking it (see opposite). Set aside to cool.

Preheat the oven to 200°C (400°F, gas 6). Finish making the stuffing by stirring the rest of the ingredients into the cooled couscous.

Remove the chickens from the marinade and, using your fingers or a spoon, fill the body cavities loosely with the couscous stuffing. Tie the legs together with string.

Place the chickens in a large roasting tin and spoon over any remaining marinade. Roast for 25–30 minutes, or until golden and the juices run clear when one of the birds is pierced in the thigh with a skewer. Remove from the oven and allow to stand in a warm place for 5 minutes before serving.

SEMOLINA: Gnocchi alla romana

Made from the endosperm of durum wheat, semolina is available in a range of grinds from fine to coarse (granular), and is primarily used to make pasta. Semolina pasta is firmer and more golden in colour than that made from other wheat flours.

Semolina can also be used in hot milk puddings, cakes, breads, and to make gnocchi alla romana. Like gnocchi di patate (potato gnocchi), these tiny dumplings are a staple of Italian cuisine. The semolina (preferably Italian semolina made from the best-quality durum wheat flour) is cooked in a similar way to soft polenta, but using milk rather than water, and the resulting paste is set and cut into shapes in the same way as polenta.

750ml (1¼ pints) full-fat milk
1 small bay leaf
1 garlic clove, crushed
170g (6oz) fine semolina
3 egg yolks
75g (2½oz) Parmesan, freshly grated
freshly grated nutmeg
50g (1¾oz) unsalted butter plus extra for greasing

1 Put the milk, bay leaf, garlic, and a little salt into a heavy-based saucepan and bring to the boil. Remove the bay leaf, then slowly rain in the semolina, whisking constantly to prevent any lumps from forming.

2 Lower the heat and cook gently, uncovered, for 12–15 minutes, whisking occasionally, until the semolina mixture is thick and starts to pull away from the sides of the pan.

5 When the gnocchi mixture is cold and set, cut into rounds with a 5cm (2in) biscuit cutter. Reform the scraps with your hands and cut out more rounds. The mixture will make about 16 gnocchi rounds.

6 Melt the remaining butter in a frying pan over a medium heat. When foaming, add the gnocchi and fry for 5 minutes on each side, or until golden and crisp. Drain on kitchen paper, then finish with a sauce or another topping (see opposite) and serve.

BAKING OR GRILLING

Instead of frying in butter, gnocchi alla romana can be baked or grilled.

■ To bake, arrange the gnocchi rounds, in one layer, in a well-greased baking dish. Dot with 50g (1¾oz) unsalted butter, cut into pieces, and sprinkle with 75g (2½oz) freshly grated Parmesan. Bake on the top shelf of a preheated 230°C (450°F, gas 8) oven for 15 minutes, or until a light golden crust has formed and the gnocchi are heated through.

■ To grill, top the gnocchi rounds with 75g (2½oz) freshly grated Parmesan and cook under a preheated hot grill until golden, bubbling, and heated through.

3 Remove the pan from the heat and beat in the egg yolks, one at a time. Stir in the cheese and a little nutmeg, and season to taste with salt and pepper. Grease a 1cm (½in) deep baking tray liberally with butter.

4 Spoon the gnocchi mixture into the tray and spread it out evenly with a wet palette knife. Melt half the butter, then brush over the surface of the mixture. Once cool, cover and put into the refrigerator to chill for 2–3 hours.

FINISHING FRIED GNOCCHI

Once fried, place the gnocchi in a greased baking dish, in one layer, then add one of the following toppings. Bake in a preheated 230°C (450°F, gas 8) oven for the timings given.

■ Top with 750ml (1¼ pints) tomato or cheese sauce and sprinkle evenly with 50g (1¾oz) freshly grated Parmesan. Bake for 8–10 minutes.

■ Top with 300g (10½oz) blanched broccoli florets, 450g (1lb) sliced, cooked spicy sausage, and 75g (2½oz) crumbled Gorgonzola. Bake for 8–10 minutes.

■ Top with 2 thinly sliced buffalo mozzarella balls and 4 thinly sliced ripe tomatoes, drizzle over 120ml (4fl oz) pesto sauce (p42) and scatter on 12 black olives. Bake for 5 minutes.

BASIC PREPARATION OF PULSES

There is hardly a country or continent that does not have its own favourite pulse-based dishes, whether it is refried beans from Mexico, hummus from the Middle East, Boston baked beans from the US, the fragrant dals of the Indian subcontinent, or the grand meat and vegetable stew cocido from Spain. The basic preparation of the pulses is simple – sort, rinse, soak if necessary, and then simmer, after which they can be used in all kinds of dishes. See the chart opposite for individual soaking and cooking times.

Sorting & rinsing

This is the first step for all pulses, whether they are lentils or split peas you are about to cook, or beans or whole peas you intend to soak. Place them in a sieve or colander and pick them over carefully to remove any dirt or grit, tiny pebbles, or other foreign material. Then rinse the pulses well under cold running water.

USING CANNED PULSES

While I prefer freshly cooked pulses, I recognize that canned pulses are very convenient. I don't recommend them for salads as they cannot absorb dressing easily and take on flavours, but the firmer beans – black and red kidney beans, for example – are fine added to stews and to make quick soups. Before using canned beans, drain and rinse them thoroughly in a sieve or colander.

Soaking

With the exception of lentils and split peas, pulses are soaked before cooking to ensure that they cook evenly and relatively quickly. Time permitting, I like to give them a long soak because I think they keep their shape better than pulses that have been quick-soaked (see below). Place the pulses in a large bowl and cover with 3 times their volume of cold water. Cover the bowl and leave to soak for 8 hours or overnight (I always refrigerate them, to avoid any chance of fermentation). The next day, drain the pulses and discard the soaking water. They are now ready to cook.

Quick-soaking

This is a great shortcut when time is of the essence. Put the pulses in a large pan, cover with 3 times their volume of cold water, and bring quickly to the boil. Reduce the heat and simmer for 5 minutes. Remove from the heat, cover with a lid, and leave to soak for 1–2 hours. Drain. The pulses are now ready to cook.

Adding flavour

Because pulses can be somewhat bland, when cooking them I often add an onion studded with a few cloves, or replace the water with a well-flavoured chicken or beef stock. Spices such as coriander, cumin, caraway, anise, and chili can be added too, as can bay leaf, thyme, and rosemary. Vegetables such as carrots will add sweetness. Wait until towards the end of cooking to add salt, and be sure the pulses are completely cooked before mixing in acidic ingredients such as tomatoes, wine, and lemon. This is because salt and acidity will toughen the skins of the pulses, preventing them from softening, and will thus prolong the cooking time.

Cooking on the stovetop

I often start with a 10-minute period of rapid boiling (this is especially important for red kidney beans and soya beans, which have harmful toxins in their skins). Then I continue cooking, monitoring carefully – if pulses are overcooked, they will be soggy, with split skins.

1 Place the pulses in a large pan and cover with 4 times their volume of cold water. To stop them sticking, add 1tbsp vegetable oil for every 450g (1lb) soaked beans. Bring quickly to the boil and boil over high heat for 10 minutes. Skim any scum from the surface.

2 Reduce the heat, partly cover with a lid, and simmer until tender (see right for timings), topping up with boiling water if necessary. Add salt 15–20 minutes before the end of cooking.

Other cooking options

The stovetop method is a slow business, but it is hard to beat. Microwaves, slow cookers, and pressure cookers are other options, but the results are seldom as good: microwaves can actually take longer to cook lentils and split peas, while the settings on slow cookers are often too high or too low. Pressure cookers do cut cooking times – by up to two-thirds – but they are not suitable if you want to add flavourings or cook more than 450g (1lb) at a time.

Soaking & cooking times for pulses

Soaking and cooking pulses can never be an exact science because much depends on the age and origin of the crop. The timings below are therefore approximate.

TYPE OF PULSE	SOAKING TIME	APPROXIMATE COOKING TIME	BEST FOR
Adzuki beans	overnight	40–45 minutes	pâtés, soups, sprouting
Black beans (Mexican)	overnight	1 hour	salads, soups, stews, refried beans
Black-eyed beans	overnight	1–1½ hours	casseroles, pâtés, salads, soups
Borlotti beans	overnight	1–1½ hours	Italian dishes, soups, stews
Broad beans (skinless)*	overnight	1½ hours	falafel, salads, soups, stews
Butter beans	overnight	1–1½ hours	pâtés, salads, soups
Cannellini beans	overnight	1–1½ hours	Italian dishes, salads, soups
Chickpeas	overnight	2–3 hours	casseroles, hummus, Middle Eastern dishes, sprouting
Flageolet beans	overnight	1½ hours	casseroles, soups, salads
Ful medames	overnight	1–1½ hours	ful medames, bigilla
Haricot beans	overnight	1–1½ hours	Boston baked beans, casseroles, cassoulet, salads, soups
Lentils (split)	not required	25 minutes	casseroles, dals, pâtés, soups
Lentils (whole)	not required	45 minutes	casseroles, dals, pâtés, salads, soups, sprouting
Mung beans (whole)	not required	¾–1 hour	salads, sprouting, stews
Peas (whole)	overnight	1–1½ hours	casseroles, mushy peas, pease pudding, purées, soups
Peas (split)	not required	45 minutes	casseroles, dals, pease pudding, soups
Pinto beans	overnight	1–1½ hours	Mexican dishes, refried beans, tacos
Red kidney beans**	boil hard for 10 minutes, then soak for 4 hours	1–1½ hours	casseroles, chili con carne, salads, soups, stews
Soya beans**	boil hard for 10 minutes, then soak for 4 hours	3–4 hours	casseroles, fritters, pâtés, tofu

* broad beans with skins need to be soaked for 48 hours in several changes of water, then skinned before cooking; skinless broad beans require only an overnight soak.

** to destroy toxins in their skins, red kidney beans and soya beans require a special soaking procedure. Follow the quick-soaking method, but boil the beans hard for 10 minutes. Remove from the heat, cover, and allow to soak for 4 hours, then drain and cook.

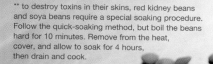

PURÉEING: Hummus

A blender or food processor take a lot of the hard work out of puréeing pulses, which would otherwise have to be done by pressing them through a sieve or food mill. The machines also give a smooth, silky finish. For the Middle Eastern dip hummus, chickpeas are puréed to the consistency of wet mashed potatoes.

150g (5½oz) dried chickpeas, soaked overnight, then drained

600ml (1 pint) water

2 large garlic cloves, crushed

juice of 2 lemons

75ml (2½fl oz) olive oil

150ml (5fl oz) tahini (sesame seed paste)

cayenne pepper

To serve

2tbsp olive oil

2tbsp chopped flat-leaf parsley

pinch of cayenne pepper or paprika

1 Put the chickpeas and water in a large pan. Bring to the boil, then partly cover and simmer for 2–3 hours, or until tender. Drain, reserving the liquid. Set aside 2–3tbsp chickpeas. Put the remainder in a blender with the garlic.

2 Add the lemon juice, olive oil, and 150ml (5fl oz) of the reserved cooking liquid. Process to a purée. Add the tahini and process until smooth. Season with salt and cayenne pepper, then transfer to a bowl.

BIGILLA

Bigilla is a black bean paste eaten as a dip. To make it, soak 450g (1lb) dried ful medames overnight, then drain and put in a pan with 1 chopped onion and 2 peeled garlic cloves. Cover with water and bring to the boil. Boil for 10 minutes, then reduce the heat and simmer, partly covered, for 1–1½ hours, or until the beans are soft. Add 150g (5½oz) sun-dried tomatoes and cook for a further 15 minutes. Drain the bean mixture and leave to cool, then put in a blender with 2 crushed garlic cloves, 3tbsp chopped flat-leaf parsley, 2 seeded and finely chopped red chilies, and salt and pepper to taste. Process, adding about 120ml (4fl oz) olive oil to form a smooth paste with the consistency of wet mashed potatoes. Chill, then serve with slices of mature goat's cheese liberally sprinkled with cracked black pepper and drizzled with olive oil, and plenty of bread.

Drizzle over the olive oil. Garnish with the parsley, cayenne, and reserved chickpeas, and serve

PASTA E FAGIOLI

This is one of the all-time great soups, a hearty rustic dish made from borlotti beans – either fresh or dried – flavoured with pork, rosemary, and tomato, and finished with pasta and a light drizzle of olive oil. There are many versions throughout Italy, but this is my favourite way to prepare it. I have to confess that on occasions of extreme hunger I have chopped up the pork hock and added it back to the soup. And why not?

4tbsp olive oil plus extra for drizzling

1 onion, finely chopped

2 carrots, finely diced

2 celery sticks, finely diced

200g (7oz) boneless pork hock, cut into large pieces

300g (10½oz) dried borlotti beans, soaked overnight, then drained

400g (14oz) canned tomatoes, chopped with juice

1tbsp tomato purée

2 sprigs of rosemary

1 litre (1¾ pints) beef or chicken stock

150g (5½oz) small tubular pasta, such as macaroni or maltagliati

50g (1¾oz) Parmesan, freshly grated, plus extra for serving

Serve sprinkled with cracked black pepper and extra Parmesan, plus a little olive oil drizzled over the top

1 Heat the oil in a large heavy-based pan. Add the onion, carrots, and celery, and cook over moderate heat for 5–10 minutes, or until the onion is translucent.

2 Add the pork, beans, tomatoes, tomato purée, rosemary, and stock. Bring to the boil. Reduce the heat, cover, and simmer for 1–1¼ hours, or until the beans are tender.

3 Remove the pork and discard the rosemary stalks. Ladle one-third of the bean mixture into a blender and process to a purée, then return to the pan.

4 Bring back to the boil. Add the pasta and cook for 15 minutes, uncovered. Remove from heat, stir in the cheese, and season. Leave for a few minutes before serving.

MASHING: Refried beans

For this dish (called frijoles refritos in Mexico), black beans are cooked, then coarsely mashed and fried in lard with bacon and chilies. Also known as turtle beans, black beans are shiny and kidney shaped with a white seam. They are popular in Latin America and the West Indies, where they are used in salads, soups, and stews.

450g (1lb) dried black beans, soaked overnight, then drained

1.8 litres (3¼ pints) water

50g (1¾oz) lard

1 onion, chopped

75g (2½oz) streaky bacon, cut into small pieces

2 small red chilies, finely chopped

1 sprig of epazote, or 2tbsp chopped coriander

To serve

50g (1¾oz) crumbled queso fresco or feta cheese

4 spring onions, chopped

2tbsp chopped coriander

fried tortilla triangles (see below)

1 Put the beans in a large pan with the water and bring to the boil. Boil for 10 minutes, then partly cover, reduce heat, and simmer for about 1 hour, or until tender. Drain, reserving the cooking liquid. Place in a mixing bowl with 100ml (3½fl oz) reserved liquid. Mash with a potato masher until lightly crushed.

2 Heat the lard in a large frying pan. Add the onion, bacon, and chilies and cook until soft and golden. Add the epazote and mashed beans. Cook, stirring, for 1–2 minutes to heat through. The mixture should be as thick as mashed potatoes; add 1tbsp reserved liquid if it is too dry. Season and transfer to a serving bowl.

Serve topped with the cheese, spring onions, and coriander, and garnished with fried tortilla triangles

FRIED TORTILLA TRIANGLES

Cut 2 corn tortillas into equal-sized wedges using a sharp knife. Deep-fry in vegetable oil heated to 180°C (350°F) for 1 minute, or until golden and crisp. Drain on kitchen paper.

STEWING: Dal

For this staple of Indian cuisine, split red lentils are gently stewed with chilies, then combined with tomatoes and a fried spice mixture. Dal can also be served with a little plain yogurt.

170g (6oz) split red lentils, rinsed	1tsp ground turmeric	½tsp cumin seeds
2 green chilies, seeded and finely chopped	1 onion, finely chopped	½tsp grated fresh ginger
	450ml (15fl oz) water	1 garlic clove, crushed
	400g (14oz) canned tomatoes, drained and chopped	½tsp ground coriander
	4tbsp ghee or vegetable oil	4 curry leaves (optional)
	½tsp mustard seeds	½tsp asafoetida

1 Put the lentils in a saucepan. Add the chilies, turmeric, onion, and water and bring to the boil. Partly cover the pan and simmer, without stirring, for 30–35 minutes, or until the lentils are soft. Stir in the tomatoes.

2 Heat the ghee in a small pan. Add the rest of the ingredients and fry over moderate heat for 2 minutes, stirring occasionally. Add to the lentils and cook, stirring, until thick. Season.

Serve with Indian bread to scoop up the dal

SLOW COOKING ON THE STOVETOP: Cocido español

Simmered gently with vegetables and meat, pulses make satisfying one-pot meals. Cocido, the national dish of Spain, is one of these, and there are as many variations of it as there are cooks. At its simplest, cocido is a peasant dish of potatoes or rice with vegetables, beans, and, sometimes, a piece of pork or a ham bone. Or, it may be rich with fatty meats like goose confit or spicy sausages. The slow, gentle cooking is considered to be the secret of its tastiness.

During cooking, keep the pan partly covered to stop the broth evaporating too much, but with enough of a gap so it will not boil over.

Following tradition, cocido is served in two parts: first the broth, then the boiled meat and vegetables. I like to finish the broth with rice instead of the traditional fine noodles.

Serves 8

5 litres (8¾ pints) water
500g (1lb 2oz) beef flank
4 ham bones, about 450g (1lb)
250g (8½oz) cured Serrano ham
200g (7oz) fatty salt pork
300g (10½oz) dried chickpeas, soaked overnight, then drained
150g (5½oz) chorizo sausage
125g (4½oz) morcilla blood sausage (optional)
½ chicken, about 675g (1½lb), cut into small joints
4 potatoes
400g (14oz) turnips, cut into large wedges
400g (14oz) carrots, halved lengthways
600g (1lb 6oz) cabbage, cut into thick wedges
3tbsp olive oil
3 garlic cloves, crushed
150g (5½oz) Valencian paella rice or risotto rice, or fine vermicelli noodles

1 Put the water in a large saucepan and add the beef flank, ham bones, Serrano ham, and salt pork. Bring to the boil, skimming off any impurities that rise to the surface. Add the chickpeas. Reduce the heat, partly cover the pan, and simmer for 1½ hours.

2 Add the sausage, chicken, potatoes, turnips, and carrots and simmer, partly covered, for a further 30 minutes. Cook the cabbage in a pan of boiling water for 10–15 minutes; drain. Heat the oil and garlic in a frying pan and sauté the cabbage for 2–3 minutes to brown. Keep warm.

4 Arrange the chickpeas and vegetables on a warmed platter. Cut the sausage into thick slices and arrange with all the meats on another platter. Serve after the broth.

3 Meanwhile, boil the rice, if using, until cooked. Lift the meat and vegetables from the broth, with enough broth to moisten the meat. Keep warm. Return the remaining broth to the boil, add the rice or noodles, and simmer for 2–3 minutes before serving as a first course.

SLOW COOKING IN THE OVEN:
Boston baked beans

Small, oval, white beans are traditionally used for America's favourite bean dish as well as for French cassoulet. The beans are cooked on the stovetop until tender before they are combined with the sauce ingredients.

| 450g (1lb) dried haricot beans, soaked overnight, then drained |
| 2 onions, finely chopped |
| 2tbsp Dijon mustard |
| 2tbsp dark brown sugar |
| 5tbsp black treacle |
| 400g (14oz) canned tomatoes, drained and finely chopped |
| 1tbsp Worcestershire sauce |
| 1 garlic clove, crushed |
| 1tsp cider vinegar or white wine vinegar |
| 150g (5½oz) piece of smoked bacon, cut into small pieces |
| 4tbsp chopped flat-leaf parsley, to garnish |

1 Put the beans into a large pan and cover with 4 times their volume of cold water. Bring to the boil and boil for 10 minutes, then reduce the heat. Partly cover the pan and simmer the beans for 1–1½ hours, or until tender.

2 Preheat the oven to 150°C (300°F, gas 2). Drain the beans and put them into a large casserole. Add all the remaining ingredients except the parsley and mix thoroughly together.

3 Cover the casserole tightly and place it in the oven. Bake for 3 hours, or until the beans are surrounded with a sauce, stirring every hour and adding a little hot water if the beans look at all dry.

4 Season the beans with salt and freshly ground black pepper. Sprinkle with the parsley before serving.

DEEP-FRYING: Falafel

A popular way to use pulses in the Middle East is to make small, deep-fried croquettes called falafel. Dried broad beans and/or chickpeas are traditionally used, and the falafel are served either as mezze (appetizers) or as a snack in pitta bread. They are accompanied almost always by a tomato and cucumber salad and tahini, a sesame and garlic sauce.

Makes 20

| 350g (12½oz) dried broad beans |
| 250g (8½oz) dried chickpeas, soaked overnight, then drained |
| 1 onion, finely chopped |
| 50g (1¾oz) flat-leaf parsley, chopped |

| 2 garlic cloves, crushed |
| 4 spring onions, finely chopped |
| small pinch of hot chili powder |
| 1tsp each ground coriander and cumin |
| 1tsp bicarbonate of soda |
| vegetable oil, for deep-frying |

1 If not using skinless broad beans, soak them for 48 hours, changing the water twice. Drain, then remove the skins by pinching the beans at one end between fingers and thumbs. Skinless broad beans only need overnight soaking.

2 Process the beans and chickpeas in a food processor to a grainy texture. Add the onion and process until fine. Transfer to a bowl and mix in the parsley, garlic, spring onions, spices, soda, and seasoning. Leave to rest for 1 hour.

3 Mould the mixture into 4cm (1½in) balls and flatten them slightly. Leave to rest for 30 minutes, then deep-fry in oil heated to 180°C (350°F) for 3–4 minutes, or until golden all over. Drain on kitchen paper and serve.

Falafel – spicy bean patties

BLACK-EYED BEAN FRITTERS

Popular throughout central Africa, these spicy bean fritters called akara make great appetizers or snacks. This recipe makes 20.

Soak 150g (5½oz) dried black-eyed beans overnight, then drain and dry well. Put the beans in a food processor with 1 finely chopped onion, 2 crushed garlic cloves, a finely chopped 4cm (1½in) piece of fresh ginger, 2 seeded and finely chopped red chilies, and 3tbsp roughly chopped coriander. Process until light and fluffy, then beat in 25g (scant 1oz) chickpea flour and seasoning to taste. Leave to rest for 15–20 minutes. Using a spoon, shape the mixture into small ovals, then deep-fry in vegetable oil heated to 180°C (350°F) for 2–3 minutes, turning to cook evenly. Drain on kitchen paper and serve.

SHALLOW-FRYING: Dosas

These crisp, eggless pancakes are a staple of south Indian cooking, and recipes for them abound. Traditionally they are made with split pulses and rice, soaked, then blended to a thick batter and left to ferment overnight. At their simplest, after frying in ghee or butter, dosas are filled with chutneys or pickles, or they can be wrapped around a filling, such as dal (p333).

Makes 8

100g (3½oz) basmati rice
75g (2½oz) hulled urad dal (split urad beans)
1tsp fenugreek seeds
600ml (1 pint) cold water
45g (1½oz) ghee or clarified butter, for frying

1 Mix the first 4 ingredients in a bowl. Leave at room temperature for 2 hours. Transfer to a blender and process to a thick batter. Add a little salt. Pour into a jug and refrigerate overnight. Heat a non-stick frying pan brushed lightly with some of the ghee. Pour in 3tbsp batter and tilt the pan to coat the bottom evenly. Cook over a moderate heat for 2–3 minutes, or until bubbles appear on the surface.

2 Using a spatula, turn the pancake over and cook for a further 2 minutes, or until golden and crisp. Remove from the pan and keep warm while you cook the rest of the pancakes in the same way.

Dosa, south Indian pancakes

SPROUTING

Sprouted pulses, such as sprouted seeds and grains, make an excellent addition to salads, stir-fries, omelettes, and sandwiches. They are low in calories, easily digested, and very nutritious.

The most popular commercial sprouts are derived from mung beans, chickpeas, lentils, and adzuki beans, but many other pulses can be sprouted successfully. When buying sprouts, choose those that are fresh and crisp, with the seed capsule still attached. Ideally use them on the day of purchase, or keep them in a plastic bag in the refrigerator for no more than two days.

Sprouting pulses at home

Growing your own sprouts is easy and satisfying. It only takes 4–5 days, and all you need is a big jar, some muslin, and an elastic band. Be sure to buy whole pulses that are labelled specifically for sprouting. As a first step, pick them over, then rinse them well and drain.

1 Place the pulses in a jar large enough to allow them to increase up to 10 times in volume. Fill with room-temperature water. Secure a piece of muslin over the mouth of the jar with an elastic band. Leave upright overnight.

2 Drain off the water through the muslin, then rinse the pulses by filling the jar with fresh cold water and draining it off again. Lay the jar on its side in a warm, dark place or covered with a towel. Twice every day, rinse the pulses and drain. They must never dry out, nor should they sit in water (they will rot).

3 Harvest the sprouts when the cotyledons (the first tiny green leaves) have appeared.

SALADS: Warm lentil salad with scallops

The best pulses to use in salads are butter beans, kidney beans, haricot beans, cannellini beans, and Puy lentils. Cook them fresh and add to the dressing while still hot – they will absorb it immediately. This is one of my favourite lentil salads, flavoured with bacon, garlic, and herbs. Cook the scallops lightly and quickly so you retain their natural juices.

225g (8oz) Puy lentils, rinsed

1 bay leaf

2tsp olive oil plus extra for brushing

1 red pepper, halved and seeded

50g (1¾oz) pancetta, finely chopped

1 red onion, finely chopped

2tbsp chopped flat-leaf parsley

1tbsp chopped coriander

12 large scallops, shelled and cleaned

For the dressing

1 garlic clove, crushed

2tsp Dijon mustard

1tbsp red wine vinegar

3tbsp olive oil

1 Put lentils and bay leaf in a pan, cover with water, and bring to the boil. Simmer, partly covered, for 20–30 minutes, or until tender.

2 Meanwhile, heat a ridged grill pan until hot. Add the oil and char-grill the pepper for 5–6 minutes, turning, until lightly charred all over. Place in a plastic bag, seal, and leave for 2–3 minutes, then skin and dice.

3 Fry the pancetta in a non-stick pan for 3 minutes, or until crisp. Meanwhile, whisk the dressing ingredients in a bowl and season.

4 Drain the lentils and put into a large bowl. Add the dressing, pepper, pancetta, onion, and herbs. Toss to combine. Return the grill pan to the heat. Add the scallops, brush with olive oil, and season. Char-grill for 2–3 minutes on each side, or until golden brown.

Serve the lentil salad on individual serving plates. Top each with 3 scallops

Soya beans

Of all the pulses, the soya bean is the most nutritious, equal in protein to meat and rich in beneficial fatty acids, iron, and calcium. However, soya beans are extremely bland and do not absorb cooking flavours, so need hearty ingredients to support them.

The common soya bean is white, but yellow, black, and red varieties can also be found. In addition, soya beans appear in many other forms, being fermented for miso, black and yellow bean sauces, and soy sauce; made into tofu (bean curd) and tempeh; and ground for flour and to make soya milk and cheese.

Tofu

Made in a similar way to soft curd cheese, tofu is available soft (also known as silken), firm, and smoked. Soft tofu, with its creamy texture, is best for dressings, sauces, and dips; firm tofu, which is similar in texture to feta cheese, can be sliced to use in stir-fries, soups, and sweet dishes. Smoked tofu, which tastes a bit like bacon, can be fried or used for kebabs.

Unlike soya beans, tofu absorbs flavours easily. Because it is very perishable, tofu should be kept covered with water and chilled. To prolong its shelf life (up to 4–5 days), transfer it to a new container, cover with fresh water, put on the lid, and refrigerate. The water needs to be changed daily.

Tempeh

Made by fermenting partly cooked soya beans with a starter culture, tempeh has a firm texture and a flavour that varies from mild to pungent, according to how long it has been ripened. It can be sliced, marinated, and deep-fried; simmered in a sauce; or chopped and added to stews and salads.

Hot Asian salad with tofu dressing

Vegetables are greatly enjoyed throughout the Far East, often parboiled in a seasoned stock or stir-fried and then topped with a warm dressing. Here, soft (silken) tofu makes an interesting dressing for fragrant stir-fried vegetables. This starter or side-dish salad is also good served cold.

2tbsp olive oil

2.5cm (1in) piece of fresh ginger, finely shredded

50g (1¾oz) shiitaki mushrooms, thickly sliced

1 carrot, cut into thick batons

100g (3½oz) Chinese long beans, blanched for 3–4 minutes, drained, and cut into 5cm (2in) lengths

1 red pepper, seeded and cut into thick strips

100g (3½oz) Chinese broccoli, cut into florets

100g (3½oz) small mangetout

2 baby pak choi, separated into leaves

For the dressing

170g (6oz) soft tofu

1tsp light soy sauce

1tsp toasted sesame oil

1tbsp toasted sesame seeds or tahini (sesame paste)

½tsp caster sugar

To make the dressing, drain the tofu in a fine sieve for 30 minutes, discarding the liquid. Press the tofu through the sieve into a bowl. Mix in the remaining dressing ingredients and set aside.

Heat the oil in a wok until hot, add the ginger, and stir-fry briefly. Add all the vegetables and stir-fry over moderate heat for 1–2 minutes, or until tender but still crisp. Add the dressing to the vegetables, season, and serve warm.

Push the tofu through the sieve with a wooden spoon

BREADS & BATTERS

DAN LEPARD

A table laid with simple things to eat is the kind of meal I most want for myself and to share with friends. Sometimes it might include a saucepan, with meat and onions bobbing in a broth made with good stock, or perhaps a warm roast chicken stuffed with lemons, olives, and garlic. A little cheese, alongside a bowl of tender salad leaves, and some good wine. And also on the table, a whole loaf of bread, baked that day but cool enough to be sliced. Perhaps it is to be expected that I should want to make bread whenever friends are due. But let me also tell you – every time I have the chance to bake some bread, I feel that I am the fortunate one.

Baking your first bread The perfect loaf is the result of care and practised method. It doesn't come from an inherited knack for baking. If you have never baked before, be reassured that with simple ingredients and tools you can make a loaf to be proud of. The measured ingredients are mixed thoughtfully, kneaded carefully, nurtured through a gentle rise, and shaped: the baking itself just seals those good things in place. Avoid becoming over concerned with perfection. In a working bakery we are obliged to sell what we make, and with that comes a pressure to make perfect bread, every day, without any dip in consistency. Uniform loaves, day in and day out, and crusts that look paint-chart perfect. That is what our customers demand, but how is it that somewhere, during our transformation from hunter-gatherers to supermarket-gatherers, we lost our acceptance of variety? I hope you will aspire to something less artificial and rather more human. Celebrate the odd tear that appears like a smile across the top of the loaf. Or the knobbly, crispy ends that make a home-made wholewheat stick something earthborn and real. Bread baking is not a ceramic art. It is, like all good cooking, about taste and the way that taste is affected by appearance, texture, and aroma.

Take a dusty, round loaf from the remarkable Poilâne bakery in Paris. Beneath its "P", cut with a razor-sharp blade into the surface of the dough, is an extraordinary texture and taste. Yet the ingredients are simple – flour, water, salt, and leaven – and the recipe is hardly complicated: mix, shape, and bake. So how can a complex, elemental flavour grow from this simplicity? The secret lies in the interaction between ingredients, nature, and science. Just as an apple can reflect the care given to the orchard, so grain can reflect the region and its soil. Careful, slow milling can preserve much of the grain's taste. Slow mixing with good water and mineral-rich salt helps to enhance it. Layered over that foundation will be the complex flavours of the leaven – yeasts that multiply slowly in a doughy mixture alongside lactic acids and healthy bacteria. For some loaves, the smoky heat of a wood-fired oven will set the crust and add a little flavour too.

Working with your ingredients The key to great bread baking is care and consideration, from the purchase of ingredients through to the final bake. Wherever you live, in a city or village, your choice of ingredients will be the cornerstone of the final quality. It is a myth that excellent bread can be baked with poor ingredients, and it is equally untrue that you need the finest ingredients to bake well. But you do need to understand and work with the qualities of the ingredients you have at hand. You must believe that each ingredient in your kitchen will perform differently in accordance to your recipe and the way you use your hands, and oven. White wheat flours, each labelled "suitable for bread making", will not necessarily perform equally well. They will probably be similar, but each will need tweaking according to your taste and intention.

My hope is that you will attempt to understand the flour you use and make sure that your recipe, technique, and dough handling serve to enhance the basic qualities of the grain. In the following chapter are recipes for breads and batters, some simple and others more demanding and complicated, to help you examine the ingredients you have and out of them create outstanding, nutritious foods that will give you pleasure for years to come.

MAKING YEAST-RISEN BREAD

The single-celled fungus *Saccharomyces cerevisiae* – more commonly known as baker's yeast – is a fermentation machine, taking the natural sugars present in a mixture and releasing carbon dioxide as a result. Fermenting yeasts give beer its fizz, champagne its pop, and leavened bread its texture with a crumb full of bubbles.

When using commercial yeast in baking, I prefer fresh rather than dried yeast, as I think it gives a better result. If you must use dried because no fresh yeast is available, then follow this method. Use half the weight suggested for fresh yeast, and stir this into 50g (1¾oz) water or liquid taken from the total amount, but at a temperature of 35°C (95°F). Stir this with 1tbsp flour, taken from the total amount of flour, and leave the mixture for 10 minutes. Then add it to the dough with the rest of the liquids, and proceed according to the recipe.

Remember, though, that by changing from fresh to dried yeast you are tinkering with the heart of the loaf, and the result will not be as certain as the one I have written.

Read through the methods shown on the following pages for mixing, kneading, and shaping before making your first loaf, as the recipes will refer you to these techniques.

SIMPLE WHITE OR WHOLEMEAL BREAD

Once you have read the sections on mixing, kneading, and shaping, you should be ready to start baking. The wholemeal loaf needs less rising time than the white: the husk and fibre in wholemeal flour mean the percentage of gluten is lower; too long an initial rise might leave the dough exhausted. Both loaves are easier to slice the day after baking.

Makes 1 loaf

10g (1½tsp) fresh yeast
350g (12oz) water at 22°C (72°F)
500g (1lb 2oz) strong white or strong wholemeal flour plus extra for shaping
10g (1½tsp) fine sea salt
olive or sunflower oil for kneading

1 Follow the steps for mixing and kneading the dough (p346). Then cover with a cloth and leave for 30 minutes before giving the dough a final knead. A wholemeal dough is now ready to be shaped, but leave a white dough to rise for a further 30 minutes before shaping.

2 Oil and flour a deep 12x19cm (about 5x8in) loaf tin. Cut the dough into 2 equal pieces, round them, and tuck side by side into the tin (p346). Cover with a cloth and leave to rise at room temperature (22°C/72°F) for 1–1½ hours, or until almost doubled in height.

3 Preheat the oven to 220°C (425°F, gas 7). Uncover the loaf. Spray the top with a fine mist of water and dust lightly with flour.

4 Place the tin on the centre shelf of the oven and bake for 15 minutes. Reduce the heat to 190°C (375°F, gas 5) and bake for a further 30 minutes, or until the bread is done.

5 Remove from the oven. After a few minutes, take the loaf out of the tin and leave to cool upright on a wire rack. When cold, wrap in greaseproof paper and store in a bread bin.

MIXING THE DOUGH

There is one commonly recommended step that I would remove from the baking lexicon: do not throw handfuls of flour into a dough to stop it sticking. When it is first made, sticky dough is exactly what it will be and should be.

Within wheat flour there are strands of protein that, after wetting, align to form the stretchy, resilient substance we know as gluten. Though it is important to make sure that the moisture is evenly incorporated through the dough for gluten to form, it is not kneading that determines whether gluten becomes elastic, as this is predetermined by the integral characteristics of the proteins. All that is required is patience: after the initial thorough mixing of the wet ingredients with the dry, leave the dough to sit for 10 minutes, covered with a cloth.

WEIGHING INGREDIENTS

In this chapter, liquid quantities larger than 4tbsp are weighed in grams rather than measured in millilitres. This is because the ingredients used in my bread and batter recipes are calculated by reference to the flour weight. If you use the same set of scales for all the ingredients, then the recipe will stay true to the original. This would not be the case if you mixed weights with volumes.

Digital scales – along with the metric system of measurement – are a great invention, and one I could not live without. It is true that skilled home bakers can create excellence while appearing to use less precise measurements, but it is their practised eye that guides them, and they are still measuring, but using their familiarity with the ingredients rather than scales. In translating recipes for others to replicate, digital scales and the metric weighing of all ingredients enables me to convey to you exactly what I am measuring.

The only point where I would advise caution is that domestic scales often weigh in increments of 5 grams, and are therefore not always so good at measuring tiny amounts accurately. So even though the recipes show salt and yeast in grams, I have given teaspoons too, as I find it is better to use an accurate set of measuring spoons for these small but vitally important ingredients.

1 In a bowl, whisk the fresh yeast and water together with a fork until the yeast has completely dissolved.

2 Combine the flour and salt in a bowl. Mix the yeast liquid with the dry ingredients, stirring in with your hand.

3 Mix thoroughly, as quickly as possible, to make a soft, sticky dough. Dig right down to the bottom of the bowl, and squidge the dough through your fingers to be sure all the flour is mixed with the liquid.

4 Scrape any dough from your fingers back into the bowl, then cover with a cloth to keep the dough moist. Leave it for 10 minutes before starting to knead, as this will give you a more elastic dough with less effort.

KNEADING THE DOUGH

I use a lightly oiled rather than a floured surface for kneading. Instead of 10 minutes of constant working, I give the dough a series of brief kneads with rests in between. This produces an elastic result, avoids the damage caused by over-zealous kneading, opens the texture by stretching the emerging gas pockets, and gives the flour time to fully absorb moisture. Forget about trying to "develop gluten". This will happen through hydration over time. What you need to do is concentrate on mixing the dough evenly.

1 Tip 1tsp of oil onto the work surface and rub it out into a circle 20cm (8in) in diameter. Also rub 2tsp oil over the surface of the dough. Scrape the dough out onto the oiled surface and cover with a cloth.

2 Before starting to knead the dough, wash and dry the bowl, then rub the inside and your hands with a little oil. Set the bowl aside. Uncover the dough and fold it in half towards you. It will be very soft and sticky at this stage.

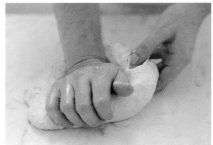

3 If you are right handed, use your left thumb to hold the fold in place, while with the heel of your right hand you gently but firmly press down and away through the centre of the dough to seal and stretch it.

WHICH OIL?

I like to use olive, corn, or sunflower oil for oiling the work surface, my hands, and the mixing bowl. The oil won't impart much flavour to the dough, as only a very small amount is needed to keep the dough moving smoothly as you knead it. Work surfaces made of laminate, marble, unvarnished wood, and stainless steel are all good for kneading dough.

4 Lift and rotate the dough a quarter turn. Repeat the folding, pressing, and rotating 10–12 times, stopping before the dough starts sticking to the surface. Then place the dough in the oiled bowl, seam-side down, cover with a cloth, and leave for 10 minutes.

5 Repeat the kneading procedure twice at 10-minute intervals. Each kneading will require less oil. The dough will change from its lumpen start to a silken and elastic finish.

SHAPING THE DOUGH

After the initial rise, the dough is divided into smaller pieces according to the use you have in mind. You could simply chop the dough in half or quarters, not worrying about the exact weight of each piece. However, as larger loaves take longer to bake than smaller loaves, it is good practice to weigh your mass of dough and divide it accurately. For shaping, the work surface should be lightly floured. This will slightly dry the outside of the dough to encourage a good crust to form during baking. Once shaped, the dough is ready for its final rise.

Shaping a tin loaf

For a tin loaf, you can just press a short, stocky baton (see opposite) down into an oiled and floured loaf tin, or even roll up the dough neatly like a swiss roll to give an even rise. Here, I've cut the dough into two equal pieces, rounded the pieces, and tucked them side by side into the tin.

Shaping a round loaf

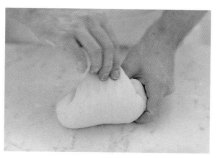  

1 If the dough has been cut in half, place a piece on the lightly floured work surface, smoothest side down. Pinch the edge of the dough and pull it into the centre, holding it in place with the thumb of your other hand.

2 Continue the pinching and pulling, rotating the dough a little each time, until you have worked your way all around the dough in 6 or 8 movements, and have shaped a rough ball. Flip the dough over.

3 Make sure that the work surface is only barely dusted with flour, then rotate and drag the ball of dough across it. As the underside of the dough catches slightly, the upper surface will be pulled taut, making a neat round loaf.

Shaping a baton

1 Shape the dough into a ball (see above), then leave to rest, covered, for 10 minutes. Turn it over, seam-side up, and pat out into a flat oval.

2 Pinch the sides of the oval farthest from you and fold them both in towards the centre, pressing them down to seal.

3 Fold the point you have made in towards the centre and press down to seal. Turn the dough around 180°, then repeat steps 2 and 3.

4 Turn the dough around 180° again and fold it lengthways in half, sealing down with the heel of your hand. Avoid trapping pockets of air.

5 Roll the dough with your hands to taper the ends, giving the loaf a baton shape.

 A PROFESSIONAL FINISH

To get an extra fine finish to their loaves, bakers prefer to shape the dough on an unvarnished wooden surface. A chopping board with a lip along one side, to rest over the edge of the worktop and prevent slipping, is ideal for this purpose.

Shaping small round dinner rolls

You can use simple white bread dough (p344) to make rolls. Put them on a baking tray to rise, covered, until doubled in height, then bake in a preheated 210°C (410°F, gas 6) oven for 20 minutes, or until golden brown.

1 Divide the dough into pieces weighing 50–75g (1¾–2½oz). Your flat hand holding the dough should be clean, and your cupped hand floured. Place one piece of dough on your clean palm, then cup your floured hand over it so your fingers claw around the dough.

2 Quickly rotate your floured hand anticlockwise, spinning the ball of dough around but letting it catch a little on the clean hand (see right). This will pull the outer skin of the dough ball taut as it turns in your palm.

Shaping breadsticks

Make breadsticks from simple white bread dough (p344) or an oil and cheese-enriched dough. Once shaped, put them on a baking tray sprinkled with semolina, cover with a cloth, and leave to rise until barely doubled in height. Bake in a preheated 180°C (350°F, gas 4) oven for 15–20 minutes, then leave in a warm place for a few hours to dry and crisp.

1 Roll out the dough on a lightly floured surface into a rectangle roughly 1cm (½in) thick. Cover and leave to rest for 5 minutes. Using a ruler or other straight edge as a guide, cut off thin, equal-sized strips with a pizza wheel or sharp knife.

2 Roll each strip back and forth on the lightly floured surface to make long, thin breadsticks.

THE FINAL RISE

Once the dough has been shaped, it is usually essential to protect its upper surface during the final rise by covering it with a cloth or plastic sheet. This helps to preserve moisture and elasticity in the "skin" of the dough so that it won't crack as the dough rises before baking. It is impossible to give exact timings for the final rise as so many variables in the dough can affect it – temperature, the amount of leavening, ingredients that can slow or hasten yeast fermentation, and the moisture content. The best guide is that the loaf should rise to at least one and a half times, but no more than double, its original volume before baking.

For a round loaf

1 Place the shaped dough, seam-side up, in a bowl lined with a floured cloth. Fold the corners of the cloth over to cover the dough.

2 Once risen, the ball of dough will be almost doubled in size.

For a baton

Set the shaped dough, seam-side up, on a floured cloth. Pull the cloth up in pleats along the sides of the dough, then twist the ends of the cloth to tighten it. Place the wrapped loaf on a tray to rise. The cloth will prevent the baton from spreading. For more than one baton, either wrap each one separately and set side by side on the tray, or use a larger piece of cloth with a fold sitting up between the two loaves and another cloth to cover the upper surface.

GETTING THE LOAF READY FOR BAKING

Once the dough has risen it needs to be baked without delay. With a naturally leavened loaf, the window in which the dough needs to be baked is quite large, perhaps an hour or more. But with many yeasted breads, the time window is perhaps 15 minutes – the rapid production of CO_2 by the yeast might cause the dough to collapse upon itself. It is better to put the loaf into the oven a little too early, rather than a little too late.

Slashing the dough

1 To prevent the dough from tearing through the crust in an unattractive way, popping out around the base rather than bursting through the top, slash it before you put it in the oven.

2 Very carefully tip the dough onto your outstretched hand, then slide it seam-side down onto a semolina-dusted baking tray. Take care not to deflate the dough. Using a sharp blade, slash the upper surface, cutting at an angle and making the slashes about 5mm (¼in) deep.

Creating a humid environment

1 Creating a perfect crust is a surprisingly tricky balance between having the skin of the dough moist enough at the start of baking for the loaf to rise to its full expanse, yet dry within minutes so that it can then harden and crisp.

2 Spray the loaf with a fine mist of water just before putting it into the oven. Alternatively – as long as your oven is not fan-assisted – spray water on the oven walls (avoiding internal lights), or throw a few ice cubes into a hot metal tray in the bottom of the oven.

CONTAINED RISE

If a shaped dough is set in a tin or in a basket or bowl lined with a floured cloth, the loaf will be forced to rise upward. This is important for naturally leavened doughs that need a long final rise, and for doughs with a high moisture content that would have a tendency to spread if risen on a tray. If rising a round loaf in a bowl, choose one that is twice the size of the unrisen dough. The diameter of the bowl will affect the final shape – the wider the bowl, the flatter the final loaf will be. Containment will result in a loaf that is high and proud, with a light aerated crumb.

CHECKING IF BREAD IS DONE

When perfectly baked, most loaves will be a good brown colour. If baked in a tin, the sides of the loaf will have pulled in slightly, away from the tin.

To check if a loaf is cooked through, tip it out of the tin or off the baking tray and into a cloth held in your other hand. The loaf should feel light and, when you rap the base with your knuckles, should sound hollow.

BAKING WITH A NATURAL LEAVEN

All artisan bakers nurture and use a natural leaven in their bakery. Kept chilled in the refrigerator, cool in a basement, or simply at the bakery temperature, this living mixture of flour and water is used to create richly flavoured breads. Making a leaven is easy and doesn't require any special ingredients or equipment. The secret – if there is one – is to refresh the mixture with flour and water every day.

Adding 1tbsp organic raisins to the initial mixture – and then straining them out after day four – appears to create a more vigorous fermentation, but is optional. After five days, visible fermentation will have begun, but the development of a complex, healthy leaven takes time. I suggest you try this as a two-week project, baking bread daily for the last five or six days.

A NATURAL LEAVEN

For the initial mixture

4tsp strong wholemeal, strong white, or rye flour

2tsp live plain yogurt

3½tbsp water at 18–20°C (65–68°F)

1tbsp organic raisins (optional, see above)

For the daily refreshment

strong wholemeal, strong white, or rye flour, depending on the bread you will make

STORING LEAVEN

You can keep the leaven between refreshments at cool room (kitchen) temperature, although that may fluctuate a little, or it can be kept in the refrigerator or a cellar. Wherever you keep it, just be sure to refresh it daily while you continue to use it. For long-term storage, place it in a sealed container and leave it undisturbed at the back of the refrigerator. After a week it may not look too pretty, as the paste sinks to the bottom and the liquid turns a grey-brown colour. But it will be fine, just dormant.

To revive it, take 2 heaped tsp of the paste and stir it in a clean lidded jar with 50g (1¾oz) water and 60g (2¼oz) flour. The following day, remove three-quarters to four-fifths of the mixture and replace it with another 50g (1¾oz) water and 60g (2¼oz) flour. Leave for a further day, then refresh once more. The leaven should now be active. If not, refresh again and check the following day. Nature will eventually allow fermentation to restart.

1 Measure the ingredients for the initial mixture into a 500ml (17fl oz) jar with a lid and stir together vigorously with a fork. Cover the jar with its lid, then leave for a day at room temperature.

2 The next day, both bacteria and yeasts will have begun to multiply, yet all you will see is a glassy layer of liquid over the solid matter. Measure 4tsp of your chosen flour and 3½tbsp water into the jar, stir vigorously, and replace the lid. Leave again until the following day.

3 On day 3, look for the odd tiny bubble on the surface of the mixture. This is the beginning of fermentation. Again, add 4tsp flour and 3½tbsp water to the jar, stir vigorously, and replace the lid. Leave until the following day.

4 By day 4, the mixture will be getting energetic and will benefit from a higher ratio of new ingredients to old leaven. Stir the mixture, then tip three-quarters to four-fifths out (throw this away). Add 100g (3½oz) water to the jar. Stir vigorously, then add 100g (3½oz) flour and stir vigorously again. The mixture will look like a thick batter. Replace the lid and leave until the following day.

5 On day 5, bubbles of fermentation will appear on the surface. Repeat the procedure followed on day 4, then put the lid back on and leave until the following day.

6 From day 6 on, the mixture will be able to raise a dough, but it will take more time for complex flavours to emerge. Repeat the day 4 procedure each day for the following 2–4 days. You will notice the aroma becoming sharper every day. After 8–10 days, you will have a healthy leaven that you can use in the recipe opposite and in the English leaven bread with potatoes and ale on p353.

SIMPLE LEAVEN BREAD

The secret to producing a good naturally leavened loaf is in the initial rise. With a commercially yeasted loaf, recipes can be precise, but for a bread raised with a natural leaven a baker must adapt the times and temperatures to suit the responsiveness of their dough.

Makes 1 loaf

120g (4¼oz) natural leaven (see opposite)
200g (7oz) water at 22°C (72°F)
7g (1tsp) fine sea salt
300g (10½oz) strong white flour
olive or corn oil for kneading

1 Early in the morning, at around 8am, combine the leaven and water, mixing with your fingers. In a large bowl, mix the salt with the flour, stirring well with a spoon.

2 Tip the leaven mixture into the flour and, using your hands, mix quickly and evenly to make a soft, sticky dough. Cover the bowl with a cloth and leave for 10 minutes. The dough temperature should be about 20°C (68°F).

3 Spoon 1–2tsp oil onto the top of the dough and rub it all over the surface. Upturn the bowl and scrape the dough out onto an oiled surface. Knead the dough (p346), repeating after 10 and 20 minutes, then cover and leave it for 30 minutes at room temperature (20°C/68°F).

4 Fold the dough by thirds (p352), and repeat this every hour for 3–4 hours. Each time, return it either to a bowl or tray, seam-side down, and cover with a cloth. At the 3-hour mark, cut a deep slash into the surface of the dough to check the aeration. If you can see a good network of air bubbles, it can be shaped.

5 Line a basket or bowl with a cloth rubbed thickly with rye flour. Shape the dough into a round loaf or a baton (p347). Place it seam-side up in the cloth, cover, and leave to rise until almost doubled in height. At 20°C (68°F), this will take 2–3 hours; rising time will be longer if the dough is cooler.

6 Preheat the oven to 220°C (425°F, gas 7). Sprinkle a little semolina or flour on a baking tray, then upturn the dough onto it. Slash the surface, then lightly spray the loaf with water. Bake for 20 minutes. Reduce the heat to 190°C (375°F, gas 5) and bake for a further 15–20 minutes, or until the loaf is a good brown colour and feels light in weight.

7 Leave the bread to cool on a wire rack. When cool, wrap in greaseproof paper and store in the bread bin.

FOLDING DURING THE INITIAL RISE

Though the procedure described here is particularly relevant to bread that relies on a natural leaven, it can successfully be applied to any dough that appears sluggish. By stretching and folding the dough during the initial rise, you can speed the fermentation and open the texture by elongating each pocket of gas produced by the yeast. Keep the dough cool, at 20–25°C (68–77°F), and try not to knock out the air. If a bread recipe contains a high proportion of water (more than 70 per cent of the flour weight), this technique will make the dough more resilient and much easier to shape.

1 Put the dough on a lightly floured surface. (For some breads, like a focaccia, an oiled surface is used.) Pat out to a rectangle about 20x30cm (8x12in). Fold a short side in by one-third, then fold the other short side over that.

2 Fold the long sides in by a third in the same way. Flip the dough over, cover with a cloth, and leave to rest. Then repeat the patting out and folding into thirds at intervals, according to the particular recipe.

3 At the end of the rising period, cut through the surface of the dough to check the aeration that has formed. What you want to see is a lot of small bubbles, caused by the yeast as it ferments the natural sugars in the dough.

4 If bubbles have formed, you can proceed to shape the loaf and then give it its final rise prior to baking. If not, press the seam back together and leave the dough for a further 30–60 minutes, then check again. If the dough is very firm, just perform step 1 at each interval.

HELPING DOUGH TO RISE

Breads that rely on natural leavens – populated by a host of bacteria, enzymes, and yeasts that ferment the natural sugars slowly in a cool place – need to be nurtured until the point where they can be baked. The yeasts in a natural leaven produce carbon dioxide in much smaller quantities than commercial cultured yeasts, which is why rising times of 8 hours or more are not uncommon with naturally leavened loaves. Attempts to speed up the rising by putting the dough in a very warm place will fail to produce the flavour and crumb texture you want, and instead will make a heavy, leaden loaf. By manipulating the dough during the first long rise, and extending the period of that rise, you will achieve a light-textured loaf with a good rounded appearance.

English leaven bread with potatoes & ale

The ale contributes both a hint of bitterness from the hops and a flavour of malt, to capture the best from England's bread-making past. Traditionally, bakers steeped hops and mashed malt before adding flour to gelatinize the mixture (called a "barm"). Today's easier way uses bottle-conditioned ale.

Makes 2 loaves

For the barm

125g (4½oz) English bottle-conditioned ale or dark beer

25g (scant 1oz) strong white flour

50g (1¾oz) natural leaven (p350)

For the dough

150g (5½oz) firm, part-boiled waxy potato, roughly diced

225g (8oz) unsalted potato cooking water, cooled to 18–20°C (65–68°F)

10g (1½tsp) fine sea salt

500g (1lb 2oz) strong white flour

olive or corn oil for kneading

The morning before baking the bread, prepare the barm. Whisk the beer with the flour in a saucepan. Heat, stirring often, until the mixture reaches 75°C (167°F) and thickens to a creamy paste. Transfer to a bowl and cool to about 20°C (68°F), then stir in the leaven. Cover and leave at room temperture until the following day, by which time the barm should be lively with fermentation.

Early on the day of baking, add the barm to the potato and its cooking water and mix well. In a large bowl, stir the salt with the flour. Tip the barm mixture into the flour and, using your hands, mix to a soft, sticky dough. Cover the bowl with a cloth and leave for 10 minutes.

Spoon 2tsp of oil onto the top of the dough and rub it all over the surface. Scrape the dough out onto an oiled surface and knead it (p346). Return to the bowl, cover, and leave for a further 30 minutes.

Remove the dough from the bowl and fold it into thirds (see opposite). Repeat every hour for 4 hours. Each time, return it either to a bowl or tray, seam-side down, and cover with a cloth. At the 4-hour mark, check the aeration. If the dough has risen enough you can shape it.

Divide the dough into 2 equal pieces and shape each into a baton (p347). Put each baton on a separate floured cloth and place on baking trays. Cover and leave to rise for 2–3 hours, or until the loaves have doubled in height.

Preheat the oven to 220°C (425°F, gas 7). Sprinkle a baking tray with semolina or flour. Tip each baton onto your outstretched hand, then transfer, seam-side down, to the tray, leaving 10cm (4in) space between the loaves. Slash them, then lightly spray them with water. Bake for 20 minutes. Reduce the heat to 190°C (375°F, gas 5) and bake for a further 15–20 minutes, or until done.

Cool on a wire rack, then wrap in greaseproof paper and store in the bread bin.

MAKING RYE BREAD

When attempting to bake a good 100-per cent rye loaf, you must first avoid any comparison with a wheaten loaf. Although rye flour contains gluten, a rye dough handles as if the flour has been mixed with glue, and it lacks the stretchy, gas-holding properties that a wheat dough has. So there is no reason to give a rye loaf an extended first rise. And thus it is impossible for rye bread to have the crumb of a wheaten bread. In countries where rye flour is the dominant milled grain, bakers have used various methods to work around these problems, like the two breads shown here and the crisp rye bread on p363.

SIMPLE RYE LOAF

Jan Hedh, Sweden's bread-maestro, gave me his method for making rye flour behave a little more like wheat flour. The flour is whisked into boiling water, then left overnight to cool. This batter becomes sweeter and almost elastic, which in turn makes the dough easier to shape. Note that the rye flour is sifted before weighing to remove the bran – if the bran is left in, the gluten it contains can make the loaf too sticky and harder to slice. Keep the bran to sprinkle over the loaf before baking.

Makes 1 loaf
For the overnight batter
150g (5½oz) boiling water
25g (4tsp) sifted light rye flour
For the dough
5g (¾tsp) fresh yeast
20g (1tbsp) honey
80g (2¾oz) water at 20°C (68°F)
300g (10½oz) sifted light rye flour
7g (1tsp) fine sea salt

1 For the overnight batter, bring a kettle of water to the boil, then measure the required amount and pour it into a large bowl. Sift the flour into the water, whisking well as you do so. You should have a thickish grey liquid. Cover the bowl and leave at room temperature overnight.

2 Add the yeast, honey, and water to the batter and whisk together, then add the rye flour and salt. Squidge with your hands to make a soft, sticky dough. Cover and leave for 10 minutes.

3 Turn the dough onto an oiled surface and knead (p346). Cover the dough with a cloth and leave for 30 minutes, then shape it into a baton (p347). Place, seam-side up, in a cloth rubbed with rye flour for a contained rise. Leave to rise at 20°C (68°F) for 1½–2 hours, or until risen by half its height again.

4 Preheat the oven to 220°C (425°F, gas 7). Sprinkle a little semolina (or sifted-out rye bran) on a baking tray. Transfer the baton, seam-side down, to the tray. Gently brush off any excess flour, then spray the loaf with a fine mist of water and dust it lightly with rye bran. Bake for 20 minutes. Reduce the temperature to 190°C (375°F, gas 5) and bake for a further 30–35 minutes, or until the loaf is done. Leave to cool on a wire rack.

WHOLEGRAIN RYE BREAD

This is a heavy, dense loaf that needs to sit for a few days before it is sliced thinly. The secret for success is to get the rye or wheat grains plump and moist before they go into the dough. Finely milled and sifted rye flour is also essential – too much of the fibre and the result will be a bread that is too sticky to cut. To make the leaven, follow the instructions on p350, using equal quantities of water and fine sifted rye flour in the refreshments.

Makes 1 loaf

300g (10½oz) whole rye grains or wheat grains
300g (10½oz) white wine, beer, or cider
200g (7oz) natural leaven, made with rye flour (see above)
175g (6oz) water at 20°C (68°F)
300g (10½oz) sifted light rye flour
7g (1tsp) fine sea salt
40g (2tbsp) honey

1 The day before, simmer the grains in water to cover for 45 minutes. Drain and put in a large bowl. Cover with the white wine, beer, or cider and leave to soak overnight at room temperature.

2 Drain the grains. Weigh out 600–650g (about 1¼lb) and return these to the bowl (discard the rest). Whisk in the rye leaven and water. Add the remaining ingredients and stir together with a spoon. The dough will be more like a paste than a dough, so don't try to knead it. Cover with a cloth and leave for 10 minutes. Then stir the dough and set aside again, covered.

3 Line a 30x11x7.5cm (12x4½x3in) loaf tin with brown paper or baking parchment rubbed with oil, taking care to fold the paper neatly so that you retain the sharp edges of the corners of the baking tin.

4 Scrape the dough into the tin and smooth the surface. Cover the tin with a cloth and leave to rise in a warm place for 3–4 hours, or until the dough has risen by almost one-third.

5 Preheat the oven to 200°C (400°F, gas 6). Cover the tin with foil and bake on the centre shelf of the oven for 30 minutes. Reduce the heat to 180°C (350°F, gas 4) and bake for 30 minutes. Then lower the heat to 150°C (300°F, gas 2) and bake for a further 1½ hours, removing the foil for the last 30 minutes. The top of the bread should be a good dark brown.

6 Cool in the tin for a few minutes, then turn out the loaf, peel off the paper, and cool on a wire rack. Wrap in a fresh sheet of oiled brown paper and tie snugly with string. Leave the loaf for 2 days at room temperature before slicing.

MAKING PIZZA DOUGH

Pizza can be the simplest of flat breads, or a complicated cheese-filled pie. I have a place in my heart for both. The quantity of yeast you use depends on when you want to bake. This recipe works best if the dough is at least 2 hours old, and it can be kept in a cool place for up to 4 hours. Reduce the yeast to 1–2g (¼tsp) if you make the dough at midday but want to bake with it that evening, and increase the yeast to 7g (1tsp) if you are running late and want to use it almost immediately.

BASIC PIZZA DOUGH

Makes about 440g (14½oz)

3–4g (½tsp) fresh yeast
150g (5½oz) water at 22°C (72°F)
10g (2tsp) caster sugar
25g (1½tbsp) olive oil plus more for kneading
150g (5½oz) "00" flour
100g (3½oz) strong white flour
5g (¾tsp) fine sea salt

1 Whisk the yeast with the water, sugar, and oil. In another bowl, lightly toss the flours with the salt. Pour the liquid into the flour and stir together into a soft sticky mass. Scrape any remaining dough from your hands, cover the bowl, and leave for 10 minutes.

2 Lightly knead the dough (p346). The combined series of light kneads and rising will take 1½ hours. Then round the dough into a ball, place in a bowl, and keep in a cool place until required.

ROLLING THE DOUGH

Roll out the dough into a circle or oval, then cover and leave to rest for 10 minutes. Uncover and roll it even thinner, as thin as you can – ideally 3–4mm (about ⅛in) thick. Dust with flour so it doesn't stick.

PIZZA DI ACCIUGATA ALLA TORRESE

I adapted this from *Il Re Dei Cuochi*, edited by Giovanni Nelli, published 1925 (mine is the revised edition). Anchovies, garlic, and parsley top a sheet of dough, which is then sprinkled with breadcrumbs to give the surface a crunch.

Makes 2 pizzas, to serve 4–8

1 quantity of basic pizza dough (see left)
olive oil for brushing
50g (1¾oz) cornmeal or polenta
8–10 salted anchovies, soaked and drained
1 garlic clove, crushed and finely chopped
25g (2 good handfuls) chopped parsley
50g (1¾oz) dry white breadcrumbs, made from a good loaf

1 Divide the dough in half. Roll out each piece into a thin circle or oval (see left). Leave to rest for 10 minutes, covered with a cloth.

2 Preheat the oven to 220°C (425°F, gas 7) or as hot as it will go. Lightly brush 2 large baking trays with olive oil, then sprinkle the surface lightly with the cornmeal or polenta.

3 Roll one of the dough circles even thinner (see left), then roll it around the rolling pin and unroll onto a baking tray. Tuck back any edges of dough that hang over. Brush the dough with olive oil, then dust lightly with sea salt.

4 Tear half of the anchovies into strips and drop them randomly on top, together with dots of crushed garlic. Finally, sprinkle with half of the parsley and breadcrumbs.

5 Bake in the centre of the oven for 12–15 minutes, or until the top is lightly browned and the edges are crisp. Repeat with the other dough circle, rolling it out and topping it just before baking. Serve hot or warm.

HOT CHEESE & RADICCHIO PIZZA PIE

You will find that you have more pizza dough than this simple pie needs, but any attempt at being economical with the dough will make lining the tin difficult. Roll out any trimmed dough into a disc and freeze it unbaked to use as a pizza base another time.

Serves 6–8

1tbsp olive oil plus more for the tin and brushing the pie
1 onion, thinly sliced
½tsp crushed dried chilies
1 small head of radicchio, thinly sliced
1 garlic clove, crushed
1tsp red wine vinegar
1 quantity of basic pizza dough (see opposite)
10 thin slices of good ham
250g (8½oz) tomato sauce (p40)
150g (5½oz) Fontina cheese, sliced
50g (1¾oz) Parmesan, freshly grated

1 First prepare the filling. In a saucepan, heat the olive oil with the onion and crushed chilies until they begin to sizzle. Reduce the heat, cover, and cook for 4–5 minutes, or until the onion becomes somewhat translucent. Add the radicchio and toss to mix. Add the garlic. Cook for 3–4 minutes, or until the radicchio has wilted. Remove from the heat, stir in the vinegar, and season to taste with salt and pepper. Leave to cool.

2 Mark the dough into thirds, then cut a third off and place to one side, covered with a cloth. Roll out the larger piece on a floured surface to a circle about 20cm (8in) in diameter. Cover it with a cloth while you lightly grease a 20cm (8in) springform cake tin with olive oil.

3 Roll out the dough into an even larger, thinner circle, measuring 40cm (16in) in diameter. Cover again and leave it to rest for a few minutes, then lift it up and lay it over the tin so that the centre droops down to cover the bottom. Gently ease the dough into the corners and up the sides of the tin, leaving some hanging slightly over the rim.

4 Lay three-quarters of the ham evenly over the bottom. Cover with the drained radicchio, then with the tomato sauce. Finish with the Fontina layered with sprinkles of Parmesan and the remaining ham.

5 Roll out the smaller piece of dough to a circle 20cm (8in) in diameter. Place this lid on top of the tin. Use a knife or scissors to trim the edges of the dough lining the tin, so that they can be folded in over the lid and overlap by a few centimetres. Brush the lid with a little olive oil, then leave the pie to rest at room temperature for 30–45 minutes.

6 Preheat the oven to 200°C (400°F, gas 6). Place the pie in the centre of the oven and bake for 40 minutes, or until the top is golden brown. Carefully remove the side of the tin and, with a palette knife, ease the pie off the metal base onto a serving plate. Leave to cool for a moment, then serve hot or warm.

MAKING LOW-RISEN BREADS

For low-risen breads, a softer flour is good – the loss of height can mean a gain in taste as there is less flavourless gluten in the loaf. The same soft dough can be used to make three Mediterranean-style breads: focaccia, pide, and paper-thin crispbread.

For Italian focaccia a little olive oil and malt are added to the dough, plus – if you can obtain it or like it – optional "strutto" (pork lard). Pide is the flat bread of Turkey, while paper-thin crispbread is inspired by the carta di musica of Italy.

Pocket breads such as pitta and naan owe their appearance to the way heat is applied rather than just to the dough used. In a Lebanese clay oven, the stone sole sits above a layer of salt, which helps to insulate it and keep it relatively cool. So most of the heat comes from above, to pull a pitta dough upwards. In a traditional tandoor oven used to bake a naan, the breads surround the central heat source. This creates a dryer heat, which blisters the outside of the bread but leaves it moist inside.

SIMPLE WHITE SOFT DOUGH

Use this dough to make pide (see below), focaccia (see opposite), or paper-thin crispbread (p363). As the dough is very soft, I fold and stretch it on an oiled surface, rather than knead it.

For the ferment

200g (7oz) water at 20°C (68°F)
150g (5½oz) "00" flour
7g (1tsp) fresh yeast

For the dough

150g (5½oz) water at 20°C (68°F)
1tbsp olive oil plus extra for folding
10g (1½tsp) malt extract for focaccia
375g (13oz) "00" flour
10g (1½tsp) fine sea salt

1 In a medium bowl mix together the ingredients for the ferment. Cover the bowl with a cloth and leave at warm room temperature (22°C/72°F) for 2 hours, giving the mixture a stir after the first hour. At the end of this time it should be bubbling and have risen to double the original height.

2 To make the dough, whisk the water and 1tbsp oil into the ferment until combined. If you are going to use the dough to make focaccia, whisk in the malt extract.

3 Mix the flour and salt into the ferment, and squidge together to make a very soft, slightly lumpy, and very sticky dough. Scrape any remaining dough from your hands, then cover the bowl and leave for 10 minutes.

4 Rub 1tbsp of oil all over the surface of the dough, then scrape it out onto an oiled work surface. Work the dough (p346) by folding and prodding at 10-minute intervals for 30 minutes, then fold the dough every 40 minutes for the next 2 hours. The dough will then be ready to be shaped.

PIDE

These flat breads are often topped with sesame seeds, nigella seeds, or fennel seeds. This is an Australian-inspired version of the popular Turkish bread – only much puffier and softer than the original.

Makes 6 breads

1 quantity of simple white soft dough (see above)
sesame seeds for the topping

1 Divide the dough into 6 equal pieces (about 150g/5½oz each). Round on a floured surface into balls, then cover with a cloth and leave for 15 minutes.

2 Roll out each ball into an oval shape about 1cm (½in) thick. Place on a floured cloth and cover with another cloth. Leave to rise for 30 minutes.

3 Preheat the oven to 220°C (425°F, gas 7). Transfer the pides to a floured baking tray. Brush lightly with water, then sprinkle with sesame seeds. Bake in the centre of the oven for 20 minutes, or until golden on the outside. Serve warm.

FOCACCIA

Rubbing a mixture of water, oil, and salt over the dough before baking is the traditional method bakers in Italy use to create a golden surface.

Makes 1 bread

good olive oil

1 quantity of simple white soft dough (see opposite)

fine sea salt

rosemary leaves (optional)

1 Rub a 30x40cm (12x16in) baking tray liberally with olive oil. Round the dough into a ball, then place it on the tray.

2 Using a rolling pin and then prodding with your fingers, lightly flatten out the dough. Don't worry at this point if it springs back. Then cover with a cloth and leave in a warm place for 20–30 minutes.

3 Preheat the oven to 220°C (425°F, gas 7). Pick up the corners of the dough and stretch them out until they reach the corners of the tray. Sprinkle a little water, olive oil, and salt on the dough, and rub these ingredients together all over the surface.

4 Lightly dimple the surface with your fingertips, pressing down without pushing too much gas from the dough. Sprinkle with rosemary, if using. Bake in the centre of the oven for 15 minutes, then reduce the heat to 200°C (400°F, gas 6) and bake for a further 15 minutes. Cool on a wire rack.

 WORKING SOFT DOUGH

When working with this sort of soft dough, it is very important to keep the work surface and your hands well oiled. The dough will gradually absorb some of the oil, but when you are folding it, as soon as the dough starts to stick, put it back in the bowl, cover it, and leave it to rest.

Flat bread with pumpkin, green olives & shallots

The combination of two starches has always been a favourite of mine, from a simple chip butty to a focaccia topped with sliced potatoes and truffle oil. For this bread, pumpkin is baked, then sliced and tossed with shallots, garlic, green olives, and olive oil before being baked again on a sheet of white dough.

Scatter the pumpkin mixture over the dough

Makes 1 bread

250g (8½oz) piece of pumpkin, seeds and fibres removed

1 large banana shallot, finely sliced

80g (2¾oz) pitted green olives, sliced

1 garlic clove, finely sliced

50g (2tbsp) olive oil

250g (8½oz) simple white soft dough, made with malt extract (p358)

Preheat the oven to 200°C (400°F, gas 6). Wrap the pumpkin in greased foil or baking parchment, place on a baking tray, and bake for 50–60 minutes, or until tender. Leave to cool, then peel the pumpkin and cut the flesh into thin slices.

Mix the pumpkin with the shallot, olives, garlic, and olive oil. Set aside.

Roll out the dough on a lightly floured surface into a large oval about 30cm (12in) long and 15cm (6in) wide. Transfer to a lightly greased baking tray.

Spread the pumpkin mixture over the top of the dough, then season with salt and black pepper. Bake for 25–30 minutes in a hot oven, or until the top is golden and the edges are crisp. Serve hot or warm.

PAPER-THIN CRISPBREAD

This thin, crisp bread can also be baked, covered, in an ungreased wok set over a heat-diffusing plate. Check after a few minutes to see that the bread is a good colour on the underside (lift it carefully with a spatula), then flip over and bake for a few minutes on the other side. Like cooking pancakes, this method requires some attention at the beginning to get the heat right.

Serves 6

1 quantity of simple white soft dough (p358)

olive oil for brushing

1 Divide the dough into 6 equal pieces (about 150g/5½oz each) and roll out into ovals as for pides (p358). Cover and leave to rise for about 30 minutes.

2 Preheat the oven to 220°C (425°F, gas 7) or as hot as it will go. Just before baking, one at a time roll and stretch each oval once more, until it is thin and the length of your baking tray.

3 Transfer to the oiled tray and brush the dough with olive oil. Bake for 12–15 minutes, or until lightly browned. Cool on a wire rack, then wrap or freeze immediately. Break into pieces for serving.

PITTA BREAD

Don't attempt to make these unless your oven can reach the required temperature. Bake another bread instead. The reason is that the dough needs to explode in the heat, causing the bread to puff like a balloon. Without a great heat, this just won't happen.

Makes 8 breads

For the ferment

3–4g (½tsp) fresh yeast

125g (4½oz) warm water at 30°C (86°F)

100g (3½oz) strong white flour

For the dough

195g (scant 7oz) water at 22°C (72°F)

200g (7oz) plain white flour

250g (8½oz) strong white flour

40g (1½oz) caster sugar

7g (1tsp) fine sea salt

1 To make the ferment, whisk together the yeast and water in a small bowl. Add the flour and stir to a smooth batter. Cover and leave in a warm place (25°C/77°F) for about 1½ hours.

2 For the dough, mix the water with the ferment. Put all the remaining ingredients in a large bowl and add the ferment mixture. Mix to a soft, sticky dough. Cover and leave for 10 minutes.

3 Knead the dough (p346), then leave it for 1 hour, giving it one more knead during that time.

4 Preheat the oven to at least 220°C (425°F, gas 7). Place a clean baking tray (or a baking stone) in the oven to heat. On a lightly floured surface, divide the dough into 8 equal pieces (about 100g/3½oz each). Round each piece into a ball and leave, covered, for 15 minutes.

5 Roll out each ball into a round roughly 5mm (¼in) thick. Leave to rest for 2 minutes.

6 Using a sturdy sheet of card as a makeshift shovel, scoop up each pitta and drop onto the hot tray (or stone). Bake, 1 or 2 at a time, for 5 minutes or until risen and barely coloured. Remove with tongs and cool under a cloth.

NAAN BREAD

This is the quickest yeast-raised bread I make at home. The recipe uses soft flour, giving a very tender crust with almost no kneading, together with both fresh yeast and baking powder. I improvise on the traditional tandoor oven by using a wok with a lid (a rather nifty and easy solution). Failing that, use a non-stick frying pan with a lid. The baked naan freeze very well. Reheat, wrapped in foil, in the oven.

Once it is made the dough must be used promptly. If you want to make the dough in the morning for use in the evening, reduce the amount of yeast to ¼tsp, and keep the dough covered and chilled until required.

Makes 4 breads

150g (5½oz) water at 22°C (72°F)
5g (¾tsp) fresh yeast
250g (8½oz) plain white flour
50g (2½tbsp) plain low-fat yogurt
4g (½tsp) fine sea salt
¾tsp baking powder
sunflower oil, ghee, or melted butter for kneading
2tbsp finely chopped coriander or parsley (optional)

1 Pour the water into a bowl. Whisk in the yeast, then add half the flour. Mix together with a fork, then cover the bowl and leave in a warm place for 30 minutes.

2 Stir in the yogurt, then add the rest of the flour, the salt, and baking powder. Mix together with your hands (or a spoon if you find it easier) into a soft, sticky ball. Spoon 2tsp oil, ghee, or melted butter into the bowl and rub it over the top of the dough, then pick the dough up out of the bowl and roughly squeeze it once or twice. Place the dough back in the bowl, cover, and leave for 15 minutes.

3 Pour another 1tsp oil, ghee, or butter onto the dough and rub lightly all over, then turn the dough out onto a lightly oiled work surface. Knead the dough lightly for 30 seconds, then return it to the bowl. Cover and leave for another 15 minutes.

4 By this time the dough should be much smoother. Knead lightly on the oiled surface for a minute, then divide into quarters. Dust with flour and leave for 5 minutes. Meanwhile, heat a wok over a moderate heat.

5 Take one piece of dough and roll it out into a teardrop shape, dusting well with flour as you go. It is important to get the dough quite thin, about 3mm (⅛in).

6 When the wok is very hot, gently lift the dough and lay it in the wok. Brush the surface of the dough with a little sunflower oil, ghee, or butter, mixed with the herbs if using. Place the lid on the wok and leave for 1 minute while you roll out another piece of dough.

7 Check the naan. It should have risen slightly and blisters of air should be forming on the top surface. With tongs, lift the bread carefully at one end and look to see whether it has browned lightly underneath. If so, flip the naan over and cook for a further 1 minute.

8 When the naan is cooked on both sides, remove from the wok. Keep wrapped in a clean cloth or tea towel while you roll out and cook the remaining naan.

MAKING CRISP, FLAT, WHEAT-FREE BREADS

Though we now think of bread as soft and leavened, the earliest breads made by man were much simpler, and were made using the grain found through foraging. For example, some Australian Aboriginals use a type of wild millet, ground into flour and mixed with water, to make a basic flat bread. The recipe below is inspired by one of the great crispbreads of Scandinavia.

CRISP RYE BREAD

Makes 2

200g (7oz) dark wholemeal rye flour plus extra for dredging

5g (¾tsp) fine sea salt

5g (¾tsp) fresh yeast

175g (6oz) water at 20°C (68°F)

1 Combine the flour and salt in a large bowl. Whisk the yeast with the water, then add to the dry ingredients. Stir together until you have a smooth, sticky paste. Cover the bowl and leave for 3 hours, or until the paste is slightly puffy.

5 Using a round-bladed knife, cut out discs the size of an LP record (see left). In the centre score a smaller circle 3–4cm (about 1½in) in diameter. Remove the paste from around the discs (the trimmings can be re-rolled to make another disc or other shapes). Alternatively, score the sheets of paste into squares or rectangles.

6 Bake in the centre of the oven for about 40 minutes, or until the crispbreads are dry and slightly crisp at the edges. Remove from the oven and, when cool enough to handle, break the breads into large pieces.

2 You need 2 baking trays, each measuring 20x30cm (8x12in). If they aren't non-stick, line them with baking parchment. Scrape half the paste onto each tray and spread out to about 1cm (½in) thickness. If the paste starts to dry out as you are scraping, sprinkle it with water.

3 Dredge the surface liberally with additional rye flour, then with a rolling pin and your fingers, roll and press out the paste to roughly 5–7mm (about ¼in) thick and smooth on the top. Cover with cloths and leave in a warm place (25–28°C/77–83°F) for 1 hour, or until the sheets of paste are doubled in height.

4 Preheat the oven to 200°C (400°F, gas 6). Uncover the sheets. With the rounded end of a chopstick, make dimples all over the surface.

OATCAKES

Makes 12–15

200g (7oz) fine oatmeal plus extra for rolling and sprinkling
4g (½tsp) bicarbonate of soda
4g (½tsp) fine sea salt
30g (2tbsp) double cream
50g (3¼tbsp) milk
50g (3¼tbsp) water

1 Mix together the oatmeal, soda, and salt in a large bowl. In a jug, stir the cream, milk, and water together, then add to the dry ingredients. Stir to form a very thick paste that will stiffen as it rests. Cover and leave for 15 minutes to firm. (If it hardens too much, work in a little water.)

2 Preheat the oven to 180°C (350°F, gas 4). Lightly dust the work surface with more oatmeal. Roll out the dough carefully until it is 3–5mm (⅛–¼in) thick. To prevent the dough from sticking to the surface as you roll, keep sliding a palette knife underneath.

3 Using an 8cm (3in) diameter cutter, cut discs from the dough. Use the palette knife to transfer the discs to a clean, dry baking tray. Re-roll the scraps and cut out more discs until you have finished the dough.

4 Sprinkle with extra oatmeal, then bake for 15–20 minutes, or until the oatcakes are dry and lightly tinged with brown around the edges. Remove the oatcakes to a wire rack. When cool, store in an airtight container.

MAKING QUICK BREADS

In countries where the summertime temperatures often made it difficult to store yeast or dough before the advent of refrigeration, bicarbonate of soda and baking powder were used as instant leavening agents for "quick" breads. These were a familiar part of home baking, from America to Australia, and are now much-loved everywhere.

CORN BREAD

I like corn bread made with a little sugar, and butter to add a creamy taste. You can vary the proportions to suit your own preferences.

Serves 6

200g (7oz) cornmeal or polenta
100g (3½oz) plain flour
100g (3½oz) caster sugar
15g (2tsp) bicarbonate of soda
300g (10½oz) semi-skimmed milk
60g (2¼oz) unsalted butter, cut into small dice
2 large eggs
275g (10oz) plain yogurt
4 long, red chilies, seeded and finely sliced lengthways (optional)

1 Preheat the oven to 190°C (375°F, gas 5). Line a deep 20–25cm (8–10in) round baking tin with baking parchment.

2 Sift the cornmeal, flour, sugar, and bicarbonate of soda into a bowl. In a saucepan heat the milk until it simmers, then remove from the heat and add the butter. Let the butter melt and the mixture cool to lukewarm, then beat in the eggs and yogurt.

3 Pour the milk mixture into the dry ingredients and whisk very lightly together. As soon as combined, pour the mixture into the tin. Arrange the chilies on top (they will sink in during baking), if using. Bake in the centre of the oven for 30–40 minutes, or until a skewer inserted into the centre comes out clean. Serve warm.

CINNAMON & DATE SCONE BREAD

Shaped into a big twist and curled in a ring mould, this scone bread is very quick to make and is served torn up in a basket. It's perfect as part of a summer brunch, or when the weather is a bit chilly as part of an autumn afternoon feast, with mugs of hot chocolate.

Makes 1 bread

40g (2tbsp) softened unsalted butter plus extra for the tin
250g (8½oz) plain flour
25g (scant 2tbsp) caster sugar
14g (2tsp) baking powder
1 large egg
75g (2½oz) milk

For layering the dough

75g (2½oz) soft brown sugar
100g (3½oz) dates, pitted and roughly chopped
50g (2½tbsp) softened unsalted butter
7g (1tsp) ground cinnamon
25g (1½tbsp) dark rum

1 Preheat the oven to 200°C (400°F, gas 6). Thickly butter a 21cm (8½in) ring mould that is 5cm (2in) deep, or a sponge tin of the same diameter. Line the bottom of the mould or tin with baking parchment.

2 Sift the flour, sugar, and baking powder into a bowl. Rub in the butter using your fingertips. In a jug whisk the egg with the milk until well combined, then stir this into the dry ingredients in the bowl. Work the mixture well together with your hands until you have an evenly mixed soft dough. Scrape the dough out onto a floured work surface and lightly knead for 10–15 seconds.

3 Mix together the brown sugar, dates, butter, cinnamon, and rum in a small bowl; keep to one side. Roll out the dough to a rectangle that is roughly 5mm (¼in) thick, 35cm (14in) long, and 20cm (8in) wide.

4 Spread the date mixture evenly over the surface of the dough, then roll it up tightly like a swiss roll. With a sharp knife cut the rolled dough in half lengthways.

5 Twist the 2 pieces together, keeping the cut surfaces facing upwards, then curl into the mould. Bake in the centre of the oven for about 30 minutes. Leave the bread to cool in the mould for 5 minutes, then turn out onto a wire rack. This is best served still warm.

MAKING BATTERS

A batter may be silky smooth, with the consistency of thick cream, or slightly puffy, due to the action of yeast or the inclusion of an aerated mixture like whisked egg whites or whipped cream. Either way, a batter is perfect for cooking simply, in a heavy-based pan or on a griddle – one of the oldest ways of baking bread – as well as in a waffle iron or in the oven.

If the heavy-based frying pan or griddle you are going to use isn't non-stick, temper it by doing the following: rub with vegetable oil, then heat until smoking hot. Remove from the heat and cool, then rub off any excess oil with kitchen paper. Before cooking, lightly grease the pan with butter or oil. For all griddle-cooked cakes, cold batter onto a hot surface produces the best results.

THIN PANCAKES

Before ovens were common, a griddle or pan placed over a fire would cook a mixture of grains and water into a flat bread – a "pan" cake. Today, pancakes may be thin and delicate, when they are often called crêpes, or fluffy and thick.

When making thin pancakes, the first few can be tricky to get right, as the heat needs to be adjusted so that the upper surface sets before the base of the pancake gets too brown.

Makes 12

125g (4½oz) plain flour
2 large eggs
20g (1tbsp) vanilla sugar (optional)
pinch of fine sea salt
250g (8½oz) cold milk
40g (2tbsp) melted butter

1 Combine all the ingredients in a bowl and whisk to make a smooth batter. Cover and leave to rest in the refrigerator for 2 hours. The batter should be the consistency of single cream. Add a little more milk to thin it, if necessary.

Serve freshly made, simply sprinkled with sugar and lemon juice, or wrapped around a lavish sweet or savoury filling

2 Heat a heavy-based non-stick pancake or crêpe pan (my pan is 25cm/10in diameter, but a pan smaller than this will be fine too). Remove from the heat and ladle a small amount of batter into the pan.

THICK PANCAKES

These can be made any diameter, although I like them king-size. Serve in a stack, with melted butter and maple syrup or preserved ginger in syrup, and some good yogurt or fresh cream.

Makes 12 big pancakes

| 150g (5½oz) milk |
| 2 large eggs plus 1 egg white |
| 40g (2tbsp) melted butter |
| 20g (1tbsp) golden syrup |
| 20g (1tbsp) caster sugar |
| 200g (7oz) plain flour, sifted |
| 14g (2tsp) baking powder |

1 Combine the milk, whole eggs, melted butter, golden syrup, sugar, flour, and baking powder in a bowl and whisk until smooth. The batter should pour from a ladle in a thick, soft ribbon. Cover the bowl and leave the batter to rest for 2 hours (or you can leave it overnight in the refrigerator if you are going to make pancakes for breakfast or brunch).

2 Just before cooking, whisk the egg white to soft peaks, then fold into the batter.

3 Heat a heavy-based non-stick frying pan or griddle until hot. To test the heat of the pan, pour 1tsp of the batter into the centre. After a minute, the upper surface of the batter should be pitted with small holes.

4 With a palette knife, flip the test pancake over. It should be an appetizing light brown on the cooked side. If it's too dark or burnt, lower the heat and test again.

5 When you've got the temperature right, make the pancakes. Ladle about 60g (4tbsp) batter into the pan and tilt it gently so the batter spreads evenly to a 15–20cm (6–8in) disc. After a minute the upper surface should be pitted with small holes and have begun to set. Carefully lift up the pancake with a spatula and flip it over to cook the other side for a minute or so.

6 Remove from the pan and keep warm while you cook the remaining pancakes. Serve the pancakes freshly made.

3 Swirl the batter around so that the bottom of the pan is evenly and lightly coated. Replace the pan on a moderate heat. Cook for 45–60 seconds, or until the edges of the pancake start to come away from the pan and are brown.

4 Peel the pancake loose and flip it over to cook the other side for 30–60 seconds. Then turn it out onto a plate. As the pancakes are made, pile them up and keep covered with a cloth while you cook the remainder.

BLINIS

These little yeasted pancakes are perfect served freshly made with a little smoked fish, soured cream or melted butter, and a mixture of grated raw beetroot and horseradish.

Makes 20

75g (2½oz) light rye flour
25g (scant 1oz) strong white flour
4g (½tsp) fine sea salt
50g (1¾oz) warm mashed potato, sieved
3g (½tsp) fresh yeast
75g (2½oz) ale or dark beer
100g (3½oz) water
40g (2 tbsp) melted butter plus extra for greasing the pan
1 large egg, separated

1 Sift the flours and salt into a bowl. In another bowl whisk the sieved potato with the yeast, ale, and water until smooth and combined. Stir in the flours, then cover and leave for 2 hours at room temperature, stirring once during this time.

2 Beat the melted butter and egg yolk into the yeasted mixture. In a separate bowl, whisk the egg white until it forms soft peaks. Fold the white gently through the batter.

3 Heat a large, heavy-based non-stick frying pan or griddle. Using a large spoon or small ladle, pour 2 or 3 discs of batter into the pan. Leave to cook undisturbed over a low heat until the edges of the discs start to matt and small bubbles open up on the surface.

4 With a fish slice, lift up the blinis and flip over. Cook for a few more minutes, then remove. Keep covered while you cook the rest.

YORKSHIRE PUDDING

This recipe varies a little from traditional versions: the addition of a small amount of melted butter and a little baking powder produces a pudding that is less likely to fall after baking. Also, I prefer it made in individual dariole moulds. A dozen small Yorkshires are produced, which may be too many but it is always a shame to have too few.

Makes 12

125g (4½oz) plain flour
2g (¼tsp) fine sea salt
¼tsp baking powder
2 large eggs
275g (10oz) milk
10g (1tbsp) melted butter
lard or olive oil for the moulds

CLAFOUTIS

Here, a batter enriched with eggs and cream is poured over ripe fruit and baked. You can also use drained, preserved fruit or soft dried fruit such as plump prunes or apricots.

Serves 3–4

125g (4½oz) caster sugar
60g (2oz) plain flour
200g (7oz) whole milk
100g (3½oz) double cream
3 large eggs, separated
½ vanilla pod, split open
butter, flour, and caster sugar for the dish
250g (8½oz) ripe black cherries, pitted (or drained canned cherries)
sifted icing sugar to dust (optional)

1 Put the sugar and flour in a bowl and slowly whisk in the milk, cream, and egg yolks to make a smooth batter. Scrape in the seeds from the vanilla pod and whisk to mix. Leave to one side for 2 hours.

2 Preheat the oven to 200°C (400°F, gas 6). Rub a 20cm (8in) round ovenproof dish liberally with butter and dust with a mixture of flour and sugar. Spread the cherries in the dish.

3 In a clean bowl, whisk the egg whites to soft peaks. Pour the batter through a sieve onto the egg whites and fold through evenly until just combined. Pour this mixture over the cherries.

4 Bake for 25 minutes, then reduce the heat to 180°C (350°F, gas 4) and bake until the edges are puffed up and the centre is set. Serve warm.

1 Combine all the ingredients in a bowl and beat together to make a smooth batter. Transfer to a jug and leave to rest in the refrigerator for 2 hours.

2 Preheat the oven to 200°C (400°F, gas 6). Place about 2tsp of lard or oil in each of 12 dariole moulds. Set the moulds on a baking tray and put into the oven to heat.

3 Remove the tray from the oven. Pour the batter evenly into the moulds, half-filling them. Return to the oven and bake for 25–30 minutes, or until well puffed and golden brown. Turn out of the moulds and serve immediately.

APPLE FRITTERS

Either as a teatime treat or as a dessert at the end of a family meal, fritters are an old favourite that deserve to see a revival in their popularity.

175g (6oz) water at 20°C (68°F)
3–4g (½tsp) fresh yeast
5g (1tsp) honey
50g (1¾oz) strong white flour
50g (1¾oz) sifted rye flour
3g (½tsp) fine sea salt
15g (1tbsp) good olive oil
light vegetable oil for deep-frying
4 dessert apples
1 large egg white
caster sugar mixed with ground cinnamon to finish

1 Pour the water into a bowl, then whisk in the yeast followed by the honey. Mix in both types of flour and the salt, then stir in the olive oil. Cover with a cloth and leave the batter to rise for 2 hours at room temperature.

2 Check the consistency of the batter. It should be like thick pouring cream. Add more water, little by little, if necessary.

3 Heat the vegetable oil in a heavy pan. For safety's sake the oil should come no more than one-third the way up the side of the pan – say 5cm (2in) depth. When a cube of stale bread dropped into the hot oil turns golden in about 60 seconds, then it is at the right temperature for cooking the fritters.

4 Peel the apples, halve them lengthways, then cut each half apple into 4 pieces, lengthways. Remove the cores from the apple pieces.

5 Whisk the egg white to soft peaks and fold through the batter. One at a time, dip the apple pieces into the batter, using a fork, then lower them into the hot oil. Fry, a few at a time, for 2–3 minutes, or until the batter is golden brown. Remove with a slotted spoon and drain on kitchen paper. Serve freshly made, tossed in a little cinnamon sugar.

WAFFLES

The most delicious waffles are made with rich ingredients. These are best eaten immediately after baking, while they are still crisp and feather-light, topped with fruit, honey, and cream. For best results use an electric waffle iron. Thicker waffles are easier to cook than thinner ones, but both will need to be watched during cooking.

Makes 5–6 large, thick waffles

125g (4½oz) plain flour
50g (1¾oz) caster sugar
14g (2tsp) baking powder
2 large eggs, separated
175g (6oz) milk
75g (2½oz) unsalted butter
½tsp vanilla extract

1 Heat your waffle iron or pan according to the manufacturer's instructions (mine makes 10cm/4in square waffles).

2 Sift the flour, sugar, and baking powder together into a large bowl. In another bowl, beat the egg yolks with the milk, then pour into the dry ingredients and stir until smooth.

3 In a small saucepan, melt the butter until liquid, but just warm rather than hot. Beat the butter into the batter together with the vanilla extract.

4 Whisk the egg whites to soft peaks, then carefully fold into the batter. Once made, the batter can safely sit for up to 30–45 minutes at room temperature before using.

5 Lightly grease the waffle iron if necessary, then, working quickly, spoon in enough of the batter just to cover the dimples evenly. Close the lid and bake for 4–6 minutes (or according to temperature and the manufacturer's instructions), or until risen and golden.

6 Open the lid and ease the cooked waffle away from one corner, then quickly peel the waffle from the iron. Keep warm while the remaining waffles are baked, then serve hot.

CRUMPETS

To make crumpets that stand tall, use greased metal rings (like egg rings). If you don't have rings, just pour the batter directly onto the griddle. They will be thinner, but just as good.

Makes 10–15

125g (4½oz) strong white flour
15g (2tsp) caster sugar
7g (1tsp) fresh yeast, crumbled
3g (½tsp) fine sea salt
50g (1¾oz) warm water at 32°C (90°F)
100g (3½oz) lukewarm milk
5g (¾tsp) bicarbonate of soda, dissolved in 1tsp boiling water

1 Combine the flour, sugar, yeast, salt, water, and milk in a bowl and beat together with a spoon to make a very smooth batter. Leave in a warm place for 45 minutes or until the batter has begun to bubble.

2 Very lightly grease a large heavy-based frying pan or griddle. If you have 8–10cm (3–4in) diameter metal rings, grease these too and place them on the pan to heat. When both pan and rings are smoking hot, reduce the heat and place a heat-diffusing pad under the pan (or turn the heat very low). Leave for a minute to cool down slightly.

Allow crumpets to cool completely before toasting or grilling them, ready for eating

3 Pour the batter into a jug and stir in the dissolved bicarbonate of soda, stirring well to make sure that it is evenly combined. Pour a little of the batter into each of the rings to a depth of 1cm (½in). If not using rings, pour the batter directly onto the hot pan in discs 8–10cm (3–4in) in diameter.

4 Leave the crumpets to cook for 3 minutes, or until the surface is full of holes and the batter almost set. Flip the crumpets over and cook on the other side until lightly coloured. (This is when you can tell if the heat is right – the bottom of the crumpets should be dark brown but not burnt; if burnt then reduce the heat.)

5 The crumpets may pop out of the rings on their own. If they don't, run a sharp knife around the inside of the rings to loosen them. Place the cooked crumpets on a wire rack to cool, then oil the rings once more and put back on the pan to heat. When the rings are hot, make another batch of crumpets.

PASTRY & SWEET DOUGHS

PIERRE HERMÉ

The art of pastry making can be traced back to the time of the Egyptians, who were the first to make yeast cakes. The Greeks baked confections of almonds, poppy seeds, honey and black pepper, enclosed in a pastry made with flour, honey, and sesame seeds. Aristophanes, a Greek playwright of the 5th century BC, wrote in the Archarnians of "sesame cakes and fruit pastries". Similar ingredients appear in classical Roman recipes, which survive in medieval transcriptions of the oldest surviving cookbook – the recipes of Apicius, a Roman epicure of the 1st century AD.

The armies of Alexander the Great brought sugar cane to the Mediterranean, the Crusaders introduced the spices and nuts of the Orient, and chocolate was carried to Spain in the 16th century by the conquerors of Aztec Mexico. As a result the cooking of medieval Europe was greatly enriched.

Italian innovation Throughout the Middle East cooks developed the art of pastry and dough making. The impact of this on Italian cooking was revealed when Bartolomeo Scappi, chef to two popes, published his cookbook, Opera, in 1570. Scappi is to cooking what Michelangelo is to the fine arts. His cookbook was printed at a time when the arts of good living, manners, stylish clothes, furniture, and fine cooking were studied and enjoyed in Italy. Scappi was the first European cook to explore the Arabic art of pastry making and he details several sophisticated methods for making sweet and savoury doughs, which he uses in over 200 recipes. One pastry, layered with melted lard then folded and rolled, marks the beginnings of what was to become puff pastry.

These new ideas travelled to France and some 85 years later the first French book devoted entirely to pastry making was published. François Pierre de la Varenne is the founder of French classical cooking. He is credited with the authorship of Le Pâtissier François, the first comprehensive French work on pastry making. It was printed in 1655, but sadly few copies now survive. The book had step-by-step instructions, accurate measurements, and instructions for temperature control. Its methods for making pie pastry, puff pastry, macaroons, and waffles are very similar to those of today, and it is the first book to mention the small baking ovens known as petits fours, a name now used for little cakes and pastries served with coffee.

Pastry making was now an established art and thoughout the 18th century cooks created new confections. During this time, millers discovered that by sieving flour through finely woven silk they could extract most of the husk. Pastry cooks no longer relied on yeast to leaven their dough and eggs alone were used to raise the now refined flour, giving light airy doughs. In 1720 a Swiss pastry cook beat egg whites and sugar together to create the first meringues.

French excellence In the early 19th century pâtisserie reached new heights of elaboration at the hands of Antonin Carême. Born in 1783 to poor parents, he was turned out onto the streets at 10 years old. He knocked on the door of a cookshop, was taken in, and began to serve a six-year apprenticeship. At 17 he went to work for Bailly, one of the most famous pâtissiers of the day. At the time the profession of pâtissier was very prestigious because they were responsible for pièces montées, the great decorative centrepieces that were the crowning glory of grand dinners. Carême excelled at these flights of fancy and he produced two books in 1815 containing hundreds of designs for ornate creations in the shape of windmills, ruins, cascades, and temples.

Pastry making increased in status and came to be seen as a formal art. The unprecedented affluence of the period prompted thousands of pastry cooks throughout Europe to establish shops, and Vienna and Budapest vied with Paris for supremacy in cake and pastry making. Today flamboyant displays are no longer fashionable, but happily the tradition of fine baking is thriving in pastry shops and cafes. By reading this chapter you can benefit from centuries of sweetmeat-making expertise and learn how to bake delicious pastries, sweet doughs, and biscuits.

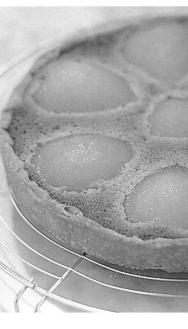

PASTRY

The old adage that a good pastry maker has "cold hands and a warm heart" is not far from the truth. Making melt-in-the-mouth pastry is not difficult but does require patience and attention to detail. Follow the instructions carefully and you will derive great pleasure from working with the ingredients and producing wonderful pastries. One of the most important things to remember when making pastry is to allow adequate time for resting and chilling. The times given in each recipe should be followed as the resting time will make the pastry easier to handle and prevent any

shrinkage. Among pastry doughs, pâte brisée or shortcrust, and its sweet variations, is justly celebrated. It bakes to a crisp, compact pastry, which makes a smooth container for tarts or a sturdy base for a layered confection. Pâte feuilletée has a complex texture as the repeated rolling and folding creates layers that, on baking, rise up to form thin, buttery flakes. Choux pastry is a moist airy paste, which puffs up in the oven to form a crisp outer shell with a hollow inside. It can be piped and shaped in many ways and makes a good container for creamy fillings.

PÂTE BRISÉE (SHORTCRUST PASTRY)

This amount of pastry is enough to make four 24–26cm (9½–10½in) tarts, or six 20cm (8in) tarts, or sixteen 10cm (4in) tarts. The pastry can be used once it has rested or can be stored for up to 2 days in the fridge or tightly wrapped and frozen in portions. Thaw slowly in the fridge before using. Do not knead again as if you do it will lose its melting texture.

Makes 1kg (2¼lb) pastry

375g (13oz) unsalted butter, at room temperature and cut into pieces

2 scant tsp salt

1 egg yolk

2 scant tsp caster sugar

100ml (3½fl oz) full-fat milk, at room temperature

500g (1lb 2oz) plain white flour plus extra for dusting

Making by hand

This is not a classic pâte brisée as it is made with milk and eggs instead of water, so the resulting dough is very crisp with a melting texture. Lightness of hand and speed are very important, and the whole process should not take longer than 4–5 minutes or the pastry will be tough.

1 Place the butter in a bowl. Beat with a wooden spoon to soften. Stir in the salt and egg yolk. Stir the sugar into the milk in a bowl. Pour this onto the softened butter in a thin stream, stirring constantly.

2 Sift the flour into a shallow bowl and steadily stir it into the butter mixture.

3 Mix by stirring with a wooden spoon or gently bring it together by hand in the bowl.

4 On a floured work surface, and using the palm of your hand, lightly knead the pastry just until it forms a soft, moist dough.

CHILLING TIME

Although the dough is made in minutes, the recommended chilling time is very important. The resting time in the refrigerator gives the gluten in the flour a chance to relax. Effective chilling will prevent the dough from shrinking too much when it goes into the hot oven.

5 Shape the dough into a ball, flatten slightly, and wrap in cling film. Leave in the fridge to rest for at least 2 hours.

Using a food processor

This is the ideal way to make pâte brisée as it is very fast. It is important to stop the machine the moment the dough gathers into a ball.

1 Fit the metal blade into the food processor. Add the butter, salt, egg yolk, sugar, and milk and process until you have a smooth cream. Sift the flour into a shallow bowl and then add to the food processor.

2 Process, using the pulse button, until the mixture just starts to come together. Stop as soon as the pastry has formed a ball. Wrap in cling film and refrigerate for at least 2 hours.

Rolling out & lining a tart tin

This dough is very rich and can be difficult to roll out. A well-floured surface makes the job easier but if you are new to pastry making you can roll the dough out between two large sheets of baking parchment. If you do this, make sure to lift the top sheet of parchment from time to time so that it does not crease into the dough.

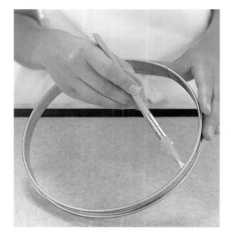

1 Butter a tart ring or a loose-bottomed tart tin. Place the ring on a baking sheet covered with baking parchment.

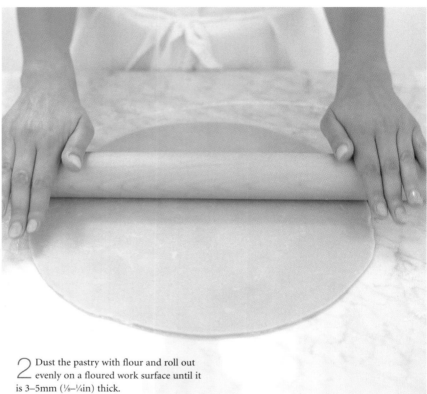

2 Dust the pastry with flour and roll out evenly on a floured work surface until it is 3–5mm (⅛–¼in) thick.

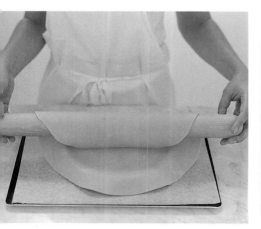

6 Dust off the surplus flour again and unroll the pastry into the tart ring.

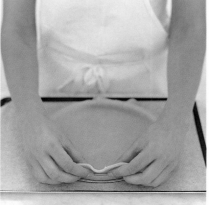

7 Press the pastry into the bottom and up the sides of the ring.

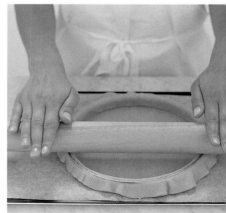

8 Roll the rolling pin over the top of the ring to cut off the excess pastry.

3 Slip a flexible spatula underneath now and again to prevent the pastry from sticking.

4 Carefully dust off the surplus flour with a dry pastry brush.

5 Drape the pastry halfway over the rolling pin to lift it over the tart ring.

CRACKING

If the dough cracks or splits as you work, then simply patch the split with small scraps of pastry. Moisten the edges to "glue" them into place and smooth gently with your finger, taking care not to stretch the pastry.

9 Using your fingertips, press the pastry into and up the sides of the ring.

10 Prick the base all over with a fork. Refrigerate for 30 minutes.

PEAR TART BOURDALOUE

A great classic of French pâtisserie, this delicious tart is named after a street in Paris' 9th arrondissement. The optional caramel coating gives a lovely deep flavour to this fruit-filled tart and is well worth the extra effort.

Makes a 22cm (8½in) tart

1.1kg (2½lb) firm, ripe William pears

6tbsp lemon juice

½ vanilla pod, halved lengthways and grated

300g (10½oz) pâte briseé (p376)

280g (10oz) almond cream (p419)

½ pot of apricot jam or quince jelly

1 The night before, peel the pears, cut in half, and remove the cores. Place in a bowl and coat with 3tbsp lemon juice. Put 1 litre (1¾pints) water, 3tbsp lemon juice, and the vanilla into a pan. Bring to the boil. Add the pears. Place a cartouche (p207) on top and simmer for 10–15 minutes. Cover and set aside to infuse overnight.

2 The next day, roll out the pastry 3mm (⅛in) thick and use to line a 22cm (8½in) tart ring (p378). Trim, then press the top of the pastry between your thumb and forefinger to ruffle the edge. Spread the almond cream evenly in the pastry case. Arrange the strained pears on top, core-side down.

3 Preheat the oven to 180°C (350°F, gas 4) and bake the tart for 30 minutes. Allow the tart to cool to lukewarm, then remove from the ring and place on a wire rack.

4 Warm the apricot jam in a pan. Liquidize with a hand-held blender then sieve to remove any bits of skin if necessary. Brush the surface of the tart with the melted apricot jam.

CARAMEL COATING

For optional caramel coating, make a dark golden caramel syrup with 30g (1oz) caster sugar and a little water (pp410–1). Remove the pan from the heat and add 10g (¼oz) butter and 20g (¾oz) crème fraîche. Just before serving, bring the caramel to the boil and immediately spread over the tart.

Crunchy tart with pistachios & cherries

This tart blends the classic flavours of pistachios and cherries, with a hint of cardamom in the streusel. The contrasting textures of crisp pastry, creamy filling, and crunchy topping make a mouthwatering dessert.

Makes a 26cm (10½in) tart

500g (1lb 2oz) frozen or fresh Morello cherries, pitted

80g (2½oz) caster sugar

300g (10½oz) pâte brisée (p376)

300g (10½oz) frozen or fresh black cherries, pitted

For the almond pistachio cream

50g (2oz) skinned pistachios

2 drops of bitter almond extract

125g (4½oz) butter, cut into pieces

125g (4½oz) icing sugar

125g (4½oz) ground almonds

12.5g (½oz) cornflour

1tbsp kirsch

2 eggs

25g (scant 1oz) skinned pistachios, crushed

150g (5½oz) crème pâtissière (p418) or crème fraîche

For the streusel

50g (1¾oz) butter, at room temperature

50g (1¾oz) caster sugar

50g (1¾oz) ground almonds

50g (1¾oz) plain white flour

pinch of ground green cardamom

pinch of salt (fleur de sel)

The night before put the Morello cherries and the sugar in a shallow bowl to macerate. The next day, strain the cherries an hour before you are going to use them.

For the almond pistachio cream, pound the pistachios with the almond extract in a mortar with a pestle to form a paste. Place the butter in a food processor and blend until creamy. Gradually add in order and one at a time, the pistachio paste, icing sugar, ground almonds, cornflour, kirsch, eggs, crushed pistachios, and crème pâtissière. Mix slowly. Place the cream in a shallow bowl and cover with cling film, making sure that the film sits on the surface of the cream. Refrigerate.

To make the streusel, put the butter, sugar, ground almonds, flour, ground cardamom, and a pinch of salt into a bowl and rub together using your fingertips. Refrigerate for 2 hours until firm. Put the streusel on a wire rack and press through to make small pieces. Refrigerate.

Preheat the oven to 180°C (350°F, gas 4). Butter a 26cm (10½in) tart tin. Roll out the pastry on a floured surface then use to line the tart tin (p378). Spread a thin layer of almond pistachio cream over the bottom of the tart. Cover with the strained Morello cherries, then sprinkle the black cherries over. Cover with the remaining almond pistachio cream. Place the tart in the

To make the streusel, press the dough through a wire rack

preheated oven. After 10 minutes remove the tart and sprinkle over the streusel. Return the tart to the oven and bake for a further 15–30 minutes. Allow to cool and then dust with icing sugar.

Baking a tart case blind

Baking blind means baking a pastry shell without a filling. Pastry cases are often pre-cooked either partially or fully, depending on the filling to be used. If a moist filling such as custard is to be cooked in the tart, the case is partially cooked to prevent the moist filling from making it soggy. The pastry has to be weighted down with beans to prevent it from losing its shape during the baking process.

1 Cut out a circle of baking parchment slightly larger than the tart ring or tin. Fold the disc in half several times to make a triangular shape, then clip the outer edge with scissors. Clipping the edge ensures a close fit against the rim when the paper is placed in the tart ring.

2 Line the tart ring or tin with the pastry (pp378–79). Cover the base and sides of the pastry with the prepared baking parchment, taking the paper above the sides of the ring. Fill with dried beans (metal baking beans are too heavy for delicate, brittle pastries).

3 Preheat the oven to 180°C (350°F, gas 4). Place the tart shell in the oven and bake for 18–20 minutes – it will be partially baked. For a fully baked case, remove the beans and lining paper, then return the tart shell to the oven.

4 Continue baking until a the pastry is a rich, golden colour, about 6–7 minutes longer. Cool the pastry case on a wire rack. Lift off the flan ring (or remove from tart tin) before or after filling, according to recipe directions.

PÂTE SUCRÉE

This amount of pastry is enough for three tarts, 26–28cm (10½–11in) or five tarts 24cm (9½in). The pastry can be frozen: divide into balls of the required quantities, and freeze. Thaw in the refrigerator the day before required. Do not work the pastry again before rolling out.

Making pâte sucrée by hand

1 Sift the flour onto a work surface. Sprinkle with salt and add the pieces of butter. Rub the flour and butter together between the palms of your hands until the mixture is the texture of fine crumbs and the butter has all disappeared.

  CHEF'S TIPS

■ When making pastry by hand it is best to use a marble or wooden pastry board and to knead the pastry as briefly as possible.

■ It is essential that the pastry rests for the time indicated. This allows it to relax and soften and will prevent it from cracking when it is rolled out and from shrinking as it bakes.

Makes 1.1kg (2½lb) pastry

500g (1lb 2oz) plain white flour

4 pinches of salt (fleur de sel)

300g (10½oz) butter, at room temperature and cut up

¼tsp powdered vanilla or the seeds scraped from ½ vanilla pod (p420)

190g (7oz) icing sugar

60g (2oz) ground almonds

2 eggs

Using an electric mixer

When using an electric mixer the ingredients will blend together quickly, so it is important to stop when the mixture just starts to cling together or the dough will be overworked. The same applies if using a food processor.

1 Sift the flour and icing sugar separately. Break the eggs into a bowl. Place the butter in the bowl of the electric mixer. Using the paddle attachment, mix until the butter softens.

2 Mix the vanilla and icing sugar together and add this, together with the ground almonds, to the flour mixture.

3 Make a well in the centre of the mixture. Break the eggs into the well.

4 Using your fingertips, mix the ingredients together to form a soft dough, but do not overwork. Press the pastry down with the palm of your hand, pushing it away from you. Bring it back towards you and shape into a ball. Wrap in cling film and refrigerate for at least 4 hours until firm.

2 Add, in order, the icing sugar, ground almonds, salt, vanilla, eggs, and, lastly, the flour. Mix slowly or "pulse" in a food processor until the pastry comes together in a ball. As soon as it does, stop processing or the pastry will lose its delicate short texture.

3 Wrap the pastry in cling film. Flatten slightly. Rest in the fridge for at least 4 hours until firm. The pastry will keep for 48 hours in the refrigerator.

TARTE AU CITRON (LEMON TART)

A familiar sight in French pastry shop windows, tarte au citron is the ideal dessert. With its crisp pastry and contrasting silky smooth filling, it is delicious on its own but equally good served with red berries, fruit coulis, or cream.

Makes a 26cm (10½in) tart

5 unwaxed lemons
240g (8½oz) caster sugar
4 eggs
160ml (5fl oz) freshly squeezed lemon juice
300g (10½oz) butter, at room temperature and cut into pieces
26cm (10½in) pâte sucrée pastry case, fully baked (p382)
apple or quince jelly (optional) for glazing

1 Zest the lemons over a large bowl. Pour in the sugar. Using both hands, rub the lemon zest into the sugar until the mixture is damp and grainy. Add the eggs and whisk everything together. Stir in the lemon juice.

2 Place the bowl over a pan of simmering water. The bottom of the bowl must not touch the water in the pan. Cook, stirring with a whisk, until the lemon cream reaches 82–83°C (180–181°F) on a digital thermometer.

LEMON CREAM

■ For a clean, sharp taste, use freshly squeezed lemon juice – nothing else will do.

■ There is a tricky moment when making the lemon cream, at the moment when the butter is added to the hot mix of eggs, sugar, and lemon juice that has been cooked over the hot water. The mixture cooks at 82–83°C (180–181°F) and should cool to 60°C (140°F) before the butter is added. If it is too hot, the butter will melt too much and the texture of the cream will be irretrievably altered.

■ To make an airy cream that is perfectly smooth, blend with the hand-held blender for the full 10 minutes. This is how long it takes for the butter to be fully incorporated.

■ To intensify the lemon flavour, sprinkle the melted and cooled glaze with little cubes of sugared lemon or thin slices of fresh lemon.

3 Strain the cream into a large bowl. Allow to cool to 60°C (140°F), stirring from time to time. Add the butter pieces one by one, whisking them into the cream with a hand-held blender. Mix the cream with the hand-held blender at full speed for 10 minutes until very smooth.

4 Pour the cooled lemon cream into the baked pastry case. Smooth the surface with a spatula. Slide the tart onto a serving plate and remove the tart ring.

5 To glaze the tart, melt some apple or quince jelly in a small pan over a low heat, or in a bowl in the microwave. Pour the cooled glaze evenly over the lemon cream filling.

Lemon tart brings a refreshing and tangy citrus finish to any meal

CINNAMON PÂTE SABLÉE (SWEET CINNAMON PASTRY)

This recipe uses cooked egg yolks. Cook 2 eggs for 10 minutes once the water has come to the boil. Drain and quickly plunge into a bowl of cold water, then shell. Allow to cool. Cut in half and push the yolks through a sieve into a bowl. The amount of pastry is enough for three 22cm (8½in) discs baked in tart rings or one 26cm (10½in) tart tin.

Makes 500g (1lb 2oz) pastry

200g (7oz) butter, at room temperature and cut into pieces

40g (1½oz) icing sugar

35g (1oz) ground almonds

8g (2tsp) ground cinnamon

2 hard-boiled egg yolks

1tbsp aged dark rum

pinch of salt (fleur de sel)

1g (¼ tsp) baking powder

200g (7oz) plain white flour

Making by hand

1 Place the butter in a bowl and beat with a wooden spoon until creamy. Add the icing sugar, ground almonds, ground cinnamon, sieved egg yolks, the rum, and the salt and mix into the butter.

2 Mix the baking powder with the flour, then add gradually to the butter mixture. Mix until all the flour is blended in. The pastry will be very soft to the touch.

3 Gather the pastry into a ball. If you are making the discs, divide the ball into 3 pieces. Wrap each in cling film. Refrigerate for at least 4 hours before using.

Using a food processor

1 Place the butter in the bowl of the food processor fitted with the metal blade and process at medium speed until the butter is creamy. Add the icing sugar, ground almonds, ground cinnamon, egg yolks, and salt.

2 Process on medium speed until the mixture is an even consistency. Add the rum. Mix the baking powder into the flour. Add the flour to the butter mixture and process, using the pulse button, until the flour is just mixed in.

3 The mixture will be very soft. Shape into a ball, divide into 3 pieces, wrap in cling film and refrigerate for 4 hours before using.

STORING PASTRY

■ The pastry will keep for 2 days in the fridge or can be vacuum-sealed.

■ The pastry should be well chilled before use. Any cracks can be patched with small pieces of pastry.

Baking a pastry disc

If making more than one pastry disc, work with one piece of dough at a time and keep the remaining dough refrigerated until needed. Be sure that the work surface and the dough are well floured, as this pastry is very soft. Any trimmings can be chilled, then re-rolled, cut into small shapes, and baked to make small biscuits.

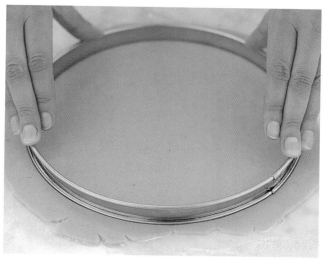

1 Flour the work-surface and the pastry. Roll out until it is 3mm (⅛in) thick. Dust off the excess flour with a dry brush. Place a tart ring on top of the pastry and press down firmly.

2 Cut cleanly round the inside edge with a small sharp knife. Remove the ring and the excess dough.

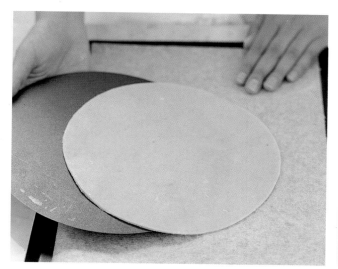

3 Either slide the base of a loose-bottomed tart tin or a cardboard disc underneath the pastry. Place a sheet of baking parchment on a baking sheet and slide the pastry disc onto it.

4 Prick the pastry with a fork. Cover with cling film. Refrigerate for 30 minutes. Preheat the oven to 180°C (350°F, gas 4) and bake the pastry for 18–20 minutes.

INVERTED PÂTE FEUILLETÉE ("INSIDE-OUT" PUFF PASTRY)

In classic puff pastry, a flour and water dough is used to encase a block of butter and then the whole is rolled and folded several times to make the many layers. This dough is different as most of the butter is on the outside and a mixture of flour, water, and melted butter is made for the inside, resulting in a crisp yet melting pastry.

Makes about 1.1kg (2¼lb) pastry

For stage 1

75g (2½oz) plain white flour

75g (2½oz) strong plain white flour

375g (13oz) unsalted butter, at room temperature

For stage 2 (the détrempe)

150ml (5fl oz) water

½tsp white vinegar

15g (2tsp) salt (fleur de sel)

175g (6oz) plain white flour

175g (6oz) strong plain white flour

110g (4oz) unsalted butter, melted then cooled

1 For stage 1. Mix the flours and butter together in a bowl until the pastry comes together in a ball. Flatten the pastry into a disc 2cm (¾in) thick. Wrap in cling film and refrigerate for 2 hours.

2 For stage 2, mix the water, vinegar, and salt together in a bowl. Mix the flours and butter together, sprinkle over the water and mix well. Depending on how much water the flours absorb, you may not need to use all the water. The dough should be soft but not too soft.

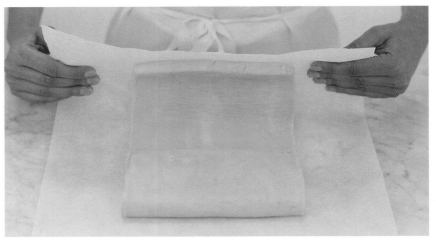

6 Pat the top of the parcel all over with your fist to spread it out. Then, using a floured rolling pin, roll it out from the centre into a rectangle 3 times as long as it is wide. Be careful not to squash the edges of the pastry.

7 Fold the top quarter of the pastry down to the middle of the rectangle, then fold the bottom quarter up to the middle, edge to edge with the top quarter.

3 Using a rolling pin, flatten the stage-2 dough (the détrempe) into a square that is 2cm (¾in) thick. Wrap it in plastic wrap and refrigerate for about 2 hours.

4 Flour the ball of pastry made in stage 1. Roll out on floured baking parchment into a circle 1cm (½in) thick.

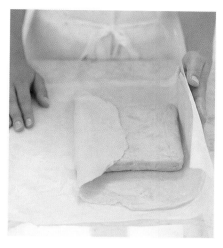

5 Place the square détrempe in the centre of the pastry circle. Fold in all the sides of the pastry taking care that the seams meet and the square of détrempe is completely enclosed.

8 Fold the dough in half at the centre. There will be 4 layers of dough. This gives you a "tour portefeuille" also called a "double turn". Flatten slightly. Wrap in cling film and refrigerate for an hour.

9 Place the pastry on a floured work surface with the fold lying to the left. Flatten the pastry again with your fist, then roll out to make a rectangle 3 times as long as it is wide. Fold the pastry as before into the "tour portefeuille". Brush off any excess flour, wrap in cling film, and refrigerate for an hour.

10 The last turn, called the "tour simple" or "single turn", is made when about to use the pastry. With the folded side on your left, roll the pastry out into a rectangle as before. Fold one narrow end to the middle and the other back over the top of it to make a square. Wrap in cling film and refrigerate for 30 minutes.

Rolling out & baking pâte feuilletée

Make sure the pastry is very well chilled before rolling out. When rolling out, use short, sharp strokes in the same direction. Firmly push in a direction away from yourself in order to extend the pastry. Do not roll backwards and forwards haphazardly or the layers will not rise evenly.

1 Roll out the pastry on a floured work surface until it is 2–3mm (1/16–1/8in) thick. From time to time, lift the pastry off the work surface by sliding your hands underneath. It is essential to do this as it will prevent the pastry from overstretching and then shrinking as it cooks. Brush off the excess flour.

CHEF'S TIPS

■ When you cut pâte feuilletée into a rectangle or a disc, there are always some trimmings left. Do not knead them together but place one on top of the other, press them down firmly, then roll out. Use to make sweet or savoury mini bouchées ("puffs" or vol-au-vents).

■ The baking parchment needs to be moistened with water when baking pâte feuilletée. This moistening helps to stop the pastry shrinking as it bakes.

2 Cover a baking tray with moistened baking parchment, then slide the pastry onto the paper. Prick all over with a fork. Leave to rest for 1–2 hours in the fridge. Preheat the oven to 200°C (400°F, gas 6). Bake for 15–20 minutes, reducing the temperature to 190°C (375°F, gas 5) as soon as the pastry goes in.

CARAMELIZED INVERTED PÂTE FEUILLETÉE

This is ideal for small and large mille-feuilles, as the caramelization will prevent the cream filling from making the pastry soggy. Once the pastry sheet has cooled, cut it lengthwise in half. Spread one half with crème pâtissière (p418), crème Chantilly (p414), jam, or fruit purée and put the other piece of pastry on top.

400g (14oz) inverted pâte feuilletée (p388), rolled out and pricked with a fork ready to be baked after its rest in the refrigerator (see left)

40g (1½oz) caster sugar

20g (¾oz) icing sugar

1 Preheat the oven to 230°C (450°F, gas 8). Sprinkle the caster sugar evenly all over the pastry. Place the pastry in the preheated oven and reduce the temperature immediately to 190°C (375°F, gas 5). Bake for 8 minutes, then cover with a wire rack to prevent it from rising too much. Bake for a further 5 minutes.

2 Remove the pastry from the oven. Remove the wire rack and cover the pastry with a sheet of dry baking parchment, then set another baking sheet, the same size as the first, on top. Turn the 2 sheets over, holding them firmly. Set them down on the work surface.

3 Remove the top (previously the bottom) baking sheet and the baking parchment. Sprinkle the pastry with the icing sugar, place in the oven at 240°C (475°F, gas 9) and bake for 5–7 minutes. The pastry should turn golden and will then caramelize.

Arlettes

Light, delicate, spicy and crunchy, these little biscuits make a very good accompaniment to ice cream.

Makes 70–80

300g (10½oz) inverted pâte feuilletée (p388)

For the spiced sugar

1 scant tsp powdered vanilla

2tsp ground allspice

500g (1lb 2oz) icing sugar

Flour the work surface and roll out the pastry until it is 3mm (⅛in) thick. Cut out a 20x40cm (8x16in) rectangle. Place it in front of you with the long side parallel to you and roll up very tightly. Cover with cling film and place in the freezer for 45 minutes. It should be quite firm. Using a sharp knife, cut evenly into slices 3mm (⅛in) thick.

Cover a baking sheet with baking parchment. Sift together the vanilla, allspice, and icing sugar. Sprinkle the spiced sugar over the work surface to make a square 5mm (¼in) deep. Take 2 rounds of pastry and place on the sugar, leaving a large space between them. Using a

rolling pin, flatten on both sides as thinly as possible. Transfer the rounds to the baking sheet. Repeat the process with the remaining slices, adding more spiced sugar as required.

Preheat the oven to 230°C (450°F, gas 8). Bake in the oven for 5–6 minutes. The biscuits should be very caramelized.

Remove from the oven and cool on a wire rack. Arlettes will not keep for more than a day. Once they have cooled, place in an airtight tin or plastic container. Serve with tea or coffee or use to accompany ice cream or as petits fours.

Using a sharp knife, cut slices 3mm (⅛in) thick

CROISSANTS

One of the more colourful accounts of the croissant's origin is set in Vienna, Austria. In 1683 bakers were working overnight when they heard invading Turkish forces tunnelling under the city walls. They alerted the authorities and the city was saved. The bakers then created a commemorative pastry in a crescent shape – the emblem on the Turkish flag. In fact, the croissant was probably created in France after 1850.

Makes 24

12g (½oz) fresh yeast or 7g (¼oz) dried yeast
200ml (7fl oz) water at 20°C (68°F)
600g (1lb 6oz) strong white flour
12g (2tsp) salt (fleur de sel)
75g (2½oz) caster sugar
35g (1oz) very soft unsalted butter
15g (½oz) full-fat milk powder
325g (12oz) unsalted butter, chilled

For the glaze

2 eggs
1 egg yolk
pinch of salt

FREEZING

It is best to make enough dough for 24 croissants, shape them, and freeze what you do not need. Freeze the unbaked croissants on the baking tray and cover tightly with cling film. Ideally they should be frozen for no more than 2 weeks to a month.

1 Dissolve the yeast in two-thirds of the water. Sift the flour into a large bowl. Mix in the salt, sugar, very soft butter, milk powder, and dissolved yeast. Knead everything together quickly. If the dough is still a little stiff, add the rest of the water. Cover with cling film. Rest at room temperature for 1–1½ hours.

2 When the dough has doubled in size, remove it from the bowl, punch it down, and return to the bowl. Cover with cling film and refrigerate for 1–1¼ hours. Remove the dough from the bowl, punch down again, cover with cling film and place in the freezer for a further 30 minutes.

6 Flour the work surface then roll out the dough until it is 3mm (⅛in) thick. Using a sharp knife, cut out triangles 20cm (8in) high by 12cm (5in) across the base.

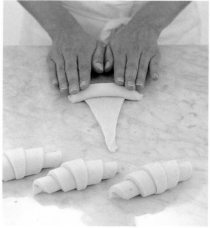

7 To shape, place a triangle with the base nearest to you, roll it up, then bring the ends round towards each other to make a crescent. Place the croissants 5cm (2in) apart on a baking sheet lined with baking parchment. Leave to rise at room temperature for 1½–2 hours.

3 Remove the dough from the freezer. Knead the cold butter until it is soft. On a floured surface, roll the dough out to a rectangle 3 times longer than it is wide. Place half the butter along the bottom edge of the dough. With the palm of your hand, push the butter up to cover two-thirds of the rectangle of dough.

4 Fold the rectangle of dough into thirds, folding the unbuttered top third down first. Wrap the folded dough in cling film. Let rest in the freezer for 30 minutes and then in the refrigerator for 1 hour.

5 Roll out the dough into a rectangle as before and spread with the remainder of the butter. Fold into thirds again and wrap in cling film. Let rest in the freezer for 30 minutes and then in the refrigerator for 1 hour.

 VARIATIONS

You can use this same dough to make almond croissants by rolling 50g (1¾oz) almond paste or 50g (1¾oz) pistachio-flavoured almond paste into the dough. To finish, sprinkle flaked almonds over the tops of the croissants. You can also make pains au chocolat. Cut the dough into rectangles 12x6cm (5x2½in) and place a small bar of chocolate on each one, fold the dough in three, and brush with glaze.

8 Preheat the oven to 230°C (450°F, gas 8). Place the eggs, egg yolk, and salt in a bowl and whisk together. Brush the croissants with egg glaze, then place in the oven and reduce the temperature to 190°C (375°F, gas 5). Bake for 20 minutes. Remove from the oven and place on a wire rack to cool.

BRIOCHE DOUGH

Delicately savoury and sweet at the same time, brioche is the ideal vehicle for a jam or fruit preserve and is an excellent partner for foie gras and blue-veined cheeses. Brioche dough needs a lot of working. It is an extremely sticky dough and is best made in an electric food mixer.

Makes 1.3kg (3lb) dough

500g (1lb 2oz) strong plain white flour
12.5g (½oz) fresh yeast or 7g (¼oz) instant dried yeast
50g (2oz) caster sugar
7 eggs
2 scant tsp salt
400g (14oz) unsalted butter, at room temperature

1 Pour the flour into the bowl of an electric mixer fitted with the dough hook. Add the crumbled fresh yeast or the instant dried yeast, and the sugar. Mix on medium speed then add 4 eggs. Mix again then add the 3 remaining eggs one by one, making sure that each is fully incorporated into the dough.

2 Once the dough comes away from the sides of the bowl, add the salt and the butter cut into pieces. The dough is ready when it comes away cleanly from the sides of the bowl again.

CHEF'S TIPS

■ To make brioche dough double in size at room temperature, the room should ideally be around 22°C (72°F). Allow at least 2 hours and 3 at most. Make sure that you cover the dough with either cling film or a clean cloth. Do not leave the dough in a draught.
■ Raw brioche dough does not freeze well, although you can keep it in the fridge for a day.

4 Lift the sticky dough out of the bowl and place it on a lightly floured work surface.

5 Punch down the dough with your fist. This will deflate the dough and it will return to its original size. Put it back into the bowl and cover with cling film again. Place in the refrigerator and let rise for 1¼ hours.

3 Transfer the dough, which should now be silky in texture, to a large bowl. Cover with cling film and leave at warm room temperature for 2–3 hours until double in size. The risen dough should be very sticky.

6 Press down on the dough to check that it has risen again, then remove it to the work surface and punch down to deflate. The brioche dough is now ready to be shaped and baked.

RAISIN BRIOCHES

Makes 12

500g (1lb 2oz) brioche dough (see opposite)
50g (2oz) white raisins
1 egg
1 egg yolk
¼tsp caster sugar

Mix the raisins into the brioche dough. Divide the dough into small, 45g (1½oz) balls and place 5cm (2in) apart on a baking sheet lined with baking parchment. Leave at room temperature until doubled in size. In a small bowl, mix together the egg, egg yolk, and sugar. Brush this glaze over the brioches. Preheat the oven to 220°C (425°F, gas 7) and bake for 12–14 minutes. Remove from the oven and cool on a wire rack.

Serve raisin brioches with tea or coffee for a satisfying snack in the morning or afternoon

KUGELHOPF

A traditional cake from Alsace, this recipe for kugelhopf is from the repertoire of M. Hermé senior, who is a pâtissier in Colmar. The cake takes its name from the pan in which it is baked, whose shape has altered very little since the 16th century. A kugelhopf pan has sloping, furrowed, and moulded sides and a central funnel. In the past the pans would have been made from tin, clay, and copper, but nowadays it is much easier to use one that has a nonstick lining.

Makes a 23cm (9in) kugelhopf

250g (8½oz) white raisins	
50ml (1¾fl oz) dark rum	
1.3kg (3lb) brioche dough (p394)	
40g (1½oz) flaked almonds	

For the syrup

200ml (7fl oz) water	
300g (10½oz) granulated sugar	
30g (1oz) ground almonds	
1tbsp orange-flower water	

To finish

80g (3oz) butter	
50g (1¾oz) caster sugar	

1 The night before, soak the raisins in the rum then add to the dough 2 minutes before you finish kneading. Flour your fingers and flatten the dough into a circle.

2 Lift the edges up and over towards the centre and shape the dough into a ball. Roll the ball on the work surface, shaping it between the palms of your hands so that it will rise evenly during baking.

3 Make a hole in the centre of the dough by pressing down with your fingertips.

4 Butter a 23cm (9in) kugelhopf mould and sprinkle evenly with flaked almonds.

5 Transfer the dough to the mould and press it down onto the almonds. Cover the dough with a clean cloth and leave it to rise at room temperature for about 1½ hours.

6 To make the syrup, pour the water and sugar into a large pan. Bring to the boil. Remove from the heat and add the ground almonds and orange-flower water. Allow to cool, then refrigerate. Clarify the butter (p24).

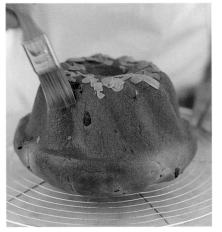

7 Preheat the oven to 180°C (350°F, gas 4). Bake the risen dough for 35 minutes. Remove the kugelhopf from the mould while it is still hot and brush with the clarified butter, followed by the syrup.

8 Spread the sugar in a shallow tray and roll the kugelhopf in it, or lightly sprinkle sugar over the kugelhopf with your hand.

BRIOCHE NANTERRE

Brioche Nanterre is baked in a loaf tin and so is ideal for slicing. Try it toasted or, even better, brush untoasted slices with melted butter and put under a hot grill.

generous ¼ quantity (13oz/375g) brioche dough (p394)

1 egg plus 1 egg yolk

¼tsp sugar

1 Butter an 18x8.5cm (7x3½in) loaf tin. Divide 375g (13oz) brioche dough (p394) into 4. Roll each piece of dough into a ball on a non-floured work surface. Stretch gently to make the pieces into ovals.

2 Set closely side by side in the tin. Leave the dough at room temperature until it has doubled in size. Brush with glaze (p395).

3 Using a pair of scissors, cut a cross in each ball. Bake in the oven, preheated to 180°C (350°F, gas 4) for 25 minutes, until well risen and golden brown. Cool on a wire rack.

SUGARED BRIOCHES

Butter 6cm (2½in) fluted brioche tins. Divide the brioche dough into small 45g (1½oz) balls. Place in the tins. Leave at room temperature until they have doubled in size. Brush with glaze (p395). Cut a cross in each ball. Sprinkle generously with granulated sugar. Bake in the oven, preheated to 220°C (425°F, gas 7), for 12–14 minutes. Remove from the oven, shake out of the tins, and cool on a wire rack. These are good with breakfast or at teatime.

PÂTE À BRIOCHE FEUILLETÉE

This dough has the taste of brioche and the crispness and lightness of a croissant. It can be used in a similar way to croissant dough (see variations, p393).

Makes 1.7kg (4lb) dough

55g (2oz) fresh yeast or 25g (scant 1oz) instant dried yeast
3 eggs, very cold
750g (1lb 10oz) strong plain white flour
50g (1¾oz) caster sugar
10g (2tsp) salt (fleur de sel)
40g (1½oz) full-fat milk powder
310ml (10fl oz) very cold water
300g (10½oz) unsalted butter, chilled

1 Place the crumbled fresh or instant dried yeast, eggs, flour, sugar, salt, milk powder, and water in the bowl of an electric mixer fitted with the dough hook. Mix together and stop as soon as the dough is smooth. Wrap the dough in cling film. Place in the freezer to cool.

2 When cold remove the dough. Cream the butter until soft. On a floured surface roll out the dough to a rectangle 3 times as long as it is wide. Place half the butter on the bottom edge of the dough. Using your palm push the butter evenly over two-thirds of the dough.

3 Fold the dough into thirds, folding the top, unbuttered third down first. Chill in the freezer for 30 minutes, then refrigerate for 1 hour. Roll out and spread with the remaining butter as before, then fold into thirds and chill in the freezer and refrigerator as before.

PAINS AUX RAISINS

A rich, sweet dough entwined with an almond cream and plump raisins. The contrasting topping of slightly acidic orange glaze makes the perfect "sticky bun".

Makes 24

1.7kg (4lb) pâte à brioche feuilletée (p399)

175g (6oz) almond cream (p419)

250g (8½oz) white raisins

For the orange glaze

150g (5½oz) icing sugar

2.5g (½tsp) powdered gum arabic (available from chemists or specialist cake shops)

2.5g (½tsp) full-fat milk powder

3 tbsp orange juice

1 tbsp Cointreau

1 Start the day before by making the orange glaze. Sift the icing sugar into a pan. Add the powdered gum arabic and the milk powder. Pour in the orange juice. Dissolve over a very low heat and warm very slightly. Remove from the heat and stir in the Cointreau. Refrigerate until the next day.

2 On a floured surface, roll the dough into a rectangle 60cm (24in) long and 2.5cm (1in) thick. Spread the almond cream over the dough, leaving 2cm (¾in) clear all round the edge.

3 Sprinkle the raisins evenly over the almond cream. Roll up like a swiss roll, starting from one of the long edges.

Made with pâte feuilletée and almond cream with an orange glaze, pains aux raisins are a richly flavoured treat

FREEZING

■ Make 24 pains aux raisins and freeze what you do not need. Freeze uncooked on a baking sheet, tightly wrapped with cling film. Do not keep for more than a month or they will become covered in ice crystals.

■ It is best to freeze choux pastry raw, shaped into choux buns or éclairs, on a baking tray. Let the buns or éclairs harden in the freezer before wrapping tightly with cling film.

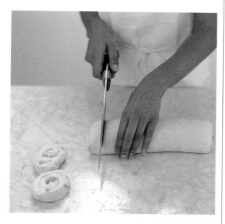

4 Using a sharp knife, cut the roll into 24 slices, about 2cm (¾in) thick. On each slice tuck the end underneath to prevent the pain aux raisin from unrolling as it expands.

5 Place the pastries 5cm (2in) apart on baking sheets lined with baking parchment. Place in the freezer to chill for 30 minutes. Remove from the freezer and let rise at room temperature until doubled in size.

6 Preheat the oven to 180°C (350°F, gas 4) and bake for 18 minutes. As soon as the pastries come out of the oven, brush them with the orange glaze. Eat warm.

CHOUX PASTRY

A great classic of French pâtisserie, choux pastry is used for making éclairs and profiteroles. The traditional cake for weddings and communions in France, the croquembouche, is an elaborate cone-shaped confection of custard-filled choux buns, caramel, spun sugar, and fresh flowers.

Makes 750g (1lb 10oz) dough

125ml (4fl oz) water
125ml (4fl oz) full-fat milk
1 scant tsp caster sugar
1 scant tsp salt
110g (4oz) butter
140g (5oz) plain white flour
5 eggs

2 Continue to beat the mixture for another 2–3 minutes until the dough dries out and comes away from the sides of the pan in a ball. Tip it into a large bowl.

1 Pour the water, milk, sugar, and salt into a pan. Add the butter. Bring to the boil. As soon as the liquid boils, add the flour all at once. Beat vigorously until the dough is smooth.

3 Add the eggs one by one, beating well so that each egg is thoroughly incorporated before adding the next.

4 When the dough falls as a ribbon, it is ready to be shaped as required by the recipe and baked straight away.

CHEF'S TIPS

■ Choux pastry is made with equal amounts of water and milk. Using water only results in rough pastry.
■ It is essential to put the dough in a bowl before adding the eggs in order to mix them in well and so make a light pastry.

BISCUITS

Biscuit comes from the words "bis" meaning twice and "cuit" meaning baked. The name referred to twice-baked pieces of bread dough that were cooked until they had completely dried out and become hard. For centuries no ship left port without a supply of biscuits to last for the months, or even years, of a long voyage.

In medieval times, cooks in wealthy households experimented with honey, eggs, spices, cream, flour, butter, and breadcrumbs, fashioning these ingredients into many kinds of sweetmeats.

By the 17th century, sweet biscuits were commonplace in prosperous households and street pedlars did a lively trade supplying biscuits to those of more modest means. Today there are many kinds of biscuits available and here you will find recipes and variations for a few of the most popular: the buttery sablé, which is the French shortbread; delicately thin, crisp tuiles; and the all-time favourite, chocolate chip cookies. Any of these biscuits are ideal to serve with creamy desserts and ice creams.

SABLÉS DIAMANT VANILLE

The French name, "sablé" (sandy), for these crunchy, crisp, and crumbly shortbread biscuits accurately describes their texture. They are especially good with tea or coffee.

Makes 50

225g (8oz) unsalted butter, at room temperature and cut into pieces

100g (3½oz) caster sugar

½tsp vanilla extract

2g (¼tsp) salt (fleur de sel)

320g (12oz) plain white flour

To finish

sugar crystals or demerara sugar

CHEF'S TIPS

■ What makes these diamond sablés special is that they are made without eggs, which are unnecessary because the dough contains a lot of butter. This makes the texture of the sablés very short.

■ To make the dough by hand, follow the same procedure as for making in the processor, taking care not to overwork the ingredients.

1 Place the butter in the bowl of a food processor fitted with the metal blade. Process until the butter is creamy then mix in the sugar, vanilla extract, and salt and process again. Sift the flour and add to the mixture, then process until the dough is smooth.

2 Remove the dough from the processor. Shape it into a ball and divide into three. Refrigerate for a while if you think the dough is too soft. Roll each ball of dough into a cylinder shape 5cm (2in) in diameter on a sheet of baking parchment. Make sure that there are no slits or bubbles of air in the dough.

3 Spread out the sugar crystals evenly on a sheet of baking parchment, then roll each cylinder in the sugar. Preheat the oven to 180°C (350°F, gas 4).

4 Using a sharp knife, cut each cylinder into slices 2cm (¾in) thick.

5 Put the slices onto a baking sheet lined with baking parchment. Bake the sablés until they are golden brown, 22–25 minutes. Transfer to a wire rack to cool.

TUILES AUX AMANDES EFFILÉES

The raw dough will keep for almost a week in the fridge and the baked tuiles can be stored for 2 days in an airtight box.

**Makes 40 small or
25 large biscuits**

125g (4½oz) flaked almonds

125g (4½oz) caster sugar

2 drops of vanilla extract or
2 pinches of vanilla powder

drop of bitter almond extract

2 egg whites

25g (scant 1oz) butter

20g (¾oz) plain white flour

1 Using a rubber spatula, mix the almonds, sugar, vanilla extract or powder, bitter almond extract, and egg whites together in a bowl.

2 Melt the butter and, while it is still hot, pour it onto the egg white mixture. Mix thoroughly. Cover with cling film and refrigerate overnight.

3 The next day, sift the flour into the bowl and mix in thoroughly. Place teaspoonfuls of dough on a non-stick baking tray, spaced well apart.

4 Preheat the oven to 150°C (300°F, gas 2). Flatten each biscuit with the back of a tablespoon dipped in cold water. Bake for 15–18 minutes. The tuiles should be an even golden colour with no white in the centre.

5 Remove the tuiles from the tray with a flexible spatula, slide onto a sheet of baking parchment, and allow to cool.

ORANGE & NUT TUILES

Makes 25

grated zest of 1 unwaxed orange

100g (3½oz) caster sugar

20g (4tsp) orange juice

100g (3½oz) chopped almonds

80g (3oz) clarified butter, melted (p26)

20g (¾oz) plain white flour

1 Put the orange zest, sugar, orange juice, and almonds into a bowl and mix together. Stir in the butter and mix well. Leave to rest for 24 hours.

2 The next day, preheat the oven to 150°C (300°F, gas 2). Stir the flour into the almond mixture. Place teaspoonfuls of dough on a non-stick baking sheet, leaving a large space between each one.

3 Flatten each biscuit with the back of a spoon dipped in cold water. Bake for 15–18 minutes. Remove from the tray and cool.

SHAPED TUILES

You can also make shaped tuiles by lifting them off the baking tray with a flexible spatula while they are still hot and draping them over a wine bottle or rolling pin so that they take on the shape of a roof pantile.

CHOCOLATE CHIP COOKIES

Real chocolate cookies, chewy in the centre, crunchy round the edges and irresistible.

Makes 30

150g (5½oz) butter, at room temperature and cut into pieces

5g (1tsp) salt (fleur de sel)

240g (8½oz) light muscovado sugar

1½ eggs

225g (8oz) plain white flour

5g (1tsp) baking powder

1.5g (¼tsp) bicarbonate of soda

120g (4oz) pecan or macadamia nuts, chopped

240g (8½oz) best-quality dark chocolate (70% cocoa solids) cut into small pieces

1 Place the butter in the bowl of an electric mixer. Beat until smooth and creamy. Add the salt and sugar and beat well.

2 Add the eggs and mix for 3 minutes. Add the flour, baking powder, bicarbonate of soda, chopped nuts, and chocolate. Mix for 2–3 minutes.

3 Shape the dough into a ball. On a sheet of baking parchment roll into a sausage shape about 6cm (2½in) in diameter. Wrap the dough in cling film and refrigerate for 2 hours.

4 Preheat the oven to 180°C (350°F, gas 4). Cut into slices 1cm (½in) thick. Place on a baking sheet lined with baking parchment. Bake for 12 minutes. Cool the cookies on a wire rack.

CAPPUCCINO COOKIES

Makes 25

115g (4oz) softened butter

125g (4½oz) light muscovado sugar

15g (½oz) acacia honey

1.5g (¼ tsp) salt (fleur de sel)

1 egg

25g (1tbsp) liquid coffee essence

2tbsp instant coffee, dissolved in 1tbsp hot water

170g (6oz) plain white flour

3g (½tsp) baking powder

1.5g (¼ tsp) bicarbonate of soda

85g (3oz) chopped macadamia nuts

140g (5oz) plain chocolate, chopped

1 Put the butter into a bowl and beat until creamy. Add the sugar, honey, and salt and mix well. Add the egg, coffee essence, and dissolved instant coffee and mix for 3 minutes. Add the flour, baking powder, bicarbonate of soda, chopped nuts, and chocolate and mix for 3 minutes.

2 Roll into a sausage shape 6cm (2½in) in diameter and refrigerate for 2 hours.

3 Preheat the oven to 180°C (350°F, gas 4). Cut the dough into slices 1cm (½in) thick; place on a baking sheet lined with baking parchment. Bake for 14 minutes. Remove and cool on a wire rack.

DESSERTS

PIERRE HERMÉ

Dessert is the last course of a meal, offered after all the other food has been "desservi": literally "unserved" (removed), which is where the word "dessert" comes from. Until the mid 19th century it was usual to offer an array of sweets, such as crystallized fruits and nuts, before the actual dessert, which might be a cream, compote, fancy cake, or pastry. Nowadays, the habit is to offer one or other of these, not both – but the importance of the dessert course remains undiminished.

Fruit desserts At its simplest, dessert can consist of fresh fruit, but with just a little more effort that same fruit can be served in ways that turn it into something really special. For that reason this Desserts chapter starts with instructions for making sugar syrups. From the basic ingredients of sugar and water you can make the lightest of syrups to enhance the individual flavours in, for example, a fruit salad. Alternatively, you can cook that basic syrup until it begins to caramelize and take on its own distinctive character. Then, depending on its colour and thickness, it can be used to glaze petits fours, coat moulds, serve as a sauce, or flavour desserts, cakes, and pastries. Continuing with the theme of simplicity, the recipes for apple and strawberry crisps really could not be easier. The finely sliced fruit is simply dried in a very low oven to preserve its colour and flavour. The result is instantly familiar yet surprisingly different – a light way of ending a rich meal. The same drying technique can be applied to any fruit that lends itself to being finely sliced, although for the best results you should use fruit that is in season and in peak condition.

Dairy classics Given France's long association with dairy farming, it is only natural that dairy products should have inspired so many wonderful desserts. Milk, cream, and crème fraîche (the last of these being cream sharpened but not soured by adding a special lactic culture in the form of sour cream or buttermilk) are important parts of numerous recipes. This chapter covers the four classic pastry creams – crème Chantilly, crème pâtissière, almond cream, and ganache (a cream made from chocolate and crème fraîche) – that are used as accompaniments, fillings, or decoration rather than being served on their own. Each of these creams may be flavoured in a variety of ways and used in desserts ranging from parfaits and charlottes to mousses and flans.

No dessert chapter would be complete without a recipe for pouring custard, called crème anglaise. Rich in egg yolks and delicately flavoured with vanilla, it transforms a simple dessert of poached fruit into a sublime experience. Crème anglaise must be watched during cooking – take care not to let the custard overheat, or it will curdle and will be spoilt.

Meringue Another classic with an undeserved reputation for being difficult to make is meringue – that light-as-air mixture of whipped egg whites and sugar. Various countries have claimed the credit for this wonderful invention, but it was the great French pâtissier Antonin Carême who exploited its versatility to make desserts of architectural splendour as well as breathtaking flavour. The method for making meringue in Carême's classic style is given, and also a recipe for Italian meringue, made with a hot sugar syrup and used to top trifle and tarts, make icing, and fold into soufflés.

The selection of desserts also includes some excitingly flavoured sorbets (water ices) and ice creams. Since the advent of refrigeration, both can easily be made at home, and more than repay the time involved. The key thing is to beat them at least twice during the freezing process so that the mixture becomes smooth and free of ice.

We hope you will see that the recipes in this chapter have been carefully chosen to link to each other in subtle but important ways. The techniques of one recipe can be applied or adapted elsewhere, and the ideas build upon each other rather than exist in isolation. Applying and combining techniques is a skill that every good cook needs to acquire, and we hope the desserts in this chapter will give you a good grounding in the most delicious ways possible.

MAKING SUGAR SYRUPS

Sugar syrups form the basis for a range of delicious desserts, from exotic fruit salads, ice creams, and meringues to confectionery. The basic mixture of sugar and water is cooked to different temperatures to produce varying concentrations of sugar that make the syrup suitable for different pâtisseries, confectionery, and chocolate products. It is essential to keep to these temperatures.

Boiling sugar temperatures

The best utensil for testing the rising temperature of cooking sugar is a sugar thermometer that reads up to 200°C (392°F). Small quantities of syrup can be hand-tested. Place a bowl of iced water beside the pan, dip your fingers in the water, then dip them very quickly into the sugar syrup and straight back into the iced water. Lift your fingers up and separate them to test the consistency. However, do not test in this way once the syrup has passed the hard crack stage as at this point it is burning hot.

SYRUP	TEMPERATURE	DESCRIPTION
Coating syrup	100°C (212°F)	Bring the water and sugar to the boil slowly over a low heat. If you dip a tablespoon in very quickly, the sugar syrup will spread and cover the back of it. At this stage the syrup is used for making babas, savarins, and fruit in syrup.
Small thread or small gloss	103–105°C (217–221°F)	The sugar syrup begins to thicken. If you take it between your wet fingers, it will make a very thin thread about 2–3mm (¹⁄₁₀–¹⁄₈in) thick that will break very easily. This syrup is used for making glacé fruits.
Large thread or large gloss	106–110°C (223–230°F)	When picked up between wet fingers, the syrup forms a thicker, stronger thread at this stage, about 5mm (¼in) thick. This syrup is used for glazing.
Small pearl	110–112°C (230–234°F)	The syrup produces small bubbles on the surface and a thick, solid thread between wet fingers. Used for making marshmallows.
Large pearl	113–115°C (235–239°F)	If you pull the syrup out with your wet fingers, it will make a long thread up to 2cm (¾in) long. Used for making marrons glacés.
Small or soft ball	116–125°C (241–257°F)	If you take a little syrup between wetted fingertips, it will form a soft, flat ball. Used for making buttercream, macaroons, Italian meringue, and nougat.
Hard ball	126–135°C (259–275°F)	When a little syrup is dropped into iced water the ball that forms does not collapse, as it is harder. Used for making caramel and sugar decorations.
Soft crack	136–140°C (277–284°F)	At this stage it is not used as it sticks to the teeth.
Hard crack	146–155°C (295–311°F)	Drop a little syrup into iced water; when the ball that forms is flattened between moistened fingers it is hard and brittle, but not sticky. It breaks easily. The sugar turns a pale straw yellow colour. Used for boiled sweets, sugar flowers, and spun sugar decorations.
Light caramel	156–165°C (313–329°F)	The syrup now contains hardly any water, and it is at this stage that it becomes caramel. Used for lining moulds and flavouring desserts and puddings.
Brown or dark caramel	166–175°C (331–347°F)	At this point the syrup takes on an intense caramel flavour as it has browned and lost its sweetening power. Used for flavouring creams, mousses, and ice creams.

Coating syrup

Small thread or small gloss

Light caramel

Dark caramel

CARAMEL SYRUP

If you want to make caramel successfully, it is best to add some liquid glucose (available from chemists) to the sugar to prevent crystallization. This recipe is for a coating caramel, which is suitable for dipping choux buns, lining moulds, and making caramel decorations.

Makes 500ml (17fl oz)

150ml (5fl oz) water
330g (12oz) caster sugar
120g (4oz) liquid glucose

1 Pour the water, sugar, and glucose into a heavy-based pan and stir together with a wooden spatula. Dissolve the sugar then bring to a boil. Use a wet pastry brush to wipe down the pan to stop grains of sugar becoming stuck, as this might make the syrup crystallize.

2 When the caramel is a light golden colour and coats the back of a tablespoon, stop the mixture cooking by plunging the base of the pan into a shallow bowl filled with cold water and ice cubes.

CARAMEL SAUCE

For an intense flavour, this sauce needs to be caramelized as much as possible.

Makes 300ml (10fl oz)

100ml (3½fl oz) liquid glucose
130g (4½oz) caster sugar
25g (scant 1oz) slightly salted butter
250ml (8½fl oz) softly whipped cream

1 Place the glucose in a heavy-based pan. Warm over a low heat without allowing it to boil or it will become sticky. Add the sugar and cook until the caramel is a lovely amber colour.

2 Remove the pan from the heat and whisk in the slightly salted butter and the whipped cream. Place the pan back over a low heat and bring gently to the boil (103°C/217°F). Allow the caramel to cool before serving.

CHEF'S TIPS

■ Always ensure the sugar has completely dissolved before bringing the syrup to the boil.

■ Do not stir the syrup once it has boiled.

■ You can add crème fraîche instead of whipped cream to the sauce, but the caramel will spatter more onto the sides of the pan.

■ Use a sugar thermometer to determine the exact temperature of the caramel.

EXOTIC FRUIT SALAD

Fruit salad always makes a light and refreshing end to a meal. As spirits and liqueurs tend to change the taste of the fruit, I have created a fresh, flavoursome syrup for this recipe.

Serves 8

For the exotic syrup

500ml (17fl oz) water

100g (3½oz) caster sugar

2 strips of unwaxed lemon zest, 6cm (2½in) long

2 strips of unwaxed orange zest, 6cm (2½in) long

1 vanilla pod

14 mint leaves

For the fruit salad

1 ruby red grapefruit

3 unwaxed oranges

1 small pineapple

3 mangoes

6 peaches

6 apricots

300g (10½oz) mixed red and black berries, such as strawberries, raspberries, redcurrants, blackberries, blueberries

1 Pour the water and sugar into a heavy-based pan. Add the lemon and orange zests. Split the vanilla pod and scrape out the seeds. Add the pod and seeds to the pan. Dissolve the sugar over a low heat, then bring to the boil. Whisk. Remove the pan from the heat and add the mint. Cover and leave to infuse for 30 minutes.

2 Remove the peel and pith from the grapefruit and oranges and segment using a sharp knife. Peel the pineapple and remove all the eyes with a sharp knife. Cut the pineapple lengthways into quarters and slice thinly. Peel the mangoes. Cut the peaches and apricots in half and remove the stones. Slice all these fruits thinly.

3 Transfer a mixture of these fruits to shallow serving plates. Sprinkle with the berries. Spoon over the very cold syrup and serve immediately.

FRUIT

■ To retain the full flavour and freshness of the fruit, prepare it just before serving.

■ I never include melon or bananas in a fruit salad as their flavours are too strong.

■ When they are in season, quartered figs and thin slices of peeled kiwi fruit can be added to the salad.

DIPPED FRUIT & NUTS

Fruit and nuts coated in sugar syrup are very easy to make. You can serve them as unusual pieces of confectionery, or use them to decorate cakes and desserts.

Serves 6–8

675g (1½lb) fruit and nuts, such as shelled almonds, kumquats, physalis (with their leaves opened out), black or white grapes, strawberries, blueberries

150ml (5fl oz) water

500g (1lb 2oz) caster sugar

150ml (5fl oz) liquid glucose

Sugar-dipped fruit are a refreshing alternative to dessert

CHOOSE THE BEST

■ Use only very sound fruit for dipping.
■ Wash the fruit before use and make sure it is well dried because the syrup will not stick to the surface of the fruit if it is damp.
■ Once dipped in syrup, these fruits will not keep for more than 5–6 hours.

1 Spear the pieces of fruit and the nuts onto the ends of cocktail sticks.

2 Place the water, sugar, and glucose in a heavy-based pan. Dissolve the sugar over a low heat and bring to the boil until the syrup reaches 155°C (311°F) – hard crack stage (p410). At this point, remove the pan from the heat and place in iced water.

3 Immediately, dip the fruit in the syrup, piece by piece, then spear them into oranges or grapefruit to set. When the syrup in the pan thickens, warm it through for a few minutes over a very low heat. Dipped fruit and nuts should be eaten on the day they are made.

CRÈME CHANTILLY

This simple cream is a classic accompaniment for desserts and it is used in many recipes, such as creams, mousses, or charlottes.

Makes 550ml (18fl oz)

500ml (17fl oz) very cold double cream or crème fraîche

30g (1oz) caster sugar

CHEF'S TIP

Use pasteurized, pouring, French crème fraîche, if available. However, double or whipping cream can be used instead. The cream must be very cold before you whip it, so always use it straight from the refrigerator. It will whip up faster and more easily if you place the bowl over a larger, shallow bowl filled with ice cubes.

1 Make sure that the cream is really cold by using it straight from the fridge. Pour the cream into a shallow bowl standing in another, larger bowl filled with ice cubes. Whip the cream with a balloon whisk or an electric whisk on medium speed until the cream thickens a little, slowly adding the sugar, whipping as you go.

2 Stop whipping once the cream is nearly firm but still fluffy. Chill until ready to use.

Chantilly ideas

All kinds of flavourings can be added to the basic Chantilly cream to create a pleasing harmony or contrast of flavours with the desserts the cream accompanies.

Coffee Chantilly

Bring 500ml (17fl oz) double cream or crème fraîche to the boil and add 30g (1oz) ground coffee. Leave to infuse for 15 minutes. Strain, then chill and whip as in the basic recipe.

Cinnamon Chantilly

Bring 500ml (17fl oz) double cream or crème fraîche to the boil and add a cinnamon stick. Cool and chill, then remove the cinnamon stick and whip as in the basic recipe. Delicious when served with muscat grapes.

Star anise Chantilly

Bring 500ml (17fl oz) double cream or crème fraîche to the boil and add 1½ star anises. Cool and chill, then remove the star anise and whip as in the basic recipe. Serve with sliced pineapple or raw figs and decorate with raspberries.

Vanilla Chantilly

Bring 500ml (17fl oz) double cream or crème fraîche to the boil. Halve 2 vanilla pods lengthways, scrape out the seeds and add these to the cream along with the pods. Leave to infuse for at least 30 minutes. Cool and chill, then strain and whip as in the basic recipe.

Fresh mint Chantilly

Bring 500ml (17fl oz) double cream or crème fraîche to the boil and stir in 30g (1oz) chopped mint leaves. Leave to infuse for 15 minutes. Strain and chill, then whip as in the basic recipe.

Other flavourings

The basic Chantilly can also be flavoured with a few drops of bitter almond extract or the finely grated zest of an unwaxed orange or lemon.

CHOCOLATE CHANTILLY CREAM

This silky chocolate cream is luscious with fresh fruit, when it can be served as a sweet dip. It can be used to fill meringues or biscuit cups.

Makes 500ml (17fl oz)

100g (3½oz) best-quality dark bitter chocolate (70–75 per cent cocoa solids)

500ml (17fl oz) crème fraîche or double cream

50g (1¾oz) caster sugar

1 Chop the pieces of chocolate very finely with a serrated edge knife.

2 Pour the crème fraîche and the sugar into a pan and bring to the boil. Remove the pan from the heat. Add the chocolate immediately, whisking vigorously. Pour the chocolate mixture into a shallow bowl and set aside to cool completely. Cover with cling film and chill the mixture for 6–8 hours.

3 Set the bowl of chocolate in a shallow bowl filled with ice cubes. Whip the chocolate cream with a balloon whisk or with an electric whisk on medium speed until firm and fluffy.

Milk chocolate Chantilly

Whisk 210g (7oz) very finely chopped good-quality milk chocolate into 300ml (10fl oz) boiling crème fraîche or double cream. Cool and chill, then whip as in the basic recipe.

TIP FOR SUCCESS

Good-quality chocolate is essential for making the best chocolate Chantilly cream. If possible, select Guanaja dark bitter chocolate, or Valrhona milk chocolate for the milk chocolate version.

CHANTILLY TUILE BASKETS

Crisp little biscuit baskets make ideal containers for smooth creams. Slightly sharp berries, such as raspberries or tiny wild strawberries, perfectly complement the baskets. Serve at coffee or teatime.

Makes 8

8 tuiles aux amandes effilées (p404), freshly baked and still soft

1 quantity of crème Chantilly or chocolate Chantilly cream (see left)

about 225g (8oz) raspberries

Shape the tuiles into baskets by placing them in small bowls or in little fluted brioche moulds while they are freshly baked and still soft. Fill with the crème Chantilly or chocolate Chantilly cream and top with raspberries.

Chantilly cream and fresh berries are enticing in crisp biscuit cups

HOT APPLE SABAYON

This recipe follows the general principle of a traditional sabayon, using apple juice rather than white wine to intensify the apple flavour. The recipe incorporates French pain d'épices: a sweet, spiced bread that usually also contains chopped almonds and candied peel. If you prefer, the cooled sabayon can be mixed into 120ml (4½fl oz) of whipped cream and served separately.

Serves 6

5 egg yolks
65g (2¼oz) caster sugar
150ml (5fl oz) apple juice
grated zest of ½ unwaxed orange
3tbsp lemon juice
small pinch of ground cardamom
½ cinnamon stick
½ tsp freshly grated ginger
3 grindings of black pepper
small pinch of salt (fleur de sel)

For the hot apple mixture

800g (1¾lb) Granny Smith apples
3tbsp lemon juice
60g (2oz) caster sugar

few drops of vanilla extract
90g (3oz) butter
80g (2¾oz) moist pain d'épices, or gingerbread, cut into 5mm (¼in) cubes
20g (½oz) flaked almonds, dry roasted (p480)
20g (½oz) pine nuts

1 Whisk the egg yolks and sugar in a bowl for 2 minutes. Place the apple juice in a pan with the orange zest, lemon juice, cardamom, cinnamon, ginger, pepper, and salt. Bring to the boil and strain. Pour one-quarter of the mixture over the egg and sugar. Whisk until frothy.

2 Pour the egg mixture into the pan containing the apple juice mixture and place over a medium heat, whisking constantly with a balloon whisk.

3 Keep whisking the mixture briskly until the sabayon thickens and becomes light and frothy. The mixture is ready when it leaves a trail when the whisk is lifted. Remove from the heat. Preheat the grill.

4 Peel, core, and dice the apples. Stir with the lemon juice, sugar, and vanilla. Melt half the butter in a frying pan. Brown the pain d'épices or gingerbread. Remove and keep warm. Heat the remaining butter in the pan over a high heat. Add the apple and brown all over. Sprinkle with the almonds, pine nuts, and gingerbread.

5 Arrange the apple mixture in neat mounds on individual flameproof plates. Spoon the sabayon over and place under a hot grill until golden. Alternatively, turn the sabayon into a non-metallic bowl and serve separately.

Sabayon turns golden under the heat of a grill

CRÈME PÂTISSIÈRE

Crème pâtissière, or pastry cream, is the classic custard-style filling for many desserts, such as profiteroles, éclairs, and the famous Gâteau St Honoré. It is also often used as a filling for Danish pastries. This cream is best made just before you are going to use it.

Makes about 300ml (10fl oz)

250ml (8½fl oz) full-fat milk
22.5g (scant 1oz) cornflour
62.5g (2¼oz) caster sugar
1 vanilla pod
3 egg yolks
25g (scant 1oz) butter at room temperature

1 Whisk the milk, cornflour, and 30g (1oz) of the sugar in a heavy-based pan. Split the vanilla pod in half lengthways and scrape out the seeds with the point of a sharp knife. Add the vanilla seeds and pod to the pan. Bring to the boil, whisking all the time.

2 In a bowl, whisk the egg yolks and remaining sugar. Pour the hot milk onto this mixture in a thin stream, whisking all the time. Transfer the mixture to a pan and bring just to the boil, whisking constantly, then immediately remove the pan from the heat.

4 When the sauce has cooled a little (to 60°C/140°F), add the pieces of butter, whisking briskly until they have melted and the sauce is smooth and shiny.

VARIATIONS

Chocolate crème pâtissière
Add 125g (4½oz) finely grated plain chocolate to the warm sauce in 3 batches. Stir until the sauce is smooth.

Coffee crème pâtissière
Dissolve 2.5g (½ tsp) instant coffee in 1tsp hot water and add 2 drops of natural coffee extract. Stir into the cream.

Alcoholic flavours
For a lift, flavour the cream with 1tbsp Cointreau, Grand Marnier, kirsch, or dark rum.

The finished crème pâtissière is smooth and glossy

ALMOND CREAM

3 Stand the pan in a shallow bowl filled with iced water. Remove the vanilla pod. Cut the butter into walnut-sized pieces on a plate.

Like crème pâtissière, almond cream is often used to fill cakes and pastries, including brioches and tartlets. It may also be baked, as in the classic Gâteau Pithiviers.

Makes about 800g (1¾lb)

135g (5oz) butter
165g (6oz) icing sugar
10g (¼oz) cornflour
165g (6oz) ground almonds
2 eggs
1 tbsp dark rum
200ml (7fl oz) crème fraîche

1 Cut the butter into pieces, then place the pieces in a bowl. Cream the butter with a spatula to soften it.

2 Combine the icing sugar, cornflour, and ground almonds together in another bowl. Sift the mixture into the softened butter and mix well. Add one egg, stirring with a spatula. Once it is well combined, add the other egg and mix again. Pour in the rum, followed by the crème fraîche, and mix until perfectly smooth. Cover with cling film and refrigerate. The cream will keep for 36–48 hours in the fridge or can be frozen until required.

CREAMING BUTTER

It is important to knead the butter without making it fluffy. If air is beaten in, the almond cream will rise during baking, but will collapse and lose its shape when it comes out of the oven.

CRÈME ANGLAISE (ENGLISH EGG CUSTARD)

This rich, thin vanilla custard is a wonderful sauce. Serve it warm or cold with many desserts. For the best result, flavour the milk the day before making, then chill the sauce overnight to allow the flavours to blend together.

Serves 10

2 vanilla pods
500ml (17fl oz) full-fat milk
500ml (17fl oz) crème fraîche
12 egg yolks
200g (7oz) caster sugar

1 Using a sharp knife, split the vanilla pod in half lengthways and scrape out the seeds.

2 Pour the milk and crème fraîche into a heavy pan and whisk to combine. Add the vanilla seeds and pod to the pan. Bring to the boil, then remove from the heat. Cover and allow the milk to cool completely, then put the pan in the fridge and leave to infuse overnight.

ICE CREAM BASE

Crème anglaise is used as the base for home-made ice cream. To make vanilla ice cream, pour the well-chilled crème anglaise into your ice cream maker and follow the manufacturer's instructions. If you do not have an ice cream maker, see p423.

3 The next day, remove the pan from the fridge and discard the vanilla pod. Bring the flavoured milk to the boil. Place the egg yolks and sugar in a bowl and whisk for 3 minutes. Pour the flavoured milk onto the egg mixture in a thin stream, whisking all the time.

4 Pour the egg and milk mixture back into the pan. Continue to whisk constantly over a medium heat until the mixture reaches a temperature of 85°C (185°F).

5 The custard is now thick enough to coat the back of a wooden spoon. Remove the pan from the heat and stir the custard very slowly for 4–5 minutes until it is smooth. Fill a large, shallow bowl with ice cubes. Place another, smaller bowl in the first and strain the custard into it. Allow to cool, stirring from time to time. Cover and chill the custard overnight so that the flavours blend successfully.

Aromatic vanilla crème anglaise pours like a thin cream.

CHEF'S TIPS

◼ If you are short of time, you can infuse the vanilla in the milk mixture for just 10 minutes rather than overnight, but the flavour won't be as pronounced.

◼ Use only fresh full-fat milk, as low-fat varieties simply don't give a rich enough flavour.

◼ Cook the sauce slowly or it will taste eggy.

◼ Crème anglaise is perfectly cooked when it is "à la rose". This is the point when you can blow on a wooden spoon coated with the sauce and it forms a perfect rosette.

◼ Once you have removed the sauce from the heat, stirring it slowly for 4–5 minutes gives it a superbly smooth texture.

CARAMEL ICE CREAM

Nothing beats home-made ice cream, especially when it has the superb flavour and texture of this recipe. It makes the perfect light dessert to round off an elegant dinner party. The salted butter balances the sweetness of the caramel, while bringing out its flavour. Serve the ice cream drizzled with caramel sauce (p411).

Makes 2 litres (3½ pints)

1 litre (1¾ pints) full-fat milk
300ml (10fl oz) crème fraîche
5 egg yolks
520g (1lb 3oz) caster sugar
70g (2½oz) slightly salted butter

1 The day before the ice cream is needed, whisk the milk and 100ml (3½fl oz) crème fraîche in a pan, then bring to the boil. Remove from the heat and cover. Whip the remaining crème fraîche to soft peaks. Whisk the egg yolks and 170g (6oz) sugar in a large, heavy pan.

5 Pour the caramel into the hot milk, whisking briskly.

2 Place 35g (1oz) caster sugar in a third, small, heavy-based pan. Melt the sugar gently over a low heat, then pour in another 35g (1oz) sugar. Repeat the process until all the sugar has been used up. Cook until the caramel turns a good dark amber colour.

3 Remove from the heat and add the butter, stirring it in a figure of eight with a whisk or wooden spoon.

4 Add the whipped crème fraîche to the pan and whisk well.

6 Pour this caramel milk over the egg yolk and sugar mixture, stirring it all together. Cook the mixture, whisking well, until it is thick enough to coat the back of a spatula or wooden spoon. Cool the cream over ice as for a crème anglaise (p420). Chill overnight.

7 The following day, transfer the caramel cream to an ice cream maker and follow the manufacturer's instructions. If you do not have a machine, see right. Serve the finished ice cream in scoops drizzled with caramel sauce.

ICE CREAM TIPS

■ It is possible to make ice cream by hand if you don't have an ice cream maker in your kitchen. Follow the steps given here up to the end of step 6. The following day, pour the mixture into a shallow freezerproof container and freeze until mushy. Turn the mixture into a cold bowl and beat until the ice crystals are broken up. Return to the container and freeze again until mushy. Repeat the whisking and freezing once more.

■ To make up a delicious sundae, serve scoops of caramel ice cream together with scoops of dark chocolate mousse (p431).

ROSE ICE CREAM

This pretty pale pink, delicately flavoured ice cream is the perfect dessert for a warm summery day.

Makes 1 litre (1¾ pints)

750ml (1¼pints) full-fat milk

200ml (7fl oz) crème fraîche

12 egg yolks

200g (7oz) caster sugar

100ml (3½fl oz) rosehip syrup

50ml (3tbsp) rose water

EXTRA SPECIAL DESSERTS

■ I like to make my favourite dessert with rose ice cream. For 4 people, arrange 12 fresh figs on a baking tray, dredge with caster sugar, sprinkle with a few drops of lemon juice, 85g (3oz) butter, 3tbsp water, a vanilla pod halved lengthways, and a small cinnamon stick and bake in the oven at 230°C (450°F, gas 8) for 20 minutes. Remove the figs from the oven and arrange on 4 plates. Coat the figs with the juice produced during cooking, add a scoop of rose ice cream and surround with fresh, crushed raspberries.

■ I also like to make up a sundae with scoops of rose ice cream, caramel ice cream, and lychee sorbet.

1 Whisk the milk and crème fraîche together and boil. Cool completely. Whisk the egg yolks and sugar in a bowl. Pour the milk onto the yolks in a thin stream, whisking, then pour back into the pan. Whisk over a medium heat until thick enough to coat the back of a wooden spoon. Cool on ice as for crème anglaise (p420).

2 Stir in the rosehip syrup and rose water. Chill overnight. Freeze as for caramel ice cream (p422). Serve the ice cream in scoops with "fairies' fingers" (p427).

MINT ICE CREAM

Don't be tempted to use dried mint in this recipe. Only fresh mint effectively imparts its distinctive flavour to this refreshing ice cream.

Makes 1 litre (1¾ pints)

bunch of mint, about 55g (2oz)

500ml (17fl oz) full-fat milk

100ml (3½fl oz) crème fraîche

6 egg yolks

120g (4oz) caster sugar

3–4 grindings of black pepper

1 Remove the mint leaves from the stalks. Set a quarter aside in the fridge and roughly chop the rest. Whisk the milk and crème fraîche together in a pan, then bring to the boil. Remove from the heat. Stir in the chopped mint, cover, and infuse for 5–6 minutes. Strain, and discard the mint leaves.

2 Place the egg yolks and sugar in another heavy-based pan. Beat for 3 minutes. Pour the infused milk in a thin stream onto the egg and sugar mixture, beating as you go. Place the pan over a medium heat and cook the cream, beating constantly, until it reaches 85°C (185°F). Season with black pepper. Remove from the heat and stir for 3–4 minutes.

3 Stand the pan in a shallow bowl filled with ice cubes. Add half the reserved mint leaves, chopped coarsely. Mix with a hand-held blender. Cover and leave in the fridge overnight.

4 The following day transfer the mixture to an ice cream machine and follow the manufacturer's instructions. If you do not have a machine, see p423. Once the ice cream starts to become firm, add the remaining coarsely chopped mint leaves.

CHEF'S TIPS

■ Do not infuse the mint for longer than indicated because it adversely affects the flavour and colour.
■ Fresh mint ice cream is best eaten on the day it is made, when its flavour is at its most intense. However, it can be kept frozen for a week.

Serve the ice cream in scoops with finger meringues (p427)

RASPBERRY SORBET

Refreshing and fruity, this sorbet makes a melt-in-the-mouth treat on a hot summer day. As the fruit content in this recipe is very high, it is essential to use only top-quality raspberries to ensure a wonderful flavour.

Makes 1 litre (1¾ pints)

150g (5½oz) caster sugar
50ml (3tbsp) mineral water
900g (2lb) raspberries
15g (1tbsp) lemon juice

1 Pour the sugar and water into a heavy-based pan and place over a low heat until the sugar has dissolved. Bring to the boil. Cool. When the syrup is cold, add the raspberries and lemon juice. Purée the mixture in a food processor.

2 Strain the puréed raspberries through a fine sieve. Transfer the mixture to an ice cream machine and follow the manufacturer's instructions. Alternatively, see p423. Serve in scoops.

BITTER CHOCOLATE SORBET

For the best result I use bitter chocolate rather than cocoa powder because it has a cleaner flavour.

Serves 6–8

200g (7oz) best-quality dark bitter chocolate (70–75 per cent cocoa solids)
160g (5½oz) caster sugar
500ml (17fl oz) mineral water
chocolate curls to decorate

1 Chop the chocolate coarsely using a serrated edge knife. Dissolve the sugar in the water in a large pan over a low heat. Bring to the boil. Add the chocolate and stir continuously for 2 minutes as the mixture will make a lot of froth.

2 Stand the pan in a shallow bowl of iced water and leave the mixture to cool completely, stirring from time to time.

3 Transfer the mixture to an ice cream machine and follow the manufacturer's instructions. Alternatively, see p423. Serve the sorbet in scoops, topped with chocolate curls.

MAKING FRENCH MERINGUE

Some people like meringue to be crunchy and caramelized; others prefer it soft and yielding. However you like it, these crisp, light-as-air meringue fingers and shells can be used as a base for all kinds of desserts, or just served simply with fresh fruit and cream.

Makes enough for about four 20cm (8in) discs, or 30 fingers or small shells

8 egg whites

500g (1lb 2oz) caster sugar

seeds from 2–3 vanilla pods (p420)

CHEF'S TIPS

■ It is best to leave the egg whites in a covered bowl for 2–3 days at room temperature. They will liquefy a little, and be easier to whisk and less likely to collapse.
■ For dry heat and best results, prop the oven door open with a spoon while the meringues are drying.

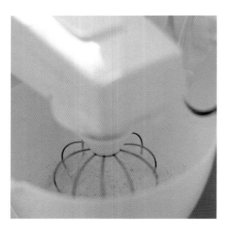

1 Place the egg whites in a large bowl and whisk on medium speed, gradually adding half the sugar and all the vanilla seeds.

2 Continue whisking until the egg whites are shiny, smooth, and very firm.

3 Gradually fold in the rest of the sugar, lifting the egg whites up with a rubber spatula, but working them as little as possible.

Piping & baking meringue shapes

Pipe the meringue shapes onto a baking sheet lined with parchment paper and bake in a preheated 120°C (225°F) oven. Then turn off the oven, prop open the oven door slightly with a wooden spoon, and let the meringue shapes dry for at least 8 hours or overnight.

Discs or layers
Use a pastry bag fitted with a No. 9 star tip. Pipe the meringue in a spiral, starting in the centre, to make a disc about 20cm (8in) in diameter. Bake for 1 hour and 20 minutes, then let dry.

Shells
Use a pastry bag fitted with a No. 14/16 round tip. Pipe the meringue in dollops about 7.5cm (3in) in diameter. Bake for 1 hour and 10 minutes (when a shell is broken open, the centre should be slightly golden), then let dry.

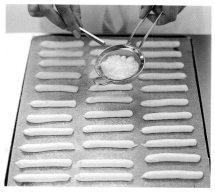

Fingers
Use a pastry bag fitted with a No. 10 round tip. Pipe the meringue in thin sticks about 7.5cm (3in) long. Dust lightly with icing sugar. Bake for 30–35 minutes, then let dry. I call these meringue sticks "fairies' fingers".

Perfectly cooked meringues are slightly golden in the centre

 MERINGUE TIPS

■ To test that the consistency of egg whites whisked to soft peaks is correct "blancs au bec d'oiseau" – "bird's beak whites", use an old trick of the trade. Dip your fingertips into the whites. When you remove them, the whites should hang off your fingers in the hooked shape of an eagle's beak.

■ Whatever shape you are making, you can "pearl" the meringues by sprinkling them with a fine coating of icing sugar before baking. When cooked, the meringues will be covered with little golden balls that are attractive to the eye and the palate. Bake for about 15 minutes until the meringues develop a light crust, then sprinkle them lightly with icing sugar and return to the oven to finish baking.

DARK CHOCOLATE TRUFFLES WITH LIME & HONEY

Surprisingly simple to create, these delicious truffles are made from a slightly bitter ganache – a richly flavoured cream that is also used to fill cakes and decorate desserts.

Makes about 50

95g (3½oz) butter

440g (1lb) best-quality dark chocolate (60–70 per cent cocoa solids)

325ml (11fl oz) crème fraîche

zest of 1 lime

50g (3tbsp) lime juice

50g (1¾oz) acacia honey

For the coating

finely grated zest of ½ lime

120g (4½oz) caster sugar

120g (4½oz) cocoa powder

1 Prepare the coating the day before it is needed. Mix the lime zest with the sugar and rub between the palms of your hands. Spread in a thin layer on a non-stick baking tray and leave to dry overnight at room temperature.

2 The following day, cut the butter into walnut-sized pieces, place in a bowl, and leave to soften to room temperature. Chop the chocolate into small pieces with a serrated edge knife and place in a large bowl.

3 Bring the crème fraîche to the boil in a pan. Finely grate the lime zest into the crème fraîche. Remove from the heat, cover, and leave to infuse for 10 minutes. Return the pan to the heat and bring back just to the boil. Remove from the heat.

4 Pour the lime juice and honey into another small pan. Warm without boiling.

 CHEF'S TIPS

■ Truffles that have not been rolled in cocoa powder can be stored for 2 weeks in the fridge in an airtight box. Remove from the fridge and the container two hours before serving.

■ This ganache can also be used as the basis of a chocolate sauce and drizzled over desserts, such as poached fruits and ice cream.

6 Once the ganache is smooth, slowly add the pieces of butter, stirring them gently into the mixture. Chill for at least 30 minutes until the ganache has thickened.

7 Stir the ganache gently before pouring into a piping bag fitted with a No.9 plain nozzle. Pipe balls of ganache onto a baking tray lined with baking parchment. Chill for 2 hours.

5 Pour half of the infused, boiling cream over the chocolate, stirring with a wooden spoon. Start at the centre with small circles, then move outwards. Add the rest of the infused cream and repeat the stirring process. Add the lime juice and honey mixture.

8 Mix the cocoa powder with the lime-flavoured sugar, making sure that the sugar is perfectly dry. Spread over a tray with a raised edge. Using a fork, roll the balls of ganache in the powder. Remove with a slotted spoon, then place in a sieve to remove the excess coating. Store in an airtight box.

Milk chocolate truffles with passion fruit

An intriguing combination of flavours makes these truffles sweet with just a hint of acidity.

Makes about 70

700g (1lb 9oz) good-quality milk chocolate

100g (3½oz) butter

20 passion fruits

40g (1½oz) acacia or flower honey

cocoa powder for coating

Shake off excess cocoa powder

Cut the butter into walnut-sized pieces, place in a shallow bowl, and leave to soften to room temperature. Chop the chocolate finely with a serrated edge knife.

Line the bottom and sides of a large rectangular dish with baking parchment.

Cut the passion fruits in half. Remove the flesh with a teaspoon, placing it in a sieve set over a shallow bowl to collect the juice. Pour the passion fruit juice and honey into a pan and bring to the boil. Add the chopped chocolate a handful at a time. Stir it gently with a wooden spoon, starting from the centre and gradually working outwards.

Once the chocolate mixture is well combined, add the butter a little at a time and stir as before. Pour the ganache into the prepared dish. Chill and leave to set for about 2 hours.

Place a sheet of baking parchment on the work surface. Remove the ganache by pulling the edges of the paper, then turn it over onto the baking parchment on the work surface. Cut the ganache into small 2.5x1cm (1x½in) rectangles.

Sift the cocoa powder onto a baking tray. Turn the truffles in the cocoa powder one by one, pushing them with a fork. Remove with a slotted spoon and place in a sieve in order to remove the excess cocoa.

DARK CHOCOLATE MOUSSE

This simple-to-make mousse has a smooth, silky texture and rich chocolate flavour. An essential lightness is achieved by whisking and folding in stages. Decorate the finished dish with dark chocolate flakes, whole or crushed raspberries, finely chopped mint, or caramelized crushed hazelnuts.

170g (6oz) dark bitter chocolate (67–70 per cent cocoa solids)
80ml (3fl oz) full-fat milk
1 egg yolk
4 egg whites
20g (¾oz) caster sugar

1 Chop the chocolate with a serrated edge knife. Place the chocolate in a shallow heatproof bowl over a pan of simmering water until it has completely melted. Remove from the pan.

2 Bring the milk to the boil. Pour onto the melted chocolate, stirring with a whisk. Add the egg yolk and mix thoroughly. Check the temperature by dipping a fingertip in the chocolate. It should feel hot (40°C/104°F) but not burning. Allow to cool.

3 Whisk the egg whites to firm peaks, adding the sugar pinch by pinch. Fold one-third of the whites into the chocolate. Whisk briskly, then fold in the rest of the whites, lifting the mousse from the middle of the bowl up and outwards and holding the bowl with the other hand, turning it round as you go.

4 Pour the mousse into individual cups or dishes or one large serving bowl. Chill for 1 hour before serving. Decorate the finished dish with chocolate curls.

CHEF'S TIPS

■ It's important to use a good-quality chocolate with a high percentage of cocoa solids for this recipe.
■ The egg whites should be very fresh. Use them cold, but not icy, and not at room temperature either.
■ If serving chocolate mousse in small cups, use a piping bag to fill the cups neatly.
■ You can flavour the milk by adding some orange zest, 1tsp of ground Ceylon cinnamon, a pinch of cardamom, or a few twists of freshly ground Sichuan pepper.

CAKES

Stephan Franz
STEPHAN FRANZ

Sweet-tasting foods have always been among life's pleasures. While not indispensable for man's survival they have, in the truest sense, sweetened our existence. Although our forebears were familiar with the sweetness of honey and fruits, they could not have dreamed of the baked pleasures to come. In 15th century Germany, the word "Torte" was already in use for round, salted, savoury pastries, but sweet "Torten" did not appear there until the 19th century. The word itself stems from the Latin "tortus", meaning "turned" or "wound".

Offerings to impress Sweet pastries were popularized by the newly prosperous burghers of the German industrial age, who were able to afford the expensive and luxurious ingredients. Wanting to show off their new-found wealth, the burghers emulated the royal households by ordering fine pastries and confections from the same bakers that served the nobility. Indeed, entertaining friends at "Kaffee Kränzchen", or coffee gatherings, became so popular that hostesses would vie with each other to offer their guests increasingly elaborate and fine fare. Still today in Germany, a home-baked cake is a highly appreciated gift for loved ones, and a special treat for oneself.

Austria gained a fine reputation for its bakery much earlier. Influences from eastern European countries, Arabia, and France were strongly reflected in Austrian culture and folk history, and the traditions of foreign kitchens were also evident in Austrian cuisine, particularly in cakes and pastries. The art of baking was held in such high esteem that a head pastry chef at one of the royal courts was actually decorated as a general. The first known recipe for a chocolate cake originated in Austria, in 1778. Later, at the court of Chancellor Lothar Metternich in 1832, a chef's apprentice, Franz Sacher, created Europe's most famous chocolate Torte, the Sachertorte. This complicated and inspired creation, consisting of flavoured sponge layers sandwiched with a thin layer of apricot jam and covered by a shiny glaze of rich, dark chocolate, is now baked in professional Viennese kitchens and despatched around the world; the recipe features in the following chapter.

The more formal "afternoon tea" that Lady Bedford devised in England in 1840 gave renewed impetus to cake making. Lady Bedford's social circle, finding the interval between lunch and dinner to be too long, craved some refreshment, especially something sweet, in the late afternoon. Lady Bedford's innovation, also known as "five o'clock tea", was to become the essence of English tea culture. It was an excuse for friends to meet each afternoon and share a cup of tea with a pastry or shortbread. The upper classes celebrated this repast between luncheon and dinner in grand style. Fine table linen, a silver tea service, and expensive porcelain decorated the table. Cucumber sandwiches and small cakes were served and scones became increasingly popular.

Modern-day cakes The cost of ingredients and basic foodstuffs is not such an important consideration today and baked confections have been adapted to meet the demands of our diet-conscious society. The elaborately prepared, layered buttercream gâteaux of earlier times very often have been replaced by lighter concoctions of cream and fruit, and small, delicate creations are preferred to larger and richer fare. Baking at home has become popular again, and the arts of our ancestors are appreciated once more. Children exchange recipes with their parents and grandparents, and grandmothers are explaining the detail of great-grandmothers' recipes. In Europe baking has customarily been part of the celebrations for Christmas, Easter, and children's birthdays, and the preparations for the forthcoming feast are just as important as the event itself.

Baking has its history and traditions, but it also reflects the spirit of our time. While some new confections pay homage to the preferences and styles of the past, they are often lighter than the old classics. In the recipes that follow, I have adapted some of the traditional techniques so that the final products benefit from simpler, more contemporary baking methods.

SPONGE CAKES

All sponge mixtures are rich in egg content, but the texture of the finished cake depends on the method and other ingredients used. Fatless sponges such as roulades are light and fluffy, ideal to hold a simple cream or jam filling. But when a firmer structure is needed, capable of soaking up flavoured syrups or supporting fresh seasonal fruits without collapsing, then a genoese sponge made with butter, whisked over heat, is most suitable. Heavier, richer mixtures have more than 20 per cent butter content.

GENOESE SPONGE

This light sponge is the base for many layered cakes, such as Frankfurter kranz (p446) and Stephan's cheesecake (p451). When beating over heat the temperature of the mixture should be 45°C (113°F) and must never exceed 50°C (122°F), otherwise the texture becomes like straw rather than moist. A digital or glass thermometer can be used to check the temperature. Or, test by putting a finger into the egg mixture and it should feel just hotter than bath water. There is no need to grease the sides of the tin as the dry surface stops the cake shrinking and losing shape as it cools.

Makes a 26cm (10½in) sponge

110g (4oz) plain white flour
90g (3¼oz) potato flour
6 medium eggs, 300g (10½oz) in total
180g (6½oz) caster sugar
20g (⅝oz) acacia honey
grated zest of ½ lemon
60g (2¼oz) unsalted butter, melted and cooled to lukewarm

1 Preheat the oven to 190°C (375°F, gas 5). Line the bottom of a 26cm (10½in) springform cake tin with baking parchment. Sift together the plain and potato flours twice, then sift onto a sheet of greaseproof paper. Set aside.

VARIATION

To prepare a dark genoese sponge, substitute half the potato flour with 45g(1½oz) cocoa powder. Reduce the amount of butter to 50g (1¾oz) and add 1tbsp water to the eggs before beating. Use grated orange zest instead of lemon.

2 Put the eggs into a heatproof bowl, add the sugar, honey, and a pinch of salt. Set the bowl over a pan of barely simmering water and whisk until the mixture is more than double in volume, and is thick, pale, and creamy. Be sure that the base of the bowl does not touch the water or the eggs will overcook.

3 Lift the bowl off the heat and whisk at high speed until the mixture has cooled and falls from the whisk in a thick ribbon. Add the grated lemon zest and continue whisking at half speed for 15 minutes with an electric hand-held mixer. The longer beating helps stabilize the eggs so they keep their volume.

4 Using a large spatula, gently fold large spoonfuls of the sifted flours into the beaten mixture until well blended. Stir 2–3tbsp of the mixture into the butter then, working quickly and taking care not to lose any volume, fold the two mixtures together until combined.

5 Pour the mixture straight into the prepared cake tin and lightly smooth the surface. Place in the preheated oven and reduce the temperature to 175°C (350°F, gas 4). Bake for 30–40 minutes until golden brown, light and springy to the touch.

6 Remove from the oven and leave to cool for 10 minutes. Slide a knife around the edge of the tin to loosen the cake. Pull back the clip of the springform to release the ring and lift it away. Remove the cake from the base and peel off the lining paper. Cool on a wire rack.

CUTTING & FILLING

An unfilled genoese sponge will keep fresh in the fridge for 3–4 days, it also freezes very well. When topped or filled it is best eaten on the day of making. The plainess of a genoese lends itself to the contrast of rich, creamy, or fruity fillings. To serve very simply, just spread a topping over the cake and cut into wedges. Genoese sponge is delicious when moistened with a flavoured syrup as in Frankfurter kranz (p446).

1 Put the cake on a firm level surface. For a simple filled cake cut into 2 layers, place a hand lightly on top to hold it steady. Use a sharp, long-bladed serrated edge knife to score a guideline round the sides, then slice through the cake, carefully following the guideline.

2 Using a spatula or the base of a tart tin to help you, carefully lift the layer and place it on a flat surface while you fill the cake. For more layers slice the sponge into 3 or 4 depending on its depth. Sometimes when the sponge is chilled the skin on top becomes soft. This should be carefully removed before cutting into layers.

QUICK & EASY FILLINGS

■ Sweetened whipped cream with fresh fruit such as red berries, grapes, and sliced kiwi fruit.
■ A thick layer of home-made or good-quality jam or lemon curd is simple but mouthwatering.
■ Flavoured buttercream.
■ For a topping, place thin strips of baking parchment at slight angles across the top of the cake. Dredge liberally with icing sugar. Carefully remove the strips to reveal the pattern, as for Roulade, p438.

Place a thin strip of greaseproof paper along the top of the roll, sieve over icing sugar and then carefully remove the paper strip

SPONGE ROULADE

This basic fatless sponge is best for thick, filled roulades or swiss rolls. Fillings such as strained strawberry, cherry, or apricot jam are delicious, as well as sweet whipped and flavoured creams. The sponge is made using the cold, separated egg method. It keeps fresh for a day. A roulade is less likely to tear if filled with jam and rolled up while still warm and flexible. Alternatively, roll with a sheet of baking parchment between and then cool before unrolling, removing the paper, and filling with cream. For a chocolate roulade, replace 1tbsp potato flour with cocoa powder and sift together with the plain flour.

Makes a 40x28cm (16x11in) roulade

50g (1¾oz) plain white flour

55g (2oz) potato flour, sifted

5 medium egg yolks, 100g (3½oz) in total

2tsp vanilla sugar

grated zest of ½ lemon

4 medium egg whites, 115g (4oz) in total

75g (2½oz) caster sugar

icing sugar for dusting

For the filling

90g (3oz) raspberry jam, strained and warmed

GRATING LEMON ZEST

Lay a sheet of baking parchment on the cutting surface of the grater. Rub the lemon across it and the zest will fall straight off without getting trapped in the cutter.

1 Preheat the oven to 200°C (400°F, gas 6). Line a 40x28cm (16x11in) baking tray or swiss roll tin with baking parchment. Sift the plain flour and 25g (scant 1oz) of the potato flour together twice and place on a sheet of greaseproof paper. Set aside.

2 Using a balloon whisk or hand-held electric mixer whisk together the egg yolks and the vanilla sugar until the mixture is pale, creamy, and falls in a thick ribbon. Stir in the lemon zest.

3 Place the egg whites, caster sugar, 30g (1oz) of the potato flour and a pinch of salt in a clean bowl and whisk together, with an electric beater set at medium speed, until the mixture is white and creamy, forms soft peaks, and has at least doubled in volume. This creates a foam that has a strong structure that will not collapse when the egg yolks and flours are folded in.

4 Using a spatula, fold one-third of the egg white mixture into the yolk mixture and gently mix together. Using a large spatula, fold this mixture into the remaining egg whites, taking care not to lose any air. Again taking care not to lose any air, carefully fold in the flours.

5 Turn the mixture out onto the baking tray and spread lightly to within 2cm (¾in) of the edge. Bake for 12–15 minutes until golden, light, and springy to the touch. Remove from the oven and sprinkle with caster sugar, cover with a clean sheet of baking parchment, and carefully turn the roulade over onto a clean tea towel.

6 Gently peel away the lining paper, pressing down onto it with a ruler to avoid tearing the cake. Spread the warm jam evenly over the sponge to within 2cm (¾in) of the edge. Support the roulade with the under paper and roll up with gentle pressure.

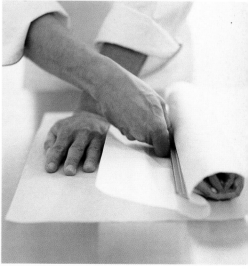

7 Lay the roulade on a spare sheet of paper and flap one end of paper over it. Hold the bottom of the paper with your left hand and push the ruler against the roll with your free hand. The paper will wrap tightly around the roll to give a good even shape. Remove the paper, cover, and refrigerate for 2 hours. Trim the ends.

2 Preheat the oven to 160°C (325°F, gas 3). Sift the plain flour again onto a sheet of greaseproof paper. Beat together the butter, potato flour, vanilla sugar, and lemon zest until thick and creamy.

3 Put the eggs, caster sugar, honey, and a pinch of salt into a large bowl and set over a pan of simmering water. Using a hand-held electric mixer whisk until pale and creamy. Lift off the water and beat for 5 minutes more, on the highest speed, until cooled. Turn the speed to low and beat 10–15 minutes longer.

4 Stir one-third of the egg mixture into the creamed butter to lighten it then gently fold in the remainder using a large spatula. Finally fold in the flour.

5 Spoon the mixture into the prepared tin and bake for 50 minutes until risen and golden brown. Test with a skewer, which should come out clean. Remove from the oven and leave for 10 minutes before turning out onto a wire rack. Dust with icing sugar to serve.

POUND CAKE

A traditional recipe in which each of the dry ingredients and the eggs weigh the same pound for pound. It is a firm favourite in the baker's repertoire. The texture is delicate, short, and crumbly and the sweet buttery taste is good plain or with added fruits, nuts, or chocolate.

Makes a 23cm (9in) kugelhopf or a 1 litre (1¾ pint) loaf cake

3tbsp toasted fine breadcrumbs
140g (5oz) plain white flour, sifted twice
175g (6oz) unsalted butter, softened
35g (1¼oz) potato flour, sifted
4tsp vanilla sugar
grated zest of ½ lemon
3 large eggs, 175g (6oz) in total
140g (5oz) caster sugar
2tsp clear honey
icing sugar for dusting

1 Prepare a 23cm (9in) kugelhopf mould or a 1 litre (1¾ pint) loaf tin. Brush with melted butter to within 1cm (½in) of the top edge. Dust with the breadcrumbs or with flour. If using the loaf tin, line it with baking parchment.

VARIATIONS

Try adding any of the following:
- 60g (2oz) raisins, steeped overnight in 2tbsp rum.
- 60g (2oz) finely chopped best-quality dark chocolate (70 per cent cocoa solids).
- 60g (2oz) chopped walnuts, roasted hazelnuts, or macadamia nuts.

Lightly fold them into the prepared cake mixture before spooning into the tin for baking.

APRICOT STREUSEL CRUMBLE CAKE

Pound cake mixture and fresh fruits taste delicious baked together in a tray, especially with the crumble topping. Other fresh fruits to use are cherries, apples, and pears.

Makes a 23x28cm (9x11in) cake

For stewing fresh apricots

750g (1lb 10oz) fresh apricots, halved and stoned

sprig of fresh thyme

1 juniper berry

500ml (17fl oz) water

300g (10½oz) granulated sugar

For the streusel

140g (5oz) chilled unsalted butter, diced

100g (3½oz) caster sugar

50g (1¾oz) marzipan, finely chopped

grated zest of ½ lemon

seeds of ½ vanilla pod

pinch of ground cinnamon

250g (8½oz) strong plain white flour, sifted

For the pound cake mixture

300g (10½oz) plain white flour

1 rounded tsp baking powder

80g (3oz) marzipan, finely chopped

6 medium eggs, 300g (10½oz) in total

225g (8oz) unsalted butter, diced and softened

225g (8oz) caster sugar

30g (1oz) liquid glucose

seeds of ½ vanilla pod

grated zest of ½ orange

grated zest of ½ lemon

50g (1¾oz) flaked almonds

1 The day before, place the fruit, thyme, and juniper berry in a heatproof bowl. Bring the water and sugar slowly to the boil, stirring until the sugar is dissolved. Pour over the fruit and leave for 24 hours. Drain the fruit and remove the loosened skins. Pat dry with kitchen paper.

2 Use a baking tin with 4cm (1¾in) sides or a 23x28cm (9x11in) roasting pan. Grease with butter. Line the bottom with baking parchment.

3 For the streusel, place the butter, sugar, marzipan, a pinch of salt, lemon zest, vanilla seeds, and cinnamon into a bowl and knead together until smooth. Sift over the flour and rub in between the fingers (do not knead) to make a light, crumbly pastry.

4 Preheat the oven to 220°C (425°F, gas 7). For the pound cake mixture, sift together twice the flour, baking powder, and a pinch of salt onto a sheet of greaseproof paper. Set aside.

5 Place the marzipan and 1 egg (50g/1¾oz) in the bowl of an electric mixer or use a hand-held electric mixer. Beat well to form a smooth paste. Add the butter and sugar and beat until lump-free. Beat in the glucose.

6 Add the remaining eggs one at a time. Beat the mixture very thoroughly after each egg is added so that the batter is completely absorbed and the mixture is smooth and shiny. Mix in the vanilla seeds and the orange and lemon zests. Carefully fold in the flour using a large spatula.

7 With a palette knife, spread the mixture evenly over the prepared cake tin. Arrange the apricots on top, closely together and cut-side up. Sprinkle over the streusel mixture. Finish with flaked almonds.

8 Place in the oven and reduce the temperature to 175°C (350°F, gas 4). Bake for 45 minutes. Remove from the oven and leave to cool in the tin. Dust with icing sugar to serve.

RICH FRUIT LOAF

This classic English fruitcake is unusually finished with a wrapping of sponge roulade – the differing textures give a pleasing crunch. If you do not wish to wrap the fruitcake in roulade, you can use marzipan or it is equally good left plain. It will keep for one week.

Makes a 1kg (2¼lb) fruit loaf

40g (1½oz) chopped almonds, lightly toasted

80g (3oz) sultanas

80g (3oz) raisins

60g (2oz) candied orange peel, finely chopped

60g (2oz) candied lemon peel, finely chopped

120g (4oz) glacé cherries, halved

3tbsp dark rum

50g (1¾oz) dark cooking chocolate (70 per cent cocoa solids), finely chopped

50g (1¾oz) hard nougat, finely chopped

40g (1½oz) plain white flour

For the cake mixture

200g (7oz) plain white flour

1 rounded tsp baking powder

80g (3oz) marzipan, finely chopped

5 medium eggs, 250g (8½oz) in total

200g (7oz) unsalted butter, diced and softened

120g (4½oz) caster sugar

3tbsp golden syrup

seeds of 1 vanilla pod

grated zest of 1 lemon

5 drops of bitter almond extract

To finish (optional)

150ml (5fl oz) apricot brandy or Cognac

150g (5½oz) apricot jam, boiled and strained

1 half quantity of sponge roulade (p584) or 500g (1lb 2oz) marzipan

80g (3oz) flaked almonds, lightly toasted

LINING THE TIN

Brush a 1kg (2¼lb) loaf tin with melted butter and dust with flour. Turn the tin over and cut a piece of baking parchment to fit the bottom and place in the tin.

1 The day before, stir together the almonds, dried fruits, candied peels, glacé cherries, and rum in a bowl. Cover and leave overnight in a warm place. Place the chocolate and nougat pieces in a bowl, cover, and refrigerate.

2 For the cake mixture, sift the flour and baking powder together twice, then sift again onto a sheet of greaseproof paper. Using a hand-held mixer beat the marzipan and 1 egg (50g/1¾oz) until smooth. Add the butter, sugar, and golden syrup and beat well.

3 Lightly whisk the remaining eggs. Add the eggs, a little at a time, to the mixture, beating well after each addition. Mix in the vanilla seeds, lemon zest, and almond extract. Gently fold in the flour in three batches. Preheat the oven to 220°C (425°F, gas 7).

4 Mix together the dried fruits, peels, cherries, chocolate, and nougat, and coat with the flour. Fold into the main mixture. Pour into the tin (see left), smooth the top, and place in the oven. Reduce temperature to 170°C (325°F gas 3).

5 Gently open the oven door after 15 minutes. Dip a knife tip in oil and make a shallow cut along the top of the cake to stop the mixture peaking.

6 After 50 minutes, insert a skewer into the centre, if it comes out with no mixture sticking to it, then the cake is ready. Remove the cake from the oven and turn out onto a wire rack. To serve, simply wrap in foil and keep for a few days before slicing.

7 If you wish to wrap the cake as shown, lightly warm the apricot brandy in a pan, put a match to it, and spoon the flaming spirit straight over the warm cake.

8 Trim the cake sides flat, brush with warm apricot glaze, and wrap the roulade or marzipan around it. Brush with remaining glaze and stud with flaked almonds.

MARBLE CAKE

An unusual and easy cake, which can be made from ingredients easily found in your cupboard. Popular in Europe and the USA where it is often called tiger cake.

Makes a 1kg (2¼lb) cake

10g (¼oz) cocoa powder
2tbsp milk
110g (4oz) plain white flour
40g (1½oz) potato flour
½tsp baking powder
80g (3oz) clarified butter (p26)
80ml (3fl oz) corn oil
140g (5oz) icing sugar, sifted
2tsp vanilla sugar, sifted
grated zest of ½ lemon
3 large eggs, 175g (6oz) in total
icing sugar for dusting

1 Use a 1kg (2¼lb) loaf tin, brush the bottom and just two-thirds up the sides with melted butter, then dust with flour. Leaving the top edge ungreased stops the mixture overflowing and gives the finished cake a better look.

2 Mix together the cocoa powder and milk to make a smooth paste. Set aside. Sift the flours, a pinch of salt, and the baking powder together twice, then place on a sheet of greaseproof paper. Preheat the oven to 220°C (425°F, gas 7).

VARIATION

For lemon cake, omit the cocoa, add 1tbsp lemon zest and 2tbsp chopped candied peel. Mix together 125g (4½oz) icing sugar, 4tsp dried milk powder, and 5tsp lemon juice and pour over the cake.

3 Heat the butter and oil very gently in a pan until warm. In a large bowl, combine the icing and vanilla sugar and the lemon zest. Add the butter and oil and mix well with a hand-held electric mixer.

4 Add the eggs one at a time, combine well, then mix in portions of flour, beating well between additions. Beat for 5 minutes longer with the machine set at maximum speed.

5 Spoon one-third of the mixture into another bowl. Add the cocoa paste to this and with a balloon whisk blend the two together until smooth.

6 For the marbled effect, spread a layer of pale mixture into the loaf tin, then place alternate spoonfuls of dark and pale batter. Top with a pale layer. Drag a fork down through the mixture in a crisscross movement.

7 Place in the oven and reduce the temperature to 200°C (400°F, gas 6). After 15–20 minutes, dip a knife tip in oil, and make a shallow cut along the length of the cake. Lower the oven temperature to 175°C (350°F, gas 4) and bake for 35 minutes more.

8 Test with a skewer. When it comes out clean, take the cake out of the oven and run a knife around the edges of the tin. Turn the cake out onto a wire rack to cool. Dust with icing sugar to serve.

HAZELNUT CAKE WITH CHERRIES

This is a cross between a cake and a tart. Equally delicious at teatime or served with cream as a dessert. To ensure a crisp pastry case the base is parbaked, and then the sides of the tin are lined with raw dough, the filling is added, and the cake is baked.

Makes a 26cm (10½in) cake

450g (1lb) pâte brisée, chilled (p376)
icing sugar for dusting

For the vanilla cream

300ml (10fl oz) milk
5 medium egg yolks, 100g (3½oz) in total
75g (2½oz) caster sugar
15g (½oz) cornflour
100ml (3½fl oz) double cream
seeds of ½ vanilla pod

For the filling

500g (1lb 2oz) black cherry jam, stoned

For the hazelnut mixture

100g (3½oz) cake crumbs or toasted breadcrumbs, finely ground
90g (3oz) hazelnuts, skinned (p480), toasted, and finely ground
pinch of ground cinnamon
100g (3½oz) unsalted butter, diced and softened
100g (3½oz) caster sugar
3 medium egg yolks, 60g (2oz) in total
seeds of ½ vanilla pod
grated zest of ½ lemon
4 medium egg whites, 120g (4oz) in total

1 Preheat the oven to 200°C (400°F, gas 6). Use a round cake tin with 4cm (1½in) high sloping sides or a tarte Tatin tin or springform cake tin 26cm (10½in) in diameter. Lightly grease the tin with butter.

2 Roll out half the pastry to a 3mm (⅛in) thickness and cut out a circle to fit the bottom of the tin. Lay in the bottom of the tin and prick all over with a fork so that no air bubbles occur during baking. Bake for 10 minutes. The pastry should be set and only very slightly coloured.

3 Let the pastry cool and lower the oven temperature to 175°C (350°F, gas 4). Roll out the remaining pastry into two equal strips, the same depth as the tin and half the circumference, and use to line the sides of the tin. Using the back of a knife, carefully trim the excess off the top edge without tearing.

4 For the vanilla cream, pour 90ml (3fl oz) of the milk into a bowl, blend in the egg yolks, 45g (1½oz) of the sugar, and the cornflour. Pour the rest of the milk into a pan and add the cream, remaining sugar, and vanilla seeds. Bring to the boil and pour onto the egg yolk mixture, stir well, and tip the mixture back into the pan.

7 For the hazelnut mixture, lightly mix together the cake or breadcrumbs, hazelnuts, and cinnamon. In a large bowl beat the butter and 30g (1oz) of the sugar until pale and creamy. Beat in the egg yolks one at a time. Add the vanilla and lemon zest and combine well.

8 In a clean bowl, whisk the egg whites, remaining sugar, and a pinch of salt to stiff peaks. Add one-third to the butter mixture and stir to combine. Carefully fold in the remaining whites using a large spatula. Fold in the nut mixture in batches.

5 Stir continuously and bring to the boil. Remove from the heat immediately so that it does not burn. Pass the cream through a fine sieve and spread evenly over the pastry base.

6 Fill a large piping bag, without a nozzle, with cherry jam and pipe the filling onto the vanilla cream surface.

9 Fit a piping bag with a large plain nozzle, spoon in the nut mixture, and pipe in a spiral onto the jam. Bake in the oven at 175°C (350°F, gas 4) for 45 minutes.

10 Remove from the oven and run a small knife around the edge of the tin to release the cake, cover with a wire rack, and turn the tin over so that the cake drops out. Remove the tin and in the same way turn the cake back over again. When cool, dust with icing sugar or glaze (see below), and serve.

FONDANT GLAZE

Simmer together 100g (3½oz) sieved apricot jam, 4tsp water, and 45g (1½oz) sugar. Brush evenly over the top of the cake. Work 150g (5½oz) fondant icing with 2tbsp William pear eau-de-vie until smooth. When the apricot glaze has set, heat the fondant glaze to 40°C (104°F) and spread over the cake. Alternatively, mix 150g (5½oz) sieved icing sugar with a little William pear eau-de-vie, and spread evenly over the cake.

FRANKFURTER KRANZ

This irresistible layered German confection is drenched with kirsch syrup and layered with a light French buttercream and cherries.

Makes a 26cm (10½in) cake

French buttercream

6 medium egg yolks, 120g (4oz) in total

100ml (3½fl oz) water

150g (5½oz) caster sugar

360g (13oz) unsalted butter, at room temperature

seeds of ½ vanilla pod

4tsp kirsch

For the croquant

450g (1lb) granulated sugar

45ml (1½fl oz) water

500g (1lb 2oz) hazelnuts, shelled, roasted, skins rubbed off in a tea towel, and chopped

For the flavoured syrup

115g (4oz) granulated sugar

115ml (4 fl oz) water

2tbsp kirsch

For the cake

50g (1¾oz) plain white flour, sifted

285g (10oz) potato flour

6 medium eggs, 300g (10½oz) in total

225g (8oz) caster sugar

4tsp water

grated zest of 1 lemon

165g (6oz) unsalted butter, melted and cooled to lukewarm

For the filling

500g (1lb 2oz) sour cherry jam, stoned

11–12 glacé cherries

1 To make the French buttercream beat the egg yolks with a pinch of salt until pale and creamy. Put the water in a small heavy pan, add the sugar, and set over medium heat. Stir until the sugar dissolves, then bring to the boil. As the syrup starts to foam, use a fine mesh strainer to remove any impurities.

2 Raise the heat, and continue boiling the syrup. During boiling, dip a pastry brush in cold water and wash down the sugar crystals from the side of the pan 2 or 3 times. Do not stir. Continue boiling the syrup until it reaches 120°C (248°F) on a sugar thermometer. Take off the heat and immediately plunge the base of the pan into cold water to stop further cooking.

3 Quickly pour the hot syrup in a thin, steady stream onto the egg yolk mixture, whisking continuously with a hand-held electric mixer. Continue beating at a lower speed until cooled to room temperature. Set aside.

4 In a separate bowl, beat the softened butter until pale and creamy. Add the vanilla seeds, mix well, then beat the butter mixture, 1 tbsp at a time, into the egg yolks and syrup. Fold in the kirsch. Cover and set aside.

5 To make the hazelnut croquant, pour the sugar and water into a heavy-based pan. Heat slowly at first to dissolve the sugar, then raise the heat and bring to the boil. Add the hazelnuts and stir well to coat with syrup. Continue boiling, without stirring, until it turns golden caramel in colour.

6 Pour the mixture straight onto a marble slab or stone and spread out with an oiled palette knife. Leave to cool. To use, break up the croquant with a rolling pin.

7 To make the flavoured syrup, bring the sugar and water to a rolling boil and skim off any froth and impurities. Remove from the heat and leave to cool. Measure out 115ml (4fl oz) of the syrup and add the kirsch. Leftover syrup can be stored in the fridge for future use.

8 Preheat the oven to 190°C (375°F, gas 5). Grease and flour a 26cm (10½in) savarin mould. Make the cake as for genoese sponge (p436). Pour into the tin. Reduce the oven heat to 175°C (350°F, gas 4) and bake for 40 minutes. Leave for 10 minutes then turn out onto a wire rack. When cold, cut cake across into 4 layers.

9 Spread just over a third of the cherry jam on the bottom layer 1cm (½in) away from the inner and outer edges. Fill a large piping bag, fitted with a plain nozzle, with three-quarters of the buttercream. Pipe a ring around the inner and outer edges. Cover with the second cake layer and press down lightly. Use half the kirsch syrup to lightly drench the cake surface, spread over half the jam, and pipe buttercream as before. Finish the third layer in the same way. Sandwich with the top layer.

10 Spread the reserved cream on the cake top, on the inside and outside of the ring. Take a strip of greaseproof paper and use to smooth the surface. Sprinkle over the chopped croquant and decorate with glacé cherries. The cake keeps fresh for up to 2 days in the refrigerator.

CHEESECAKES

Cheesecakes are traditionally baked from fresh soft cheeses, cream, eggs, sugar, and spices on a pastry or sponge base. They have been made in Europe and other places around the world since the 15th century. Made in many varieties from light and fluffy to dense and very rich, they usually use a local dairy product such as ricotta, mascarpone, quark, cottage or curd cheese.

APPLE CHEESECAKE

The base of shortcrust pastry topped with sponge can be made a day ahead. Baking in three stages prevents the surface from cracking.

Makes a 26cm (10½in) cheesecake

1 pâte brisée base (p376), about 100g (3½oz), parbaked in a 26cm (10½in) springform cake tin

30g (1oz) apricot jam, boiled and sieved

1 thin, half-quantity sponge roulade (p438), baked in a 26cm (10½in) springform tin

For the apple filling

30g (1oz) unsalted butter

60g (2oz) breadcrumbs, lightly toasted

600g (1lb 6oz) Cox's apples or similar, peeled, quartered, and cut in thick slices

50g (1¾oz) caster sugar

grated zest and juice of ½ lemon

grated zest and juice of ½ orange

40g (1½oz) walnuts, finely chopped

pinch of ground cinnamon

30g (1oz) raisins

1tbsp rum

For the cheese mixture

75g (2½oz) vanilla sugar

35g (1¼oz) custard powder

pinch of ground cinnamon

800g (1¾lb) cottage cheese, sieved

150ml (5fl oz) full-fat milk

150ml (5fl oz) double cream

5 medium egg yolks, 100g (3½oz) in total

grated zest of 1 lemon

2tbsp lemon juice, sieved

4tsp kirsch

50g (1¾oz) unsalted butter, melted

5 medium egg whites, 150g (5½oz) in total

110g (4oz) caster sugar

30g (1oz) potato flour

1 Preheat the oven to 190°C (375°F, gas 5). Leaving the cooked pastry base in the tin, brush with apricot jam and slide on the sponge layer using a cake tin base as support. Clip the springform ring around the cake. Set aside.

2 For the apple filling, melt the butter in a pan, stir in the breadcrumbs, and brown lightly. Mix in a third of the apple slices and coat well. Add the sugar, citrus zests and juice, walnuts, cinnamon, raisins, and rum. Stir together and mix with the remaining apples.

3 For the cheese mixture, mix together the vanilla sugar, custard powder, and cinnamon. Set aside. In a separate bowl, stir thoroughly together the cottage cheese, milk, cream, and egg yolks.

4 Add the lemon zest, juice, and kirsch and combine well. Fold in the vanilla sugar mixture. Mix 2 tbsp of the cheese mixture with the melted butter then fold this into the main mixture. Avoid stirring or the cheese cream might separate. Set aside.

5 Whisk together the egg whites, a pinch of salt, 30g (1oz) of the sugar, and the potato flour until pale and creamy. Gradually add the remaining sugar and whisk to a firm and creamy snow. Using a whisk, stir one-third of the egg whites into the cheese cream. Gently fold in the remaining egg whites using a spatula.

6 Spread the apple mixture evenly in the bottom of the prepared tin. Pour the cheesecake mixture onto the apples and spread out gently with a spatula.

7 Place the cheesecake in the hot oven for a short time until the top starts to set. Open the door carefully and quickly slide an oiled knife around the inside edge of the tin to release the cheesecake mixture. Return to the oven and continue baking.

A light fruit cheesecake for any occasion

8 Once the cake has risen, take it out of the oven, and reduce the temperature to 170°C (325°F, gas 3). Allow the surface to sink level with the top of the tin, then put the cheesecake back into the oven. Repeat this twice more. The overall baking time is 50–60 minutes.

9 Remove the cake from the oven and run a knife around the edge to loosen the sides. Leave to cool and then unclip and remove the springform ring and slide the cheesecake off the base and onto a serving plate. The cheesecake will keep fresh for 2 days.

NEW YORK CHEESECAKE

This is an unbaked cheesecake made with white chocolate. Its rich, creamy filling contrasts well with the crunchy almond base. It is easy to make and you can vary the toppings as you wish. Try red berries, orange or banana slices, or simply spread the top with soured cream.

Makes a 28cm (11in) cheesecake

For the base

120g (4oz) unsalted butter

250g (8½oz) amaretti biscuits, crushed

For the filling

380g (13oz) white chocolate, finely chopped

380ml (13fl oz) full-fat milk

750g (1lb 10oz) full-fat cream cheese, at room temperature

seeds of 1 vanilla pod

60g (2oz) icing sugar, sifted

dark and white chocolate scrolls to decorate

LINING THE TIN

To line the cake tin place a large piece of baking parchment on the base of a 28cm (11in) springform cake tin. Put on the outside ring and clip in place. Trim the paper with scissors .

1 Preheat the oven to 180°C (350°F, gas 4). Melt the butter in a pan and mix in the biscuit crumbs. Press into the bottom of the prepared cake tin (see left) and bake for 12 minutes. Set aside to cool.

2 For the filling, place the chocolate pieces and milk in a heatproof bowl set over barely simmering water. When melted, gently stir using a hand-held blender, avoiding beating in any air. Leave to cool, stirring now and then to prevent a skin forming on the surface.

3 Meanwhile, beat together the cream cheese, vanilla seeds, and icing sugar until creamy. Stir in half of the white chocolate mixture and then fold in the remainder. Pour into the cake tin and spread level. Chill for at least 6 hours.

4 Run a sharp knife carefully round the edge of the tin to release the cheesecake and unclip the springform ring. Place on a serving plate and decorate with chocolate scrolls.

Stephan's cheesecake

This is my own recipe for a very special occasion. Use a 26cm (10½in) springform cake tin (no base needed), the sides lightly brushed with unflavoured oil and lined with strips of foil. The cheesecake keeps fresh for 1–2 days.

Makes a 26cm (10½in) cheesecake

For the cake

1 baked 26cm (10½in) pâte brisée base (p376)

30g (1oz) apricot jam, boiled and sieved

26cm (10½in) genoese sponge cake (p436), cut into 2 layers, with the bottom layer cut to 25cm (10in)

12 bottled or canned peach halves, drained and dried on kitchen paper

icing sugar for dusting

For the cheese cream filling

340g (12oz) curd cheese, sieved

75g (2½oz) soured cream

90ml (3fl oz) full-fat milk

140g (5oz) caster sugar

5 medium egg yolks, 100g (3½oz) in total

4tsp lemon juice

seeds of ½ vanilla pod

grated zest of ½ lemon

8 gelatin leaves or
14g (½oz) powdered gelatin

568ml (1 pint) whipping cream, lightly whipped

Place the shortcrust pastry base on a baking sheet. Brush with apricot jam and cover with the (25cm/10in) sponge layer. Arrange the peaches, cut-side down, on the surface. Set the prepared springform ring (see above) over the cake layers. Set aside.

For the filling, place the curd cheese, soured cream, milk, sugar, egg yolks, and a pinch of salt in a large heatproof bowl set over barely simmering water. Whisk until the mixture is light and airy and doubled in volume. Mix in the lemon juice. Remove from the heat and stir in the vanilla seeds and lemon zest.

Soften the gelatin leaves in a large bowl of cold water for 2 minutes, remove, and squeeze gently or dissolve the gelatin powder according to the packet instructions. Immediately fold into the warm cheese mixture to dissolve.

Set the bowl over crushed ice cubes and stir continuously until the mixture starts to thicken to the consistency of raw egg white. At this point the mixture is beginning to set so remove from the crushed ice and whisk in one-third of the whipped cream. Use a spatula to fold in the remainder. Reserve one-quarter of the filling, cover, and keep in a cool place.

Carefully spoon the cheese cream over the peaches, spreading evenly down the sides and filling all the gaps. Smooth the top. Chill for at least 4 hours. Remove the ring and finish the cake shortly before serving.

To finish the cheesecake, cut the remaining top sponge layer into 12 triangles. Fit a large plain nozzle into a piping bag and fill with the reserved cream. Pipe 12 rosettes on the cake top and arrange the sponge triangles at an angle with points to the centre. Dust with icing sugar and serve.

YEAST CAKES

When fresh yeast is unavailable use dried yeast granules, substituting 20g (¾oz) fresh yeast with 7g (1 rounded tsp) dried yeast. A fresh yeast sponge batter takes about 20 minutes to rise; a dried yeast batter takes 40 minutes. The general rule for testing the rise in both is to push a finger into the batter – the dough should spring apart and then shrink back in on itself.

BUTTERCAKE

A simple version of one of the most traditional German cakes baked in a tray. As yeast activates better in a large mixture, the yeast dough quantity is enough for 2 trays. If making one tray, wrap half the finished dough in foil and a freezer bag. Freeze up to one month. The topping and finishing ingredients are for one tray only.

Makes 2 trays, or 1 tray and 1 portion dough for freezing

For the yeast sponge batter (2 trays)

35g (1¼oz) fresh yeast or 12g (⅓oz) dried yeast

125ml (4½fl oz) milk, warmed to lukewarm

150g (5½oz) strong plain white flour, sifted twice

For the main yeast mixture (2 trays)

350g (12oz) strong plain flour

1tsp salt

75ml (2½fl oz) milk

4 medium egg yolks, 80g (3oz) in total

60g (2oz) caster sugar

50g (1¾oz) quark or curd cheese, sieved

grated zest of 1 lemon

seeds of 1 vanilla pod

100g (3½oz) unsalted butter, beaten until smooth

2tsp dark rum

100g (3½oz) soured cream

For the butter topping (1 tray only)

200g (7oz) unsalted butter, diced and softened

200g (7oz) crème pâtissière (p418)

1 medium egg yolk, 20g (¾oz) in total

To finish (1 tray only)

175g (6oz) caster sugar

25g (scant 1oz) vanilla sugar

2tsp egg yolk (10g/¼oz)

80g (3oz) flaked almonds

50g (1¾oz) honey

100ml (3½fl oz) double cream

1 For the yeast sponge batter, crumble the fresh yeast, or sprinkle the dried, onto the warm milk in the mixing bowl of an electric mixer or food processor with the dough hook attached. Sift in the flour.

2 Set the machine at slow speed and knead until the mixture is smooth and rolls off the sides of the bowl. Remove to another bowl, cover with a cloth, and leave to rise in a warm place for 20 minutes.

3 To make the main yeast mixture, sift the flour and salt together twice, then sift into the mixing bowl of the electric mixer. Add the milk, egg yolks, sugar, cheese, lemon zest, and vanilla. With the dough hook, slowly knead until it forms a firm, smooth dough.

4 Drop the risen sponge batter into the bowl and continue kneading with the dough hook, until it has large air bubbles. Mix in the softened butter and rum. Gather the dough and place in a large bowl, covered with a cloth, and leave to rise for 20 minutes in a cool place.

5 Grease a 30x20cm (12x8in) baking tray and line with baking parchment. Roll out half the dough to fit in the base of the prepared tray. The remaining dough can be frozen or used to make a second buttercake. Cover with a damp cloth and set aside to rise again for 20 minutes.

6 Using a large palette knife spread the soured cream over the risen dough in the tray. Do this as carefully as possible so as not to deflate the risen dough.

7 Lightly press your fingertips into the mixture, at regular intervals. Preheat the oven to 200°C (400°F, gas 6).

8 For the butter mixture, beat together the butter, crème pâtissière, and egg yolk. Fit a plain nozzle into a large piping bag, fill with the mixture, and pipe diagonally across the surface. Fork the sugars and egg yolk together and sprinkle over the top. Scatter over the flaked almonds. Place in the oven and reduce the temperature to 175°C (350°F, gas 4).

9 After 40 minutes switch the oven onto top heat only and set the temperature to 220°C (425°F, gas 7) or use a hot grill to toast the nutty surface for 5 minutes. Bring the honey and double cream to the boil, and brush over the top of the hot pastry. Cut in squares before the topping hardens and leave to cool in the tin for 30 minutes. Best eaten freshly made.

Dresden stollen

Christmas stollen first appeared as a festive bread in 1427 in the court of Saxony. This recipe is a modern version, buttery and spicy, full of nuts, marzipan, and candied fruits. Stollen should be left to mature for 2–3 days before being eaten.

Makes two 950g (2lb 2oz) stollen

For the fruits

480g (1lb 1oz) sultanas

60g (2oz) candied lemon peel, chopped

120g (4oz) candied orange peel, chopped

1tbsp dark rum

120g (4oz) almonds, nibbed or flaked

2tsp vanilla extract

3tbsp water

grated zest of 1 lemon

For the yeast sponge batter

200g (7oz) strong plain white flour

40g (1½ oz) fresh yeast or 15g (½oz) dried yeast

150ml (5fl oz) cold milk

15g (½oz) caster sugar

For the main mixture

250g (8½oz) strong plain white flour

1tsp salt

1tsp mixed spice

90ml (3fl oz) milk

1 medium egg, 50g (1¾oz) in total

4 medium egg yolks, 80g (3oz) in total

20g (¾oz) caster sugar

20g (¾oz) cream cheese

140g (5oz) marzipan, diced

150g (5½oz) unsalted butter, chilled and diced

pinch of grated lemon zest

few drops of vanilla extract

20g (¾oz) candied orange peel, finely ground

To finish

250g (8½oz) unsalted butter, clarified (p24)

250g (8½oz) icing sugar

Start the day before and place all 8 ingredients for the fruits in a bowl. Stir well, cover, and leave at room temperature overnight.

For the yeast sponge batter, bring all the ingredients to room temperature. Sift the flour into the bowl of an electric mixer, crumble in the fresh yeast or sprinkle over the dried yeast, and add the milk and sugar. With the dough hook fitted, knead for 15 minutes at slow speed. Cover with a clean cloth and leave to rise for at least 30 minutes in a cool place.

For the main mixture, sift the flour and salt into a bowl. Add the mixed spice, milk, egg and yolks, sugar, and cream cheese. Knead to a very soft dough. Incorporate the sponge batter and continue kneading for 5 minutes.

Add the marzipan pieces and knead until the mixture rolls off the sides of the bowl. Add the butter, piece by piece, and knead until the mixture is elastic and smooth. Add lemon zest, vanilla, and candied orange. Knead well.

Turn the dough out onto a floured surface and with floured hands knead in the drained dried fruit mixture. Cover with a cloth and leave to rest for 20 minutes. Gently shape the dough into a ball, cover, and leave for 10 minutes.

Preheat the oven to 200°C (400°F, gas 6). Grease a large baking sheet and line with baking parchment. Divide the dough into 2 pieces. On a floured surface, using a rolling pin, roll out one piece into a rectangle and gently knock flat. Fold both long sides into the middle. Finish by folding in only one long side, into the middle, curling it over slightly on the top. Repeat with the second piece.

Lay the stollen on the prepared baking sheet with the raised seam upwards. Leave to rest for 5 minutes. Place in the hot oven, reduce the temperature to 175°C (350°F, gas 4) and bake for 50–60 minutes. As soon as the stollen are baked turn straight onto a wire rack. Immediately brush the surface with clarified butter and dredge with icing sugar.

SMALL CAKES

This section includes some all-time favourites such as scones, doughnuts, and chocolate-covered flapjacks. These small cakes may be less grand than their elaborately decorated sisters, but they make up for this by being some of the most addictive to eat. Who hasn't found it hard to resist yet another chocolate brownie or warm-from-the-oven muffin?

SCONES WITH RAISINS

As traditional as cucumber sandwiches on the tea table, scones originated in Scotland. They taste best filled with strawberry jam and clotted cream. Failing that whipped cream or mascarpone blended with cream also taste good. The raw dough freezes well for up to a month.

Makes 10 scones

115g (4oz) raisins
1 cup of black tea, cold
1tbsp dark rum
270g (10oz) plain white flour
90g (3oz) strong plain flour
4tsp baking powder
100g (3½oz) unsalted butter, softened
85g (3oz) caster sugar
grated zest of ½ lemon
2 small eggs, 85g (3oz) in total, lightly mixed together
100ml (3½fl oz) milk
1–2tbsp double cream

1 The day before, soak the raisins in the tea and rum and leave overnight.

2 Sift the two flours and the baking powder together twice and then sift onto a sheet of greaseproof paper. Set aside.

3 In a large mixing bowl, beat together the butter, sugar, and lemon zest until thick and creamy. Mix in the eggs in three stages, and then add the milk a little at a time. Stir well until the mixture is smooth and lump-free.

4 Add the sifted flour in stages and knead lightly until smooth and elastic in texture. Mix in the drained raisins. Shape into a ball, wrap in cling film and refrigerate overnight.

5 The next day, grease a large baking sheet and line with baking parchment. Roll out the scone dough on a lightly floured surface, until 2cm (¾in) thick. Preheat the oven to 210°C (400°F, gas 6).

6 Using a 6cm (2½in) round cutter, stamp out circles. Place them slightly apart on the baking sheet. Lightly beat the cream with a pinch each of salt and sugar. Use this to glaze the tops of the scones. Bake in the preheated oven for 15–18 minutes. Cool on a wire rack.

FLAPJACKS

For plain flapjacks, omit the white chocolate and serve after step 3. In an airtight tin, the flapjacks will keep fresh for 4–5 days.

Makes 16 flapjacks

250g (8½oz) unsalted butter, cut into pieces

200g (7oz) golden syrup

100g (3½oz) light muscovado sugar

250g (8½oz) porridge oats

100g (3½oz) plain white flour, sifted twice

150g (5½oz) dried cranberries

100g (3½oz) white cooking chocolate, finely chopped

1 Grease and line the base of a deep 23x23cm (9x9in) baking tray with baking parchment. Preheat the oven to 170°C (350°F, gas 4).

2 Melt the butter, golden syrup, and sugar gently in a small pan until foaming.

3 In a mixing bowl, stir together the oats, flour, and cranberries. Add the warmed butter and sugar mixture and blend well. Press the mixture into the lined tin and bake for 25–30 minutes. Cool. Cut into small rectangles.

4 Melt the chocolate pieces in a heatproof bowl set over barely simmering water. Pour half the melted chocolate onto a clean marble slab or stone surface. Cool it down by tempering it – moving the chocolate back and forth using a scraper and a spatula until it firms up.

5 Scrape the couverture back into the hot chocolate before it hardens and gently stir the mixture to combine; it should be no warmer than 29°C (84°F). Repeat this process and then use as required. If it has cooled too much replace the bowl over the hot water.

6 Dip each flapjack diagonally in the chocolate and leave to set on a wire rack covered with baking parchment.

SOURED CREAM DOUGHNUTS

Purists argue whether a true doughnut is made with yeast or baking powder. The yeasted version traditionally springs from 18th century Austria. This recipe for the more recent "donut", made with a raising agent, takes much less time to prepare. Eat the same day.

Makes 28 doughnuts

440g (1lb) strong plain white flour
1tsp salt
pinch of ground nutmeg
1tbsp baking powder
2 medium eggs, 100g (3½oz) in total
250g (8½oz) caster sugar
200g (7oz) soured cream
3tbsp full-fat milk
45g (1½oz) unsalted butter, melted
1tbsp orange marmalade, sieved
2tsp grated orange zest
groundnut oil for deep-frying
icing sugar for dusting

VARIATION

The finished doughnuts are also good rolled in desiccated coconut. Alternatively, brush with sieved apricot jam and coat with glacé icing or couverture chocolate.

Dust the warm doughnuts with icing sugar to serve

1 Sift together the flour, salt, nutmeg, and baking powder twice, then sift onto a sheet of greaseproof paper.

2 Whisk the eggs in a large bowl. Whisk in the sugar, a tbsp at a time, until pale, thick, and creamy. Stir in the soured cream, milk, butter, marmalade, and orange zest. Blend together well.

3 Carefully fold in spoonfuls of the flour mixture with a large spatula until just combined. With lightly floured hands shape the mixture into a ball, cover with a cloth, and leave to rest in a cool place for 20 minutes.

4 Roll out the dough to a 5cm (2in) thickness. Using a 6cm (2½in) and 1.5cm (½–¾in) pastry cutter, cut out large circles, then stamp out the centres. Gather up the scraps, knead together, roll out, and cut as before.

5 In a deep pan heat the oil to 180°C (350°F). Use a draining spoon to gently lay 2–3 doughnuts at a time in the hot oil. They must not touch each other. Fry for 1½ minutes on each side until golden brown. Lift out using two skewers. Drain on kitchen paper.

BROWNIES WITH CHEESECAKE FILLING

Who created brownies? Folklore suggests a librarian, Miss Brown from Maine, USA, forgot to use baking powder in her chocolate cake mixture. It came out of the oven completely flat. Despite this she served it to her friends, who loved it. The test of time and the huge popularity of brownies have overcome all professional criticism. Brownies keep fresh for one week.

Makes 24 brownies

For the cheese filling

250g (8½oz) full-fat cream cheese, sieved

140g (5oz) curd cheese, sieved

60g (2oz) caster sugar

15g (½oz) plain white flour

1 medium egg, 50g (1¾oz)

2 medium egg yolks, 40g (1½oz) in total

For the brownie mixture

200g (7oz) pecan nuts, toasted and coarsely chopped (p480)

200g (7oz) plain white flour, sifted twice and then into a bowl

6 medium eggs, 300g (10½oz) in total

450g (1lb) caster sugar

200g (7oz) best-quality dark chocolate (70 per cent cocoa solids), finely chopped

300g (10½oz) unsalted butter

For the glaze

85g (3oz) unsalted butter, diced

120ml (4fl oz) water

250g (8½oz) best-quality dark chocolate (70 per cent cocoa solids), finely chopped

1 Use a 28x23x4cm (11x9x1¾in) brownie cake tin or deep roasting tin, greased with butter and the bottom lined with baking parchment. Preheat the oven to 170°C (350°F, gas 4).

2 For the cheese filling, stir all ingredients together in a large bowl. Cover and set aside.

3 For the brownie mixture, stir the nuts into the flour. Place the eggs in a separate large bowl with a pinch of salt and 200g (7oz) of the sugar. Whisk until pale and foamy, then gradually whisk in the rest of the sugar.

4 Melt the chocolate pieces in a heatproof bowl set over barely simmering water. Heat the butter until foaming, slowly whisk in the melted chocolate, and stir until the temperature has dropped to body heat, 40°C (104°F). Leave to cool.

5 Stir 2–3tbsp of the egg mixture into the butter and chocolate to lighten it, then fold in the remainder with a large spatula taking care not to lose air. Fold in the flour and pecan mixture a spoonful at a time. Pour into the prepared cake tin.

6 Put the cheese filling into a large piping bag fitted with a plain nozzle. Pipe down 2cm (¾in) into the chocolate surface, close together, at regular intervals.

7 Bake for 35–40 minutes. When the cake centre starts to thicken and set, remove from the oven. Leave in the tin until cold.

8 To make the glaze, put the butter and water into a pan and bring just to the boil. Ladle the chopped chocolate pieces into the centre, remove from the heat, and wait for a few moments.

9 Using a heatproof spatula and working from the middle, start stirring, gradually drawing the liquid into the chocolate. Always work from the centre outwards. Stir until well blended, taking care not to beat in air while stirring. The glaze will develop a slight sheen.

10 Spread in a smooth layer on the brownie surface and drag a confectioner's comb or a fork across it in a wavy line. To serve, cut in squares using a knife dipped in hot water.

APRICOT MUFFINS

Considered now to be traditional American fare, muffins made with yeast originated on the English table for high tea. Emigrants in the mid-19th century took the traditional recipe with them to the USA, found the yeasted method rather laborious and, to save time, used baking powder instead.

Makes 10 muffins

| 250g (8½oz) dried apricots, finely chopped |
| 100ml (3½fl oz) fresh orange juice, strained |
| 375g (13oz) strong plain white flour |
| 4tsp baking powder |
| 125g (4½oz) unsalted butter, diced and softened |
| 125g (4½oz) caster sugar |
| 2 large eggs, 110g (4oz) in total, lightly mixed together |
| 250ml (8½fl oz) plain yogurt |
| grated zest of 1 orange |

1 Soak the apricots in orange juice for at least 3 hours.

2 Preheat the oven to 200°C (400°F, gas 6). Grease a 12-hole muffin tin with butter. Sift the flour and baking powder twice, and then sift onto a sheet of greaseproof paper. Set aside.

3 In a large bowl, mix together the butter, sugar, and a pinch of salt until light and fluffy. Add the eggs to the mixture in three stages, beating well between each addition. Should the mixture curdle, stir in a small amount of flour to bind. Add the yogurt, orange zest, and drained apricots and stir lightly together until just mixed.

4 Gently mix in the flour until just blended. Avoid over mixing as it makes the mixture heavy. Spoon into 10 of the muffin moulds and pour a little water in the two empty spaces.

5 Reduce the oven temperature to 180°C (350°F, gas 4) and bake the muffins for 25 minutes until well risen and golden.

PERFECT MUFFINS

■ Butter the muffin tin, then place the tray in the freezer briefly. The muffins will pop out of the tins more easily.
■ Steam from the water in the empty moulds makes the baked buns soft, light, and moist.

6 To test if the muffin is cooked, prick the centre with a toothpick and it should come out completely clean and dry.

7 Remove the muffin tin from the oven and place on a damp cloth for 5 minutes. This makes it easier to release the muffins from the baking tin. Eat on the same day.

FRUIT & NUTS

SHAUN HILL

Today, fruit has a healthy aura, but it was not always so. In Roman times fruits, especially soft fruit, were regarded with some disdain. The great physician Galen saw moist fruits as little better than a laxative, claiming that their nutrients are easily leeched away. In fact, fruits are among the few foodstuffs that evolved to attract the hungry, their perfume and sweetness being nature's way of enticing those creatures able to eat them and distribute their seeds. Before Adam's unfortunate episode with the apple, fruits were the nourishment of the Garden of Eden.

Seasonal fare Fruits and nuts are emblems of their seasons. Just as the first strawberries represent all the freshness and vitality of early summer, apples are as much wedded in the mind with Hallowe'en as pumpkins and ghosts, and nuts, tangerines, dates, and figs with Christmas. The recipes and dishes that have developed around specific fruits reflect the seasonal desire for appropriate fare. Most apple and pear dishes are served hot rather than cold, whereas fresh stone fruits and berries are associated more with light desserts and refreshing ice creams.

Dried fruits such as figs, dates, sultanas, raisins, and currants are store-cupboard items, ingredients for winter cakes and puddings. Candied and preserved stone fruits such as cherries are also welcome by-products of the pre-freezer era, ingredients that brighten up a range of winter dishes and are closely linked in most people's minds with Christmas feasting.

All-year availability Fruits have their seasons, but many of us expect to eat all kinds of fruits and nuts all year round. While most fruits naturally ripen on the bush or tree, imported fruit has to be gathered under-ripe to survive the long journey from grower to kitchen. Of course, these fruits continue to ripen after purchase and, if kept too long or in overly warm conditions, will overripen and spoil. This process can be slowed by chilling the fruit and by isolating it from other fruits, since gases given off by ripening fruit help to ripen the fruit around them. Conversely, you can speed up the ripening process by placing ripe fruits with unripe ones.

While it is convenient to buy fruits according to whim, the shopper has to be alert to practices that favour those supplying fruit, rather than those buying and eating it. Irradiation of soft fruit in countries where this is permitted encourages lazy handling and storage. Excessive spraying worldwide with pesticides is a menace in foodstuffs that are likely to be eaten raw. Even the standard treatment of citrus fruits makes it necessary for organic or unwaxed fruit to be specified if the peel is to be used in the recipe. Genetic engineering and changes in horticultural technique have extended the season for most soft fruits and, while the result has been cheaper fruits and better availability, there is a danger of less prolific fruit varieties becoming rare as we select newer strains that crop more heavily or store better, but possibly have inferior flavour and character.

The value of nuts Unlike fruits, nuts are more often used as ingredients than served as a separate course in a meal. In the past, some nuts played a much more significant part in the diet – even the humble acorn was ground and used as a flour substitute when food was short. Acorn flour is rarely on offer now but you can buy chestnut flour in Italian shops for making into fritters and cakes.

Many nuts are now cultivated primarily for their oil. For a long time groundnut oil was a major kitchen ingredient but the burgeoning sensitivity of many people to nut products has reduced its importance. Walnut oil is second only to olive oil as a salad dressing ingredient, and hazelnut, coconut, and almond oils are all used to flavour both sweet and savoury dishes.

Nuts are high in oil and vitamin B and, like anything oily, turn rancid if stored badly or for too long. The best way to keep nuts is to refrigerate them in their shells, sealed in glass or plastic containers to avoid being tainted by other odours. Almonds and cashews are among the most hardy; walnuts and pecans are most prone to deterioration in storage.

PREPARING FRESH FRUIT

Fruit has evolved to be eaten. When it is ripe it is at its best and little of the chef's art is called for to improve matters. The citrus family forms segments and all members are easily tackled in the same way as oranges. Those fruit that are awkward to peel, like peaches, can be dropped into boiling water for a few moments to blanch and loosen the skin for easy removal.

SEGMENTING AN ORANGE

1 With a sharp knife, cut a small piece of skin from the top and tail of the orange. Hold the orange firmly with a fork or your other hand and slice down and round the flesh. Try to take off as much pith as possible. Use a small knife to cut away any left clinging to the fruit.

2 The orange will now show the contours of each segment, separated from the next by a membrane. Cut into and along the edge of a segment. Cut the segment back along its outer edge, leaving behind the membrane, so that it is free. Repeat this process with all the segments.

CUTTING PINEAPPLE RINGS & CHUNKS

1 Cut off the stalky top and then the base of the pineapple. Stand the fruit upright and then slice off the skin in long strips. Cut from top to bottom and follow the contour of the fruit so that no flesh is lost where it bulges towards the middle.

2 For pineapple rings, turn the fruit on its side and slice into whatever thickness suits. Take a round pastry cutter and cut out the centre of each slice. For pineapple chunks, cut the fruit into thicker slices and again remove the hard centres before segmenting.

PREPARING A MANGO

Mangoes must be ripe unless they are an ingredient of a savoury stew or chutney. It is unnecessary to peel them. The best method is to make mango hedgehogs. The stone is surrounded by hard fibres and the extent to which these affect the surrounding flesh varies. Least is best.

REMOVING POMEGRANATE SEEDS

1 Stand the fruit on its side and slice down and into the middle. The fruit has a large flat stone so your knife must follow the soft flesh around it to the chopping board. Repeat the exercise with the other side.

2 Place the mango halves flesh-side up. Cut the flesh into strips lengthways, then crossways until you reach the skin. Do not cut through the skin. Press the skin so that the fruit bursts upwards into segments.

Cut the fruit in half and carefully scoop out the seeds with a teaspoon. The pithy membrane is bitter so discard this.

PEELING PEACHES OR NECTARINES

TOPPING & TAILING GOOSEBERRIES

1 Cut a small cross in the skin at the base of the fruit.

2 Immerse the fruit in boiling water for 30 seconds. Remove from the water and pull the skin off with your fingers.

With a sharp knife or scissors cut off both ends. Frozen gooseberries are already topped and tailed, but you still need to remove any stalky bits for a smooth dessert like gooseberry fool.

PURÉEING FRUIT

Soft fruits like raspberries and strawberries need no cooking before being puréed. Most other fruits need to be braised or poached in advance to soften them. This gives an opportunity for judicious spicing and for the sweetness of the fruit to be altered to suit the treatment – ice creams need more sugar than a mousse that is served at room temperature, and ripe fruit need little sweetening.

GOOSEBERRY FOOL

There are differing degrees of smoothness desirable in a purée, from the completely smooth and homogenous result from a blender to mashing in a food mill or pressing the cooked fruit through a coarse sieve. Gooseberry fool is best served by the latter for the texture and specks of fruit still remaining are part of the dish's appeal. Most gooseberries need to be cooked with sugar. Their bright green colour turns yellow during the process and the firm texture softens – not an aesthetic improvement but essential to a successful dish. Gooseberries have an affinity with elderflowers, which blossom at the same time. A few drops of elderflower cordial work well with this or any other gooseberry dish. Rhubarb makes an excellent alternative to gooseberries.

Serves 4–6

500g (1lb 2oz) gooseberries
20g (¾oz) unsalted butter
200g (7oz) granulated sugar
few drops of elderflower cordial (optional)
300ml (10fl oz) double cream

1 Top and tail the gooseberries (p465). In a heavy-based saucepan, heat them gently in the butter along with the sugar. Once the gooseberries start to cook they produce plenty of liquid, but if they or the sugar catch on the surface of the pan before softening they will caramelize to produce a different flavour from that wanted. Cook for 10–15 minutes until soft.

2 Mash the cooked fruit or pass through a coarse sieve, then leave to cool. Add a few drops of elderflower cordial, if using.

3 Whip the cream. When it has thickened, but is not yet fully whipped, fold in the fruit purée. Check for sweetness – a tart, refreshing flavour is the objective – then spoon or pipe into glasses and refrigerate until needed.

BANANA MOUSSE

The smooth purée achieved by a blender is called for here, and also the use of gelatin to set the mousse properly. Most mousses are set with gelatin. Use as little as possible so that the finished mousse is soft and delicate rather than rubbery. If liked, combine a fruit mousse with a layer of the same fruit in jellied form (p468) to make a more complex dish with varying textures.

Serves 4–6

250g (8½oz) ripe bananas
juice of 1 lemon
juice of 1 orange
125g (4½oz) caster sugar
2tbsp crème de banane liqueur
1tbsp water
3 gelatin leaves, soaked for 10 minutes then squeezed dry, or powdered equivalent (see steps, right)
360ml (12fl oz) double cream

1 Peel the bananas and cut into pieces. Purée in a blender with the fruit juices and sugar.

2 Warm the water and crème de banane, then, away from direct heat, stir in the gelatin leaves. When the gelatin has completely dissolved, stir the mixture into the puréed fruit. Whisk the cream until thick but not fully whipped and fold into the fruit purée. Spoon the mousse into individual ramekins or dishes of your choice and refrigerate until set.

USING GELATIN

Gelatin comes in two forms, leaf and powder. Whichever you use, the principle is the same: the gelatin must be soaked in a little cold liquid for at least 10 minutes before being dissolved in warm, but not boiling, liquid. Gelatin is added to warm liquid so that it will melt and disperse evenly before the mousse is chilled and set. A leaf of gelatin weighs only 3g, equivalent to about ½tsp powder. The powdered variety is more powerful and is sold in sachets marked with the equivalence in weight to leaf gelatin rather than by its actual weight.

Leaf gelatin

1 Soak 3 leaves of gelatin in cold water to cover for at least 10 minutes. Squeeze out as much water as possible.

2 Warm 3tbsp water or flavoured liquid in a small saucepan. Remove from the heat and stir in the gelatin to dissolve.

Powdered gelatin

Soak 3 leaves' worth – about 1½tsp – of powdered gelatin in 3tbsp cold water until it becomes spongy. Dissolve in warm liquid as for leaf gelatin.

JELLY

For successful jelly, you need just enough liquid, at a high enough temperature, to melt the gelatin. Too much gelatin and the jelly will set like rubber, too little and it may not set at all. Jellies in the past were regularly made too hard in order to produce moulded shapes for dessert trolleys or table decoration and it may be memories of

these chewy and wildly coloured confections that lowered their popularity as a pudding. The vegetable counterpart – aspic – has suffered a fall from grace for the same reasons. The best advice is to err on the side of softness and refrigerate the jelly until it is to be eaten rather than displaying it on the sideboard.

ROSÉ WINE JELLY WITH BERRIES

All rosé wines work in the recipe but the style and weight of the finished dish will be affected by your choice. I have used hefty Californian blush as well as fruity Anjou and Australian rosés. The wine need not be extra sweet for it is its tartness balanced by sugar that produces the right effect. The fragile nature of berry fruit is well served by this treatment. The recipe makes enough for six 150ml (5fl oz) dishes and the result can be spooned from these dishes or unmoulded.

Serves 6

750ml (1¼ pints) rosé wine

600g (1lb 6oz) caster sugar

8 gelatin leaves, soaked for 10 minutes and then squeezed dry, or powdered equivalent

6 heaped tbsp mixed blueberries, raspberries, and blackberries

1 Heat the wine and sugar together. When this syrup reaches boiling point, remove the pan from the heat and stir in the gelatin leaves. When the liquid is lukewarm, pour a 3mm (⅛in) layer into each dish. Refrigerate until this starts to set.

2 Arrange the fruit on top of the first layer of jelly. Pour on the remaining cool syrup and refrigerate overnight. The jellies will be set. Serve with cream or ice cream.

POACHING FRUIT

Poaching is an extension of the ripening process with the fruit intensifying in flavour but deteriorating in texture. It also gives an opportunity to add complementary flavours, such as vanilla to pears or sweet wine to plums. There are two main categories of poached fruit. In compotes, the fruit retains its shape, while in dishes like summer pudding and rote grütze, any loss of texture is more than compensated for by the juices and extra flavour. Large fruit are suited to poaching as compote: apples, pears, and quinces in autumn; apricots, peaches, and plums in summer. The sweeter the syrup used to cook the fruit, the better it will retain its shape.

SUMMER PUDDING

The essence of summer, this pudding contains whatever summer fruits are at their best and transforms them by first poaching, then pressing in white bread. The bread becomes saturated by the warm fruit juices and when chilled tastes completely of these fruits, lending just texture and body to the finished dish. My own fruit preference is to add stoned cherries to the mixture as berries soften completely, losing all texture, and currants can feel almost gritty if used to excess. The objectives are a deep red colour, fruitiness, and a touch of tartness to balance the sweetness of the sugar and ripe fruit.

1kg (2¼lb) fruit, such as raspberries, stoned cherries, and redcurrants; peaches, plums, blackcurrants, and strawberries can also be used

250g (8½oz) caster sugar

I white loaf, sliced then crusts removed

1 In a saucepan, toss the fruit in the sugar then bring to the boil, stirring to prevent burning. Simmer gently, uncovered, for 2 minutes or until plenty of juice is produced. Add more sugar if necessary, or a few drops of lemon if too sweet.

2 Cut a disc of white bread to fit the base of a pudding bowl and cut the remaining slices into triangles. Fit these alternately into the basin so that it is completely lined, then pour in the fruit and cooking juices. Cover the basin with more slices of bread.

3 Place a small plate on top of the pudding with weights on top. Stand in a dish to catch any drips of juice. As soon as it is cool, refrigerate. Leave at least overnight and preferably for a few days before turning out and serving in wedges with thick double cream.

POINTS TO WATCH

■ The fruit must produce enough juice to completely soak the bread. Should you be short of juice at the crucial moment, heat a few more raspberries in sugar and water to produce extra.

■ The pudding shouldn't be overly sweet. Err on the side of less sugar and adjust while the poached fruits are still hot enough to melt any additional sugar needed.

■ Summer pudding's flavour develops over a few days as the bread and juices combine, so it is best made well in advance.

ROTE GRÜTZE

Germany's take on summer berry fruit translates as "red grits" or "red gruel", not the marketing manager's ideal title, but the stuff of nostalgia for many nonetheless. Throughout Germany, Austria, and Denmark there are many variants, some thickened with sago, some with gelatin, and some with cornflour. This recipe uses potato flour, sometimes sold by its French name fécule de pommes de terre. Raspberries are the only truly essential ingredient, with whatever else you want to keep them company. The objective is a slightly thickened pudding with an almost porridge-like consistency.

2tbsp potato flour
300ml (10fl oz) water
200g (7oz) raspberries
200g (7oz) redcurrants
150g (5½oz) granulated sugar
squeeze of lemon juice
few drops of vanilla extract

1 Dissolve the potato flour in 200ml (7fl oz) of the water. Whisk until smooth. Bring the fruit, sugar, and the remaining water to the boil in a medium saucepan.

2 Whisk the flour solution again and stir into the fruit. Bring back to the boil to thicken. Add the lemon juice and vanilla extract. Decant into a serving dish and cool.

FRUIT COMPOTE

If fruits are to be kept long term, they have to be preserved to stay in perfect condition. Use heat-resistant preserving jars that have a rubber seal, and wash and sterilize the jars before use. Most fruits with a reasonably firm texture can be substituted for the figs in this recipe. Pears and peaches also work well. Like figs, they need to be poached by simmering, covered, in enough water to cover until tender. Cherries can be made into compote without poaching. The syrup's flavour can be tailored to your own taste by adding, say, preserved ginger to pears or vanilla to cherries.

1 litre (1¾ pints) water
500g (1lb 2oz) granulated sugar
1tsp lemon juice
3 cinnamon sticks
3kg (6½lb) figs, stalks removed and poached in enough water to cover for 10–15 minutes until tender, then drained

1 Bring the water, sugar, lemon, and cinnamon to the boil. Fill the sterilized jars with the fruit then pour on the hot syrup.

2 Close the jars and place in a pan half-full of water. Bring to the boil, reduce the heat and simmer for 5 minutes, with the lid on.

Poached pears with cinnamon ice cream

The choice of pear variety is important. Williams is the best suited to poaching. The recipe works equally well using red wine but produces a slightly different dish, not just darker but with the wine predominating over the delicate pear flavour. The ice cream recipe produces about 1 litre (1¾ pints). If this is slightly more than needed, then use the remainder some other time for it is really not worth making less. If you do not have an ice cream maker, whisk periodically while it is freezing to break up the ice crystals. It will have the texture of a parfait rather than ice cream.

4 small or 2 large firm, or under-ripe, pears

500ml (17fl oz) white wine

75g (2½oz) granulated sugar

strip of lemon peel

For the ice cream

600ml (1 pint) full-fat milk

300ml (10fl oz) double cream

250g (8½oz) granulated sugar

4 cinnamon sticks, broken into pieces

1 vanilla pod, halved lengthways

6 egg yolks

Peel the pears. If they are large enough to make 2 portions apiece, then core and halve them. Place the pears in a saucepan and add the wine, sugar, and lemon peel and enough water to cover the fruit. Bring to the boil, then immediately reduce the heat to a simmer. Cover and poach for 15–20 minutes until soft – the timing will vary with the size, variety, and ripeness of the pears. Leave the fruit to cool in the cooking liquor.

For the ice cream, heat the milk and cream with half the sugar, the cinnamon and vanilla. Bring to just below boiling point, then cover and leave off the heat for 20 minutes to become infused with the flavours of the spices.

Whisk the remaining sugar and egg yolks together. Reheat the milk and cream to near boiling point, then whisk slowly onto the egg and sugar mixture. Return the mixture to a clean saucepan, preferably one with rounded edges so that the custard does not coagulate in the corners. Stir slowly for 5–8 minutes over a low heat until the custard thickens perceptibly. The custard must not come to the boil or it will curdle.

Strain the custard into a bowl or jug and cool, preferably overnight in the refrigerator. Churn in an ice cream maker.

Serve each pear next to or fanned across a scoop of the ice cream with the cooking liquor as sauce.

The pears keep best if left in their poaching syrup

BAKING FRUIT

Peaches and nectarines suit baking (or roasting with a coating of oil or butter to caramelize the outside), but the star performer is apple. When available, the finest cooking apple variety is the Bramleys. This is the fruit equivalent of the floury maincrop potato for the flesh disintegrates into a soft, tart mush while cooking and takes on the flavour of whatever sugars, dried fruit, and spices are mixed in with it. As no extra liquid like syrup or wine is used to affect flavour, a moist fruit, or one to which butter or oil has been added, works best.

BAKED APPLES

4 cooking apples, such as Bramleys
4tbsp granulated sugar
1tsp ground cinnamon
1tbsp sultanas

1 Core each apple, stopping just short of the bottom, but do not peel them. Mix the sugar, cinnamon, and sultanas together and use to fill each core cavity.

2 Make a small incision around the centre of each apple to prevent bursting. Bake at 190°C (375°F, gas 5) for 1 hour then serve whole with cream or ice cream.

BAKED PEACHES WITH AMARETTI

In Italy roasting and baking peaches are regular treatments. This recipe uses ground amaretti biscuits. These sometimes come in pairs attractively wrapped like sweets.

| 4 ripe peaches |
| 8 amaretti biscuits |
| 50g (1¾oz) caster sugar |
| seeds from 1 vanilla pod (p89) |
| 1 egg yolk |
| 25g (scant 1oz) unsalted butter |

1 Cut the peaches in half and remove the stones. Enlarge the space left by the stones by removing and reserving 1tsp peach flesh from each. Grind the biscuits to the consistency of breadcrumbs in a food processor. Take care not to overprocess.

2 Mix the peach pulp, sugar, vanilla, and egg yolk into the amaretti crumbs. Butter a baking dish and place the peaches, cavity-side up, inside. Spoon the amaretti mixture into the cavities and dot with a little more butter. Bake at 190°C (375°F, gas 5) for 40 minutes, until the peaches are soft and the filling crusty.

FRYING FRUIT

Banana and pineapple are often served as fritters, but apples, pears, peaches, rhubarb, and orange work just as well. A light batter is essential to success. The fritters should be dry and crisp with no hint of greasiness. A bland oil like sunflower or corn oil works best as no additional flavour is needed. Most all-purpose cooking oils have a high flash point – they survive high temperatures before burning – but there are variations among oils. The surface should be still and hot, but not giving off any sign of smoke. Should it become too hot, it is best corrected by the addition of a little more oil.

FRUIT FRITTERS

Fritters rarely suit an accompanying sauce, certainly never any custard-like confection, and are best dusted with icing or caster sugar and served hot. This still leaves scope for vanilla or cinnamon sugar if that partners the fruit in question to its advantage.

| 6 bananas or 12 pineapple rings |
| 4tbsp caster sugar |
| 2tbsp kirsch (optional) |
| oil for deep-frying |
| **For the batter** |
| 150ml (5fl oz) semi-skimmed milk or water |
| 125g (4½oz) self-raising flour |
| 1tbsp olive oil |
| 2 egg whites |
| 1tsp caster sugar |

1 For the batter, mix the milk or water, flour, and oil together until smooth. In a separate bowl, whisk the egg whites until stiff. Add a pinch of salt and the sugar to the egg whites at the final stages of whisking. Fold the egg white into the milk, flour, and oil mixture.

2 Sprinkle the fruit with the sugar and, if using, kirsch. Dip the fruit into the batter and fry in hot oil until golden brown, 3–5 minutes. Drain.

STEAMED & BOILED PUDDINGS

Steamed puddings and dumplings are made from similar mixtures of flour and fat as puddings that are baked. But steaming is a slower process, and you will need to check water levels in the pan or steamer regularly to be sure that it hasn't boiled dry. The size of the pudding and its content will decide cooking times: a family-sized Christmas pudding will need 6 hours or more.

PLUM DUMPLINGS

This is a Hungarian dish in which the plums are covered in a potato dough and then boiled. In Hungary they roll the dumplings in fried breadcrumbs, but for me this is a heftiness too far.

8 plums
4tbsp caster sugar
1tsp ground cinnamon
500g (1lb 2oz) potatoes, peeled and boiled
25g (scant 1oz) butter, softened
1 egg
75g (2 1/2oz) plain flour
1tbsp ground poppy seeds
1tbsp icing sugar, sifted

1 Dig out the stones with a sharp knife and fill the plums with the sugar and cinnamon. Push the cooked potato through a sieve or ricer. Using a fork, mix in a pinch of salt, the butter, and egg.

2 Add as much flour as you need to form a firm dough, then roll out as thinly as possible and cut into 8 squares. Draw the dough up over each plum to form a sealed dumpling. Drop the dumplings into boiling water and cook for about 5 minutes until they rise to the top.

3 Lift out the dumplings with a slotted spoon and dust with a mixture of ground poppy seeds and icing sugar.

STICKY TOFFEE PUDDING

This recipe comes from the late Francis Coulson of Sharrow Bay in the Lake District. He may have invented the recipe or collected it locally, but however it originated, it has become a standard.

Serves 6

For the sponge
75g (2 1/2oz) unsalted butter
200g (7oz) caster sugar
3 eggs
200g (7oz) self-raising flour, sifted
375ml (12 1/2fl oz) water
200g (7oz) pitted dates, coarsely chopped
1 1/2tsp baking powder

For the sauce
75g (2 1/2oz) dark brown or demerara sugar
300ml (10fl oz) double cream or condensed milk
50g (1 3/4oz) unsalted butter

1 For the sponge, cream together the butter and sugar. Beat in the eggs and fold in the flour. Bring the water to the boil in a small pan. Add the chopped dates and simmer them, uncovered, for 2 minutes.

2 Remove from the heat and add the baking powder to the pan. Mix the date mixture into the batter then pour into a 23cm (9in) square, deep-sided baking dish. Bake at 200°C (400°F, gas 6) for about 30 minutes until set.

3 Stir all the sauce ingredients together in a saucepan and bring to the boil. Pour half of the sauce onto the cooked sponge then put it back in the oven for 2 minutes to soak in. Cut into squares and serve with the remaining sauce.

Steamed orange pudding

Traditionally steamed puddings used suet (hard kidney fat), but a softer, lighter texture can be obtained with butter. The recipe calls for individual pudding basins, of a size and type known as dariole moulds, most often used for crème caramels. The mixture can be steamed in a larger pudding basin then divided into portions but needs longer cooking, about 1½ hours. If you have no steamer or your steamer is too small, place the dishes of uncooked pudding mixture in a roasting pan half-filled with boiling water, then transfer this to an oven preheated to 200°C (400°F, gas 6) and bake for 40 minutes.

Spoon the batter on top of the syrup

100g (3½oz) unsalted butter, softened

100g (3½oz) caster sugar

100g (3½oz) self-raising flour

½tsp baking powder

2 eggs

2tbsp semi-skimmed milk

grated zest and juice of 2 oranges

4tbsp golden syrup

Cream the butter and sugar together then stir in the flour and baking powder. Beat in the eggs, one at a time, then beat in the milk, orange zest, and juice.

Butter the inside of 4 dariole moulds or ramekin dishes. Put 1tbsp golden syrup in each then pour over the batter. Fasten foil loosely across the tops to act as lids.

Place the moulds in a steamer and cook for 40 minutes. Turn the puddings out into warmed bowls. Serve with cream or crème anglaise (p420), if wished.

NUTS FOR SWEET USE

The most versatile nuts for sweets and puddings are almonds – sweetened almond preparations are a cornerstone of every classic pastry and confectionery kitchen. Both almonds and walnuts can be made into "milk" by finely grinding the nuts and steeping in boiling water, then straining (see below). Vegans and those with dairy allergies can use nut milk like soya milk.

PREPARING ALMONDS

You can buy almonds ready blanched, flaked, chopped (nibbed), and ground, but it is easy to prepare them yourself. Dry-roasting (p480) intensifies their flavour and crunch.

Blanching

1 Place the almonds in a bowl and cover with boiling water. Leave them for 2–3 minutes, then drain in a colander. Set aside until they are cool enough to handle.

2 Pinch each almond between your thumbs and index fingers to slip the nut out of the skin. Alternatively, rub the nuts in layers of kitchen paper (p478) to remove the skins.

Flaking

Use a large, sharp knife and hold each nut flat on the cutting board. Cut into slices of the required thickness. To sliver almonds, cut each slice lengthwise into fine sticks.

Chopping

Using a large, sharp knife, chop the nuts into pieces of the required size – coarse or fine – guiding the knife with your knuckles. Other nuts can be chopped in the same way.

Grinding

Grind almonds (and other nuts) in a blender or food processor to the consistency of fine breadcrumbs. If using a food processor, take care not to overprocess, as nuts release their natural oils during grinding and you could end up with a nut butter.

Almond milk

Put ground almonds into a bowl and cover with double their volume of boiling water. Let steep, covered, for 30 minutes. Pour the mixture into a fine-mesh sieve held over a bowl. Press the ground nuts in the sieve to extract all of the milk, then discard the nuts.

PRALINE

As in any specialized craft, there is a jargon used in pastry-making. A mixture of caramelized sugar and almonds is known as croquant or nougat, and is used for petits fours (small fancy biscuits) and to make baskets to serve them in. Once crushed or ground into a paste, croquant changes its name to praline, which flavours tarts, soufflés, and ice cream.

480g (1lb 1oz) granulated sugar

juice of ½ lemon

360g (13oz) flaked or chopped almonds

1 Stir the sugar and lemon juice in a pan over a gentle heat until the sugar melts into syrup. A few drops of water may make this easier, but slows the process as the water has to evaporate before the sugar will caramelize. Bring the syrup to the boil, then cook for about 20 minutes until pale amber in colour.

2 Warm the almonds, then add them to the sugar and cook for a moment. Pour the mixture into an oiled pan, and let cool to set.

3 Grind the croquant in a food processor or mill. The resulting paste is praline.

BAKED ALMOND PUDDING

Bitter almonds have a stronger flavour than sweet almonds and can make you seriously ill if eaten in any quantity. However, they are made into an essence that can add depth and balance to a sweet almond preparation. If you can track down bitter almond essence, add a few drops to the batter for this dessert.

125g (4½oz) unsalted butter
250g (8½oz) ground almonds
2tbsp double cream
1tbsp Cognac
grated zest of ½ lemon
5tbsp caster sugar plus extra for sprinkling
2 eggs
2 egg yolks

1 Preheat the oven to 190°C (375°F, gas 5). Melt the butter and stir in the almonds, cream, Cognac, zest, and sugar. Finally stir in the whole eggs and yolks.

2 Oil or butter a shallow pie dish, then pour in the batter. Bake in the oven for 40 minutes. Sprinkle with caster sugar.

NOUGAT MONTELIMAR

In my childhood this confection was sold in sweet shops everywhere. It has improved its status in the meantime and can now be found gracing the petits fours selection in grand restaurants. The recipe calls for pistachio nuts. The unsalted variety – which is what you need – comes shelled but with a pale outer casing that has to be removed and discarded (see below). Use the bright green nuts whole. You need edible rice paper or cling film to line the tray.

Makes about 1 kg (2¼lb)

420g (15oz) granulated sugar
120ml (4fl oz) water
115g (4oz) clear honey
1tbsp glucose
1½ egg whites, 45g (1½oz) in total
55g (2oz) glacé cherries, coarsely chopped
55g (2oz) pistachio nuts
30g (1oz) flaked almonds
30g (1oz) nibbed almonds

SKINNING PISTACHIOS

Blanch as for almonds (p476), then rub the skins off between your hands or 2 pieces of kitchen paper.

1 Dissolve the sugar in the water then bring rapidly to the boil. Boil until the syrup reaches 107°C (224°F). The water will have evaporated by this stage, and the hot syrup will have begun a series of changes that thicken and eventually would colour the sugar – it should be sticky but without any sign of caramelization.

2 Add the honey and glucose and boil until it reaches 135°C (275°F). Whisk the egg white to stiff peaks then spoon over the hot syrup, off the heat, whisking continuously. This is best done with an electric hand-held mixer operating at maximum speed.

3 Warm the cherries and nuts then stir into the mixture. Line a baking tray with rice paper or cling film. Pour the nougat onto the tray, spread evenly, then cover with a layer of paper or film. Press down the surface with a weighted flat board and leave to cool overnight. Cut the nougat into small rectangles with a knife dipped in hot water.

Serve nougat with the rice paper attached

NUTS FOR SAVOURY USE

Many nuts can be used in savoury dishes as well as sweet ones. Hazelnuts, for instance, can be toasted then tossed with boiled brussels sprouts to partner game or poultry or ground and used to flavour meringues. Nuts can also be used as a flour substitute or in stuffings. Bear in mind when swapping ground nuts for any dry ingredient that their natural oils will soften the texture of the dish.

SHELLING WALNUTS & PECANS

You need a nutcracker to shell pecans and walnuts. The inner skin is too difficult to peel off and can be eaten.

TOASTING HAZELNUTS

To remove the papery skins of hazelnuts, spread them out on a baking tray and grill them under medium heat for 3–5 minutes until golden. Alternatively, place them in an oven preheated to 180°C (350°F, gas 4) for 7–12 minutes. Shake the tray frequently to stop the nuts burning. Wrap the nuts in a cloth and rub off the skins. Browning them also enriches their flavour and makes them more crunchy.

PARSLEY & SPRING ONION TART WITH WALNUT PASTRY

The ground walnuts substituted for some of the flour in this pastry impart an interesting taste and texture. The pastry is easier to handle if made in advance then rested in the refrigerator for an hour or so, plus another hour's resting after lining the tin. Walnuts aren't sold ready ground so use a food processor, pulsing the nuts to avoid overworking them. Take care that the food processor is completely dry before grinding the nuts or it will produce paste rather than flour.

For the pastry

170g (6oz) unsalted butter at room temperature
1 small egg
150g (5½oz) plain flour
100g (3½oz) walnuts, ground

For the filling

3 eggs and 1 yolk
300ml (10fl oz) double cream
3tbsp semi-skimmed milk
1 heaped tbsp chopped parsley
6 spring onions, chopped
25g (scant 1oz) Cheddar cheese, grated
pinch of freshly grated nutmeg

1 Mix the butter with the egg and a pinch of salt. Stir in the flour and walnuts and knead once or twice to make sure that all the ingredients are mixed. Refrigerate for at least 1 hour.

2 Roll out the pastry and line a 25cm (10in) tart tin. Refrigerate for 1 hour then bake blind in an oven preheated to 200°C (400°F, gas 6) for 15 minutes. Leave to rest for 10 minutes. If the pastry has slid down towards the base, repair any gaps with leftover pieces of raw pastry. Turn the oven down to 180°C (350°F, gas 4).

3 Whisk all the filling ingredients together and season. Place the pastry shell on a baking tray in the lower shelf of the oven and pour in this filling. Bake for about 30 minutes until the top is brown and the filling set but still soft.

PEELING CHESTNUTS

Chestnuts come in several guises: raw, sweetened, or plain in vacuum wrapping, cans, or jars. You can roast raw chestnuts by heating them on a griddle or open fire. You can also shell them after deep-frying, grilling, or blanching for a few minutes.

1 Whichever method you choose, pierce the top of each chestnut with the point of a sharp knife to stop it exploding when hot.

2 Grill or deep-fry the chestnuts for about 3 minutes until the shells split. Once they are cool enough to handle, peel off the outer and inner skin. Alternatively, blanch the chestnuts by bringing them to the boil in cold water. Remove a few at a time and peel before they cool down.

3 For stuffing, coarsely chop the chestnut flesh with a sharp knife.

CHESTNUT STUFFING

The stuffings and accompaniments to Christmas dinner are often more interesting than the celebratory birds they adorn. This stuffing goes well with both goose and turkey but is fine with chicken or any white game bird too. If you do not wish to shell the chestnuts yourself, buy them ready shelled but unsweetened.

Serves 6

25g (scant 1oz) butter
1 shallot, finely chopped
400g (14oz) sausage meat
100g (3½oz) fresh breadcrumbs
2 apples, peeled, cored, and diced
1 pear, peeled, cored, and diced
200g (7oz) unsweetened chestnuts, coarsely chopped

1 Preheat the oven to 200°C (400°F, gas 6). Heat the butter in a medium pan and sweat the shallot until cooked but not coloured. Stir in all the other ingredients and check for seasoning.

2 Roll the stuffing in well-buttered foil so that it is the shape of a thick sausage. Bake for 1 hour and serve in slices.

GLOSSARY

Acidulate To add an acid such as lemon juice to cooking or soaking water to prevent vegetables or fruit discolouring.

Al dente Literally "to the tooth". Pasta, rice, and vegetables may be cooked until al dente, which is until just tender yet still offering a slight resistance when you bite into them.

Amaretti biscuits Small almond biscuits, which sometimes come in pairs attractively wrapped like sweets.

Annatto and annatto oil Orange-red seeds from a small tropical tree, used to give colour to Asian and Latin American cooking. Fat or oil in which the seeds have been fried turns deep orange and can be used to add colour in cooking.

Armagnac A brandy, from south-west France, sometimes used to flavour desserts or pâtés.

Aspic Savoury jelly made from meat, fish, or vegetable stock, usually set with gelatin.

Bain-marie A "water bath" used to cook foods slowly and keep sauces warm. A bain-marie can be a double-boiler, just a saucepan of simmering water over which a pan or bowl of sauce is set, or a baking tin in which another dish is placed.

Bake blind To bake a pastry shell without the filling to set it. The pastry is weighed down with beans while in the oven to prevent it from losing its shape.

Banana shallot Also called a French shallot, this close relative of the onion has an elongated bulb shape and golden skin.

Baste To spoon fat over food as it cooks to prevent it drying out and for flavour.

Beurre manié Meaning "kneaded butter", this paste of butter and flour is added at the end of cooking to thicken a sauce.

Bhuna An Indian sautéing technique that lightly toasts spices, releasing their essential oils to flavour meat, fish, or vegetable dishes.

Bitter almond essence A flavouring made from bitter almonds that can add depth and balance when used alongside sweet almonds.

Blanch To immerse in boiling water for a very short time. Blanching is done to set colour (vegetables); to eliminate strong flavours (some vegetables, sweetbreads); and to loosen skins before peeling (tomatoes, stone fruit, some nuts).

Boiling fowl An older bird generally raised for egg production. It is only really good in cooking for flavouring stock.

Brioche A delicate, lightly sweetened dough. It is traditionally served plain or toasted and partnered with jams for breakfast, or at lunch or dinner with foie gras and strong cheeses.

Brunoise Very finely diced vegetables.

Buckwheat A grain used to make flour for pasta, dumplings, pancakes, and Japanese soba noodles.

Bulgur Also burghul and bulgar, wheat grains that are boiled until they crack. Bulgur is a staple in the Middle East and used to make kibbeh and tabbouleh.

Buttermilk Originally a by-product of butter making, today it is made by adding bacteria to milk to thicken and sour it.

Caramel Sugar syrup heated above 156°C (313°F) until it contains very little water and takes on a dark colour. Caramel is used as a topping for desserts and to make sweets.

Caramelize To heat a food until its surface sugars break down and turn brown. Savoury and sweet foods can be caramelized.

Cartouche A disc of baking parchment cut to fit a pan and laid directly on the surface of food to prevent evaporation and to keep it from drying out during cooking.

Ceviche A South American and Caribbean technique of "cooking" seafood without heat. A lime juice marinade partially cooks thinly sliced raw fish, which is served cold, sometimes accompanied by boiled vegetables or salad.

Chiffonade Thinly shredded herbs or leafy vegetables, made by placing leaves on top of each other, rolling them tightly, and then cutting into strips.

Clarify To skim or filter a liquid, such as a consommé or melted butter, until it is clear and free of impurities. Egg whites are sometimes used because they can entrap particulate matter. Butter is gently heated until the milk solids separate from the clear liquid fat. The clarified butter can then be poured off.

Compote Fruits poached gently in a sugar syrup so they hold their shape.

Confit Meat or poultry cooked in its own fat to preserve it.

Cornflour A white corn (maize) powder used to thicken sauces. It needs to be mixed with cold water before being heated.

Cornichons The French name for gherkins, cornichons are a small variety of pickled cucumbers.

Cornmeal Fine, medium, or coarse meal ground from dried corn. In North America, it used to make cornbread and other breads; in northern Italy, it is known as polenta and cooked to make a dish of the same name.

Court bouillon A poaching stock, most commonly used for cooking fish.

Couscous A mixture of fine and coarse semolina, in which the finer flour binds itself around the coarser grains to form granules. Traditionally couscous takes a long time to cook, but instant couscous is pre-cooked and needs only to be rehydrated.

Couverture A high-quality chef's chocolate that melts and coats easily to give a glossy finish.

Crème anglaise A thin, vanilla-flavoured English egg custard, served warm or cold with many desserts.

Crème fraîche A fermented, thickened cream with a tangy flavour.

Croquant Sugar and nuts, usually almonds, caramelized together and used to make petits fours and sweet baskets. Once crushed or milled into a paste, it is known as praline.

Croûtons Small cubes of bread fried until crisp.

Crustaceans Shellfish, such as lobsters, prawns, and crabs, which have an exterior skeleton, segmented body, and jointed limbs.

Cure To add flavour and preserve fish, poultry, and meat by drying, salting, and smoking or by marinating in an escabeche or ceviche.

Dashi A tuna and seaweed-based fish stock used in Japanese cooking.

Deglaze To use the caramelized juices released by roasted or fried meat, or vegetables to make a sauce or gravy. A pan is deglazed by adding stock, water, or wine and scraping it to loosen the juices and flavours that stick to the bottom.

Devein To remove the dark vein from prawns.

Durum wheat The hardest of all wheat grains with a high proportion of gluten, durum wheat is mostly used to make dried pasta.

Duxelles A classic mixture of cooked chopped shallots and mushrooms.

Egg wash A glaze made from egg or egg yolk and water or milk, used for browning baked foods.

Emulsion A suspension of droplets of fat, such as oil or melted butter, in liquids such as water, vinegar, or lemon juice. Emulsified sauces include mayonnaise and hollandaise.

En papillote Food sealed in a package, a "papillote", and steamed delicately in the oven to retain its texture, flavour, and aroma.

Escabeche Fried fish pickled in a spicy warm vinegar and served cold as a starter. Vegetables and chilies are also pickled in this way.

Escalope A thin cut of meat, often chicken or veal, flattened to tenderize it and to help the meat cook evenly.

Fillet A boneless piece of meat or fish.

Flash point The temperature at which an oil starts to burn and give colour. Oils with a low flash point, such as olive oil, are unsuited to cooking at high temperatures.

Flour Strong, or bread, flour has a high proportion of gluten to allow the gases from the yeast to rise and keep the bread light. Rye flour comes in light or dark varieties and produces a less airy loaf than wheat flour. Soft, or plain, flour is used for making cakes, batters, and pastries. Doppio zero, "00", flour from Italy is the finest grade of soft flour and is used to make low-risen breads such as focaccia and pasta.

Foie gras The fattened liver of a duck or goose. Goose liver is more expensive and more pronounced in flavour.

Fumet Concentrated fish stock.

Fungi porcini Also known by their French name "ceps", porcini are an excellent species of boletus fungi. They are used fresh or dried to give a rich flavour to a variety of dishes.

Galangal A spicy pink root used in Southeast Asian cooking and prepared in a similar way to fresh ginger.

Ganache A chocolate cream that is used to fill cakes, decorate desserts, and fill truffles.

Garam masala Meaning "hot mixture", this north Indian spice blend is usually added at the end of cooking.

Gelatin A setting agent available in leaf or powder form, gelatin must be soaked in cold water before being dissolved in a warm liquid.

Ghee A clarified butter used in Indian cooking and capable of being heated to a high temperature without burning.

Gum arabic Available from chemists or specialist shops, a powdered, tasteless gum that helps gels stick and prevents sugar from crystallizing.

Gut To remove the viscera (everything in the stomach cavity) of a fish before cooking.

Hang To let meat hang after slaughter to disperse the lactic acid present in muscles, maximize tenderness, and enhance flavour.

Heritage varieties Vegetables and fruit that have not been hybridized to "improve" them. They often have a more natural, less perfect appearance than standard varieties.

Jicama A bulb-shaped root vegetable native to Mexico and also used in Southeast Asian cooking.

Jus French term for a light sauce produced by reducing a well-flavoured stock. If thickened, it is called a jus lié.

Kadhai An Indian wok. Kadhai cooking combines stir-frying and sautéing and uses specific spices.

Kaffir lime A knobbly citrus fruit whose leaves and zest are used in Southeast Asian, particularly Thai, cooking.

Kirsch A clear "eau-de-vie" made from black cherries.

Leaven (natural leaven) A living mixture of flour and water that causes breads to rise without the use of commercial yeast.

Lemon-grass A thick grass used, particularly in Thai cooking, to add a lemon flavour and aroma to dishes.

Liaison A thickening agent, most often a mixture of eggs and cream, that is added to soups or sauces.

Liquid glucose Available from chemists, liquid glucose is added to sugar syrups to reduce the risk of caramel crystallizing.

Malt extract A thick, brown liquid made from barley that, when added to bread, gives extra flavour and a good texture.

Marinade A liquid for soaking or basting that adds flavour to food and protects it from drying out. If the marinade has an acid component, such as lemon or lime juice, it can also have a tenderizing effect on meat, poultry, and fish. Often used for grilled or roasted foods.

Masa harina A finely ground powder made from corn that has been simmered with mineral lime, then dehydrated. Masa harina is used throughout Mexico, Central America, and South America to make tortillas.

Matzo Unleavened Jewish flat bread that resembles a cracker and is traditionally eaten during Passover. Matzo is also ground into a meal and used to make matzo balls, called "kneidlach" in Yiddish which are often served in a rich chicken broth.

Meringue A light-as-air mixture of whipped egg whites and sugar, baked for a dessert or topping.

Mirepoix A mixture of finely diced or chopped aromatic vegetables, usually carrots, onions, and celery, used as a flavouring.

Miso A paste of fermented soya beans and other flavourings used in Japanese cooking as a flavouring and as a condiment.

Mole A spicy Mexican sauce of which there are many varieties and colours, most famously from Oaxaca.

Mollusc A soft-bodied creature that usually has a hard shell. Molluscs include single-shell univalves, such as conch shells, and two-shell bivalves, such as mussels. Cephalopods, such as octopuses and squid, don't have a shell.

Morels Stubby, short wild mushrooms/fungi that resemble sponges. They are usually bought dried.

Mount To emulsify a sauce and make it richer and smoother by adding butter. Also, a way of adding volume to egg whites or cream by whipping in air.

Mousseline A very delicate culinary mixture, such as puréed seafood and cream, often made into quenelles.

Nam pla (fish sauce) A salty flavouring and dipping sauce used particularly in Thai cooking.

Nibbed Chopped. Often used to describe chopped almonds.

Okra A ridged pod eaten as a vegetable or powdered and used as a flavouring. It adds a gelatinous, thickening quality to stews and soups.

Palm sugar A sugar obtained from the sap of sugar palm trees and used in Southeast Asian cooking. It is usually sold in a block, and is added to sweet and savoury dishes. There are pale and dark versions of palm sugar.

Pancetta Italian cured pork belly, similar to bacon but not smoked. It can be bought as cubes or very thin rashers.

Pandanus leaf A long green leaf used in Thai cooking to wrap parcels of foods or to flavour sweets.

Papillote see en papillote.

Parboil To partially cook in boiling water.

Parfait An ice cream-like dessert made from egg custard enriched with cream.

Pâtisserie The art of pastry making and a collective name for the cakes and pastries sold at a pâtisserie.

Pea aubergine A small, pea-like variety of aubergine with a bitter taste used in Thai cooking.

Petits fours Small, fancy biscuits or cakes served at the end of a meal.

Pickle To preserve foods, especially firm vegetables, in a brine or acid to give a sweet-and-sour taste.

Pilaff A method of cooking rice so that every grain remains separate, and also the name of the resulting dish. Pilaff may be plain or flavoured with meat or vegetables.

Pot-roast To braise a whole bird or joint of meat in a small amount of liquid.

Poussin A small, baby chicken.

Praline Nuts, especially almonds, that have been caramelized in boiling sugar and then crushed to a paste. See also Croquant.

Prosciutto Italian for ham. Prosciutto generally refers to cured Parma ham.

Pulses Also known as legumes, pulses include beans, peas, and lentils. The term usually refers to the dried seeds, which are a valuable source of protein.

Purge To prepare sandy molluscs for cooking by putting them in a large bowl of cold water with some cornmeal or polenta and letting them soak overnight in the refrigerator. The molluscs eat the meal and expel the sand.

Quick bread A bread made with an instant leavening agent, such as bicarbonate of soda or baking powder.

Radicchio The Italian for red chicory, this leafy vegetable can be eaten raw in salads, braised, or sautéed.

RAW A style of vegetable preparation where nothing is heated above 48°C (118°F) to prevent enzymes being destroyed and food losing its nutritional value. Techniques include soaking and sprouting nuts and legumes and marinating vegetables to break down their undesirable starchy complexity.

Reduce To boil rapidly in order to evaporate excess liquid. Reducing intensifies flavour and thickens sauces.

Refresh To cool down in ice water. A way of quickly stopping the cooking process for vegetables that have been blanched.

Rehydrate To add water to a food that has been dried, such as mushrooms, to reconstitute it.

Rendered animal fat An animal fat, such as bacon grease or duck fat, that can be used for shallow-frying and roasting.

Rest To rest meat after roasting allows the muscles to relax so that the juices are retained within the meat. The taste and texture of the meat is better, and carving is easier. Resting also refers to chilling pastry so that it can relax and soften. A batter is rested so the flour particles can expand in the liquid.

Rice vinegar Usually mildly acidic and sweet, Asia's many varieties include Chinese red, black, and white vinegars and Japanese vinegars based on mirin.

Risotto A rice dish from northern Italy in which hot stock is stirred into short-grain risotto rice until the grains are creamy, but still firm and separate.

Roasted shrimp paste (gapi) A strong paste made from salted and fermented dried shrimps and used in Thai cooking.

Roe Fish eggs, most notably caviar eggs from sturgeon.

Roux A cooked mixture of butter and flour used to thicken white sauces such as béchamel.

Saffron threads The dried red stigmas of the saffron crocus are one of the most expensive spices in the world. They add colour and a warm, musky flavour to dishes.

Salsify A long root vegetable that has a waxy texture and is eaten peeled.

Semolina The endosperm of durum wheat, available in a variety of grinds and primarily used to make pasta. See also Couscous.

Shiitake Brown cap mushrooms that can be bought fresh or dried and are often used in Asian cooking.

Shortening The fat or oil used in pastry to achieve a "short" crumbly texture.

Shuck To remove the outer covering, such as the shells of oysters or scallops or the husks and silk from ears of corn.

Skim To remove fats and other impurities from a sauce or liquid using a perforated skimmer.

Smoked sweet paprika Also called "pimentón", this is a mild Spanish paprika.

Soft peaks Egg whites whisked until their peaks are still soft. To whisk to stiff peaks means to whisk until the egg whites are stiff throughout.

Soft-shell crab A blue crab that has moulted its hard shell. The entire crab is eaten.

Spatchcock To remove the backbone from a bird and then flatten it. A spatchcocked bird will grill more evenly.

Spätzle Dumplings made from a batter-like dough pressed through the holes of a special strainer.

Squab The American name for a pigeon, which has been commandeered in Britain to mean a bird reared for the table. It has a pale flesh and less gamey taste than wild wood pigeon.

Star anise A star-shaped, anise-flavoured spice that is used in Asian cooking.

Streusel A crumble topping sprinkled over tarts.

Suet The hard white fat that surrounds sheep or beef kidneys and may be used in cooking to make pastries or puddings,

Sugar syrup Sugar and water cooked together to different temperatures to produce varying concentrations of syrup for many pâtisserie, confectionery, and chocolate products.

Tadka An Indian cooking technique in which foods usually prepared with few spices, such as lentils, are spiced just before serving.

Tamarind A tropical pod that contains a sour pulp used in curries, chutneys, and sweets.

Temper To mix something until it reaches the correct consistency. For instance, chocolate can be tempered by heating and cooling it until its fats stabilize and it becomes glossy and easy to set.

Tofu Also called bean curd, tofu is made from soya beans in a similar way to soft curd cheese. Tofu absorbs flavours easily and is used widely in Asian cooking.

Tomatillo A green husk tomato that is a distant relative of the tomato. Its citrus flavour is often combined with coriander in Mexican cooking.

Tomato passata Sieved, smooth tomatoes that can be bought in bottles or cartons.

Tortilla Corn or wheat flat bread that is an essential part of Mexican cooking. Tortillas are often filled.

Turmeric A rhizome that is an important spice and food colouring, particularly in Indian cooking. In Thailand, the red (yellow) variety is added to curry pastes, while a white variety is eaten raw as a vegetable.

Turning A cutting technique that shaves vegetables into seven-sided football shapes. Commonly used for roots and tubers.

Vanilla sugar Caster sugar flavoured by vanilla extract or by leaving a vanilla pod in it.

Wild ginger (fingerroot or grachai) A lemon-flavoured rhizome available fresh or pickled.

Yeast A fungus that uses the natural sugars in a mixture to release carbon dioxide to ferment beer, champagne, and bread. Yeast can be bought fresh or dried and needs to be activated by mixing with a liquid before use.

Yuzu A citrus fruit with an agreeable sour taste. The bottled, salted juice and the zest are much used in Japanese cooking.

Zest The coloured, outer skin of a citrus fruit.

INDEX

Roasting temperatures & times

When you do not have a recipe for roasting a joint of meat, this chart will provide you with a foolproof formula for working out the roasting time. To calculate the time accurately, weigh the joint once it is ready for the oven, after stuffing if applicable. To test for doneness, pierce the meat in its thickest part (away from any bones) with a metal skewer. When withdrawn after half a minute it should come out warm for rare meat, fairly hot for medium, and very hot for well done. For greater accuracy, use a thermometer.

SUITABLE JOINTS, ON OR OFF THE BONE	ROAST AT 220°C (425°F, GAS 7) FOR THE FIRST 15 MINUTES, THEN AT 180°C (350°F, GAS 4)	
BEEF forerib, sirloin, top rump, topside	rare	15 mins per 450g (1lb) + 15 mins
	medium	20 mins per 450g (1lb) + 20 mins
	well done	25 mins per 450g (1lb) + 25 mins
fillet (châteaubriand end) weighing 1.5kg (3lb 3oz)	all at 220°C (425°F, gas 7)	
	rare	25 mins
	medium	30 mins
VEAL breast, loin, shoulder, topside	well done	25 mins per 450g (1lb) + 25 mins
LAMB best end (rack), breast, leg, saddle, shoulder	rare	15 mins per 450g (1lb) + 15 mins
	medium	20 mins per 450g (1lb) + 20 mins
	well done	25 mins per 450g (1lb) + 25 mins
PORK belly, leg, loin, shoulder	medium	25 mins per 450g (1lb) + 25 mins
	well done	30 mins per 450g (1lb) + 30 mins
VENISON haunch, saddle	medium	20 mins per 450g (1lb) + 20 mins

Grilling times

The timings below are for meat that is cut about 4cm (1½in) thick, cooked in a ridged cast-iron grill pan, under the grill, or on a barbecue. Timings given are the total time, and will vary depending on the type of pan, the exact degree of heat used, and the quality and thickness of the meat.

CUT	RARE	MEDIUM	WELL DONE
BEEF STEAKS Fillet	4 minutes	5–7 minutes	–
Rump	6–8 minutes	10–12 minutes	12–14 minutes
Sirloin/Entrecôte/ Porterhouse	6–8 minutes	10–12 minutes	12–14 minutes
T-bone	6–8 minutes	10–12 minutes	12–14 minutes
VEAL Chops/Cutlets	–	12–14 minutes	–
LAMB Best end cutlets	4–6 minutes	8–10 minutes	10–12 minutes
Butterflied leg	–	30 minutes	–
Chump chops	6–8 minutes	10–12 minutes	12–14 minutes
Fillet (eye of loin), cubed en brochette	6–8 minutes	8–10 minutes	10–12 minutes
Leg steaks	6–8 minutes	8–10 minutes	–
Loin chops	8–10 minutes	10–12 minutes	12–14 minutes
PORK Thin belly rashers	–	–	6–8 minutes
Chump chops/steaks	–	12–14 minutes	–
Leg steaks	–	12–14 minutes	–
Loin chops/steaks	–	12–14 minutes	–
Sparerib chops/steaks	–	12–14 minutes	–

PUBLISHER'S ACKNOWLEDGEMENTS

Dorling Kindersley would like to thank the following:

Hugh Thompson, for his initial planning and management of the project.

Bridget Sargeson, food stylist, for her unfailing professionalism and good humour in preparing and presenting for the camera over half of the techniques and recipes in this book.

All of the chefs who generously made available their facilities and materials for photography.

Editorial assistance
Valerie Barrett, Shannon Beatty, Stuart Cooper, Roz Denny, Barbara Dixon, Anna Fischel, Kay Halsey, Karola Handwerker, Eleanor Holme, Katie John, Bridget Jones, Jenny Lane, Beverly le Blanc, Irene Lyford, Marie-Pierre Moine, Connie Novis, Gary Werner, Fiona Wild, Jeni Wright.

Design assistance
Maggie Aldred, Briony Chappell, Murdo Culver, Jo Grey, Toni Kay, Elly King, Luis Peral-Aranda, Judith Robertson, Liz Sephton, Alison Shackleton, Penny Stock, Sue Storey, Ann Thompson.

DTP design assistance
Alistair Richardson, Louise Waller.

Editorial consultation
Rosie Adams, Henja Schneider, Margaret Thomason, Jill van Cleave, Kate Whiteman.

Translation
Janine Broom, Cristina Garcia, Barbara Mayer.

Index
Valerie Chandler & Dorothy Frame.

Chefs' liaison
Marion Franz (for Stephan Franz); Rosie Gayler (for Paul Gayler); Barbara Maher (for Stephan Franz); Anne Roche-Nöel (for Pierre Hermé); Rochelle Smith (for Charlie Trotter); Jane Wareing (for Marcus Wareing); David Whitehouse (for Dan Lepard).

On behalf of the contributing chefs
The following chefs prepared and styled food and demonstrated cooking techniques for photography: Sébastien Bauer (for Pierre Hermé), Julien Tessier (for David Thompson), Guiseppe Tentori (for Charlie Trotter).

Food stylists
Stephana Bottom, Angela Nilsen, Lucinda Rushbrooke, Nicole Szabason, Linda Tubby, Kirsten West, Sari Zernich. Susanna Tee for recipe testing.

Hand models
Virpi Davies, Harriet Eastwood, Saliha Fellache, Caroline Green, Jane Hornby, Olivia King, Emma McIntosh, Carlyn van Niekerk, Brittany Williams, Bethan Woodyatt, Tanongsak Yordwai (for David Thompson).

Props stylists
Victoria Allen, John Bentham, Bette Blau, Andrea Kuhn, Hendrik Schaulin, Helen Trent.

Photographic studio production
Carol Myers and Alex Grant at Divine Studio/Piquant Productions, New York; Sid Kelly at Code Management Inc, Miami; Oliver Beuvre-Méry at Blanc Loft, Gentilly, Paris; Nicole Werth and Stefan Richter at Lightclub Photographic, Hamburg.

Administrative assistance
Laura Dixon, Alex Farrell, Zoe Moore, Jolyon Rubinstein.